TRADERS PRESS, INC.

P.O. BOX 6206
GREENVILLE, SOUTH CAROLINA 29606

BOOKS AND GIFTS FOR
INVESTORS AND TRADERS

800-927-8222

Inside Japanese Financial Markets

Inside Japanese Financial Markets

Aron Viner

DOW JONES-IRWIN
Homewood, Illinois 60430

Dow Jones-Irwin is a trademark of Dow Jones & Company, Inc

This book was set in Century Schoolbook by Eastern Graphics.
The editors were Richard A. Luecke, Paula M. Buschman, Joan A. Hopkins
The production manager was Carma W. Fazio.
The drawings were done by Tim Keenan.
Arcata Graphics/Kingsport was the printer and binder.

ISBN 1-55623-020-6

Library of Congress Catalog Card No. 87–71357

Printed in the United States of America

2 3 4 5 6 7 8 9 0   K   5 4 3 2 1 0 9 8

This book is dedicated to
Hiroshi Katsuta
who during a career spanning 40 years has tried to bridge the gap between East and West.
Although he may disapprove of my lack of tact and disagree with my opinions, he encouraged my interest in Japanese financial markets.

On a cool spring day in 1986, a wrecking crew completed the job of destroying the century-old Tokyo Stock Exchange building. Meanwhile, on an adjacent site, a larger, more modern stock exchange building had been open for trading since June 1985. The construction of a new stock exchange building and the dismantling of the old one a year later provide an apt symbol of the destruction and creation taking place in all of Japan's financial markets.

Of course, in Japan, as elsewhere in the world, the new relentlessly replaces the old. However, institutions and the regulations that protect them are usually slower to change in Tokyo than in New York or London.

In November 1983, under direct pressure from the U.S. Treasury Department, the "Working Group of the Japan-U.S. Yen-Dollar Committee" was created. At the Bank of Japan, the joint committee was termed, without humor, the "arrival of the American 'black ships,'"—a reference to Perry's use of force as a means of pressuring Japan to open its markets to international trade.

Commodore Perry arrived in Japan in the mid-nineteenth century and used a style of gunboat diplomacy characteristic of his era. The threat implicit in a demonstration of superior fire power precipitated a period of modernization and industrialization of dazzling speed. The Meiji Restoration (1868–1912) saw medieval swordsmen become bankers and industrialists. A government which in 1865 still collected its taxes in the form of rice, had no navy, and had few guns in its standing army, won a war against Russia by 1905.

The "black ships" of 1983, like their namesakes, are triggering a transformation. Changes which in their own way are as remarkable and as sweeping as those that occurred under Meiji, are altering the character of Japan's financial sector. The ramifications extend far beyond the narrow purview of bankers and brokers.

In 1985, while the United States became a debtor nation, Japan became the world's largest creditor. According to a leading country credit rating survey, in 1986 Japan replaced the United States as the number one sovereign risk in the world. Yet, at the time of writing, the yen is not an international currency and derivative securities have no place in Japan's financial sector.

During the late 1980s Japan will catch up. The final years of the decade will be a period in which global financial markets adjust to new patterns in the flow of funds. Twenty-four hour securities trading, made possible by international financial marketplaces in North America (New York), Europe (London), and eventually Asia (Tokyo), will lead to a standardization of products and procedures. It is only a matter of time before Japan's adeptness at creating and marketing leading edge international financial instruments will replicate its manufacturing prowess. Japanese financial products will someday rival in competitiveness those of Europe and North America.

Japanese financial institutions, despite their emerging international role, are still the product of a uniquely Japanese social structure and culture. An understanding of Japan's financial markets requires some sensitivity to attitudes and perspectives that may diverge from prevalent views in the West. The historical imperatives that shaped Japanese banking and securities markets are present today in a web of regulations. Japan is, and will continue to be for quite some time, the most tightly regulated and compartmentalized economy in the free world.

Despite the vast size of the Japanese financial sector, little information has been available in any language other than Japanese. The limited materials that are written in English are often inaccessible. There has been a growing number of securities analysts, based permanently in Tokyo, writing about Japanese investment opportunities in English. The institutional investor has been the direct recipient of their unpublished reports. Individual investors have sometimes benefited indirectly by consulting with a broker with access to such reports or by purchasing a mutual fund heavily oriented toward Japanese security investment. These reports cannot usually be purchased because they are available to large institutional clients on a "soft dollar" basis. Similarly, comprehensive information about Japanese banking and money markets has been available to professionals. A small number of densely written monographs and privately circulated memoranda have provided detailed information regarding the structure of Japanese institutions and money market instruments. Such sources are difficult to locate and difficult to read.

This book is designed to give the non-Japanese investor an easy-to-read overview of all Japanese financial markets. The character of the Japanese economy and the social and political imperatives that made it the most regulated in the free world are explained. In this way, the various Japanese markets are not divorced from their wider context.

A perusal of the chapters will give the investor enough information about Japanese financial markets to begin a program of investment diversification in Japan. Although no prior knowledge of Japanese financial markets is assumed, the book is sufficiently detailed to serve as a reference for both individual and institutional investors who have invested in Japan in the past.

The book assesses the role government plays in shaping the structure and function of securities companies, banks, and regulations governing the stock exchange, and how the interplay of these financial forces shapes the investment climate in Japan. The Japanese socioeconomic structure and value system are examined in order to reveal how they influence Japanese investors. The psychology and behavior of Japanese investors affect opportunities available to foreign investors just as Japanese investment patterns increasingly are affected by foreign markets.

Aware that the majority of North Americans and Europeans with an interest in international investment are most likely to be concerned with capital markets, particularly equities, I have given detailed attention to the securities markets and only brief coverage of the money markets and the market in foreign exchange. Foreign bankers working in Japan have their own sources of information about money markets and foreign exchange, while most nonbankers have little need—or opportunity—to participate in them.

Just as a guidebook written for the tourist points out interesting sights and puzzling rarities, I have made every effort to draw attention to the unique and sometimes enigmatic characteristics of Japan's financial markets. Greatest emphasis is, of course, given to the major attractions: the stock market, bond market, and banking. Whenever possible, I have attempted to draw attention to special attitudes or approaches which distinguish the financial markets in Japan from their U.S. or European counterparts.

Each of the following chapters is written as an autonomous unit and can be read separately, without reference to the book as a whole. However, if the chapters are read in sequence they can give the reader who may have little familiarity with Japan a comprehensive survey of the Japanese financial system. Certain terms peculiar to Japanese finance are briefly explained when they first appear in a chapter. A glossary of commonly used terms is provided as a reference tool.

For the reader with little exposure to Japanese financial markets who is seeking a deeper understanding and appreciation of Japanese business, there is no better way to approach the subject than through the financial market structure. Although financial markets are fundamentally similar throughout the world, each of the nation's markets wears the national costume. A comprehension and appreciation of Japan's markets can lead to an enhanced understanding of Japanese approaches to business and international finance.

ACKNOWLEDGMENTS

The people who have assisted, directly or indirectly, in the preparation of this book are far too numerous to mention. It's a good thing. Many of them would prefer to remain anonymous.

Special thanks, however, are due to the following: James Hegarty, Eve Kaplan, Robert McGarry, Hilary McLellan, Lisa Moore, Paulette Pugh, Nicholas Reitenbach, Andrew Simons, Thomas Smith, Samara Viner-Brown, and John Wheeler.

Aron Viner

While this book has been in the process of being published, Japan's stock markets have been growing like bamboo. The Tokyo Stock Market is now the largest in the world (in terms of capitalization), while the Osaka Stock Market ranks third after Tokyo and New York. In just six months, the average price-to-earnings ratio for all issues listed on the first section of the Tokyo Stock Exchange has risen by nearly 50 percent. The sharp rise in the market has been accompanied by volatility: the Nikkei stock average has been a swinging pendulum. The index broke the 25,000 barrier on June 4. Just eight days later, it flew dizzily above 26,000 before drifting into the doldrums at 23,500 one month later. Japanese real estate has paralleled the stocks with the choicest pieces of land in Tokyo costing as much as $200,000 per square foot.

Less impressive changes have occurred in Japan's financial markets. None of these developments is surprising. Most of them are the direct result of deregulatory actions taken by the Ministry of Finance. While Japanese government bond futures contracts are being traded in London, Japan's domestic financial institutions have been allowed to deal in foreign financial futures and options markets. A full-fledged credit rating system for Japanese companies is now being routinely applied to their issues of bonds and debentures.

The changes will continue. By the end of 1987, stock brokerage commissions will be cut yet again. In 1988, more foreign securities firms will join the stock exchanges. Stock index futures will be traded in Tokyo. Shelf registration, floating rate notes, domestic commercial paper, as well as other new instruments and procedures, will be introduced. More government bonds will be sold at auction and a growing number of foreign institutions will be bidding for them.

* * * * *

Today, the total market value of Japan's land (which is roughly the size of California) exceeds the value of the entire United States. Nomura Securities Company is capitalized at more than all the securities firms on Wall Street. In terms of stock market capitalization, 9 of the world's 10 biggest banks are Japanese. Momentary aberrations? Perhaps.

The rapidity with which Japanese finance has pushed its way into the headlines and the hearts and minds of the world's financial leaders is dazzling. Last year, it was reasonable to assume that the soaring stock market and astronomical Japanese real estate prices were a fragile South Sea bubble. Indeed, most investors are waiting for the bubble to pop. They may not be disappointed. However, I think that they will wait for an eon.

CONTENTS

PART THREE
FUND MANAGEMENT   271

CHAPTER ONE

Introduction

Prior to World War II, Japanese financial markets led a marginal existence. Although a stock market had been created in 1878 (see Chapter 3) for the trading of government bonds, capital markets constituted a minor and minuscule part of Japanese financial activities. Similarly, the short-term money markets, created in 1902 (see Chapter 8), consisted entirely of call-money transactions and did not achieve a major role in the implementation of monetary policy for quite some time. The emergence of zaibatsu holding companies was far more important to Japan's economic and financial development than financial market activity.

The **zaibatsu**, the world's first multinational conglomerates, were family-owned bank-centered holding companies. During the first four decades of the 20th century, the zaibatsu combines expanded through vertical integration of manufacturing and acquisition of raw materials while simultaneously diversifying horizontally into nearly all industrial and financial sectors. Most Japanese corporate equity and debt was held by zaibatsu members. Thus, the financial market history of prewar modern Japan (which begins with the Meiji Restoration in 1868 and concludes with the beginning of the Occupation in 1945) is largely the story of the flow of funds and goods among Japanese government institutions on the one hand and zaibatsu controlled entities on the other.

In August 1946, a Securities Holding Company Liquidation Commission, created by the Occupation authorities, began the task of overseeing the dissolution of the zaibatsu combines. Eighty-three holding companies, containing roughly 4,500 subsidiaries, were reorganized. More than 50 members of zaibatsu families were required to relinquish their securities holdings. By the time it was disbanded in 1951, the Holding Company Liquidation Commission had redistributed more than 200 million shares of stock with a value of ¥9.1 billion. In its attempt to fully democratize Japanese industrial structure, hundreds of corporate officers were purged and all corporate officials were prohibited from serving more than one corporation at a time.[1]

After the end of the Occupation in 1952, a gradual regrouping of zaibatsu interests occurred. The new groupings were termed **keiretsu,** derived from the word *kei* meaning "faction or group" and *retsu* meaning "arranged in order."[2] In common parlance, the term refers to the successors of the prewar zaibatsu. There are also, however, many types of keiretsu based on a variety of types of relationship. The keiretsu utilized interlocked cross-shareholding as a means to seal the control of group companies within the collective organization. Thus, each company owned from 1 to 3 percent of the equity in each keiretsu member,[3] resulting in the majority of corporate shares being held by member companies.

During the era of post-Occupation reconstruction (which extends roughly from 1952 to 1960), the Japanese government deployed the nation's financial institutions as levers carefully designed to lift domestic industrial capability from rubble to full production levels. With this motivation, Japan's financial institutions were given special rights, obligations, and limitations by law. Thus, for example, the Long-Term Credit Bank Law, promulgated in 1952, established that the three credit banks would provide long-term capital to corporations. Certain industrial

---

[1] Hadley's *Antitrust in Japan* discusses the dissolution of the zaibatsu conglomerates and the deconcentration of monopolies in considerable detail. The interlocking of particular industries in the prewar era and their transformation during the postwar era are described thoroughly in this study.

[2] Hadley, p. 257.

[3] In 1972 this percentage was increased further (see Chapter 3).

areas specified by the government (such as power companies and chemicals) were given privileged treatment in the allocation of funds.

During this postwar period, Japan's financial institutions were oriented exclusively toward domestic recovery. Favored industries were nurtured and protected. At that time, Japanese international finance consisted primarily of the foreign exchange dealings conducted by the Bank of Tokyo on behalf of the government and those corporations involved in the exportation of manufactured products. Nearly all imports (97 percent) and the majority of exports (more than 60 percent) were denominated in foreign currencies and the yen was not used as a reserve currency by the world's major central banks. Japan under reconstruction was a provincial nation.

During the 1970s, the market value of Japan's stock exchanges grew at a rate that paralleled the nation's remarkable economic expansion, growing from ¥25 trillion in 1971 to ¥100 trillion in 1982. Concurrently, the government was forced to abandon its balanced budget policies (see Chapter 5) and issue debt to finance its deficits. Japan's capital markets, for the first time in history, began to rival in size those of Europe. Meanwhile, the protected enclaves of specialized financial institutions (see below) became anachronistic. As Japan joined the leading industrial nations as a major world economy, the compartmentalized structure and function of the banking and securities industries were rendered unnecessary. At the same time, foreign banks and securities companies were demanding opportunities to set up operations in Tokyo with equal access to domestic sources of funds.

Thus, under combined domestic and international pressures, Japan's Ministry of Finance was forced to undertake a process of amending the financial regulatory structure. While the Japanese government wanted to limit the speed of change to the minimum, foreign governments insisted upon rapid modifications which would guarantee equal foreign access.

The basic constituents of Japan's financial system are much the same as those of other industrialized nations:

1. A *commercial banking system* accepts deposits, extends loans to businesses, and deals in foreign exchange.

2. *Specialized government-owned financial institutions* help to fund various sectors of the domestic economy.
3. *Securities companies* provide brokerage services, underwrite corporate and government securities, and deal in the securities markets.
4. *Capital markets* offer the means for financing public and private sector debt and for selling residual corporate ownership.
5. *Money markets* offer banks a source of liquidity and provide the central bank with a tool for the implementation of monetary policy.

Ten years ago, in 1977, the Economic Research Department of the Bank of Japan, Japan's central bank, prepared an English language brochure entitled, "The Japanese Financial System."[4] In four succinct parts, the book explains the structure and function of Japan's institutions and the financial markets in which they participate. Figure 1–1, below, is reproduced in full from the book and today still serves as an accurate summary of Japan's financial institutional structure.[5]

In the postwar Japanese financial system upon which Figure 1–1 is based, city banks (large commercial banks based in cities) provided short-term lending to major domestic corporations. Regional banks (smaller commercial banks scattered throughout Japan) took deposits and extended loans to medium- and small-size businesses. The commercial banks could not issue, sell, or underwrite bonds. All of the commercial banks were strictly domestic institutions and engaged in little international business other than a small volume of foreign exchange trading. A special foreign exchange bank, the Bank of Tokyo, took care of most of the government's foreign exchange needs and functioned as the nation's foreign banking representative. Although classified as a commercial bank, the Bank of Tokyo could issue debentures.

---

[4]Economic Research Department, The Bank of Japan, *The Japanese Financial System* (Tokyo, 1978).

[5]The numbers of institutions have changed little since 1977. For example, there are now 64 regional banks (not 63), foreign banks now number 79 (not 55), and trust banks now include 9 foreign institutions and so number 16.

FIGURE 1–1 Financial Institutions in Japan

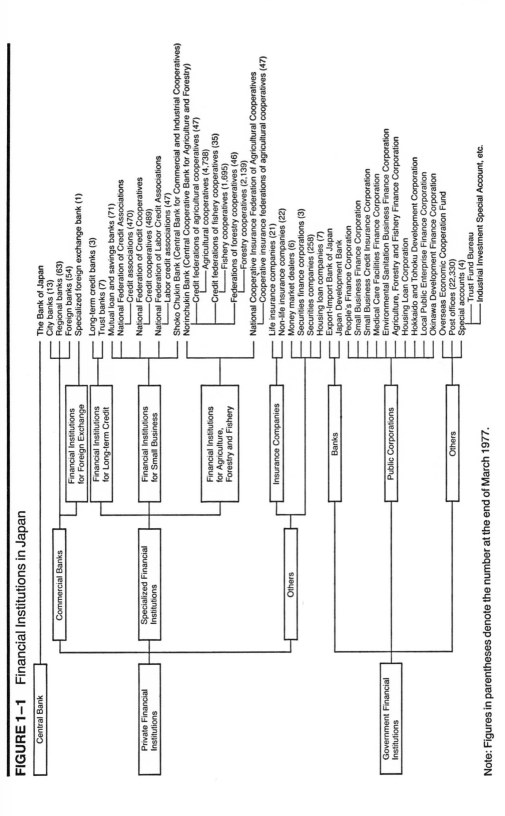

Central Bank
 — The Bank of Japan

Private Financial Institutions
 — Commercial Banks
   — City banks (13)
   — Regional banks (63)
   — Financial Institutions for Foreign Exchange
     — Foreign banks (54)
     — Specialized foreign exchange bank (1)
 — Specialized Financial Institutions
   — Financial Institutions for Long-term Credit
     — Long-term credit banks (3)
     — Trust banks (7)
   — Financial Institutions for Small Business
     — Mutual loan and savings banks (71)
     — National Federation of Credit Associations
       — Credit associations (470)
     — National Federation of Credit Cooperatives
       — Credit cooperatives (489)
     — National Federation of Labor Credit Associations
       — Labor credit associations (47)
     — Shoko Chukin Bank (Central Bank for Commercial and Industrial Cooperatives)
   — Financial Institutions for Agriculture, Forestry and Fishery
     — Norinchukin Bank (Central Cooperative Bank for Agriculture and Forestry)
       — Credit federations of agricultural cooperatives (47)
         — Agricultural cooperatives (4,738)
       — Credit federations of fishery cooperatives (35)
         — Fishery cooperatives (1,695)
       — Federations of forestry cooperatives (46)
         — Forestry cooperatives (2,139)
     — National Cooperative Insurance Federation of Agricultural Cooperatives
       — Cooperative insurance federations of agricultural cooperatives (47)
 — Insurance Companies
   — Life insurance companies (21)
   — Non-life insurance companies (22)
 — Others
   — Money market dealers (6)
   — Securities finance corporations (3)
   — Securities companies (258)
   — Housing loan companies (7)

Government Financial Institutions
 — Banks
   — Export-Import Bank of Japan
   — Japan Development Bank
 — Public Corporations
   — People's Finance Corporation
   — Small Business Finance Corporation
   — Small Business Credit Insurance Corporation
   — Medical Care Facilities Finance Corporation
   — Environmental Sanitation Business Finance Corporation
   — Agriculture, Forestry and Fishery Finance Corporation
   — Housing Loan Corporation
   — Hokkaido and Tohoku Development Corporation
   — Local Public Enterprise Finance Corporation
   — Okinawa Development Finance Corporation
   — Overseas Economic Cooperation Fund
 — Others
   — Post offices (22,330)
   — Special accounts (4)
     — Trust Fund Bureau
     — Industrial Investment Special Account, etc.

Note: Figures in parentheses denote the number at the end of March 1977.

The long-term credit banks were intended to complement rather than compete with the commercial banks. Authorized to issue debentures and prohibited from taking deposits (except from borrowers and the government), the banks specialized in long-term lending to Japan's blue chip corporations. The trust banks, authorized to conduct retail banking and trust banking, straddled the fence between commercial and long-term credit banks. The trust banks were portfolio managers on the one hand while on the other hand they raised funds through the sale of negotiable loan trust certificates (see Glossary).

Only the trust banks and life insurance companies were permitted to manage the nation's corporate pension funds. Meanwhile, the Trust Fund Bureau, an arm of the Ministry of Finance, collected public pension funds which were excluded from private sector management. No private institutions, other than the trust banks and the life insurance companies, were permitted to provide discretionary management services to domestic institutions or individuals. They were allowed to provide investment advice, but portfolio management services were formally prohibited.

Mutual loan and savings banks, credit associations, credit cooperatives, and labor credit associations collected small individual deposits from a population that has long maintained, by far, the highest ratio of savings to disposable income in the world. These deposits were loaned to cooperative members and to the liquidity starved city banks via the money markets or were transmitted to central cooperative banks which in turn loaned the money to small businesses and corporations.

More than 8,000 agricultural, forestry, and fishery cooperatives took deposits from the rural areas and, like other cooperatives in Japan, loaned the money to members or passed funds along to Federations which in turn transmitted a large percentage of liquidity to a central bank. This central institution, the Norinchukin Bank, today has the obscure status of being the largest bank in the world in terms of domestic deposits alone.

Six specialized call loan dealers (the **Tanshi**), operating in the money markets and the foreign exchange markets, have been brokers *par excellence*. Traditionally, the money markets (at first consisting entirely of call-money and later expanded to

include bond repurchase agreements and bill discounts) operated entirely through the six specialized dealers.[6]

Several hundred securities companies functioned as brokers
in the equity and bond markets, areas from which the banking
industry was absolutely excluded. Securities finance companies
acted as intermediaries between the money markets (a banking
sector) and the securities markets (a broking sector) by financing the margin borrowing, through the securities companies, of
individual investors.

Complementing this private sector structure was a parallel
structure of government financial institutions.[7] The Export-
Import Bank of Japan, the Japan Development Bank, and a
number of finance corporations (see Figure 1–1) were intended
to promote the growth of specialized sectors of the domestic economy. All of these institutions derived their funding from the deposits collected by the Postal Savings System and deposited with
the Trust Fund Bureau.

In this system, most of the more than 23,000 post offices
throughout the archipelago accepted deposits or collected funds
by means of a variety of vehicles including savings, annuities,
and insurance. The post offices (administered by the Ministry of
Posts and Telecommunications and *not* the Ministry of Finance)
offered higher interest rates than cooperatives or commercial
banks (see **teigaku** in the Glossary). Because each individual
saver was allowed ¥3 million of tax-free savings (see Appendix
I) and identification was not required for opening accounts, the
Postal Savings System collected more deposits and accounts
than any other institution in the world. Indeed, the total deposits of the postal system today exceeds the aggregate deposits of
the world's four biggest commercial banks.

This necessarily abbreviated summary of Japan's postwar
financial institutional structure does not begin to convey the
remarkably compartmentalized character of the total system.
Furthermore, although government institutions are clearly distinguished from the private sector, nonetheless the demarcation

---

[6]Bond repurchase agreements (**gensaki**) were introduced in 1949.

[7]These institutions (which do not play a significant role in the financial
markets) are not discussed in this book.

between public and private "interests" is far less distinct in Japan than in the West. Thus, the long-term credit banks and especially the Bank of Tokyo (see Chapter 7) often act on behalf of, or in concert with, the Ministry of Finance.

Today, the traditional divisions among the discrete sectors of the Japanese financial system are slowly breaking down. The deregulation of the money markets and capital markets has resulted in the introduction of new short-term instruments (see Chapter 8). Simultaneously, foreign participation in the domestic financial system is increasing (see Chapters 2 and 7). Concurrent with these developments, the Euroyen bond market has grown geometrically and now exceeds in size the Samurai bond market (see Chapter 6).

As a result of the enormous structural changes now occurring in the financial sector, as well as the considerable liquidity available to domestic institutions and corporations, Japanese finance is becoming an exciting field. A once static and closed system is being transformed into a dynamic open market.

The revision (or outright abandonment) of regulatory laws, followed by the establishment of a diversity of new capital market and money market instruments, is now exerting crucial influence on global markets. The formerly musty and dusty house of Japanese finance is being renovated. There is no master plan for the complete series of alterations currently in progress. The precise form and content of future Japanese financial markets are not known.

PART ONE

Capital Markets

CHAPTER TWO

Securities Firms

OVERVIEW

In December 1986, *Financial World* magazine, a U.S. trade publication, selected Yoshihisa Tabuchi, President of Japan's largest securities company, Nomura, as "Man of the Year." The choice was "as much for the enormous potential of the juggernaut he heads as for what he himself has managed to accomplish," the magazine explained. The attention given to Nomura by *Financial World* was just one of hundreds of articles in the non-Japanese financial press during 1985 and 1986 that focused on the growth and competitiveness of Japan's leading securities firms. If Nomura (and its coevals—Daiwa, Nikko, and Yamaichi) had been content only to amass profits and consolidate domination in the home market, then its activities would be of limited interest to the practitioners of international finance. Two factors, however, ordained otherwise.

Money. The clients of the Big Four securities firms (ranging from institutional investors, to corporate treasurers, to individuals) are the richest group of investors in the world. Beginning in 1985, liquidity in Japan far exceeded private and public demand for funds. Partly as a result, Japan became the "cash cow of the industrial world," surpassing OPEC as the world's biggest creditor. In 1985, Japan's long-term capital outflow was $65 billion and during that year, Japanese investors,

---

TABLE 2–1 Japanese Investment in Foreign Currency Bonds ($ millions)

Foreign Currency Bonds	1983	1984	1985	1986*
Purchases	26,510	77,587	291,376	1,347,000
Sales	12,822	47,108	237,860	1,254,000
Net	13,688	30,479	53,516	93,000

---

*Figures for 1986 accurate to the nearest billion.

SOURCE: Ministry of Finance

on a net basis, bought roughly $53.5 billion of foreign bonds (double the 1984 level), of which more than half was U.S. government debt (see Table 2–1). These figures increased by roughly 75 percent in 1986. Indeed, at the end of 1986, total Japanese holdings of U.S. Treasury issues were estimated to be about $100 billion.

Long-term capital outflow for 1986 is estimated to exceed $100 billion and Japanese net purchases of U.S. government securities (despite the depreciation of the dollar against the yen[1]) are estimated to be higher than $50 billion. The sudden and dramatic ascendancy of Japanese investors in the U.S. mar-

---

[1]The yield spreads between long-term U.S. Treasury issues and Japanese long-term government bonds have been considered sufficient, even at their narrowest, to justify exchange loss over the medium- and long-term (see Figure 2–1). Japanese institutional investors have considered 300 basis points (3 percent) to be the minimum acceptable spread between the yields on long-term U.S. Treasury bonds and Japanese 10-year government bonds. During 1986, however, the spread fell lower than 200 basis points. Nonetheless, Japanese investors have managed funds in accordance with the unspoken view that unrealized paper losses can be ignored because only yields are used as a performance measure for the funds managed by trust banks and life insurance companies (see Chapter 9). (It has been estimated that the 21 Japanese life insurance companies suffered paper losses of an aggregate ¥4 trillion, or about $25 billion, on their investments in Treasury issues during the period September 1985 to August 1986.) If the 30-year U.S. Treasury issues are held to maturity, their annual yield advantage against a yen security is more than sufficient to counterbalance the declines in the value of the dollar. However, if the spread falls significantly below 200 basis points (to 150 or less), then Japanese institutional investors are likely to substantially decrease investments in dollar-denominated bonds and instead focus their spending on foreign real estate and equity.

FIGURE 2-1 Yield Spreads between U.S. and Japanese Long-Term Bonds

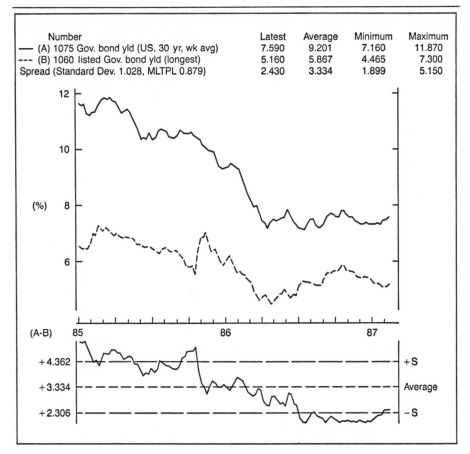

Number	Latest	Average	Minimum	Maximum
—— (A) 1075 Gov. bond yld (US, 30 yr, wk avg)	7.590	9.201	7.160	11.870
--- (B) 1060 listed Gov. bond yld (longest)	5.160	5.867	4.465	7.300
Spread (Standard Dev. 1.028, MLTPL 0.879)	2.430	3.334	1.899	5.150

ket astounded many observers, giving Nomura and other Japanese institutions unprecedented notoriety.

Euromarket. In 1986, Nomura became the second biggest underwriter of Eurobonds, and Daiwa and Nikko ranked among the top 10. The dominant Japanese presence in the Euromarket resulted in large part from the predatory pricing of debt issues in order to give institutional clients the cheapest rates and swaps in the market. In this way, domestic profits were used to buy a substantial share of the new Euromarket (see Chapter 6).

At about the same time, Japanese investors demonstrated a

new interest in Euroequities. In late 1984, Nomura securities underwrote 100 million shares (nearly 25 percent of the total overseas allotment of 415 million shares) of newly privatized British Telecommunications. Nikko, Daiwa, and Yamaichi together underwrote an additional 80 million shares. In sharp contrast to U.S. investment banks which sold their British Telecom shares back to U.K. investors, the Big Four sold 85 percent of the shares to Japanese investors who, to date, have retained an estimated two-thirds.

Although only about 6 percent of Japanese foreign securities investments are in equities, during the first nine months of 1986, the net share purchases in the United States by Japanese investors rose nearly nine times from the 1985 level, to $2.6 billion (compared to $298 million during the same period of the preceding year).

The concept of prospective Japanese dominance of the international securities industry was novel to European and U.S. investment banks. Thus, Japanese financing of international issues, combined with the capacity to fully distribute a range of securities to the home market, made Japan's leading securities firms a new and surprising force in international finance. It is likely that as Japan's trade surpluses increase, Japanese securities companies will play an increasing role in directing the flow of surplus funds by bringing domestic investors and international borrowers together.

Prior to World War II, Japanese securities firms were small and derived most of their business from trading in bonds. Because most corporate equity was held by the zaibatsu conglomerates, stock trading was thin. The dissolution of the zaibatsu and the privatization of some government institutions under the direction of Occupation authorities, led to the emergence of a new Japanese stock market in which individual investors initially held the majority of shares (69.1 percent in 1949).

Since the reopening of the stock exchanges in 1949, the history of securities firms in Japan has been characterized by the occasional opening of new firms and the frequent absorption or mergers of existing companies. Often encouraged and engineered by the Ministry of Finance in order to prevent bankruptcies, the mergers gradually reduced the number of firms from the 1,152 registered in 1949 to 244 at the end of March 1986.

Securities companies in Japan can be classified into three categories or "tiers." The first tier consists of the "Big Four" securities houses which rank among the six biggest securities firms in the world: Nomura, Daiwa, Nikko, and Yamaichi. The second tier includes 10 significantly smaller companies. The third tier is an agglomeration of all the remaining registered securities firms in Japan. Many of the second- and third-tier firms are the affiliates or "satellites" of the Big Four (more than 30 are affiliated with Nomura and 19 are affiliated with Yamaichi), some are affiliated with banks, and 83 are members of the Tokyo Stock Exchange.[2] Within the Tokyo financial community, the second- and third-tier firms are referred to as the **chusho shoken** in contrast to the Big Four which stand alone as the **yondai shoken.**

Japan's securities firms derive most of their income from brokerage fees, underwriting, and dealing. In addition, ancillary services yield incremental income and the administration of investment trusts provides considerable revenue. The Big Four control more than 80 percent of all domestic underwriting; the remainder is taken by second-tier firms. All securities companies deal in securities for their own account and carry substantial inventories. Second- and third-tier securities firms rely heavily on brokerage commissions and do little underwriting.

In such areas as international bond underwriting and Eurobond bookrunning, the four biggest Japanese securities firms rank among the leading financial institutions in the world. The Big Four are members of the New York Stock Exchange and, in March 1986, Nomura became the first Japanese member of the London Stock Exchange. Two of the Big Four (Nomura and Daiwa) are primary dealers in the U.S. Treasury market, and Japanese securities firms will eventually become primary dealers in the British gilts market.

In their home market, the Big Four securities firms have collectively cornered almost half of all equity and bond trading. In 1986, the Big Four were among the most profitable financial institutions in the world. A combination of powerful domestic

---

[2] Of the 93 members of the Tokyo Stock Exchange, 6 are foreign firms (discussed later in this chapter). The remaining 87 include the Big Four, the second tier of 10 securities firms, and 73 third-tier firms.

marketing, fixed commissions with high stock exchange turnover, and considerable margin trading by individuals resulted in record earnings. A large part of the profits are now being invested in extensive and costly computerization programs as well as the development of overseas operations.

It is likely that as deregulation loosens the Big Four's stranglehold on stock exchange trading, brokerage earnings will decline. In anticipation of that event, the Big Four and some of their second-tier colleagues are preparing to replace domestic profits with the largess of international business. Outside the domestic market, the Big Four must compete on equal terms with the universal banks, merchant banks, and investment banks of Europe and North America. In 1986, the Big Four began deploying their troops in preparation for the battles of the late 1980s in which market share will be won or lost on the basis of innovative financial developments and cut-rate deals.

The three-tier structure of securities companies in Japan is paralleled by a separate and rapidly growing category: foreign securities firms. At first marginal and insignificant players in the domestic securities industry, the foreign firms are determined to gain a major segment of Japanese securities business. Salomon Brothers, for example, was the 11th largest securities firm in Japan in 1986 in terms of operating profits (with pretax profits of ¥ 9.1 billion for the six months to March 1986) and was the third largest trader in the new bond futures market (see Chapter 5). In January 1987, the firm increased its paid-in capital from ¥5.1 billion to ¥52 billion, making it the fifth largest securities company in Japan in terms of capitalization. In November 1986, Merrill Lynch became the first foreign securities firm to list its shares on the Tokyo Stock Exchange, joining the dozen domestic securities firms listed in the first section. Two months later, the firm received authorization from the Ministry of Finance to open a branch of its London banking subsidiary in Tokyo, making it the first securities company to conduct banking operations in Japan.

THE BIG FOUR

Domestic Dominance

The Japanese leader in all domestic markets is Nomura Securities Company. During the 1980s, the value of Nomura's share-

TABLE 2–2 Share of Domestic Yen
Bond Transactions

Firm	1985 (percent)
Nomura	13.22
Nikko	9.80
Daiwa	9.46
Yamaichi	8.42
Total	40.90

holders' equity grew dramatically, reaching $34 billion at the end of 1986 and towering above Merrill Lynch. Nomura's net capital, in excess of $10 billion in 1986, exceeds Merrill Lynch, Salomon Brothers and Shearson Lehman combined. For the 1986 fiscal year,[3] Nomura increased its pretax profits (on a consolidated basis) by 86 percent to ¥428.72 billion ($2.7 billion). This was the biggest profit ever recorded by a Japanese institution, making Nomura the second most profitable institution in the world in 1986, trailing only Citicorp in pretax income. By comparison, in 1986, Dai-Ichi Kangyo Bank (the largest commercial bank in the world in terms of assets) recorded half of Nomura's profits and half of Nomura's return on equity.

As Tables 2–2 and 2–3 indicate, Nomura alone handles nearly 14 percent of all stock transactions and more than 13 percent of all bond transactions in Japan. Together the Big Four account for roughly 44 percent of all stock transactions and 41 percent of all bond transactions. If those third-tier firms that are affiliated with the Big Four were also included, these numbers would be higher still.

Prior to 1986, the Big Four handled virtually all transactions of foreign shares on the Tokyo Stock Exchange. Nomura was the most active trader in foreign shares, followed by Daiwa, Nikko, and Yamaichi. Since all dealing in foreign shares listed on the exchange is transacted on behalf of domestic investors, it is not likely that foreign branches will gain more than an incremental portion of this business.

Brokerage fees in Japan are based upon a commission scale which is nonnegotiable and relatively inflexible (see Chapter 3

---

[3] Japanese securities firms have a fiscal year ending September 30, while the Japanese government's fiscal year ends March 31.

TABLE 2–3 Share of Equity Transactions on the First
Section of the Tokyo Stock Exchange

Firm	1985 (percent)
Nomura	13.9
Daiwa	10.4
Yamaichi	10.4
Nikko	9.6
Total	44.3

for a more detailed discussion). Institutional investors are often granted a 20 percent discount as well as unofficial rebates; nonetheless the commission fees have been far higher than those in New York or London. Although commissions for large trades were reduced in November 1986, individuals continue to pay rates that are among the highest in the world.

During the 1980s, the Big Four gradually lost a small part of their share of brokerage business to second-tier firms. Nonetheless, because computerization and software refinements vastly reduced the back office cost of processing small accounts, profits increased. As a result, income for each of the Big Four rose at a dramatically rapid rate, establishing new records every year since 1982. The bond market rally in the first half of fiscal 1986 and the stock market boom later that year stimulated profit growth further, resulting in combined pretax recurring profits of ¥986.6 billion ($6.25 billion) for fiscal 1986 (see Table 2–4). This compares with the corresponding figure for the 13 city banks of ¥1,129 billion. Similarly, the 10 second-tier securities houses and the leading 10 third-tier firms all reported record earnings for fiscal 1986 with combined pretax profits rising an average of 80 percent from the preceding year.

The key to the exceptional success of the Big Four is marketing. The leader, Nomura, learned retail sales techniques from a tie-up with Merrill Lynch in the 1960s. Today, Nomura maintains a sales staff of approximately 4,800, including 2,300 women employed to sell investment trusts (mutual funds) and bonds to housewives on a door-to-door basis. Salaried salesmen based in one of the 116 Nomura branch offices throughout Japan consult convenient references published by the Tax Bureau (re-

TABLE 2–4 Nonconsolidated Big Four Pretax Profits

Firm	Pretax Recurring Profits* (¥ billions) Year Ending Sept. 30, 1986	Percent Change from Previous Year**
Nomura	390	+85.0
Daiwa	235	+91.2
Nikko	205	+82.3
Yamaichi	180	+74.0

*On a nonconsolidated basis.

**The consolidated figures are incrementally higher for Nomura (86 percent) and Daiwa (92 percent) and lower for Nikko (77 percent) and Yamaichi (68 percent).

SOURCE: Nihon Keizai Shimbun

gional lists of the biggest taxpayers) in order to select targets for telephone solicitation. "Stocks of the week" are promoted to regular customers.

Nikko, Daiwa, and Yamaichi, like Nomura, each maintain more than 100 domestic sales offices as well as thousands of sales personnel (including women employed to ring doorbells in order to persuade housewives—who usually manage the domestic budget—to buy a range of financial products). In the United States and the United Kingdom, the door-to-door approach to selling securities was abandoned by such firms as Prudential Assurance because increasing wages undermined its cost effectiveness. The system remains viable in Japan due to low wages and incentives derived from sales. In addition, Japan's high savings rate provides a base of available funds from which individual investors can draw. Thus, for example, regular Nomura customers maintain a Nomura savings box in much the same way that Americans of a bygone era placed pin money in piggy banks and cookie jars.

Each of the Big Four is structured like a zaibatsu in miniature. The parent securities firm, resembling the omnipotent prewar bank, occupies the center of a constellation of companies. These companies can best be viewed by the Western analyst as departments of the parent securities firm rather than as subsidiary enterprises. A subtle hierarchical status ranking of the group companies is not articulated but is known to all employees. Below the dozen or so subsidiary companies are 15 to 30 affiliated second- and third-tier securities firms.

At the top of the group of companies under a Big Four umbrella is the "investment trust and management" subsidiary. The single biggest producer of brokerage commissions, the investment trust subsidiary manages stock and bond investment trusts purchased by corporations and individuals (see below). The investment trust company of Yamaichi, the smallest of the Big Four, managed ¥2.628 trillion ($14 billion) at the end of fiscal 1985.

Each of the Big Four maintains a "research institute" which provides a home for its securities analysts, economists, and data bank. The research institute, near the top of the internal hierarchy, usually has the largest staff of all the subsidiary members. Immediately below the research institute is the "international capital management" subsidiary. Although of relatively recent origin (see Chapter 9), these companies, first by managing OPEC funds and subsequently domestic specified money trusts (**tokkin**), have been a major source of brokerage commissions. Additional subsidiaries within a group include (but are not limited to), real estate, venture capital, computer, and credit card companies.

The presidents and chairmen of virtually all of the group companies are seconded by the parent securities firm. Usually corporate directors or executive vice presidents who are in a weak political position within the parent firm are farmed out to the subsidiaries as chief executive officers. Those individuals given such lateral transfers and paper promotions receive no cut in salary or privileges, but suffer an enormous decline in status within the total corporate structure. Obliged to resign from the parent securities company, they can never return to it.

The system of moving employees from one company to another within the group is not limited to senior executives. Young employees are routinely shifted among the companies, experiencing little or no change in salary and prestige as a result. However, a move from one of the dozen group companies to an affiliated company is a severe demotion, often resulting from an act of wrongdoing or incompetence. All of the Big Four practice a system of "lifetime employment" in which, after several years with the company, an employee is given special status, ordinarily assuring a position until retirement. In such a system, firing can rarely be the most severe expression of official dissatisfaction with employee performance. Instead, a company's black sheep are exiled for their working lives to a minor affiliated company. There is no return.

Foreign Inroads

During the postwar period, in 1953, the first overseas office of a Big Four firm was opened in New York by Yamaichi. By the mid-1960s, each of the Big Four had established offices in North America and Europe. Offices in Singapore, Hong Kong, and the Middle East followed in the 1970s. The primary purpose of these overseas operations was the sale of Japanese securities to foreign institutional (and individual) investors and, after it became legal, the sale of foreign securities to Japanese investors. With the exception of Chinese entrepreneurs—who have an insatiable appetite for speculation of all kinds—few foreign investors initially made significant commitments to the Japanese stock market. As a result, prior to 1979, virtually all of the overseas operations lost money, except for Hong Kong.

In 1980, the new foreign exchange law stimulated Japanese investment in foreign securities. At the same time, a stock market boom (which began in 1979) in Japan encouraged foreign investors to buy Japanese equities. As a consequence, equity sales in the Big Four's overseas subsidiaries began to surge. By 1984, each of the Big Four had offices in 8 to 11 countries, including China. The profitability of these overseas operations varied considerably.

In the mid-1980s, the Big Four expanded their New York and London operations. Nomura's London subsidiary, for example, grew from 2 employees in 1964 to more than 400 in 1986, while its New York office grew from fewer than 100 employees in 1980 to roughly 400 in 1986. Approximately 70 percent of the employees at these foreign subsidiaries are non-Japanese. Thus, by the time foreign firms acquired membership on the Tokyo Stock Exchange, the Big Four were as well established overseas as were foreign firms in Tokyo.

Beginning in 1982, active campaigns to procure underwriting business in Europe (see Chapter 6 for a discussion of the Euromarket) and the United States were implemented. The

1982 establishment of shelf registration in the United States increased Big Four competitive opportunities in the American underwriting market. Shelf registration regulations eliminated much of the paperwork and time that had been previously necessary to float a primary issue. Consequently, the 1982 regulations vitiated the long-term relationships that had existed between established investment banks and their corporate clients. U.S. corporate treasurers took advantage of this newly acquired latitude to give underwriting business to those firms offering the best terms. As a direct result, Japanese securities houses had the opportunity to compete on an equal basis with such blue blood investment banks as Morgan Stanley. Japanese failure to make significant inroads in the U.S. underwriting market was due to a variety of factors. Chief among them was the in-house absence of the skills necessary to cultivate key relationships with U.S. companies. Furthermore, the Japanese staff assigned to U.S. positions lacked the training, the experience, and the authority to quickly design and implement vital deals. However, the Big Four are forging links with U.S. corporations by managing their Eurobond issues. Nomura, for instance, lead managed Euroyen issues in 1986 for such U.S. companies as AMEX, Coca-Cola, and Dow Chemical. In late 1986, Nomura replaced the president and chairman of its New York subsidiary with specialists in corporate finance. The decision can best be interpreted as an indication of Nomura's determination to gain more than a toehold in U.S. investment banking.

In 1985 and 1986, Japan's record current account surpluses, conjoined with extraordinary national liquidity, triggered a frantic interest in the U.S. Treasury market. Because the market in U.S. government debt was the only market capable of absorbing the vast sums of Japan's institutional money, neither declining U.S. interest rates nor the revaluation of the yen discouraged Japan's institutions from buying and holding Treasury issues.

The market in U.S. government debt, with a daily turnover of more than $100 billion and $2 trillion of securities outstanding, is by far the largest capital market in the world. In order to finance the biggest budget deficit in history and to simultaneously keep interest rates low, the U.S. government has developed an increasing dependence on foreign investors. Seeking minimal political risk, a relatively sound currency, and high interest rates, foreign institutions have turned to the market in U.S. Treasury issues.

In 1985 and 1986, no foreign buyers displayed a more voracious appetite for the products of the U.S Treasury Department than the Japanese. Indeed, during that two-year period, Japanese investors pumped an estimated $3 billion per month into U.S. securities. In the summer of 1986, for example, Japanese buyers alone bought roughly $4 billion of a $9 billion Treasury bond offering. Gross trading volume (total sales and purchases) of U.S. government securities by Japanese investors averaged more than $150 billion per month in 1986. As a result, by 1985, the U.S. Treasury Bond market in Japan (the **Tokyo dollar bond market**—see Glossary) had become second only to New York. The Big Four cornered this market, handling more than 75 percent of Japanese trading in American treasury bonds in 1985 and an estimated 65 percent in 1986.

In May 1986, when the U.S. Treasury auctioned a record $27 billion in notes and bonds to help finance the Federal debt, the leading four Japanese securities firms purchased roughly 18.5 percent of the total (about $5 billion). Dissuaded neither by declining U.S. interest rates nor by the depreciation of the dollar against the yen, Japanese investors hungrily snapped up the U.S. securities. Had the Big Four not participated in the auction, the Treasury would have been obliged to pay higher interest rates on the 30-year bonds that constituted one-third of the total auction. Higher interest rates on these bellwether bonds would invariably have affected the entire bond market, raising rates for all Treasury issues.

The impact of the Japanese positions in the May 1986 Treasury auction was not limited to its effect on interest rates. U.S. securities firms lost an estimated $300 million by misjudging Big Four investment strategy. U.S. traders expected the Japanese securities houses to sell older bond holdings in order to finance new purchases in the May auction. Consequently, many U.S. firms sold short on older bonds in anticipation of a price drop. The Big Four, however, held the older bonds and the expected price decline did not occur.

In 1985, Nomura and Daiwa (followed by Nikko and Yamaichi in 1986) applied to become primary dealers in U.S. government securities. Primary dealers are required to report their financial status to the Fed on a daily basis. They are committed to making markets in all Treasury issues and they must meet minimum levels of trading in Treasury auctions. The benefits of the status include substantial prestige (many large institutions only do business with primary dealers) as well as the privilege and advantages of conducting business directly with the Fed. At the end of June 1986, there were 35 primary dealers and, according to *Dow Jones Capital Market Report*, 16 applicants.

Each of the Big Four regarded joining the leading group of 35 firms that transact directly with the New York Fed as validating its position as a leader in world financial markets. Each firm believed that the magnitude of its trading in Treasury issues merited primary dealer status. Perhaps the greatest advantage derived from admission to the elite circle was in the Japanese domestic market. Nomura, or Nikko, or Daiwa could proclaim to its Japanese corporate clients, "We are second to none in the U.S. Treasury market; therefore, there is no reason to deal with foreign firms when buying or selling Treasury issues for your portfolios." This is a powerful argument in Japan, where institutions have a deeply embedded preference for conducting transactions with familiar and indigenous entities.

U.S. congressmen opposed to Japanese applications for primary dealer status argued that until U.S. firms could trade freely in Japanese markets, the Fig Four should be excluded from the exclusive club of primary dealers. The leader of the opposition, representative Charles Schumer, observed in a letter to the President of the Federal Reserve Bank of New York that a 1986 offering of 20-year Japanese government bonds was awarded to a syndicate of six Japanese firms, which gave less than 1 percent of the total issue to U.S. securities firms.

Nonetheless, in December 1986, the U.S. units of Nomura Securities and Daiwa Securities were granted primary dealer status, making them leading participants in the U.S. securities market. This decision exemplified the vital role played by Japanese securities firms in the U.S. securities industry.

In August 1984, the management consulting firm, McKinsey & Co., advised Nomura Securities to conform to local business practices and corporate structure in order to compete successfully in foreign markets. Nomura planners took this recommendation seriously. Indeed, they had already begun to staff their New York and London offices with experienced and high-salaried natives. Nomura's U.S. unit hired the former head of the Drexel Burnham government bond trading department as its chief bond trader. Other "local hires" in the U.S. included an assistant deputy secretary to the Secretary of the Treasury. In July 1986, Nomura appointed a former U.K. government official, Sir Douglas Wass, ex-permanent secretary to the Treasury, as the chairman of its London subsidiary. Daiwa, Nikko, and Yamaichi followed in step.

In the summer of 1986, for example, Nikko International America hired the Federal Reserve's top ranking staff official and perhaps the second most powerful decision maker at the Fed. Given the title of vice chairman (of the New York subsidiary *only*) and an annual salary of $700,000, he was an expression of the driving ambition to gain primary dealer status in the U.S. government securities market. Shortly afterward, Yamaichi International America hired a former senior vice president of the New York Federal Reserve Bank, also given the title of vice chairman. Similarly, Daiwa spent considerable sums to hire a former U.S. Treasury official and a former Salomon Brothers partner. In 1985 and early 1986, each of the Big Four's New York offices hired a leading American bond trader to set up and direct their bond dealing departments. These head traders received combined salaries and commissions that far exceeded the total compensation of the presidents and chairmen of the parent companies in Tokyo.

During the 1980s, and particularly in recent years, the Big Four have used their record profits to subsidize the development of international business. Vast sums were spent on the expansion of overseas offices, primarily operations in London and New York. In the spring of 1986, for instance, Nomura purchased the old London post offfice building in a $200 million cash deal. During fiscal year 1986, all of the Big Four dramatically increased the number of staff employed in their U.S. units. The "local staff" of Yamaichi International America, for example, grew sevenfold—from 21 staff members at the end of 1985 to a staff of 145 at the end of 1986, with a further doubling of local employees anticipated for 1987. At the same time, the Big Four substantially increased the capitalization of their U.S. subsidiaries. By the end of 1986, each of the firms maintained that U.S. clients constituted roughly half of all the business conducted by its U.S. operations. Such claims are difficult to verify. Nonetheless, true or not, 1986 was a watershed year for the New York and London subsidiaries of the Big Four. Trading operations in U.S. Treasury issues were vastly expanded, while trading activities were diversified to include corporate bonds and mortgage-backed securities.

As Table 2–5 indicates, for fiscal year 1986, the overseas subsidiaries of the Big Four posted pretax profits of more than ¥80 billion ($500 million), constituting a little less than 10 percent of the total profits of the parent companies.

It is noteworthy, however, that the methods for calculating subsidiary overhead are rather murky since some of the operational costs of the subsidiaries are assumed by the parent company. Thus, for example, the salaries and expenses of many Japanese employees sent to the subsidiaries are paid by the parent company. Overall, the profit gains were largely the result of expanded Japanese investments in U.S. government securities. In addition, all transactions derived from the overseas subsidiaries of Japanese corporations are regarded as overseas rather than domestic business even though the transactions are usually conducted in Japan with only formal reference to the overseas office. In this way, it is probable that each of the Big Four claimed excessive success in their total international enterprises. It is likely that in this early stage of implementing new international strategies and objectives, the overseas operations of at least several of the Big Four are far less profitable than the balance sheets indicate.

Even if each of the Big Four were currently posting losses for international business, which is not the case, the eventual success of the "internationalization" programs now underway is a

---

TABLE 2–5   Big Four Overseas Subsidiaries

Firm	Number of Units	Pretax Profit Fiscal 1986 (¥ billions)	Percent Change from Previous Year
Nomura	10	38.2	110
Daiwa	7	20.8	170
Nikko	8	12.5	130
Yamaichi	11	11.8	150

SOURCE: Nihon Keizai Shimbun

virtual certainty. The Big Four possess the capital needed to buy out any competitor in Wall Street or The City. A deterrent to such foreign acquisitions has been the fear of local staff attrition. In the securities industry, unlike the manufacturing industry, staff represent the greater part of goodwill. Were the employees of a recently acquired firm to resign *en masse*, there would be little of value remaining. The smooth acquisition of foreign banks by Japanese banks has been providing an encouraging example for the securities firms. There were few resignations at J. Henry Schroder Bank and Trust; and the employees at the Bank of California and Banca del Gottardo, institutions recently acquired by Japanese banks, have chosen to keep their jobs.

In 1985, Nomura bought 20 percent (later increased to 50 percent) of a U.S. leasing firm, Babcock & Brown. A year later, Nomura Babcock & Brown, in turn, acquired a 50 percent stake in Eastdil Realty Inc., a real estate investment banking firm. The Eastdil acquisition will be used by Nomura to exploit U.S. real estate investments by its domestic corporate clients. In 1986, Nikko acquired Fraser Green, Ltd. and may purchase a U.S. firm in 1987 or 1988. It is likely that, by 1990, all of the Big Four will have made foreign acquisitions.

ARTICLE 65: DECLINE AND FALL?

Prior to 1945, Japanese securities firms were small institutions specializing in bond trading. Although the dissolution of the zaibatsu was a key factor in their ascendancy, of even greater importance was Article 65 of the Securities and Exchange Act of 1948—Japan's version of the 1933 U.S. Glass-Steagall Act.

The Glass-Steagall Act created a barrier between commercial banks and investment banks by means of functional separation. Under the Act, banks are prohibited from owning broking or dealing companies. The Act proscribes commercial banks from underwriting or trading corporate securities for proprietary accounts. In addition, banks are banned from underwriting most municipal securities. The primary purpose of the Act was to prevent conflicts of interest while promoting the soundness of the banking system.

Article 65 of Japan's Securities and Exchange Act prohibits

banks from participating in the domestic securities industry and bans securities companies from domestic banking activities. Banks are not permitted to own more than 5 percent of a Japanese securities company (or any domestic company) and they are banned from selling equity or underwriting primary securities issues in Japan. At the same time, securities companies are not allowed to take deposits or give loans in the home market. The Act also requires the registration of securities and the registration of broker-dealers. In addition, the Act separates the insurance industry from the securities industry. As a result, the insurance industry retains responsibility for real estate investment with the consequence that securities companies are prohibited from dealing in real estate investment trust shares.[4]

Article 65 was designed to protect securities firms from the consolidated prewar power of the zaibatsu banks. The separation of commercial and investment banking was intended to dilute the concentration of funds and financial power held by the banks. Today, many securities firms, including the Big Four, maintain relationships with banks. Nomura, established in 1925, was a spin-off from the bond department of Daiwa Bank (then named Osaka Nomura Bank). Each of the Big Four currently has a loose relationship with banks within the keiretsu framework (the heir to prewar zaibatsu): Yamaichi Securities Company (est. 1896) with Fuji Bank and the Industrial Bank of Japan; Daiwa Securities Company, which traces its antecedents to Fujimoto Bill Broker, (est. in 1902) with Sumitomo Bank; and Nikko Securities Company with Mitsubishi Bank.

The complementary relationships between the securities firms and the banks in the postwar era were possible only because of the protective territories established by Article 65. Had this proviso not existed, there can be little doubt that the powerful city banks, with their extensive networks of branches (an average of more than 200 per bank—see Chapter 7) and corporate relationships, would long ago have absorbed or destroyed the majority of securities firms.

The U.S. Glass-Steagall Act was the model on which Article 65 was fashioned and, not surprisingly, the vitiation of the Act

---

[4]Consequently, the U.S. real estate industry has been constrained in its opportunities to tap the Japanese capital market.

has been perceived as an exemplar by Japan's regulatory authorities. As U.S. banks began to provide products and services previously the exclusive domain of brokers and as U.S. brokers began to provide cash management services bearing a remarkable resemblance to savings accounts, the "Chinese wall" separating banking and broking activities promised slow dissolution. Japan followed suit.

The medium-term government bond funds pioneered by Nomura in 1980 functioned like savings accounts. Indeed, since 1980, the Big Four have been promoting the concept of domestic financial deregulation. If given total freedom, the Big Four would manage pension funds, deal in foreign exchange and commodities, take personal deposits and extend loans, and offer every form of insurance from golf insurance to variable life policies.

The government's decision to permit banks to be secondary dealers in public bonds (see Chapter 5), further eroded a critical distinction between the banking and securities industries. All the while, however, the Ministry of Finance was acutely aware that if Japan's banks were permitted to encroach too deeply and directly into the securities service sector, then the more than 200 third-tier securities firms would rapidly disappear through bankruptcy, mergers, and acquisitions. Whether the Big Four could maintain their wide margin of profitability in the absence of Article 65 remains moot. Nonetheless, the leading four securities firms are confident that they will prevail in a financial free-for-all.

Meanwhile, the city banks have been lobbying with the Ministry of Finance for a full—or at least partial—demolition of Article 65. The recent liberalization of some interest rates has resulted in increased borrowing costs while, simultaneously, global interest rates have been declining. Furthermore, Japan's massive liquidity has resulted in a supply of funds that far exceeds demand, rendering the domestic loan business a game of diminishing returns. To make matters worse, during the course of the next five years, interest rates on small deposits will be deregulated. While banking profits have stagnated, Japanese corporate borrowers have been using their excess funds to pay down bank debt and invest directly in the capital markets. As a result, more than ever before, the city banks want a portion of the fat brokerage income that has made securities business the most profitable financial industry in Japan.

The inevitability of a major change was foreshadowed in late 1983 when Citicorp (the parent holding company of Citibank) bought a majority share in the Far Eastern operations of Vickers da Costa (which had been a full service securities branch in Tokyo since 1978). With strategic savvy, Citicorp announced the acquisition during a visit to Tokyo by President Reagan. The presence of the U.S. president in Japan placed the Ministry of Finance in an awkward and, from the Japanese perspective, embarrassing position to object. Under these circumstances the Ministry of Finance decided not to revoke Vickers da Costa's securities branch licenses. In this way, a securities firm owned by a bank suddenly appeared on the Japanese financial stage.

In 1985, the West German bank, Deutsche Bank, was granted a securities license for its 50 percent-owned subsidiary, DB Capital Markets. This event was followed in 1986 by government approval of a bevy of foreign securities branches with bank or bankholding company ownership (see Table 2–9). However, bank involvement in the securities branches was limited by Ministry of Finance policy to a maximum of 50 percent ownership in accordance with the Foreign Securities Company Law. In order to obtain a securities branch license for an operation which, in effect, combines banking and broking, foreign banks were advised by the Ministry of Finance to detach half the equity in the securities firm and allot it to a nonfinancial institution. This is a simple matter for the German and Swiss universal banks which have close underwriting relationships with major corporations in their home territories. Thus, Deutsche Bank, for example, brought in Siemans and Bayer while the Swiss Bank Corporation made a similar arrangement with Ciba-Geigy. Many foreign banks wih branches in Tokyo (particularly trust banks—Barclays is waiting in the wings) may use this method during the late 1980s in order to establish securities operations. However, the expected approval of a securities branch license for the American bank, Morgan Guaranty, may simplify this procedure.

At the time of writing, Vickers da Costa remained the only securities branch in Japan with the *majority* of shares owned by a bank holding company. Meanwhile, Japanese banks were proscribed from owning more than 5 percent of a securities company.[5] The other side of the coin, however, was equally significant.

On September 2, 1986, Nomura obtained a license from the Bank of England (application was made in 1980) to establish Nomura International Finance Ltd., a full-service bank capitalized at 50 million pounds. All of the Big Four have unprofitable banking subsidiaries in Amsterdam and Luxembourg. However, London, the global leader in international banking, promises a broad client base. In January 1987, Daiwa was granted deposit taking rights for Daiwa Europe Finance Ltd., its London subsidiary. Also capitalized at 50 million pounds, the Daiwa bank will be operational in mid-1987. Meanwhile, Nikko and Yamaichi have been waiting impatiently for approval of their own applications for banking licenses, which have been pending with the Bank of England for more than six years.

A London bank enables a Japanese securities firm to smoothly complete all of the arrangements for a Eurobond swap (for nonresident corporations) without the mediation of the overseas subsidiary of a Japanese bank. The interest rate swap markets became so important in 1985–86 that in 1987 several of the Big Four established swap-intermediary subsidiaries in New York. By 1988, each of the Big Four will have developed sufficient risk-management capability to begin taking positions in the market.

In 1986, Sumitomo Bank announced its intention to invest $500 million in a 12.5 percent stake in the U.S. investment bank, Goldman Sachs (discussed in Chapter 7). Not coincidentally, Goldman Sachs was one of the foreign firms permitted to become a member of the Tokyo Stock Exchange. Thus, Sumitomo Bank became the owner of far more than 5 percent of a firm directly involved in the Japanese securities market. Meanwhile, Sumitomo had been bringing Banca del Gottardo (in which it owns a majority share—see Chapter 7) into the underwriting business. Finally, in late 1986, J. Henry Schroder Bank & Trust Co. paid $234 million to acquire Aubrey G. Lanston & Company: Aubrey G. Lanston is a primary bond dealer and the

---

[5] Many banks own 5.5 percent of the shares of second-tier securities firms.

majority interest in J. Henry Schroder Bank & Trust was acquired by the Industrial Bank of Japan in 1985.[6] In this way, the Industrial Bank of Japan indirectly joined Nomura and Daiwa in the special group of 40 primary dealers in the U.S. Treasury market.

In the Euromarket, Japan's city banks have competed with the Big Four for underwriting business. In this activity, the banks are impeded by a prohibition (the **Three Bureaux Agreement**—see Glossary) against the lead management of overseas Japanese issues. The city banks, the traditional leaders in Japanese finance, are far from satisfied with playing second fiddle to the Big Four securities companies.

Recently, the London subsidiaries of many city banks have begun to exploit the domestic orientation of Article 65. Employees of overseas bank branches are used as salesmen to solicit securities business from the overseas offices of Japanese corporations *and*, it is rumored, from the home offices of domestic companies. In addition, the London-based finance subsidiaries (discussed in Chapter 9) of the major city banks have opened "representative" offices in Tokyo. These offices sell Euroyen bonds over-the-counter to domestic institutions (see Chapter 6). In this way, the city banks have made clear their intention to subvert and undermine Article 65 in every manner possible. In late 1986, the Ministry of Finance chose to be blind to these "representative offices" whose activities constituted a flagrant breach of Article 65.

While the overseas offices of banks sought securities business, the Big Four securities firms experimented with the development of banking instruments. In 1985, Yamaichi, for example, introduced a service combining securities and banking functions for European institutions investing in Japanese stocks. Termed the "automatic cash management system," the product was designed to provide a settlement system for accounts involving transactions in Japanese equities by means of deposit accounts opened by investors at Yamaichi International

---

[6]In 1985, the Industrial Bank of Japan (IBJ) purchased 75 percent of J. Henry Schroder Bank & Trust from Schroders, the U.K. merchant banking group. In early 1987, IBJ increased its stake to 95 percent and changed the name of the bank to IBJ Schroder Bank and Trust Company. Schroders now owns 4.9 percent of the voting stock of IBJ Schroder.

Nederland N.V. Yamaichi invested the deposited funds in the Euro-interbank market. The accounts carried an interest rate 375 basis points below the London interbank offered rate (LIBOR).

In 1985–86, the Big Four were authorized to deal in such money market instruments as yen denominated bankers acceptances, domestic certificates of deposit, and "money market funds" (replicas of money market certificates) which had been the exclusive purview of the banking industry (see Chapter 8). In this way, securities companies were permitted to embrace some banking activities in the domestic market without first doing so in the Euromarket.

A major event presaging an eventual amendment or reinterpretation of Article 65 occurred in January 1987 when Merrill Lynch was given approval to open a Tokyo branch of its London Banking subsidiary. This move was generally interpreted as a demonstration by the Japanese government of regulatory reciprocity following Nomura's establishment of a banking subsidiary in London and achievement of primary dealer status in the United States. As a result of this decision, a securities company (*through a subsidiary*) is now qualified to engage in foreign exchange business. Prior to 1987, only banks could conduct foreign exchange business in Japan,[7] giving them tight control of the profitable swap market.

Japanese regulatory authorities have been closely watching the fate of America's Glass-Steagall Act. The degree of its decline (or its demise) will provide a guideline for decisions regarding Article 65. A 1984 U.S. Supreme Court interpretation of Glass-Steagall concluded that bank holding companies are not banks and therefore can own discount brokerage companies. In January 1987, the Supreme Court decided that bank-owned discount brokerage offices are not bank branches and therefore are not subject to the restrictions imposed by federal law on where federally chartered banks may open branches. As a result of this decision, U.S. bank subsidiaries of holding companies were allowed to maintain discount brokerage operations. Decisions such as these, which serve to blur the distinction between com-

---

[7]With the exception of the Tanshi companies (e.g. Forex, the foreign exchange subsidiary of Tokyo Tanshi). See Chapter 8.

mercial and investment banking in the United States, will have an indirect, but clear, impact on future interpretations of Article 65. At the time of writing, although futher relaxation in the enforcement of Article 65 is expected, full abandonment during the next several years is improbable.

Foreign institutions in Japan are often used as a means for preparing indigenous markets for planned changes. That a horde of foreign banks in 1986–87 were permitted to set up securities branches in Tokyo leaves no doubt about government plans for Japan's banks. Thus, an indicator of the future of Article 65 lies in the imminent Ministry of Finance decision to permit domestic banks to open securities subsidiaries and domestic securities companies to open banking subsidiaries in Tokyo. When the government gives domestic financial institutions the same freedom allotted to foreign institutions, a portion of Article 65 will have been eroded. Article 65 and the Glass-Steagall Act are Siamese twins with a peculiar relationship: The Japanese side of the pair is immortal so long as its elder American brother survives. The death of the senior twin, however, will assure the demise of the junior.

SECOND- AND THIRD-TIER SECURITIES FIRMS

The Big Four securities companies often send stock orders to the smaller securities firms as a means of obscuring their transactions. This need for concealment need not be (although it sometimes is) the result of shady market operations (see Chapters 3 and 4). Each of the Big Four invariably uses its own affiliated firms when making such orders. Because the smaller firms usually specilize in dealing in second-section (small capitalized) companies, they are especially suited as accomplices in a variety of speculative activities.

The second-tier firms fall between the Big Four's dominance of institutional transactions and the third-tier dependence on individual transactions (or Big Four orders). While second-tier firms maintain institutional relationships and occasionally underwrite primary issues, the third-tier firms depend upon an affiliation with a major financial institution and an individual client base.

Article 65 created a rigid compartmentalization between

banks and securities firms, prohibiting banks from owning more than 5 percent of the shares in a securities company. However, for some of the leading second- and third-tier securities firms, banks have been the controlling force in the determination of business objectives and profitability.

Excluded by law from direct participation in the securities industry, many banks developed close relationships with securities companies. In this way, while not necessarily prospering *directly* from the profits of conducting securities business, banks were able to benefit from the strategic advantages of key decision making.

The ability of small securities firms to procure enough brokerage business to survive or sufficient commissions to thrive, is seriously constrained by the formidable presence and marketing power of the Big Four. The underwriting capability of second- and third-tier firms is even more directly smothered by the magnitude of Big Four capitalization and monopolization of corporate relationships. Some of the leading medium and small securities firms have depended upon the ability of banking "affiliates" to provide critical corporate introductions (without which institutional business cannot be conducted in Japan), personnel, and financial support (including secondary business).

The linkages between banks and securities firms, although not clandestine, are not limpid. Thus, for example, NKK (Nippon Kangyo Kakumaru), one of the largest second-tier firms, is "associated" with the Dai-Ichi Kangyo Bank (DKB). For decades, every president and chairman of the NKK was a seconded (or retired) DKB executive, assigned to the position at NKK by the bank's President and *not* by NKK decision.[8] Yet Dai-Ichi Kangyo Bank owns only a 5.5 percent share of NKK. Similarly, New Japan Securities Company and Wako Securities Company are "associated" with the Industrial Bank of Japan (IBJ) and many of their top executive officers are former IBJ employees. However, the IBJ owns less than 5 percent of the shares in each of those companies. Thus, banks such as DKB and IBJ are not majority shareholders in the securities companies with which they are affiliated. Nonetheless, the relationships between the

---

[8]The current president of NKK, Hisatoshi Iwamura, is the first exception to this pattern.

banks and their securities company associates are intimately close.

Faced with the prospect of increased financial deregulation, city banks have been strengthening their relationships with their affiliated securities companies. In July 1984, for example, Sumitomo Bank prompted its affiliate, Meiko Securities Company, to double its capitalization and Mitsubishi Bank "encouraged" its affiliate, Ryoko Securities Company, to triple its capitalization. Simultaneously, Sumitomo and Mitsubishi dispatched additional personnel to the affiliates. Other keiretsu banks used cross-shareholding as a means to increase their influence in the management of affiliated securities companies. The Sanwa Bank *group*, for instance, increased its shareholding ratio in Towa Securities Company to more than 30 percent and seconded dozens of personnel to the firm.

The motive for banks to participate directly in the business of the securities firms is not difficult to fathom. The second- or third-tier securities firms can be used as vehicles for promoting relationships with a range of clients (for example, by providing occasional underwriting services). They provide a means of monitoring securities markets from the inside and they assure efficient execution of the bank's securities transactions. Most importantly, *the affiliated securities company functions as a surrogate stock and bond department for the associated bank*. In this way, bank employees can receive full training in all aspects of the securities industry in anticipation of an amendment or abolishment of Article 65.

The securities company, in turn, relies substantially on the brokerage business directed to it by the bank. The bank's corporate or political relationships and intelligence are at the firm's disposal. If needed, the bank can provide a source of capital, funding increases in capitalization which have become necessary in recent years.

The symbiotic relationship that has resulted from the fraternization between banks and small securities companies exemplifies a type of compromise characteristic of Japan. Just as water adopts the shape of its container, the apparent rigidity of a formal framework is altered to satisfy vital needs and exigencies. The alteration occurs with the full knowledge and tacit approval of all concerned. Although the letter and spirit of the law

TABLE 2–6 The Second Tier: The Fiscal Year Ending
September 30, 1986

Firm	Pretax Recurring Profit	Percent Change from Half Year Earlier
New Japan	15,018	−8.2
Sanyo	14,726	93.2
Wako	12,639	95.0
Cosmo	10,388	159.3
Nippon Kangyo Kakumaru	10,055	−21.9
Kokusai	9,703	29.8
Okasan	8,178	96.4
Yamatane	6,565	75.5
Dai-Ichi	5,983	22.7
Tokyo	5,326	53.8

may be circumvented, the needs of participating parties are sufficiently satisfied. Balance is achieved at the expense of fidelity to structure while formal appearance remains intact.

In addition to relationships with banks, many second- and third-tier firms are affiliates of the Big Four. For example, Sanyo Securities, controlled by the Tsuchiya family, is an affiliate of Nomura Securities. Kokusai Securities is similarly affiliated. Recently, a number of these affiliated companies have merged to create larger companies. In 1984, for instance, three Yamaichi affiliates, Koyanagi Securities Company, Daifuku Securities Company, and Yamaichi Investment Trust Sales Company were merged to create Pacific Securities Company. This merger followed similar mergers organized by each of the Big Four during the period 1981–84.[9] The decision to institute

---

[9]In 1981, Nomura Securities Company merged three affiliates (Yachiyo Securities, Koa Securities, and the Nomura Securities Investment Trust Sales Company) in order to create Kokusai Securities. In 1982, Nikko Securities merged three affiliates (Tokyo Securities, Toyama Securities, and the Nikko Securities Investment Trust and Sales Company) in order to create a larger firm which retained the Tokyo Securities Company name. In October 1984, Daiwa Securities merged two firms (Toko Securities and Daiwa Securities Investment Trust Sales Company) in order to establish Universal Securities. Thus, Yamaichi was the last of the Big Four to conduct an identical operation, consolidating affiliated securities companies with an affiliated Investment Trust Company. This case of sequential mergers exemplifies a pattern in

these mergers was motivated by concerns about increased competition in the securities industry—particularly competition from foreign firms. The growing profitability of the leading second- and third-tier firms (see Table 2–6) does not obviate the threat of invincible competition if the future attenuation of Article 65 sires a new era of universal banking.

SECURITIES FINANCE COMPANIES

Securities Finance companies are anomalous entities peculiar to Japan. Created in 1950 with the mandate of stimulating trading in the quiet securities markets, they are a unique amalgamation of securities company and banking institution. Although securities finance companies were opened in each city with a stock exchange, the majority of the new companies were simply resurrections of the prewar securities delivery agents.

Six years after they were established, the nine companies were consolidated into three: the Japan Securities Finance Company, the Osaka Securities Finance Company, and the Chubu Securities Finance Company. Focused on the Tokyo, Osaka, and Nagoya stock exchanges, respectively, the three companies provided equity and bond financing through their associated exchanges. Each of the companies commanded a portion of the financing business congruent with the size of the market it dominated. Thus, the Japan Securities Finance Company, based in Tokyo, controlled the majority (roughly 75 percent) of market share.

Today, securities finance companies extend loans to members of the stock exchanges as well as to securities companies and their clients. Securities companies that are not members of the exchanges provide bonds as collateral for the loans and their clients are required to provide stock certificates as loan collateral.

Borrowing frequently on the call and gensaki markets, the leading finance company is the lender of last resort for securities firms. It functions as a conduit between individuals requiring margin accounts on the one hand and liquidity in the banking

---

which Nomura institutes a policy decision, Nikko and Daiwa subsequently take actions which mirror the Nomura move, and Yamaichi, trailing the other three, belatedly conforms to the already established practice.

sector on the other hand. In this way, securities finance companies link the securities markets with money markets.

The liberalization of the financial markets may gradually render the securities finance companies obsolete. The vitiation of Article 65 will increase the feasibility of new types of financing provided by securities companies and banks. Thus, for example, in 1985 a system of securities-based collateral financing was introduced. The scheme permits investors who have stocks and bonds at securities companies to borrow from banks using the securities as collateral. Each of the Big Four utilized its keiretsu bank (Daiwa Bank-Nomura, Mitsubishi Bank-Nikko, etc.) to implement the new financing. Meanwhile, banks and securities companies are also able to extend small loans to investors using public bonds as collateral.

INVESTMENT TRUST MANAGEMENT COMPANIES

There are 11 investment trust management companies in Japan, each the subsidiary of a securities company. Collectively, the investment trust companies comprise one of the major institutional investors in Japan with assets at the end of November 1986 of ¥30.8 trillion ($200 billion), exceeding private pension fund assets. As a result, the investment trust companies can be movers in the domestic securities markets.

Because investment trusts contributed to the stock market crisis of 1965 (see Chapter 3), the ratio of stock investment trusts (equity mutual funds) to total outstanding investment trusts was usually kept below 20 percent during the 1970s. However, during the 1980s, the proportion of stock investment trusts to total investment trust net assets rose steadily until, in 1985 and 1986, the equity trusts surpassed in volume the bond trusts. At the end of 1986, equity investment trusts exceeded ¥19 trillion ($125 billion).

Although intended to be a vehicle for the small investor to benefit from a cross section of market activity, plummeting interest rates and a bull stock market in 1986 prompted institutional investors to participate in the trusts. As a result, special investment trusts were created for financial institutions and other large investors. From their inception to March 1983, total assets of the trusts never exceeded ¥10 trillion. In January 1986, the net assets of the trusts reached ¥20.31 trillion, increasing by more than ¥10 trillion ($66 billion) during the course of the year. Not surprisingly, stock investment trusts (equity mutual funds) attracted considerable investor interest.

Because the investment trust companies are units of the major securities firms, they direct most of their brokerage business to the parent, thus representing a vital source of revenue and a conflict of interest.[10] Often the securities companies have dumped poorly performing issues into the investment trusts, rendering the trusts a rubbish receptacle for in-house trading errors. The investment trusts are also used as sponges to absorb issues that the parent securities company has underwritten and cannot sell. Although investors seldom lose a portion of their principal investment, returns on the trusts are notoriously poor (see Chapter 9). Few stock investment trusts, for example, have ever beaten the Nikkei Stock Averages.

The investment trusts consist of funds derived from individual and institutional investors throughout Japan, and placed in pooled fixed-income and equity portfolios. Indeed, one of the functions of the Big Four sales forces is to solicit money to be invested in trust shares. The trusts are sold with a sales charge. Management fees as well as trust fees and transactions costs are deducted from trust fund proceeds.

Initially introduced in 1937, the investment trusts ceased to exist during the war years and were not reactivated until 1951. Prior to 1962, all investment trusts were managed directly by the securities companies. The frequent and systematic manipulation of the investment trusts by their managers led the Ministry of Finance to separate the management of investment trusts from securities company activities. At government behest, each of the major securities companies created an investment trust management subsidiary by excising investment trust management functions from its investment trust sales department. This divestment was cosmetic and the abuses continue to this day, albeit with some abatement.

There are two fundamental types of domestic trusts, both based on a U.K. model:

---

[10]Third-tier securities firms are given brokerage business as a reward for selling a firm's investment trusts.

Unit Trusts. Shares in these closed-end trusts are sold by the parent securities firm (the trustor) through the sale of beneficiary certificates, customarily priced at ¥10,000 ($63) per share. The funds procured in this way are placed in the custody of a trust bank (the trustee). Each of the investment trust management companies maintains a relationship with three to six trust banks. When the full complement of shares has been sold, the trust company invests the funds in securities in accordance with the directions of the investment trust management company. In practice, however, the trust management companies freely invest the funds with the trust banks receiving fees for nominal participation. Many of the unit trusts are perpetual; some have fixed lives, ranging from 3 to 10 years. "Spot trusts" (created "on the spot," often during bonus seasons) consist of a variety of specialized funds of fixed duration. Some of the trusts pay out dividends annually, while others systematically reinvest accrued dividends.

Open Trusts. The initial subscription period for these trusts can extend over a period of years and new funds can usually be added at any time. Like the closed trusts, these funds are nominally managed by trust banks with the investment advice of the management companies. There are a range of types of open trusts such as bond investment trusts and foreign investment trusts.

The foreign trusts are nondomestic mutual funds sold to Japanese investors by the securities companies. Since their sale in Japan was first permitted in 1972, these foreign mutual funds have provided Japanese investors with capital growth and returns far superior to the domestic trusts. At the end of November 1985, foreign investment trusts were worth ¥557 billion ($2.7 billion) and were rapidly growing in popularity as Japanese investors selected them in preference to the poorer performing domestic trusts (see Chapter 9). As a result, the Big Four began to offer new types of trusts to compete with the foreign models. Daiwa, for example, marketed a "domestic and foreign bond" trust fund and Nomura created a "Japan-U.S. small capital stock" trust fund. Under new guidelines, these new funds were authorized to have a foreign allocation of up to 50 percent of portfolio holdings.

FOREIGN SECURITIES FIRMS IN JAPAN

During the postwar era, Japanese residents were prohibited from buying foreign securities. In 1970, facing the novelty of current account surpluses, the government authorized investment trusts to place a limited proportion of assets in foreign capital markets. A year later, life insurance companies and trust banks were allowed to invest 10 percent of the pension funds they managed in foreign securities.[11] Finally, in 1972, Japanese individuals were legally permitted to buy foreign stock through the medium of mutual funds and, also in that year, several foreign securities firms were granted the licenses necessary to establish branch offices in Tokyo.[12]

From 1972 to 1978, Merrill Lynch was the only foreign securities firm with a substantial presence in Japan, and earned most of its revenue by selling foreign stocks to Japanese institutional investors.[13] In 1978, a U.K. firm, Vickers da Costa, was granted the necessary branch licenses by the Ministry of Finance and focused its business development on the sale of Japanese equities to foreign investors, particularly mutual funds. A year later, Bache, Halsey, Stuart, Shields Inc. (the precursor of Bache Securities) received the necessary licenses.

Although many investment banks in the United States and Europe sought branch status in Tokyo, the Ministry of Finance limited its approval of licenses to one per year during the period 1979–83. In 1984, three licenses were approved, bringing the number of foreign securities firms with branch status in Tokyo to 10. The figure jumped to 20 in 1985, and reached 34 at the end of 1986.[14]

---

[11] Increased to 25 percent in 1986 (see Chapter 9).

[12] Four kinds of license are necessary:

1. A dealing license (for trading in securities for the firm's account).
2. A broker's license (for taking clients' orders for securities transactions).
3. An underwriting license (for underwriting primary issues).
4. A selling license (for handling securities subscriptions and offers).

[13] The Arthur Lipper Corporation and Burnham & Co. were also licensed, during the early 1970s, to conduct securities business in Japan.

[14] In addition, Merrill Lynch maintained branches in Osaka and, beginning in 1985, in Nagoya. (The Nagoya office was opened primarily to strengthen ties with Toyota Motor Corporation, which is based near Nagoya.) Including these, there were 36 branches in Japan at the end of 1986.

In the spring of 1986, the Ministry of Finance announced that it would approve seven or eight additional licenses biannually (every November and May). Sixteen more foreign branch licenses are expected to be approved in 1987.

The foreign securities companies listed in Tables 2-8 and 2-9 were, by no means, the only foreign securities businesses operating in Japan. In 1986, more than 100 foreign securities companies maintained representative offices in Tokyo. Most of these representative entities, although not legally entitled to conduct securities business in Japan, were engaged in far more than market research.

Of the 20 foreign securities company branches in Tokyo at the end of 1985, 6 were allowed to become members of the Tokyo Stock Exchange (see Chapter 3 for a more detailed discussion). In this way, foreign membership as a portion of total membership rose instantly from 0 to 6.5 percent. Although the Tokyo Stock Exchange and the Ministry of Finance have not set a timetable, new stock exchange seats will be created in order to accommodate additional foreign securities firms. When that happens (probably in 1988), the oldest foreign branches in Tokyo will be given preference. The seats on the exchange, while providing foreign brokers with incrementally more commissions, promise additional advantages—chief among them, the enhanced opportunity to underwrite domestic equity offerings.[15]

Foreign securities companies in Japan pursue the gamut of securities industry activities, ranging from fixed income and equity sales to trading to research to underwriting. Some firms made strong profits in 1986 from U.S. government bond dealing (e.g. Salomon Brothers). Other foreign firms specialized in Austrialian dollar bonds (S.G. Warburg and Schroder) and convertible bonds (Morgan Stanley), and a few (Jardine Flemming, W.I. Carr) concentrated on dealing in Japanese equity.

Although the underwriting of foreign issues in Japan (or Euroyen issues in the Euromarket) should be a promising area for the foreign firms, it will be slow to develop. The Big Four's retail distribution networks are extremely strong. In addition, they can exert a determining influence on the price of a compa-

---

[15] In 1986, Goldman Sachs became the first foreign firm to co-lead a domestic equity offering (see Chapter 3).

ny's shares. This is vital power if a foreign company intends to issue bonds convertible into equity or bonds with warrants attached.

Salomon Brothers has been the most profitable foreign securities company in Japan with more than double the revenues of other foreign firms. An early understanding of the Japanese securities industry lies behind its success. In 1979, Salomon Brothers began trading in the domestic government debt market, establishing relationships with key Japanese institutional investors. Recognizing that Japan's deficit financing would lead to a vast increase in government bond trading, the firm poached a senior Japanese government bond trader from Yamaichi. Because the behavior of the yen bond market correlates closely with moves in U.S. interest rates, Salomon Brothers was able to coordinate its U.S. research expertise and involvement in the U.S. Treasury market with its Tokyo dealing. In this way, Salomon could execute trades in Tokyo that anticipated the effects of its own market making moves in U.S. Treasury issues. During the surge of Japanese buying of U.S. debt in 1985–86, Salomon used its relationships with Japanese institutions to sell more U.S. bonds to Japanese investors than any other foreign firm in Tokyo.

In 1986, Salomon poached another Yamaichi employee (with an expertise in marketing Japanese equities to the overseas affiliates of Japanese corporations) as its chief equity trader. Determined to become as strong in equities as it is in bonds, the Japanese branch of Salomon is one of four or five foreign branches likely to become a member of the Tokyo Stock Exchange when new seats are opened for nondomestic institutions.

Salomon Brothers' bid for membership was refused once. In late 1985, when the six foreign firms were granted permission to become members of the Tokyo Stock Exchange (TSE), Salomon Brothers was one of three major American firms rejected. (First Boston and Smith Barney were the others.) These three firms had a smaller volume of equity business than the six firms approved, a key (although not decisive) factor in the TSE selection. Thus, in order to become a TSE member, Salomon Brothers is forced to increase its equity business.

The corporate finance arena, although promising, has not yet become a lucrative source of income for the foreign firms.

The total volume of Japanese corporate international financing in 1985 was roughly $21 billion. Associated with interest rate or currency swaps, most of this amount was handled by the Big Four.

Many of the foreign securities firms in Tokyo have their gaze fixed on mergers and acquisitions (M&A), an area of vast potential profitability. Japanese companies have demonstrated an interest (fast becoming a passion as the result of the depreciation of the dollar against the yen) in acquiring U.S. as well as European entities (and real estate). During the period 1984–86, Japanese corporations and institutions spent an estimated $4.5 billion on U.S. corporate acquisitions alone. The other side of Japanese M&A, the foreign purchase of Japanese corporations, is in an inchoate stage. Some of the problems involved in foreign acquisition of indigenous entities are discussed in Chapter 4.

Like M&A, private placements promise future opportunities for foreign firms to manage Japanese investment capital. To date, Japanese institutional investors have only been interested in the highest quality corporate debt (see the discussion of Shogun bonds in Chapter 5) or sovereign credit risk (including Canadian provincial credits). Government restrictions limit the number of institutions authorized to take private placements and dictate acceptable ratings and levels of capitalization. However, as Japanese institutions seek higher yields from their investments (see Chapter 9), it is likely that a market for triple B utility paper and similar weaker credits will develop.

By virtue of their origin, an obvious niche for foreign securities firms has been the sale of foreign (primarily U.S.) stock to Japanese institutional investors and the sale of Japanese equity to foreign investors. Although Japanese investment in foreign equity has been increasing during the past several years, it is only a small fraction of the size of the market in foreign bonds.

While some of the foreign firms have earned substantial brokerage from their Tokyo branches, the bulk of the profits have been from nondomestic institutional investments in Japanese blue chip issues. A growing number of U.S. and U.K. firms have begun making markets in a handful of Japanese stocks and there are signs that block trading will develop substantially in Tokyo. Merrill Lynch, for example, began trading for its own account after becoming a Tokyo Stock Exchange member, and

TABLE 2–7   Japanese Investment in Foreign Stock ($ millions)

Foreign Equities	1983	1984	1985
Purchases	2,080	2,318	5,484
Sales	1,276	2,185	4,489
Net	804	133	995

SOURCE: Ministry of Finance

Goldman Sachs, the leading market maker in Japanese American Depository Receipts (ADRs), also took significant equity positions in 1986.

All of the foreign securities companies in Tokyo have publicly voiced considerable optimism about the growth of domestic brokerage business. Privately, however, many admit that the small portion of total domestic brokerage commissions that can be pried away from established relationships cannot be satisfactorily divided among the 34 foreign companies licensed to do business in Japan at the end of 1986. Furthermore, the Big Four are likely to retain their massive share of equity trading because of their market moving capability. As more and more foreign representative offices are licensed as full branches, competition for a share of the pie will be fierce. The advantages of Tokyo Stock Exchange membership could be decisive in deciding which foreign branches will close their doors in the 1990s.

The wild card in the struggle for survival is a probable future decision by the Ministry of Finance to deregulate brokerage commissions (see Chapter 3 for a further discussion of commissions). In April 1984, Toshio Kusaba, then head of Japan's Bankers' Association, spearheaded a drive to eliminate the fixed commission schedule. The Big Four receive roughly 40 percent of annual income from stock brokerage commisions and many third-tier firms obtain as much as 85 percent of their income from this source. Fixed commissions were abolished in the United States on May 1, 1975, and in the United Kingdom on October 27, 1986. It is unlikely that Japan can maintain its fixed brokerage commission system indefinitely. A change to negotiable commissions, however, would lead to a spate of bankruptcies and mergers among the ranks of third-tier firms reminiscent of the Japanese stock market crisis of 1964–65. That is something the Ministry of Finance wishes to avoid. During the final years of the decade, the government will be faced with the thorny problem of how to compete with London and New York without destroying the stability of a system which, for 30 years, has been protected through a web of regulations and keiretsu ties.

Ultimately, Japanese officials may have little choice in deciding the commission issue. During the course of the next several years, offshore trading in Japanese stocks will defy the government regulatory requirement that maintains that domestic commission schedules have global application. Foreign Japanese equity specialists (especially those with a well-established presence in Hong Kong) will offer discounts that will undermine the fixed scale *and* divert business from Japan.

Many foreign brokers would thrive in a new Japanese world of negotiated commissions. Nonetheless, the six foreign firms that joined the Tokyo Stock Exchange in 1986, although quite vocal when discussing the slow pace of liberalization and deregulation of Japanese financial markets, have remarkably little comment regarding this issue. Having paid the price and joined the club, they are content to rake in brokerage commissions and support the status quo.

Perhaps the greatest strength of foreign securities firms in the domestic equity market is research coverage of Japanese stocks. Each of the Big Four research institutes (as well as some of the leading second-tier securities companies) produces a vast volume of reports on Japanese companies and the Japanese economy. While rich in statistical information, these reports are of little value in assessing the fundamental prospects of a potential investment. Japanese securities firms, which often maintain close relationships with those companies that are the subjects of reports, never offer negative assessments and rarely, if ever, make sell recommendations. This bias, combined with the current inability of Japanese securities analysts to apply sophisticated fundamental analysis to Japanese corporations, renders the bulk of Japanese corporate analysis useless to foreign investors. By contrast, the foreign securities firms in Tokyo produce some of the finest securities research in the world. Indeed,

---

TABLE 2–8   Foreign Members of the
                 Tokyo Stock Exchange

Tokyo Stock Exchange Member	Date Establishment of Branch Office	Bank Parent
Merrill Lynch	1971	
Vickers da Costa	1978	Citicorp*
Jardine Fleming	1981	
Morgan Stanley	1984	
Goldman, Sachs	1984	
S. G. Warburg	1984	

---

*Since 1983. In November of that year, Citicorp acquired 29.9 percent of Vickers da Costa plus 80 percent of Far Eastern operations.

the high quality of this research has enabled foreign managers of all Japan equity portfolios to consistently outperform Japanese managers of Japan dedicated portfolios.

Tables 2–8 and 2–9 are lists of the foreign securities branches permitted (in early 1987) to undertake the full range of securities business in Japan. In addition to providing such direct information, the tables contain several other messages written in the oblique code of Japan's Ministry of Finance.

MESSAGE #1:   *"Come one, come all."*

All qualified foreign securities firms will gradually be granted the four licenses necessary to establish a full branch office in Japan. It is in Japan's best interest to permit *all*, rather than just a few, qualified foreign institutions into the business. If only a handful of foreign firms were allowed to set up shop in Tokyo, they would have the opportunity to establish themselves as firmly and as successfully as Salomon Brothers. A small number of foreign companies could compete successfully with indigenous firms, slowly bleeding away market share from the entrenched establishment. Such a process would eventually weaken the government's ability to influence the financial sector through such indirect means as "administrative guidance." In any case, no authority in Japan wants the equivalent of an IBM occupying a key place in the domestic securities industry. However, a multitude of foreign firms, say 70 or more, would

TABLE 2–9   Additional Foreign Securities Branches in Japan

Firm	Date Branch Established	Bank Parent
Bache Securities	1979	
Smith Barney	1980	
Salomon Brothers	1982	
Kidder, Peabody	1983	
W. I. Carr Overseas	1985	Banque Indosuez*
First Boston	1985	
Kleinwort, Benson	1985	
D.B. Capital Markets	1985	Deutsche Bank
Drexel Burnham Lambert	1985	
Paine Webber	1985	
Hoare Govett	1985	Security Pacific†
Schroder	1985	
Cazenove	1985	
E. F. Hutton	1985	
Shearson Lehman	1986	American Express
Baring Far East	1986	Baring Brothers
UBS/Phillips & Drew	1986	Union Bank of Switzerland
SBCI Securities (Asia)	1986	Swiss Bank Corp.
Dresdner-ABD	1986	Dresdner Bank
Sogen	1986	Societe Generale
County Bank	1986	NatWest Bank
DG Bank	1986	DG Bank
Morgan Grenfell	1986	
Montagu Securities	1986	Midland Bank
James Capel (Pacific)	1986	Hong Kong and Shanghai Bank‡
West LB Securities (Asia)	1986	Westdeutsche Landesbank Girozentrale
Commerz Securities (Japan)	1986	Commerzbank A.G.
Amro (Finance and Securities)	1986	Amsterdam-Rotterdam Bank
Paribas Asia	1987	Banque Paribas
LM Securities	1987	Chase Manhattan Bank§

*Branch purchased from Exco in 1986 and license approved 1987.

†Since 1982.

‡Since 1984.

§The Ministry of Finance classifies this British firm (Laurie Milbank and Co.) which is owned by the U.S. bank, Chase Manhattan, as a British broker and not as the securities subsidiary of a bank.

SOURCES: *The Economist, The Financial Times*, Nihon Keizai Shimbun

fight among themselves to gain a toehold in the competitive market. This process is the most likely way to prevent several foreign institutions from consolidating a significant share of the market under one roof.

MESSAGE #2: *Domestic banks will be allowed to have brokerage subsidiaries, but. . . .*

Article 65 will not be discarded. Banks will not be permitted to use their branches to sell stocks. The second- and third-tier securities firms will be given the protection they need in order to conduct business as usual. Given such added deregulation, how many of the securities branches owned by foreign banks will survive the severe competition Japan's banking establishment will dole out?

CHAPTER THREE

The Stock Market: History, Structure, Dynamics

OVERVIEW

On February 1, 1986, for the first time since its creation, the Tokyo Stock Exchange (TSE) permitted non-Japanese brokerage firms to become members. This development paralleled similar changes occurring throughout Japan's financial sector. Simultaneously, foreign investors have become increasingly interested in the Japanese stock market. For example, during the 12-month period ending March 1986, most U.S. and U.K. firms doubled and tripled the number of securities analysts employed at their Tokyo branches.

Although there are eight stock exchanges in Japan, the Tokyo Stock Exchange represents 83 percent of the nation's total equity trading volume. Of the 1,848 publicly traded domestic companies in Japan at the end of 1986, 80 percent were listed on the TSE. In terms of market scale and activity, the Tokyo Stock Exchange is the second largest exchange in the world after New York.

The total value traded on the Tokyo Stock Exchange in 1985 was $437 billion, about 45 percent of the turnover of the New York Stock Exchange for the same period. During the six-month period, March 30, 1986 to September 30, 1986, the total value traded on the TSE increased by 250 percent over the preceding six months, reaching ¥663.3 billion ($4.1 billion) per day.

Similarly, volume traded is also second among world exchanges. Total volume traded on the Tokyo Stock Exchange was

428.5 billion shares in 1985—roughly 44 percent that of the New York Stock Exchange. During the six-month period ending September 1986, however, trading volume increased 1.8 times over the preceding half year, reflecting increased individual and institutional trading during the bull market.

At the end of March 1986, the market value of all stocks (250 billion shares) listed on the first section of the TSE was ¥200 trillion. This was equivalent to 63 percent of Japanese GNP. As the result of the sharp rise in the exchange's stock average during 1986, the market value of these shares grew with extraordinary rapidity. The stock value of the 1,096 companies listed on the first section of the TSE grew to ¥277 trillion at the end of 1986 and exceeded ¥300 trillion before the end of January 1987. The exceptional performance of the financial sector (representing roughly 30 percent of the total market value) contributed to this rise. Indeed, a brief continuation of this growth rate will result in a market value on the TSE first section exceeding the value of all shares listed on the New York Stock Exchange.

In January 1982, the Computer Assisted Order Routing and Execution System (CORES) was introduced in the second section of the Tokyo Stock Exchange. This new automated system replaced the standard display board which had been in use since 1974. In June 1985, with the opening of the new stock exchange building, the first section of the Tokyo Stock Exchange was placed on CORES. At about the same time, CORES was tied in with the computer systems of member securities firms.

The 250 most actively traded issues, however, continue to be bought and sold on the floor with traders using traditional hand signals. While hand signals on the New York Stock Exchange and most other exchanges communicate numbers, on the TSE trading floor, hand signals are also used to convey names of companies. Thus, for example, the shape of a *V* made with the palms represents Victor Company or the shape of an *S* written in the air is Sony Company. The sign for IBM is a finger pointing to the trader's eye followed by the writing of the letters *B* and *M* in the air. Experienced floor traders are not only able to deploy the sign language with exceptional speed and accuracy but also study the trades of rival firms in order to detect trading patterns or intentions. In 1988, when a new annex to the Tokyo

Stock Exchange building is opened, the number of issues traded on the floor will be reduced from the current 250 to 200 or less.

Japanese companies, unlike corporations in the West, have traditionally operated with funds derived primarily from indirect rather than direct financing. Funds have been borrowed indirectly from banks rather than directly from the capital markets. This has long been congruent with Bank of Japan policy which stresses the control of credit availability via corporate dependence on large bank loans, rather than money supply, in monetary policy.

While the Bank of Japan has not significantly changed its method of implementing monetary policy, Japanese corporations in the newly deregulated financial environment have begun to rely more on direct financing than ever before. Partly as a result, the Tokyo stock market has been steadily increasing in importance with trading volume and stock prices rising steadily.

Although the Japanese stock market is as rigorously regulated as the American markets, regulations are not stringently enforced. Consequently, insider trading and other marginal activities influence stock prices. As foreign participation in the stock market increases and investor knowledge of illicit practices expands, however, it is possible that Japanese authorities will take a firmer position on shady market activities. Meanwhile, stock price manipulations must be considered as a factor when evaluating some market opportunities (see Chapter 4, Pitfall #13).

There are five types of securities traded on the Tokyo Stock Exchange: shares of stock (common, preferred, deferred, without voting rights, foreign issues), bonds (government bonds, bonds of local public bodies, Samurai bonds, convertible debentures, and debenture bonds with separate warrants), investment trusts, rights, and warrants alone. On October 19, 1985, a bond futures market was initiated on the TSE; a stock *average* futures market will begin on the Osaka Stock Exchange in April 1987; and a stock *index* futures market is likely to be established on the TSE in 1988. Stocks, warrants, and rights will be discussed in this chapter; bonds and the bond futures market are discussed in Chapter 5, and investment trust performance is discussed in Chapter 9.

HISTORY

The history of the New York Stock Exchange can be followed back to May 17, 1792, when 24 traders signed a document agreeing to trade securities only among themselves and to maintain fixed commission rates. The London Stock Exchange is older still, its antecedents traceable to trading in late seventeenth century coffee houses.

The first stock exchanges in Japan are far more recent. They were created in May 1878 in Tokyo and Osaka as marketplaces for the trading of public bonds issued to former feudal lords (*daimyo*) and their retainers (*samurai*). Within three years, 137 stock exchanges had opened throughout Japan. Each of the exchanges functioned as a profit making entity, deriving revenue from commissions. Some of the exchanges issued their own stock. Although equity issues were traded side by side with bonds in the exchanges, only a small number of stocks were traded, with infrequent trades and volatile prices rendering the incipient stock market territory for speculators only. By the beginning of World War I, the government had reduced the number of exchanges to 10. It was not until this time that the trading of equities began to have an impact on the national economy.

During the period, 1914–1920, Japan's emerging industrial enterprises, stimulated by growing profits derived from the war, sought financing on the exchanges. Trading volume and stock prices rose steadily until a panic caused stock prices to plummet in March 1920. By the end of the 1920s, a half century after their formation, the stock exchanges had acquired an important role in Japan's financial structure.

During the 1930s, equity trading on the stock exchanges steadily declined. By 1937, when all capital markets were placed under wartime controls, trading volume was negligible. At this time, most equity issued by industries was purchased by member companies within zaibatsu constellations. Few shares were traded publicly and most activity on the exchanges was controlled by speculators attempting to profit from market volatility. New industries not affiliated with a holding company seldom attempted to raise funds on the stock market. Borrowing from banks was the customary avenue for raising funds.

At the beginning of the Second World War, the Tokyo Stock

Exchange was replaced by a governmental institution, the Japan Securities Exchange, which absorbed the regional exchanges. Trading throughout the war was slight and by January 1945, although the prices of most commodities had increased astronomically (particularly on the black market), stock prices were only about 20 percent higher than before the war. The end of the war in August 1945 resulted in the suspension of trading. The Tokyo Stock Exchange building was requisitioned by the Supreme Commander of the Allied Powers (SCAP) and used as a billet. Although occasional equity transactions were conducted on an unofficial over-the-counter market, the Japanese stock market was frozen.

In April 1948, a Securities and Exchange Law, similar to the American Securities Act of 1933 and the Securities Exchange Act of 1934, prepared the way for the reestablishment of stock exchanges (legally referred to as "securities exchanges") in Japan. In accordance with the new law, the Tokyo Stock Exchange and two regional exchanges (in Osaka and Nagoya) were made nonprofit membership organizations and were reopened on May 16, 1949. Simultaneously, the Nikkei Stock Average, based on the arithmetical stock price average of the Tokyo Stock Exchange (see *Indicators*), was initiated with a first-day average of 176.21. Later the same year, six new regional exchanges were established in Kyoto, Kobe, Hiroshima, Fukuoka, Niigata, and Sapporo, increasing to nine the total number of stock exchanges in postwar Japan. The Kobe Stock Exchange (first established in 1883) was merged with the Osaka Stock Exchange on October 31, 1967, reducing to eight the number of exchanges in Japan. At the time of writing, there are still eight exchanges and there is little likelihood that others will be merged or created.

During the Occupation, SCAP dismantled the zaibatsu combines, with the intention of converting their components into American-style public corporations. Thus, equity in the members of zaibatsu conglomerates was sold to Japanese individuals. Within a year after the reopening of the stock markets, more than 69 percent of all outstanding shares were owned by individuals (see Table 3–1 on page 101).

However, the American industrial experts who engineered the demolition of the combines did not grasp the critical role of banks within zaibatsu structures. By failing to dismantle the banking infrastructure, the Occupation authorities left the roots of the zaibatsu intact. Acting as a new center, each zaibatsu bank arranged a regrouping of prewar components in such a way that U.S.-introduced antitrust regulations were not broken.

Each company within a combine purchased a small percentage (from 0.5 to 3 percent) of equity in each of the other members. When necessary, the member bank provided loans to finance the equity purchases. In this way, new combines emerged. Termed **neo-zaibatsu** by foreign analysts and **keiretsu** (see Glossary) by insiders, the new organizations existed by means of mutual agreement rather than by *de jure* ownership. Each firm within a keiretsu agreed not to sell the shares it owned in members of the group. The mutual shareholding helped prevent investor takeovers and assured beneficial mutual relationships which placed the interests of member companies before the interests of shareholders. Thus, even if management behaved in a manner contrary to the wishes of large numbers of shareholders, companies could not be threatened with reprisals (such as takeovers or pressure to change management). The major shareholders in keiretsu companies are invariably keiretsu insiders. If the share price of a company were to decline to the extent that public offerings were insufficient to raise capital for the company, then financial institutions within the keiretsu would meet the financial needs of the company.

The keiretsu created a precedent for other companies in Japan which were not the descendants of the prewar zaibatsu. Nonkeiretsu companies modeled their strategies on the keiretsu example. They relied on indirect financing through bank loans rather than through equity or debt offerings on the market. As with keiretsu firms, a high percentage of outstanding shares were held by financial institutions and other friendly corporations.

More than 65 percent of all equity in all listed companies on the Tokyo Stock Exchange is now held in this way. In addition, because corporations and financial institutions do not usually sell their equity holdings, not only has individual ownership dwindled but also the float on many issues has declined significantly. The thin volume of shares has contributed to share price volatility.

As the postwar depression continued, trading was slight, with only 256 million shares traded in Tokyo in 1949. By July 1950, the Nikkei Stock Average had fallen to ¥85.25. The Korean war, however, stimulated the Japanese economy and marked the beginning of Japan's rapid rise as a global industrial and financial power. Stock market prices rose steadily and Japan's first stock market boom was soon underway. The boom reached its zenith on February 4, 1953, with a Nikkei Stock Average high of 474. Nearly three years in duration, the stock market boom paralleled a period of great industrial growth which rendered postwar shortages and suffering a specter of the past. The announcement of Stalin's death, on March 5, 1953, triggered a 10 percent decline from the previous day's closing. Termed the *Stalin plunge* by Japanese stock market historians, it remains the largest single day proportional decline in Japanese stock market history.

In 1956, the Japanese government issued an "Economic White Paper" which announced with finality that the "postwar period has ended." During the next five years, high economic growth accompanied by the development of the industrial sector (particularly heavy and chemical industries), stimulated stock market activity. During this era, two stock market booms were separated by a period of desultory market growth.

In 1961, a second section was added to the Tokyo Stock Exchange with Osaka and Nagoya quickly following suit with new second sections of stocks. Listing requirements for the new second section were less stringent than for the first section.

Also by 1961, investment trusts (see discussion in Chapter 2), revived by the Ministry of Finance in 1951 as a means to stimulate the growth and development of Japan's postwar capital markets, began to adopt a central role in stock market activity. By offering a variety of institutionalized investment vehicles, particularly equity mutual funds, investment trusts appealed to a wide range of investors. Corporate funds as well as individual capital were given to the investment trusts for securities investments. As a result, by 1961, the investment trusts had risen to 17 times 1955 levels (reaching ¥1.4 trillion). At their peak in late 1961, investment trusts represented 10 percent of stock market capitalization.

For the first time in Japanese history, the stock market

seemed to offer a means of obtaining consistently high returns with little risk. By investing large blocks of capital in the equity market, the investment trusts further stimulated prices. On July 18, 1961, the market reached a record high of 1,829.74 with the investment trusts the primary market movers. By the end of the summer of 1961, tightening credit led to a gradual withdrawal of investment trust funds from the stock markets. As the market fell, the per-share net asset value of the investment trusts also declined. This in turn led to additional redemptions of the trusts prior to maturity. As investment trust redemptions increased, the market fell further as the direct result of the sale of equity holdings to meet the redemptions. The more the market fell, the more early redemptions of the trusts induced further market declines.

The possibility of a stock market panic was recognized, and under the direction of the Bank of Japan, actions were taken to prevent a collapse. However, two years later, in the spring of 1963, cancelled orders of investment trusts began to proliferate. In early 1964, the Japan Joint Securities Corporation, consisting of banks and securities firms, was created. The central bank provided the Corporation with substantial loans. At about the same time, the Japan Securities Holding Association was created by the Big Four securities houses. The Holding Association was designed to purchase stock resulting from the cancellations of orders from the investment trusts. The creation of these temporary institutions as a last moment effort was perhaps designed to create the semblance of emergency action when it was nearly too late to prevent a market collapse.[1]

With the opening of the second section of the Tokyo Stock Exchange in 1961, the major securities houses were pressured by the exchange administration to purchase blocks of stock in virtually all of the newly listed second section companies. As investors, particularly the investment trusts, liquidated holdings and fled from the market, the securities firms were left with possession of second section stocks which had drastically declined in market value and could not be sold.

---

[1]The Japan Securities Holding Association was terminated in January 1969 and the Japan Joint Securities Corp., Ltd. was dissolved exactly two years later.

By mid-1965, the Nikkei-Dow Jones Stock Average had plummeted 44 percent from the high of July 18, 1961. The largest of the Big Four securities firms, Yamaichi Securities Co., was the largest holder of second section stocks. During the bull market of 1960–61, Yamaichi derived the bulk of its profit from trading on its own account.[2] During this period, the firm utilized borrowed funds to accumulate large holdings in "growth companies," particularly issues it had underwritten. The market decline not only left the company with enormous paper losses but also with crushing interest payments.[3]

In order to save the stock market from a severe, debilitating crash, the Central Bank intervened in what was termed the "securities panic of 1965." Yamaichi Securities Company as well as a smaller firm, Oi Securities Company (the precursor of Wako Securities Company, a leading second-tier firm), were rescued from imminent bankruptcy by 18-year lifeboat loans from the Bank of Japan.

The stock market and the economy weathered the storm. The market recovered and the recession of 1965 was left behind in the wake of renewed economic growth. However, of the roughly 600 securities firms registered in Japan in 1960, only 430 remained in 1965.

The market recovery led to increased commission revenue for Yamaichi Securities Company and an increased value in the second-section stocks held in its vaults. As a result, Yamaichi repaid its ¥28.2 billion debt to the Bank of Japan in a little more than three years. However, the firm never recovered its preeminent place in Japan's capital markets and during the ensuing 20 years became the fourth of the Big Four firms (see Chapter 2). Not until the end of fiscal year 1970 could Yamaichi (or Wako Securities) issue a dividend.

In order to prevent future securities panics and debacles, the Securities and Exchange Law was amended in 1965. Securities

---

[2]Until 1964, all of the major securities companies derived roughly 50 percent of their income from trading on their own account. Regulations that followed the securities panic of 1965 limited the amount of trading securities companies could transact on their own account.

[3]The securities panic of 1965 and the Yamaichi rescue are described in detail by T. F. M. Adams and Iwao Hoshii, *A Financial History of the New Japan*, pp. 170–72.

companies and their sales personnel were required to be licensed (rather than registered). The system of investment trusts was revised in order to protect investors and a variety of rules and regulations were introduced. In addition, the financial statements of corporations listed on the exchanges were to be more carefully monitored under an amendment of the Certified Public Accountant Law. In 1970, securities companies were ordered by the Ministry of Finance to invest no more than 5 percent of their net assets in shares of any single listed company and to reduce mutual stockholdings to no more than 10 percent of net assets.

By 1970, substantial growth in the national economy saw parallel growth in trading volume and stock prices on the Tokyo Stock Exchange. From 1970 until the first oil crisis in 1973, trading volume rose to 100 billion shares. In 1973, in order to address a problem of spiraling inflation, the Bank of Japan tightened credit, raising the prime rate from 4.25 percent to 9 percent. Equity trading sagged and the volume of new issues plummeted.

Although the first oil crisis led to a market decline, ultimately it revivified the stock market, forcing corporations to reduce overhead. For the first time, an attempt was made to reduce the indirect financing of industrial growth. This served to wean Japanese industry from a traditional dependence on bank loans, instead directing fund raising efforts toward the securities markets. New equity issues began to appear and regulations pertaining to the introduction of new issues on the stock market were relaxed.

The market gradually recovered, and the late 1970s saw a steady growth in trading volume and the stock index averages. During the first six years of the 1980s, the Nikkei Dow Jones Stock Average (renamed the Nikkei Stock Average in May 1985) nearly trebled in value, rising from 6,560 at the close of the first trading day in 1980 to 18,820 at the close of the first trading day in 1987. In 1986 alone, the stock average increased by nearly 50 percent.

THE PRIMARY MARKET

The volume of equity within a corporation's financial structure is a function of the cost of equity within a particular market and the traditions of that market. Thus, in the United States, for example, the average debt/equity ratio is roughly 1:1 so that the total outstanding debt is roughly equal to total equity. In Japan, by contrast, debt/equity ratios are often as high as 4:1. When offering new shares on the Japanese stock market, the traditional acceptance of the company's stock with investors is a key consideration.

Overall, new issues of stock represent only a small portion of the total capital raised by industries and thus have financed only a small part of industrial capital expenditures. Currently, Japanese corporations have become powerful investors rather than borrowers (see Chapter 9). As a consequence, the major Japanese corporations do not need to raise capital through new share issues, resulting in a substantial decline of new equity in Japan.[4]

In the past, more than 80 percent of new issues were offered to existing shareholders at par (¥20, ¥50, ¥500). The new issues were distributed directly to shareholders without recourse to underwriters. Usually, shareholders are invited to subscribe to a new issue with payment for shares made in cash (or, rarely, in kind). Sometimes such new issues are offered at market value (unsubscribed new offerings are sold at market value) and occasionally new issues are offered at a price between par and market value. Following the issuance of new shares, the corporation's share price in the secondary market invariably declined as a result of the increased capitalization. During the past 15 years, there has been a rise in the number of market price issues for public subscription. For example, in 1986, roughly 90 percent of all paid-in capital increases were at market price.

There are thus three types of possible new issue subscriptions:

1. The allotment of shares to *existing shareholders*. Such shares are usually issued at par. If the shareholder relinquishes the right to subscribe to a new offering, the unsubscribed shares are distributed through a public offering.
2. The allotment of shares to *third parties*. Third-party allocations of new shares represent only a very small part of

---

[4]Roughly 0.3 percent of stock market capitalization in 1985 compared with 2.1 percent in 1971.

all new offerings. They are usually confined to individuals (such as employees or corporate directors) or institutions with special relationships with the company. Because third-party allotments are offered at below market prices to insiders, the offerings are regarded as exceptional, are discouraged by the Ministry of Finance, and are considered acceptable only in cases of corporate reorganization, rare instances of consolidating corporate relationships, or as profit sharing plans for employees.

3. The allotment of shares through *public offerings*. Invariably at market price, public offerings are now the most common method of raising capital on the stock market. Because of the strong traditional preference for indirect financing, Japanese corporations never undertook public offerings prior to 1969. In January 1969, Nihon Gakki (today, the largest manufacturer of musical instruments in the world), offered new shares at market price. The burgeoning of new share issues which began in the 1970s and accelerated in the 1980s has encouraged a growing commitment to direct financing. By providing a source of capital less expensive than bank loans, public offerings have become a valuable source of funds for Japanese companies. The public offerings are purchased by underwriting syndicates, usually led by one of the Big Four securities firms, with the underwriters earning a substantial 3.5 percent commission.

In addition to paid-in capital increases, gratis capital increases are also utilized. In this manner, a corporation increases its capital through the granting of new stock subscription rights to all registered shareholders without cash payment. The volume of new shares issued is limited to the amount of the company's total reserves—capital reserves plus retained earnings—or to the amount of capital raised in the last share offering (minus the total par value of all issued shares). Less common are combined capital increases in which new shares (issued at par or market price) are combined with a gratis issue. In this way, shareholders can elect not to subscribe to the new issue but at the same time receive a gratis allotment of shares. Another technique sometimes used for the creation of new equity is the conversion of stock dividends into new shares which are distributed to shareholders in lieu of the dividend.

Stock splitting is also a method for increasing the volume of stock outstanding in a corporation. A stock split can be in any proportion, although two-for-one splits, in which the number of outstanding shares doubles, is the most frequent format for stock splits. The 1950 Commercial Code stipulated that stock splits were only permissible for stocks with a par value of ¥500 and prohibited the conversion of par stocks into nonpar stocks. This inhibiting regulation[5] was amended in 1982, making it possible to split nonpar stocks (i.e. convert par to nonpar prior to the split) and permitting (under some conditions) the splitting of stocks with a par value of less than ¥500.

It became legally possible, after 1970, for non-Japanese corporate entities to offer new equity issues in Japan. The first company to do so was the General Telephone and Electric Company (GTE) which offered 750,000 shares at market price in 1973. GTE was followed by public offerings from Paribas and IU International as the first step in listing their shares on the Tokyo Stock Exchange. In 1976, BankAmerica Corporation offered simultaneous public offerings in the United States and Japan. Only a small portion of these offerings were placed with domestic subscribers. As a result, foreign motivation for placing new issues in the Japanese capital market disappeared until deregulation in 1984 led to a resurgence of interest (see below).

THE SECONDARY MARKET

The secondary market consists of exchange markets and the over-the-counter market (OTC). The eight stock exchanges represent the core of the Japanese equity market with the Tokyo Stock Exchange handling the lion's share of trading volume. The Tokyo, Osaka, and Nagoya exchanges together account for 99 percent of total trading volume in Japan. Only a small number of unlisted stocks, registered with the Securities Dealers Association of Japan, are traded on the OTC (see below). Listed

---

[5]Very few issues have par values of ¥500.

securities alone are tradable and forward transactions are prohibited.

STOCK EXCHANGE MEMBERSHIP

Trading on the stock exchanges is limited exclusively to licensed member securities firms. All other types of entity as well as individuals are proscribed from membership. Stock exchange members consist of two basic types and two special categories:

1. The *regular members* consist of securities firms or "dealers" (including six foreign firms on the Tokyo Exchange) which trade on the exchanges for clients and for their own accounts. Although the number of membership positions is fixed, the Tokyo Stock Exchange is likely to increase its membership from 93 members (at the end of 1986) to 100 (or more) in 1988. Each member firm appoints a floor representative and traders. The allotment of traders allowed for a firm is based on business volume and the member's capitalization.

2. *Saitori members* (termed **nakadachi** on the Osaka Stock Exchange) are limited to 12 in Tokyo, 5 in Osaka, and 3 in Nagoya. They are securities firms operating in an intermediary capacity in securities trading for regular members. This intermediary function is analogous to the activities of specialists on the New York Stock exchange. Saitori are not permitted to compete with regular members for commission business by taking orders from ordinary investors. Unlike specialists on the New York Stock Exchange, they are proscribed from trading for their own accounts. Saitori members, like regular members, appoint a representative and traders.

3. In addition to the regular and saitori members, there is a *special member* category. This refers to the status of a securities firm licensed to deal with the purchase and sale of stock orders which cannot be met on the smaller regional exchanges. Thus, when orders cannot be executed on the regional exchanges, special members bring their orders to the Tokyo Stock Exchange or the other Central Exchanges.

4. Finally, Tokyo Rengo Securities and Naniwa Securities companies have the anomalous roles of taking stock orders from those of their own shareholders who are not members of the exchanges.

FOREIGN STOCK EXCHANGE MEMBERSHIP

Non-Japanese securities firms were prohibited by Article 8 of the Tokyo Stock Exchange charter from becoming members of the Tokyo Stock Exchange. Article 8 was amended in 1982 so that foreign firms were legally permitted to join the TSE; however, there were no available seats. Regular membership was limited to 83 seats (by comparison there are 1,366 on the New York Stock Exchange) and an opening could only occur if a member decided to sell a seat—an improbable occurrence. The improbable happened in 1984 when three Yamaichi affiliated securities firms (two with seats on the TSE) merged to create Pacific Securities Company. A seat was released and offered for auction with Yamaichi Securities Company acting as broker. Although more than 90 foreign securities firms maintained a presence in Tokyo in 1984, only Merrill Lynch placed a bid. The extremely high expected market price for a stock exchange seat (roughly $5 million) was one reason why there were no other foreign bidders. When the bidding had closed, Yamaichi rejected the highest bid (roughly $8 million) as well as Merrill Lynch's bid and awarded the seat to Utsumiya Securities Company, a small Yamaichi affiliated firm based in Hiroshima. Utsumiya paid $6.6 million.

Many investment professionals believed that Merrill Lynch had lost the opportunity to purchase the seat because it was a foreign firm, and pressure on the Ministry of Finance to admit foreign members mounted. As a result, in late 1984, the Ministry of Finance ordered the Tokyo Stock Exchange governing committee to expedite alterations in the TSE's membership regulations. Nothing less than a major concession would assuage the growing resentment of the U.S. Treasury Department over the issue of equal access to financial markets.

A year later, the Tokyo Stock Exchange announced the first membership expansion since the exchange had reopened in 1949. Ten new seats would be created, the majority reserved for non-Japanese firms. Applications from foreign securities firms with branches in Tokyo were accepted in late 1985, and in January 1986 the TSE announced that six foreign members had been accepted (see Chapter 2, Table 2–8). As a result—although the significance is open to considerable interpretation—in 1986 the

Tokyo Stock Exchange consisted of 6.5 percent foreign membership, in contrast to the New York Stock Exchange whose non-American members numbered 17, or 1.2 percent. At the end of 1986, in addition to the six foreign firms holding regular membership on the TSE, there were also 28 non-Japanese securities firms with full branch status in Tokyo.

Following the completion of a new annex to the Tokyo Stock Exchange (scheduled for the spring of 1988), stock exchange membership will be increased again. Pressure from the United States and the United Kingdom was largely responsible for the decision to implement another expansion of membership. An estimated 6 to 10 new membership positions will be created and at least half of these will be reserved for foreign securities companies with branches in Tokyo.

In order to establish foreign membership on a basis equal with Japanese members, Merrill Lynch informed the TSE in late 1985 that it wanted to serve on its board of governors. In addition, the firm told the TSE that it expected foreign securities companies to sit on the Exchange's various operating committees. Although it may be quite some time before these demands are realized, in principle there are no obstacles to full foreign participation in all sectors of the stock exchange's institutional framework.

LISTING OF FOREIGN ISSUES

Listed securities are those issues qualified for stock exchange transactions. Listing criteria include specific minimum levels of capitalization, assets, liquidity, and other key financial factors. Delisting criteria also exist in order to insure the removal of listed companies which, at any time, fail to meet the listing criteria. The Central Stock Exchanges (Tokyo, Osaka, and Nagoya) are divided into first and second sections with all new listings placed in the second section. As of the end of December 1986, there were a total of 1,848 domestic companies listed on all eight stock exchanges. Of these, 1,075 were on the first section of the TSE and 424 on the second section of the TSE.

Foreign stocks were first allowed to be traded on the Japanese stock market in 1973, with trading limited to the first section of the TSE. GTE, the first foreign firm to raise capital on the primary market, was the first to list its shares. The Big Four securities firms aggressively encouraged foreign firms to list their stock in Japan.

However, the burden of considerable documentation, the requirement of a second audit by a Japanese accounting firm, and exorbitant costs inhibited most foreign firms from considering a listing. The dual accounting requirement particularly offended many American corporations for several reasons. First, U.S. accounting procedures and disclosure requirements have been, and continue to be, far more comprehensive and substantive than requirements for Japanese companies. Second, Japanese corporations listed on the U.S. stock exchanges are not required to conform to U.S. accounting and disclosure regulations. As a result, from 1973 to 1976, only a dozen U.S. financial and industrial firms and five European firms listed their stock on the TSE. Motivated as much by the intention of promoting their corporate name in Japan as by the expectation of raising capital in an environment with low interest rates, the foreign companies achieved very little. Although the foreign shares were denominated in yen and received some marketing promotion from the Big Four, local interest was muted.

The failure of the foreign shares to have significant trading volume was partly due to limitations on their sale. Local institutional investors were prohibited from purchasing foreign stock, and, significantly, foreign shares could not be purchased on margin (although they could be used as collateral). In addition, the Ministry of Finance imposed a quota on the total value of foreign stocks held by Japanese securities firms.[6] Finally, the foreign shares did not conform to two special expectations of Japanese investors:

1. U.S. blue chip stocks provide an average yield more than six times higher than Japanese shares (the average dividend yield for the first section of the Tokyo Stock Exchange was 0.69 percent at the end of 1986). However, because dividends are *taxed* as income in Japan, dividends are not usually an objective

---

[6]For example, at the time of writing, Nomura Securities Company is limited to total holdings of foreign stock equal to ¥15 billion. Each of the other Big Four securities firms is limited to ¥5 billion. It is likely that the quotas will be increased in 1987.

of the individual Japanese investor and may be deliberately avoided.

2. Foreign shares are, on average, less volatile than Japanese shares. The typical Japanese individual investor seeks capital gains (which are currently *untaxed*) through share price appreciation.[7] Often the hope of short-term capital gains is a major investment incentive. From this perspective, many Japanese issues are far more appealing than the foreign stocks listed on the exchange.

Trading on the foreign section of the TSE occurs during two half-hour slots each day: 10:30 A.M. to 11 A.M. and 2:30 P.M. to 3 P.M. Transactions are settled by means of a depository system with no actual shares traded.

Originally, volume in foreign stock trading during these brief periods was small (IBM and General Motors were exceptions) and, overall, little public relations benefit was derived. In 1976, just one firm (Robeco) listed its stock and then for *nine* years there were no further foreign stock listings. Because the cost of maintaining share listings was extremely high and the benefits limited, GTE and Borden delisted their shares in 1977. In 1982, Amax Inc., disgruntled by negligible trading (including an eight-month period when there were no trades in the stock) and high listing costs, delisted, followed by Paribas and Atlantic Richfield.

In 1984, the Ministry of Finance eliminated the dual audit requirement, reduced the number of documents required for application, placed dividend taxation on the same basis as domestic corporations, and reduced listing fees. At the same time, the Big Four were advised through **administrative guidance** (see Glossary) to use the marketing capability of their New York and London subsidiaries to encourage foreign listings. Later that year, Sears Roebuck listed its stock. In 1985, 5 U.S. firms and 5 other foreign firms also listed and in 1986, 32 additional foreign

---

[7]Capital gains will be taxed in the near future. Such taxation could very well reduce trading on the TSE. Opponents to a Japanese capital gains tax have long pointed out that because corporate income tax is levied on corporate profits, taxation on dividends and capital gains is equivalent to double taxation. However, such double taxation (without reduced taxes for long-term capital gains) obtains in the United States under new tax regulations. Japanese regulators are likely to follow the U.S. example.

firms listed their shares, bringing to 52 the total number of foreign listed firms (see Appendix III). The trading value of foreign issues listed on the TSE reached roughly ¥1.2 trillion ($7.5 billion) in 1986, a 40 percent increase over the preceding year.

Total initial listing fees (including legal, registration, and brokerage costs) exceeded $200,000 in 1986,[8] with the annual cost of maintaining a listing equivalent to roughly 25 percent of the one-time expense. Nonetheless, as individual Japanese investors become increasingly receptive to buying foreign equities *and* as the Tokyo securities markets open further to foreign participation, growing numbers of foreign firms will list their shares on the TSE. In 1987, about 20 additional foreign firms are expected join the club. It is assumed that a listing on the TSE will facilitate participation in Japan's capital markets. Perhaps for this reason, more than 30 percent of the foreign listed firms are financial institutions.

Trading volume in foreign firms also increased after 1984 (see the discussion of churning below), rising from 134 million shares in 1985 to 185 million shares during the first six months of 1986. Japanese investors and institutions purchased 15.5 million shares of foreign listed stock in July 1986 and nearly double that amount during the market rally the following month. Some domestic individual investors, perhaps attracted by the relatively low P/E ratios of foreign firms, by the opportunity to gain foreign currency diversification, and occasionally by high yields, gravitated toward the foreign issues. *However, a large portion of the turnover was the result of trading among TSE members.*

During 1985–86, the flowback of newly listed issues to the home markets was substantial. The flowback was considered disturbing to the corporations whose shares became unexpected boomerangs. Furthermore, market conditions provided little indication and sparse promise of a decline in the flowback phenomenon.

In order to qualify for TSE listing, a non-Japanese corporation is required to have a minimum of 1,000 shareholders in Japan. This requirement is usually fulfilled through a public offer-

---

[8]This includes a one-time listing fee of ¥2.5 million, a one-time stock exchange fee of ¥1 million, a fee per share of ¥0.0045–0.0225, as well as a variety of legal and administrative expenses.

ing on the primary market or through sales on the secondary market. Foreign share placements are permitted to range from a minimum $30 million to a maximum $200 million. The gross commission for a private placement of shares or for a public offering is 3.5 percent. In those instances in which an issue consists of tranches being placed in a range of stock markets throughout the world, the gross commission is negotiable and usually falls within the 2.5 percent to 3 percent range.

SECTIONS

The Tokyo, Osaka, and Nagoya stock exchanges are divided into a first section (**ichibu**) which includes the top rated and most actively traded companies and a second section (**nibu**) which consists of additional stocks able to meet less severe listing requirements. The over-the-counter market (see below), a small segment of the equity market, includes roughly 150 equities which do not meet listing requirements on the exchange but which are registered.

TRADING LOTS

Trading lots (the unit of trading securities) vary in size on the exchanges. Trading is usually limited to round lots, with a round lot equivalent to 1,000 shares of a stock with a par value of ¥50 (most old-line companies issued ¥50 par value shares) and 100 shares of an issue with a par value of ¥500. Shares issued prior to 1952 often have a par value of ¥20 and trade in 1,000-share lots. Certain stocks that trade at unusually high prices are sometimes, at the behest of the exchange, traded in 100-share lots. The par value of shares of a company established after October 1, 1982, is required to be ¥50,000 or more. These issues ordinarily are traded in single-share lots. Foreign stocks are traded in four units of 1,000, 100, 50, and 10 shares in accordance with relative price level.

In 1982, an amendment to the Commercial Code prohibited the issuance of odd lot shares. Prior to this amendment, certificates were issued for all odd lot purchases. After 1982, however, trading in odd lots on the exchanges began to decline, certificates ceased to be issued for odd lot transfers, and owners of odd lots without certificates could only sell the odd lot back to the issuer. As a result, from January 1982 to January 1986, the number of odd lot shares outstanding fell 16 percent, to 85.2 million shares. Currently, odd lots can only be purchased on the stock exchanges by contracting to obtain pre-1982 odd lot certificates, a practice which has become quite rare.

TRANSACTIONS

Transactions on the stock exchanges only may occur during ordinary market hours, which for the Tokyo, Osaka, Nagoya, and Kyoto Exchanges are from 9 A.M. to 11 A.M. Monday to Saturday and 1 P.M. to 3 P.M. Monday to Friday. Trading hours on the Fukuoka, Hiroshima, Niigata, and Sapporo exchanges are from 9 A.M. to 11:30 A.M. Monday to Saturday and from 1 P.M. to 3:30 P.M. Monday to Friday. The stock exchanges are closed the second and third Saturday of each month as well as Sundays and national holidays. In 1985, the Tokyo Stock Exchange began to study the possibility of eventually introducing a 24-hour trading system. The establishment of around-the-clock trading is not likely to occur until it has been established on other major world stock exchanges. However, TSE officials have recognized that a 24-hour stock trading system would help to consolidate Tokyo's position as a major player in global equity trading.

Roughly 2,000 people work on the floor of the TSE, making it the most densely populated stock exchange floor in the world. Floor traders are reputed to be selected on the basis of size so that they can successfully push their way through the thronging melee which characterizes daily trading. Indeed, a large number of floor traders are heavy and relatively tall. The floor traders are distinguished by their blue jackets which contrast with the black jackets of exchange staff and the brown jackets of the saitori.

There are two methods of determining the prices of buy and sell orders on the exchange. Under the **zaraba** system, which is used throughout the trading day, buy and sell orders are consummated at auction with the highest price taking precedence for all buy orders and the lowest price for all sell orders. The

itayose method is used for opening trades at the beginning of each session. Under the itayose method, all buy and sell orders are matched by the saitori in order to establish opening prices.

There are four types of stock transaction: *regular way, cash, special agreement*, and *when issued*. In regular way transactions, accounting for 99 percent of trading volume, transactions are settled on the third business day after the contract or the fourth business day if the third day falls on a Saturday. In cash transactions, settlement occurs with the exchange of cash on the day of contract. Special agreement transactions, now rarely used, extend the settlement to an agreed-upon day within 14 days following the contract. When issued transactions are confined to the issuance of new shares by listed companies. The settlement date is declared by the exchange and usually falls from two to four months after the contract.

MARGIN TRADING

Margin transactions in the Japanese stock market began in 1951. Based on the American margin transaction system, the introduction of margin trading was the logical continuation of Occupation policy intended to stimulate free market activity and to decentralize corporate ownership by encouraging individual ownership of stock. Margin trading involves the purchase of securities on credit extended by a securities firm involved as the agent in the securities transaction. Very common in the United States (indeed, it was instrumental in the stock market crash of 1929), it is rare in Europe and is not currently practiced in the United Kingdom.

By means of margin trading, an investor can use leverage to buy shares at a fraction of the price involved. In Japan, margin collateral requirements (set by the TSE), range from 30 percent to 70 percent of the cost of the transaction or ¥300,000, whichever is higher (different rates obtain for different securities). In March 1986, margin collateral requirements were raised from 50 percent to 60 percent, with margin trading accounting for almost 40 percent of trading volume. Non-Japanese investors are prohibited from engaging in margin transactions, unless they can use a substantial portfolio as collateral.

In a typical margin transaction, the securities firm effects the transaction, holding the shares as collateral. In a margin sale, the securities firm lends shares for sale and holds the proceeds from the sale as collateral against the stock lent. Settlement must occur within six months after the contract date. Thus, margin transactions can be used to profit through price differentials between date of purchase and date of sale and to hedge against possible losses resulting from price declines in shares already owned.

In 1978, a designated issues system was created with the expectation that it would function as a measure of market trends. Twelve representative stocks believed to be sensitive indicators of market movements were selected from the first section of the TSE. Margin trading in these issues occurs under special terms. Designated issues were also selected for each of the other stock exchanges.

Nearly half of all margin transactions in Japan are handled by the Big Four securities firms. If stock exchange officials believe that a particular issue has become too speculative, then margin long/short positions may be announced on a daily basis. In addition, collateral requirements may be increased and the daily price range allowable may be narrowed. In rare cases, the stock exchange may place a temporary ban on the trading of an issue.

If the ratio of margin long to short selling exceeds 10:1 in value terms, the market is considered "overbought." Japanese investors monitor the ratio of margin long/capital of the Tokyo Stock Exchange first section in value terms. If this ratio exceeds 2 percent, then the market is again considered "overbought." As a result, investors carefully consider whether or not stock exchange authorities will increase margin collateral requirements. This, in turn, leads directly to speculative decisions. If it is believed that officials will increase margin requirements, investors may decide to liquidate long margin positions in anticipation of an imminent announcement. In this way, a brief concentrated period of selling can pull the two ratios (margin long/short positions; margin long/first section TSE capital) down to levels considered acceptable by investors and officials.

Although individual investors and corporate traders are allowed to utilize margin trading, financial institutions are prohibited from margin transactions on their own account. Trust banks and life insurance companies are allowed those margin sales that will be liquidated by the subsequent transfer of negotiables (i.e. for hedging only). Securities firms and foreigners are also allowed margin transactions for hedging only. In practice, nearly all margin trading in Japan is contracted by individual Japanese investors.

SETTLEMENT

Each stock exchange has clearing facilities that effect settlements. Two basic methods are used:

1. *Delivery.* The stock certificates (or bond certificates) are delivered to the exchange member making the contract.
2. *Book entry.* The settlement is made by the transfer of stock certificates in the books of a central depository institution.

Although all regular way and when issued transactions could easily be settled though book entry, delivery has been the preferred method in Japan.

Thus, the processing of share ownership transfers has been the last sector of the Japanese stock market to modernize. A new centralized computer clearing system will probably encourage the elimination of the unwieldy and expensive delivery system. Nonetheless, many Japanese individual investors are likely to continue demanding physical delivery of certificates for some time to come.

THE OVER-THE-COUNTER MARKET (OTC)

Registered stocks and stocks delisted from the exchanges can be traded in Japan's over-the-counter market. In 1976, the Japan Over-the-Counter Securities Company was created in order to promote trading. However, the primary function of the OTC market has been secondary trading in government bonds (see Chapter 5).

Until 1983, the prices of stocks traded on the OTC were determined through private communications among brokerage firms. In 1983, registration criteria for the OTC market were relaxed with the intention of establishing a market similar to the

U.S. OTC. It was hoped that small corporations would successfully raise capital in the OTC. However, in order to prevent the ascendancy of a competitive market, the Tokyo Stock Exchange responded to the new OTC by modifying its own listing requirements. This facilitated the entry of many additional firms into the second section, thus preventing the OTC from realizing its potential. Instead, the over-the-counter market was effectively absorbed by the second section of the TSE. In this way, the second section of small-capitalized stocks resembles the National Association of Securities Dealers Automated Quotations (NASDAQ) in the United States.

Prior to 1985, when a computer monitoring system for OTC issues was introduced by the Japan Securities Dealers Association, investors were obliged to telephone as many as 20 dealers in order to locate the best quotations. Dealer prices were known to vary considerably and irrationally. Although not always current, prices for all OTC issues can now be determined by consulting the video terminal of an on-line computer service.

In the summer of 1986, Goldman Sachs became the first U.S. investment bank to co-lead an equity offering in Japan. With Nikko Securities, Goldman Sachs co-led a six million share offering for Shaklee Japan K.K. (a subsidiary of the U.S.-based Shaklee Corporation) on the over-the-counter market. In this way, the OTC functioned as a trial area in which new types of foreign participation in the domestic securities market could be discretely attempted.

The variety of stocks registered on the OTC includes unusual issues, such as bill brokers, which have never been traded on the exchanges, and a handful of venture businesses. However, total over-the-counter trading during the past three years has been slight. Turnover in the OTC during 1985 was 192.2 million shares (far less than a half day of transactions on the Tokyo Stock Exchange) worth about ¥195 billion. During the first nine months of 1986, turnover increased, reaching 203.3 million shares valued at roughly ¥290 billion. Because the OTC is so small, large buy or sell orders from major investors can cause market agitations. The absence of market depth, which precludes smooth and rapid sales of blocks of stock, has motivated many investors and speculators to avoid OTC investments.

OTC issues are recognized as collateral for margin trading of stocks (as well as bond futures transactions) and consequently individual investors have accounted for a large part of trading volume. During 1987, trading volume on the OTC will probably reach double 1986 levels, with individual investors accounting for the lion's share of transactions. As the Japanese securities markets develop during the deregulatory period of the late 1980s, a new OTC may emerge in Tokyo. Nonetheless, at the time of writing, the OTC is a minuscule sector of Japan's equity markets.

COMMISSIONS

The commissions received by regular members of the stock exchanges from investors are fixed in accordance with a nonnegotiable schedule determined by the TSE and approved by the Ministry of Finance. All nonmember securities firms pay a brokerage fee of 27 percent of the normal commission rate to the exchange member executing the transaction.

Discounts of up to 20 percent (the discount limit allowed by exchange regulations) are negotiable for large transactions. Block transactions on a net price basis enable some institutional investors to procure lower commission rates. Additional hidden discounts are provided to select clients in a number of ways. Small securities firms are known to "buy" corporate "research" from institutional clients. The research purchased is not needed by the firms and may be worthless; it functions as a means of offsetting commission fees. Other means of circumventing the nonnegotiable character of the commission schedule include billing "errors" in which a securities firm "inadvertently" provides a favored client with below cost brokerage.

The TSE does not practice continuation (the process of treating an order carried out during a period of several days as a single order for the purpose of calculating commissions). As a result, those large orders placed by institutional investors that require an extended period of time for execution often cost more than the levels indicated by the commission scales.

Brokerage commissions constitute a major portion of securities firms' revenue. The Big Four derive 40 to 50 percent of their revenue from brokerage fees, while brokerage commissions constitute from 75 to 85 percent of the revenue of the smaller securities companies. During the fiscal years 1985 and 1986, the Big Four posted profits from 40 to 80 percent above the preceding years. In September 1985, the Tokyo Stock Exchange (at the instigation of major institutional investors) undertook an investigation of brokerage commissions.

Intermediary transactions, in which securities firms function as nominal intermediaries, are fully deregulated. In intermediary transactions, buyers and sellers find each other and bypass the exchanges. Because the commissions paid to the brokers are small, these transactions have been of increasing popularity among Japanese institutional investors.

The dismantling of all commission requirements would have a severe impact on Japan's securities firms. Many small firms could not survive without the guaranteed commissions which they receive from individual and institutional investors. Even the Big Four would experience a disturbing decline in revenue if forced to compete with foreign brokerage firms in a free-for-all environment.

By the end of 1986, one year after they became stock exchange members, the six foreign firms had succeeded in winning very little commission business. Collectively, the foreign members accounted for roughly 1 percent of the TSE daily turnover. Nonetheless, the foreign members, by using their New York and London offices, enabled some Japanese institutional investors to avoid the relatively high Japanese brokerage commission rates through off-market block trading.[9]

In November 1986, the Tokyo Stock Exchange lowered brokerage fees on transactions above ¥10 million. Fees on transactions of more than ¥10 million but less than ¥30 million (roughly $62,000–$185,000) were cut to 0.7 percent of the transaction from 0.75 percent, and fees on transactions above ¥30 million but less than ¥100 million ($308,000–$617,000) were reduced by 40 percent, from 0.55 percent to 0.3 percent. It is

---

[9]In off-market block trading, large institutional investors are invited to arrange for their New York or London offices to place block orders for Japanese shares through a foreign broker's New York or London office. When the broker locates the ordered shares (or the buyers) offshore, both sides of the transaction are completed on a negotiated commission basis, resulting in substantial commission savings.

probable that the decision to lower the rates resulted from concerns that deregulated commission rates in the United Kingdom (which were initiated on October 27, 1986) would result in a surge in Japanese equity transactions in the London market. Further deregulation of the commission schedule is likely to occur if it appears that lower London commission fees are responsible for an outflow of equity business from Japan to the United Kingdom.

The 12 major securities firms in Japan do not favor systematic reductions in the schedule of brokerage commissions. However, as Tokyo becomes increasingly integrated into the 24-hour global securities market, the day in which commissions will be fully negotiable will relentlessly approach. When this occurs (in the early 1990s or perhaps sooner) Japanese and foreign brokers will engage in fierce wars in which weapons consisting of discounts and rebates will clutter the brokerage industry with casualties.

DEPOSITORY RECEIPTS

The Securities and Exchange Law of Japan does not recognize foreign depository receipts as negotiable securities and securities firms are prohibited from dealing in them. Consequently, depository receipts for foreign stocks are not sold on the Japanese stock exchanges. Only foreign stocks listed on the Tokyo Stock Exchange are available to domestic investors wishing to purchase foreign stock locally with yen. The actual stock certificates for the foreign listed equities are not imported but are instead held in the name of the appropriate Japanese clearing institution at custodian institutions in the stock's country of origin.

There are no restrictions on Japanese corporations wishing to issue depository receipts abroad. The first American Depository Receipt (ADR) for a Japanese company was an issue by Sony in 1961. In 1963, the U.S. Interest Equalization Tax (11.25 percent of the purchase price of foreign securities) stifled U.S. interest in foreign equity investment.[10] Although several Lon-

---

[10]The Interest Equalization Tax (IET) did *not* apply to ADRs. Nonetheless, most U.S. institutional and individual investors during the 1960s turned

don Depository Receipts were issued, the market in depository receipts for Japanese corporations was negligible until the mid-1970s. During the period 1975–1985, more than 100 Japanese ADRs were registered in the United States, the majority on the over-the-counter market (see Appendix II). In addition to American Depository Receipts, Japanese shares are available as European Depository Receipts (EDRs), Continental Depository Receipts (CDRs), Hong Kong Depository Receipts (HKDRs), and Singapore Depository Receipts (SDRs).

DETACHED WARRANTS

A stock purchase warrant permits the holder to buy the common stock of the issuer at a future date at a specified price. In technical parlance, a warrant is a long-dated call option. Usually issued as a detachable portion of a bond, warrants contribute to the attractiveness of a bond issue. They also enable the issuer to increase capital structure at a future time. Whereas rights are often granted to shareholders and expire within six months, warrants usually have a five-year life. Unlike convertible bonds (which can be converted into a specified number of ordinary shares at a fixed price), a bond with attached warrants enables an investor to subscribe to shares at a fixed price (by detaching the warrants) and simultaneously retain the bond.

Warrants are issued at a premium price, the premium being the difference between the cost of buying the warrant and exercising it immediately, and the current share price. Warrants issued by Japanese corporate entities can be detached from foreign currency denominated bonds and traded separately. Prior to January 1986, warrants could not be detached from domestic issues (see Chapter 5).

Many investors have used warrants as a leveraged method for building an equity holding. For example, a warrant attached to a $2,000 bond might entitle the investor to purchase a fixed number of shares for $2,000 up to five years in the future. The

---

away from foreign securities. Many were unaware that ADRs offered a means for avoiding the tax on those equities available. Others spurned foreign investment as undesirable for a variety of fallacious reasons. The IET was repealed in 1973.

warrant, when first traded, may be valued at only $400, which assumes a 20 percent growth in the value for the next five years, giving the warrant a future value of $2,400 at the end of the period. Thus, for a $400 warrant price, the investor can gain the same profits as an investor who paid $2,000 for each share. If the warrant rose in price by $400 to $800, this would constitute a 100 percent gain for the warrant holder, whereas the percentage increase for a normal shareholder would be only 20 percent.

Although trading in Japanese warrants alone began in September 1967, the instrument did not gain popularity until the early 1980s. Since 1982, many Japanese corporations have used detachable foreign currency denominated equity warrants to sweeten fixed interest rate bond offerings in the Euromarket. From 1982 to 1985, 132 Japanese companies raised more than $6 billion by issuing 170 bonds with warrants attached.

Japanese companies using warrants issue them in larger quantities than is normally the case in Europe or the United States. For the Japanese firms, warrants provide an immediate opportunity to raise capital at low interest rates: about 5 percentage points lower on the bond portion of a warrant issue than is normally paid on a straight bond issue.

In April 1986, in a 400 million Eurodollar issue, Mitsubishi Corporation sold a novel type of warrant bond in which the exercise price on the warrant could be changed once after issuance of the bond. Thus, if the share price declines, the exercise price can be lowered.

When warrants first appeared in Japan's capital markets, few domestic institutional investors were familiar with them and most eschewed the market. Today, warrants are well understood and are sometimes used as a hedging instrument by Japanese institutional fund managers. The size of the Japanese warrant market at the end of 1986 is estimated at $10 billion with the total market capitalization which the warrants could purchase worth roughly three times that amount. From January 1986, Japanese investors were permitted to purchase foreign currency warrants (i.e. nonyen overseas issued warrant bonds). Warrants thus have a potential of becoming an attractive means of raising capital in the Japanese domestic market. However, currently the warrant market is dominated by non-Japanese investors in Europe.

MARKET INDICATORS

There are 10 indicators commonly used by investors, economists, and analysts to interpret the Tokyo stock market.

Nikkei Stock Average (225). The most prominent market indicator is the Nikkei Stock Average based on 225 issues (see Appendix V.). From 1949, when the Tokyo stock exchange reopened, until 1969, the average (then named the "Nikkei-Dow Jones Average") was calculated and published by the Tokyo Stock Exchange. In 1969, the Exchange abandoned the Nikkei Average and adopted the Tokyo Stock Exchange Average (see below). The change occurred because the average of the 225 stocks was considered to overstate and distort price movements. Because the index is adjusted for new issues, it is roughly 13 times higher than the simple arithmetic average and, as a consequence, price movements are amplified 21 times. Furthermore, the average ignores the capitalization of component companies resulting in erratic and nonrepresentative price fluctuations. In 1975, the Nikkei Keizai Shimbun Company negotiated with the Dow Jones Company to calculate and publish the "Nikkei-Dow Jones Average." In 1985, the average was renamed the Nikkei Stock Average. The Nikkei Average is the arithmetic mean of the stock prices of 225 representative issues multiplied by a constant which is regularly adjusted. The method for calculating the average is given in Appendix V. There have been few changes in the identity of the 225 issues that constitute the basis for calculating the average. In those cases in which mergers or bankruptcies occur and issues cease to be listed, a new issue is added. Thus, in 1985, Sanko Kisen was delisted following bankruptcy and was replaced by Yamanouchi Seiyaku.

Nikkei 500 Stocks Average. (Formerly the Nikkei-Dow Jones 500.) The Nihon Keizai Shimbun Company also provides a stock average based on 500 representative issues.

Nikkei Over-the-Counter Average. Beginning in April 1985, an OTC stock average has also been published by the Nihon Keizai Shimbun Company.

The Tokyo Stock Exchange Average. In 1969, the Tokyo Stock Exchange discarded the Nikkei-Dow Jones Average which it considered insufficiently representative of the market as a whole. The Tokyo Stock Exchange Average was based on a value of 100 for the average of all listed shares on opening day in 1968. The average is regularly adjusted for new listings and changes in capital. Although less popular than the Nikkei 225, the TSE Average is considered the most representative indicator of the total market.

Tokyo Stock Exchange Yield Average. Determined by dividing the total dividends paid by all first-section and most second-section issues by the total market value of those issues.

The average daily trading value of listed stocks. The closing price of each listed issue is multiplied by the number of shares outstanding. The total for all companies then yields the indicator. The value has been rising steadily, from ¥260.2 billion in 1984 to ¥264.7 billion in 1985. During the bull market of 1986, the average daily trading value exceeded ¥500 billion during many months.

Turnover ratio. This is the ratio of all outstanding listed shares to the volume of shares traded. The turnover ratio on the TSE is larger than the ratio for any U.S. or European exchange. The ratio usually exceeds 50 percent and is perceived by foreign investors as evidence of market volatility.

Average daily turnover of the Tokyo Stock Exchange. The total volume of shares traded on the exchange has risen dramatically from roughly 345 million shares per day in 1984 to 414 million shares per day in 1985. For the first time in TSE history, the billion share level was reached in August 1986.

Average price/earnings ratio for all issues. The PER is calculated by dividing share price by earnings per share. The average PER for all stocks listed in the first section of the TSE is given scant attention by most Japanese analysts. Japanese P/E ratios are difficult to interpret and greatly exceed their U.S. or European counterparts (see Chapter 4, Pitfall #2). On the last trading day of 1986, the average PER was 49.22.

Market performance of Heiwa Real Estate Company, Ltd. Although this is the most unusual market indicator applied to the Tokyo stock market, it is regarded seriously by Japanese investors and analysts. Heiwa (which means *peace*) was created in 1949 as a holding company for the buildings occupied by the stock exchanges. A small real estate firm, Heiwa derives the bulk of its profits from renting office space and trading space to stock exchanges and stock brokers. Through an unusual agreement, Heiwa's rental income is tied to stock exchange volume. Indeed, more than 50 percent of Heiwa's revenues are derived from rental of the stock exchange buildings and, in turn, more than 70 percent of that revenue is derived from the Tokyo Stock Exchange. Thus, when market activity is strong, Heiwa profits and when market activity is sluggish, Heiwa's financial results are poor.

Because stock exchange members are the controlling shareholders of Heiwa, every two years they review the formula that determines Heiwa's rental income and alter the formula's components so that, although Heiwa may profit, it does not profit excessively. This in turn increases the likelihood that Heiwa's share price movements will continue to reflect average stock exchange growth (see Figure 3–1).

NTT: THE WORLD'S BIGGEST STOCK

Nippon Telephone and Telegraph (NTT) was a state-run telephone monopoly wholly owned by the Ministry of Finance. On April 1, 1985, it was privatized in order to improve the efficiency of Japan's telecommunications industry and to raise cash to help finance the budget deficit. In late 1986, the government began to sell half of its 15.6 million shares with a plan to sell roughly 1.95 million shares per year for four years (thus ending the sale of newly offered public shares in 1989). The shares were given a par value of ¥50,000 ($310).

In order to determine a price for the limited sale of shares before the stock was listed on the eight stock exchanges, 200,000 shares were tendered at public auction for large lot investors in October 1986. Foreign investors were excluded from the offering.

The response to this initial auction was astounding. Domestic institutional investors, corporations, and some individuals

FIGURE 3–1 Comparison of the Nikkei Stock Average and the Share Price of Heiwa Real Estate Company

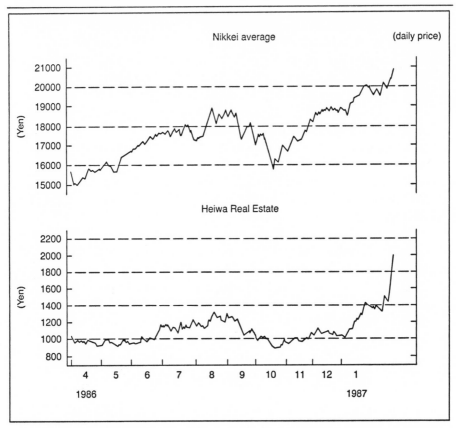

offered bids for nearly six times the number of shares available at prices per share ranging from ¥1.02 million to ¥2.4 million ($6,375 to $15,000). Based on these bids, the Ministry of Finance set the initial price per share at ¥1.197 million ($7,480), giving NTT a price-to-earnings ratio of about 130 times. At this price, the total value of NTT shares would equal ¥15.6 trillion ($97.5 billion), placing it well ahead of IBM as the largest capitalized company in the world.

In late November 1986, 1.65 million shares of NTT were offered for sale at the fixed price (¥1.197 million) with the right to buy determined by lottery. An additional 100,000 shares were held in reserve by the Ministry of Finance in order to reduce the market price if trading in the stock became overheated. The appreciation of the share price of recently privatized British Telecom (the 50p paid price rose to 95p on the day of listing) gave investors a tempting example of what could happen to NTT stock. In addition, the record low interest rates and stampeding bull market heightened public enthusiasm for the issue. As a result of these and more elusive reasons, investor response to the offering was so powerful that many securities firms announced expectations that 20 million people would join the lottery. Although the number of applicants did not reach the rosy expectations of brokers, the total, at 10.4 million (plus 38,750 companies), was roughly double the total number of resident stockholders in Japan.

Investor interest in NTT mirrored the rationality of the Japanese stock market. During 1986, pretax profit was only 6.2 percent of sales and prospects for improved earnings were bleak. Yet domestic portfolio managers and individual investors expressed an enthusiasm for owning NTT which was reminiscent of an earlier national passion for koala bears.

The successful applicants for the purchase of shares were selected by means of a lottery in late December and were required to make payment after January 5, 1987 and before the stock was officially listed on February 2.

At the time of writing, it is not known whether the fixed share price will be maintained after NTT is listed on the exchanges in 1987. Nonetheless, it appears probable that the share price will rise substantially. According to market rumors in December 1986, the Big Four are expected to respond to government "encouragement" by driving up the share price. In any case, once listed, NTT will constitute at least 5 percent of the total market capitalization of the TSE.[11]

CHURNING

Churning is a term used to describe excessive trading in an equity account with the implication that the buying and selling ac-

---

[11] As this book goes to press (in April 1987), the price of NTT shares has doubled, reaching 3 million yen and yielding a price-to-earnings multiple of nearly 270. As a result, NTT's market capitalization has grown to 11 percent of the Tokyo Stock Exchange and exceeds the total capitalization of the West German Stock Market and the Hong Kong Stock Market combined.

tivities of the broker or fund manager are contrary to the best interests of the client. The motive for such unnecessary trading is the generation of brokerage commissions. In the United States, churning is illegal and is actionable by law. Churning is also illegal in Japan where it is alleged to be a common practice among domestic securities firms.

It is impossible to ascertain the verity of claims made by some foreign investors that Japanese securities firms routinely churn all equity accounts. An article in *Businessweek* magazine (October 15, 1984) described a Japanese doctor who, in a culture where litigation is rare, chose to sue his broker at one of the Big Four securities firms. According to the article, the broker made "1,599 stock trades in 25 months, running up commission fees of $250,000, and incurring losses of $500,000." The article reported that a spokesman from the securities firm rebutted that "only 900 trades were made, the period in question was 21 months, and the doctor had signed his approval for the transactions." Law suits brought by disgruntled clients against brokers are extremely rare in Japan and Japanese courts have not decided in favor of the plaintiffs.

However, in January 1987, a Tokyo District Court judge ruled that Nomura Securities Company had betrayed a client's trust. Two Nomura salesmen executed unauthorized trades for the client's margin account, causing more than ¥50 million in losses. The court ordered Nomura to pay damages to the plaintiff equivalent to roughly one-third of the alleged loss. This decision represented the *first* instance of a court ruling in favor of a plaintiff against a broker.[12]

The possibility of churning has raised some concern among foreign issuers considering listing on the Tokyo Stock Exchange. After the Ministry of Finance relaxed requirements for foreign listings in an attempt to encourage foreign firms to list their shares in Tokyo, trading in foreign stocks on the Tokyo Stock Exchange increased remarkably. From December 1983 to

---

[12] It is noteworthy that the plaintiff was not a Japanese citizen and therefore may not have felt constrained against litigation by social tradition. It is also interesting to observe that a tape recording in which Nomura employees unambiguously acknowledged the illegal transactions was used as evidence in the case. (Perhaps only with such irrefutable proof could a plaintiff have hoped to win a decision against a broker.)

April 1984, trading volume in the 11 listed foreign stocks *increased* 13 times while, simultaneously, trading in Japanese stocks listed on the first section of the Tokyo Stock Exchange *declined* by 4 percent. Thus, in March 1984, the trading volume in Sears stock on the TSE was 8.9 million shares and exceeded the monthly volume for Sears stock on the New York Stock Exchange. Yet, at that time, only about 50,000 Sears shares were held in Japan.

In 1985, the monthly trading volume in foreign issues listed on the TSE was ¥141 billion, more than five times the average monthly trading volume for foreign shares in 1984. Monthly trading volume for foreign stocks in 1986 averaged roughly 30 percent more than the 1985 level. Yet, there was little evidence of strong sustained Japanese investor interest in the foreign issues.

It cannot be proven that Japanese securities firms were systematically crossing (mutually trading) foreign shares in order to produce an artificially high trading volume so that foreign firms would be encouraged to list their shares in Tokyo. It is known, however, that between 75 and 80 percent of all trading in foreign shares was carried out by TSE members on their own accounts. Thus, the circumstantial evidence is persuasive. Churning in the management of equity portfolios is discussed further in Chapter 9.

HOSTILE CORPORATE TAKEOVERS

Because of the system of mutual shareholdings in Japan (discussed in more detail in Chapter 4), corporate takeovers are uncommon and are discreetly handled with little publicity. Private negotiations resulting in the transfer of large blocks of stock have occurred behind the scenes for decades in Japan. Mergers intended to avert bankruptcies are encouraged by the Ministry of Finance, while secret transfers of enormous blocks of shares have been used to establish new affiliations among corporations. In such cases publicity is shunned. On rare occasions, Japanese corporations will buy large quantities of shares (on and off the stock exchanges) in companies in related industries in order to guarantee optimal service. Thus, for example, a company dependent upon scarce supplies will invest in all of its suppliers.

Cases of *hostile* takeovers in which a firm assembles a controlling block of stock in another company by buying stock inside and outside the market are rare in Japan. In 1971, an amendment of the Securities Exchange Law introduced a system of notification for takeover bids and, in 1972, Bendix Corporation made a tender offer for part of the equity in a small firm (Jidosha Kiki). These events prompted Japanese corporations to consider measures that would prevent foreign firms from initiating hostile takeovers of domestic companies. Thus, it was decided that mutual shareholding, if established on a more widespread basis, could render foreign takeovers virtually impossible in many cases. With this in mind, hundreds of corporations (with unofficial Ministry of Finance encouragement) that were not members of a keiretsu systematically expanded their mutual shareholdings. Companies within keiretsu increased mutual shareholding to the legal limit.[13] As a direct result of this strengthening of interlocking ties, the total percentage of shareownership of all outstanding listed shares by individuals declined by 12 percent in just one year, 1971–72. Simultaneously, the percentage of shares held by corporations rose 12.7 percent. This was to be an enduring redistribution in which the shares acquired were permanently removed from the float. Indeed, the redistribution was so effective that during the period 1978–84, the number of foreign acquisitions of Japanese companies numbered just 20. Of these, only two were of substantial size.[14]

In early 1986, the Ministry of Justice and Daiwa Securities Company surveyed 6,689 companies in Japan and found that 53 percent of the respondents claimed to be employing lawyers specializing in corporate acquisitions. More than 12 percent of those surveyed stated that they had made acquisitions during

---

[13]Japanese antitrust law imposes limits on cross-shareholding. Large corporations are prohibited from acquiring shares of other domestic companies in excess of their owned capital or net assets, whichever is larger. Under the revised L977, banks and other financial institutions will be prohibited from holding more than 5 percent of the shares in a domestic corporation beginning in December 1987.

[14]Namely, the BOC group's takeover of Osaka Sanso in 1982 and the acquisition of Banyu Pharmaceutical by Merck in 1983.

the preceding five years. However, nearly a third of the respondents stated that their corporate image would be tarnished if they attempted a takeover bid. Nevertheless, as Japan's capital markets continue to deregulate, it will become increasingly likely that warrants and convertible bonds (see Chapter 5) will be used in conjunction with purchases of stock to permit a hostile takeover bid or facilitate greenmail.

Unlike the United States, Japan does not harbor an indigenous society of corporate raiders, although a few exceptional individuals do engineer corporate acquisitions. Japanese industry's most flamboyant maverick is Takami Takahashi, the 60-year-old president of Minebea Company. Takahashi (who, with his family, owns roughly 13 percent of Minebea) utilized acquisitions as the primary strategy for building Minebea from a small domestic manufacturer of miniature ball bearings to a global firm which currently has 14,000 employees producing products ranging from computer keyboards and computer peripherals to handguns. Today, Minebea controls a 50 percent share of the U.S. miniature ballbearing market. Takahashi masterminded 15 corporate takeovers in Japan, and, in 1985, acquired a controlling interest in the U.S. company, New Hampshire Ball Bearings, Inc., the only remaining U.S. producer of miniature bearings and a supplier of parts to the Pentagon.

Also in 1985, through purchases of convertible bonds in the Euromarket, Minebea secretly acquired a 19 percent share of Sankyo Seiki Manufacturing Company, a Japanese precision equipment producer which controls 75 percent of world market share in musical box movements. Takahashi attempted to use his stake to undertake a hostile takeover of this medium-sized company listed on the first section of the Tokyo stock exchange.

While Minebea was occupied with the task of attempting to force a merger with unwilling Sankyo Seiki, other investors were purchasing Minebea convertible bonds and warrants. The reality of a hostile takeover of a major Japanese company by a *non*-Japanese organization was foreshadowed at this time. Ironically, it was Minebea Company, engaged in its own hostile takeover bid and the most feared raider in Japan, which was the acquisition target. Warrants issued by Minebea were purchased in the Eurobond market by a small U.K. investment group, Glen

International Financial Services Company, led by Terry Ramsden.

Ramsden, a self-made English millionaire financier, discreetly acquired Minebea warrants. Because warrants (and other securities) trade anonymously in the Euromarket, Ramsden and his associates were able to buy virtually all of the Minebea warrants on the market without Minebea's knowledge. Ramsden later claimed that the warrants were accumulated at extremely low prices because they were selling cheaply at a time when investors were wary of them (*and* they were purchased prior to the appreciation of the yen). Ramsden then added convertible bonds to the holdings, giving him a strategic stake in Minebea (50 million shares, equivalent to about 23 percent of total equity) and several other Japanese companies. Ramsden subsequently contacted Minebea and offered to sell back the stake at a price nearly double the market value.

Takahashi refused to succumb to the first *foreign* attempt at greenmail in Japan. Ramsden then sold the stake to Trafalgar Holdings, Ltd., the Los Angeles based investment company created by Charles Knapp. Knapp quickly discovered, however, that a hostile takeover bid in a financial world bitterly opposed to unfriendly mergers and foreign encroachment was difficult. According to a foreign banker quoted by *Euromoney* magazine, Knapp "could not find a single Japanese bank or securities house to help in any capacity with his bid."[15]

In order to battle Knapp's attempts to takeover Minebea, Takahashi merged Minebea with Kanemori Company (a producer of apparel) and placed the equivalent of 20 million shares in convertible bonds with institutions having close relationships with Minebea. By diluting Knapp's stake, the takeover attempt was thwarted.

This episode functioned as a warning to other small Japanese corporations considering issuing bonds with detachable equity warrants and convertible bonds in the Eurobond market. Once introduced, the specter of a hostile takeover will continue to haunt small-capitalized firms considering raising capital abroad. It is only a matter of time before another foreign in-

---

[15] Eamonn Fingleton, "Tokyo Takeovers Are for Japanese Only," *Euromoney*, February 1986, p. 114.

vestor, with superior planning and *tact*, succeeds where Trafalgar failed.

SHAREHOLDERS' MEETINGS AND THE SOKAIYA

In Japan, as in the United States, shareholders' meetings ideally provide a forum where corporate management affirms the effectiveness of management policy and the sufficiency of corporate performance. The few shareholders who attend the meetings are usually large institutions, with perhaps a handful of individual stockholders. Within this ideal model, no formal allowance is made for an institution peculiar to Japanese corporate culture: the **sokaiya.**

Sokaiya have attended the meetings of virtually every company listed on Japan's stock exchanges. Directly translated as "shareholders' meeting men" or "specialists," the term refers to a type of financial racketeer, specializing in attending **sokai,** shareholders' meetings. Although the sokaiya tradition is at least as old as the reopening of the stock exchanges in 1949, the institution did not become a corporate problem until the late 1960s.

The typical sokaiya groups initiate a form of blackmail. By purchasing shares in a company, they become shareholders in the corporation. Subsequently, the sokaiya searches for scandalous information, including details about the peccadilloes of top management. The sokaiya then directly approaches corporate officials demanding payment in exchange for silence. If the officials succumb to the extortion, the sokaiya departs cheerfully. If, on the other hand, management refuses to cooperate, the sokaiya makes his angry exit with a promise to attend the next shareholders' meeting. Both corporate management and the sokaiya know what will happen in such instances. As soon as the general meeting begins, the sokaiya will loudly interrupt the proceedings. He will announce all that he has unearthed about the company and its management. The disruption is often so complete and the embarrassment so overwhelming that corporate representatives gladly pay a premium to avoid a repetition. In Japan, where appearances are of paramount importance and publicly voiced dissent is anathema, sokaiya threats provide sufficient pressure to force corporations to yield to blackmail. Whereas in the United States, major corporations scoff at strong-arm tactics, Japanese executives find it more convenient and expeditious to pay a fee rather than meet an ugly confrontation.

Sokaiya blackmail may take a variety of forms. The sokaiya groups sometimes represent themselves as economic research institutes or consultants involved in the collection of "corporate data." The "corporate data" consist, however, of intimate details about the personal finances and relationships of corporate executives. Corporations pay a consulting fee, listed on the books as a business expense, in order to "acquire" the information. In much the same way, sokaiya sell subscriptions to magazines or financial newsletters. The periodicals are thin and the "subscriptions" disproportionately expensive.

Kaplan and Dubro (1986), in their study of the **yakuza** (Japanese crime syndicates), describe a variety of types of sokaiya ranging from skilled extortionists who extract $100,000 in a single instance to *banzai sokaiya* who walk the corridors of corporate headquarters shouting "banzai!" and depart after receiving a small cash payment. "So lucrative is the field that many corporate officials who once dealt regularly with sokaiya have switched roles and turned up as sokaiya at company meetings."[16]

The sokaiya operate in groups, the larger groups usually belonging to one of many underworld organizations. The biggest sokaiya groups sell their services to companies in another way. They function as "guards" intended to intimidate dissident shareholders. Thus, a shareholder attempting to express an opinion or raise a question embarrassing to management would encounter a sokaiya response. Such responses range from loud heckling by the sokaiya to physical abuse.

Kaplan and Dubro cite a 1981 police survey which "revealed 6,800 sokaiya in 500 separate groups extorting as much as $400 million annually."[17] In 1982, Japan's commercial code was re-

---

[16] David E. Kaplan and Alec Dubro, *Yakuza. The Explosive Account of Japan's Criminal Underworld*, p. 173.

[17] *Ibid.*

vised, making payments to sokaiya illegal and prescribing prison sentences for guilty sokaiya *and* cooperating corporate officials. Although a number of arrests were made (including a senior official of Isetan, a department store chain), the law was not rigorously enforced. As a response to the law however, large cash payments to the sokaiya have been partially replaced by perquisites such as travel, gift certificates, and, according to *Newsweek* magazine (August 11, 1986), "tips on buying and selling company shares."

In early 1984, the annual meeting of Sony Corporation lasted for more than 13 hours while sokaiya interrogated corporate officials. The meeting proved to be a landmark in the resurgence of sokaiya activity. Hundreds of major Japanese corporations are reported to have made payments to sokaiya groups during the weeks following the Sony meeting. Currently, many shareholders' meetings in Japan are dominated by sokaiya who disrupt normal proceedings. In addition, the overseas affiliates of Japanese corporations have also been victims of increasing sokaiya extortion.

Sokaiya are generally viewed in Japan as a minor intrusion within the corporate sector. Particularly following the amendments of the Commercial Code, corporations do all that they can to promote this view. Nonetheless, few, if any, major corporations in Japan have avoided the problem. The vast majority of companies listed on the stock exchanges have cooperated with the sokaiya, either by paying extortion money (through one of many disguised avenues of solicitation) or by hiring them to directly intimidate dissenting shareholders.

The systematic cooperation of Japan's major industrial and financial institutions with extortionists and thugs raises more general questions about the conduct of the firms themselves. Can a corporation that hires sokaiya to shout down shareholders be trusted to provide accurate financial data regarding corporate performance? Can a corporation, which by bowing to corporate blackmail breaches the Commercial Code, be trusted in other instances? The international reputation of Japan's most eminent blue chip corporations is impugned by their willingness to cooperate with blackmailers and thugs who are often members of organized crime syndicates.

GREENMAIL

The activities of Japan's sokaiya are not the only form of questionable pressure placed on corporations. No more subtle than the sokaiya, but certainly more legal, are the tactics occasionally used by "corner groups" (**kaishime**). Groups of speculators, often operating under separate names in order to conceal their activity, systematically purchase on margin substantial blocks of shares in listed corporations. Subsequently, using a technique not unfamiliar to American and European investors, the speculator group resells the block of shares at a large premium. In rare cases, a kaishime will attempt to purchase most of the float of a listed corporation. The corporation, in order to prevent delisting from the stock exchange, will seriously consider direct share tender of the issues. The price negotiated is usually far higher than the market price. Because Japanese corporations are prohibited by law from holding their own shares, an affiliated corporation or a friendly financial institution will transact the purchase and hold the shares. The rumor that such a cornering operation is underway will almost always drive up the stock price.

In 1986, a kaishime, after accumulating 47.6 percent of the outstanding shares in Fujiya Company, one of the largest confectioners in Japan, was repeatedly rebuffed by Fujiya's chairman and president. In late November 1986, after nearly a year of unsuccessful approaches, the speculator group informed Fujiya that it had found a U.S. buyer for the shares. Fujiya immediately capitulated and arranged for the purchase of the 61.4 million share block. The price agreed upon, although less than half the current market price of the shares, is believed to have been more than the investor group's purchase price. Fujiya thus became the first Japanese company to yield to greenmail under the threat of a potential foreign takeover. Although an actual U.S. buyer may not have existed, the case set a precedent which will be repeated many times in the future. Hostile acquisitions of Japanese firms by foreign companies, with Japanese cornering groups acting as agent, are likely to begin to occur in the late 1980s.

SHARE PRICE MANIPULATION: RAMPING

Although the Big Four securities firms will grudgingly admit that they have engineered ramping operations in the past, their spokesmen insist that the firms no longer participate in the activity. In one type of ramping ploy, an incentive issue (**zairyo**), with good fundamentals or the rumor of an exciting new product, is selected by the securities firm initiating the operation. The firm instructs its floor traders to discretely begin buying the stock. After a core inventory has been gradually assembled, the firm initiates a marketing campaign promoting the stock. Termed *lighting the lantern* (*chochin o tsukeru*), this promotion is recognized by investors as a choice opportunity to grasp a rising star. Often stock market commentators are encouraged to discuss the stock in their newspaper or magazine columns. Rumors may be promulgated. Simultaneously, firm traders are instructed to begin buying the issue in significant amounts for the firm account. When it is decided that the stock has begun to approach its zenith, the company (and those it selects to advise) liquidates its holdings as rapidly as possible. The share price plummets. Examples abound.

During a two-day period in July 1986, trading volume in the shares of Tokyu Department Store, one of the largest department store chains in Japan, increased by about 30 times while the share price rose 15 percent. The sudden interest in Tokyu stock was triggered by a rumor, reported in the financial press, that Nomura Securities Company was planning a substantial real estate deal with Tokyu. The rumor proved to be unfounded, and the share price, as well as trading volume, returned to previous levels.

The case of Tokyu Department Store shares was an unambiguous and simple instance of a ramp. Often, however, a stock's price may rise during a prolonged period of time without the circulation of rumors. Thus, for example, the rapid rise in the share price of Japan Airlines (JAL) in 1986 (see Figure 3–2) bears the outward signs of manipulation. A major plane crash in 1985 (520 people died) caused a significant decline in JAL share price. The gloomy prospects for JAL were compounded by poor earnings for fiscal year 1986 (resulting directly from a decline in rev-

FIGURE 3–2 Japan Air Lines (JAL) Share Price Movements

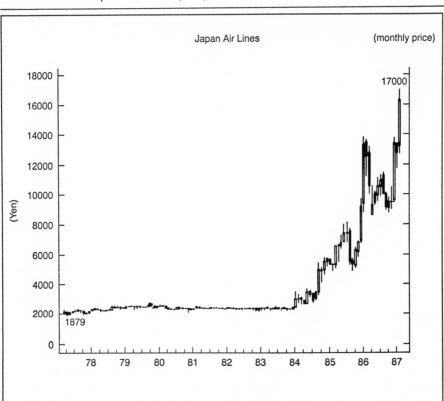

enue following the crash) and middling earnings forecasts. However, in 1986 (and again in early 1987), the price of JAL stock rose steadily, increasing by more than 200 percent. Nonetheless, it is impossible to prove that manipulation occurred.

It has been hypothesized that the Japanese government, which is planning to sell its 34.5 percent share of the national flag carrier, encouraged the Big Four securities firms to promote JAL stock. Similarly, the government is alleged to have directed the Big Four to promote the shares of Tokyo Electric Power (which rose from ¥3,000 in January 1985 to ¥8,500 in January 1986) in order to prepare the market for the launch of NTT (discussed above).

Although the ramp does increase the revenue of the securities firm involved, direct profit is not necessarily the underlying motive for the activity. Instead, the advance information that a stock will be ramped is used as an asset in itself. Such market tips are given gratuitously to those individuals the firm wishes to cultivate. Corporate leaders with whom an underwriting relationship is vital, politicians whose support can be indispensable, and others deemed useful by the firm are given advance warning of the ramp and are told when to sell. In addition, valuable clients who have recently lost money by purchasing stock at the firm's recommendation are informed about the ramp as a compensatory and conciliatory act by the securities firm.

In addition to securities firms, a second type of market participant also sometimes engineers a ramp. Full-commission stockbrokers from small securities firms (termed **gaimuin**) can conspire with colleagues to select a specific issue and systematically promote it to professional traders and wealthy clients. Little is known about gaimuin manipulations except that they do occur.

In rare cases, a **sobashi**, an unaffiliated market expert with considerable cash backing, may undertake a ramping operation on his own. If a famous sobashi is known to be involved in heavy buying of a particular stock, individual investors quickly jump on the wagon, further raising the share price.

Ramping is also undertaken by elusive groups of market experts who pool their funds and agree to buy on margin a particular stock in order to drive up the price. Because the group has no formal affiliation, market orders are channeled through dozens of securities houses and hundreds of brokers. At an agreed upon time, stockholdings are liquidated as smoothly as possible.

Finally, brokers and companies planning a public offering in the primary market are known to collaborate in a ramping operation designed to inflate share prices prior to the offering. This type of manipulation, which provides corporations with increased premiums and brokers with proportionately higher commissions, are often planned long in advance. As a result, a gradual rise in share prices prior to the offering may disguise the artificially induced price levels. After the offering, intervention having been discontinued, the stock price descends to earlier levels.

A ramping operation can be passed along like a football from one group to another. Invariably, however, it is the ill-informed individual investor who loses when share prices tumble. Although not clearly documented, it is well known in Japan that politicians procure campaign funds from stock market investments. That many securities firms ramp stocks in order to fill political campaign coffers is also well known. Indeed, many individual Japanese investors will buy any stock rumored to be on the current buy list of a politician. Although fund raising through stock market manipulation is illegal in Japan, authorities are not motivated to conduct investigations or prosecutions.

The Securities and Exchange Law of Japan does prohibit insider trading, including the manipulation of information in order to cause investors to buy or sell a stock (company directors are specifically excluded from these regulatory restrictions and are freely permitted to deal in their own company shares). Nonetheless, only a handful of insider trading cases have ever gone to court.[18] Furthermore, when the TSE discovers flagrant abuses of the law and decides to reprimand the culprits, its discoveries and decisions are treated as confidential and are never publicly released. As a result, individual investors are denied the opportunity to avoid future dealings with known miscreants.

In May 1986, the Ministry of Finance agreed to exchange information with the United States Securities and Exchange Commission (SEC) regarding possible securities abuses. To what extent the Ministry of Finance will pressure the Tokyo Stock Exchange to provide such information is not known.

NIKKEI STOCK INDEX FUTURES

The Singapore International Monetary Exchange (SIMEX) began trading Nikkei Stock Average futures on September 3,

---

[18] A major stock swindle case in 1980 (which resulted in a $3 million loss for Bache Halsey Stuart Shields, the precursor of Prudential Bache) led to a number of arrests. The stock fraud, considered one of the biggest ever recorded in Japan, was the result of complicity between Nihon Tanko Company (listed on the Osaka Stock Exchange) and the International Division of Okasan Securities Company (a second-tier securities firm). The perpetrators were not convicted, while Okasan paid the customary penalty: its international division was closed for three days. The first conviction for share price manipulation occurred in July 1984. Seven defendants (five brokers and two company officials) were sentenced for the 1982 manipulation of the share price of a primary offering of Kyodo Shiryo Company.

1986. The contracts traded are based on the Nikkei (225 stocks) Average. Stock index futures have only been traded for a short time. The modern development of this vehicle and the first trading of it began at the Kansas City Board of Trade in early 1982. Japanese securities regulations, which prohibit Japanese residents from trading any product which is not backed by a physical commodity, proscribed Japanese participation in the new market. Although stock index futures trading quickly spread to the Chicago Mercantile Exchange and the New York Futures Exchange, the ban on Japanese participation was not lifted. As a result, because there has been no Japanese trading in SIMEX's Nikkei Index Futures contracts, trading activity was muted during the market's brief existence in 1986. Beginning in 1987, the SIMEX Nikkei futures contract was sold in the United States by brokerage houses (including the New York subsidiaries of Japanese securities companies). The improved availability of the contract may encourage U.S. institutional investors to hedge their Japanese equity positions. Eventually, the contract will be traded on the Chicago Mercantile Exchange.

Stock futures contracts, based on a "package" of 50 blue chip firms selected from the 225 issues which constitute the Nikkei Stock Average, will be traded on the Osaka Stock Exchange beginning in spring 1987.[19] Because the package of equities can be delivered like a commodity to the investor when the contract expires, the stock futures contracts are legally permissible. The proposed contracts would have durations of 3, 6, 9, 12, and 15 months with maximum permissible fluctuations of 3 percent per

---

[19]The proposed futures "package" consists of the following 50 issues: Kajima, Daiwa House Ind., Meiji Seika, Kirin Brewery, Ajinomoto, Toyobo, Teijin, Toray Industries, Ashai Chemical Industries, Oji Paper, Sumitomo Chemical, Mitsubishi Chemical Industries, Toyo Soda Mfg., Denki Kagaku Kogyo, Kanegafuchi Chemical Industries, Kyowa Hakko Kogyo, Takeda Chemical Industries, Fuji Photo Film, Nippon Oil, Nippon Sheet Glass, Onoda Cement, Mitsubishi Mining & Cement, Nippon Steel, Kawasaki Steel, Sumitomo Metal Industries, Mitsubishi Metal, Nippon Mining, Sumitomo Electric Industries, Komatsu, Nippon Seiko, Hitachi Ltd., Matsushita Electric Industries, Nissan Motor, Toyota Motor, Cannon, Dai Nippon Printing, Mitsui & Co., Mitsubishi Corporation, Mitsukoshi, Sumitomo Bank, Tokio Marine & Fire Insurance, Yasuda Fire & Marine Insurance, Mitsubishi Estate, Kinki Nippon Railway, Nippon Express, Nippon Yusen, Kansai Electric Power, Osaka Gas.

day. Margin requirements would be set at 9 percent of the contract value (18 percent if only one package is traded).

Meanwhile, the Ministry of Finance and the TSE are expected to promote a revision of securities regulations in order to make the trading of stock index futures legal in Japan. With the expectation that a new market in Nikkei Stock Index futures will begin on the TSE in 1988, TSE officials signed an agreement with Nihon Keizai Shimbun Co. Inc. which would allow use of the Nikkei Index for futures trading.

It is virtually a certainty that the planned Stock Average futures market in Osaka will be successful. The Big Four securities firms, by virtue of their enormous market share, are well positioned to move futures prices at will. Although individual investors may participate heavily in the new futures trading, the Big Four will carefully watch activity and take all actions necessary to insure the success of the trial market. When Stock Index futures begin trading on the TSE in 1988, the Big Four will become major participants in the type of program trading that has caused substantial price fluctuations on the New York Stock Exchange.

THE JAPANESE INDIVIDUAL INVESTOR

The percentage of individual share ownership of all listed companies on all stock exchanges in Japan has been steadily declining. From 69.1 percent when the stock exchanges were reopened after the War, the percentage dropped to 46.3 percent in 1960, falling below 40 percent in 1970 (see Table 3–1). Between 1970 and 1972, the percentage of individual ownership declined a formidable 18 percent. This was the direct result of institutional consolidations of cross-shareholding (discussed earlier) designed to preclude foreign takeovers in a future "internationalized" domestic financial environment.

From 1972 to 1986, the percentage steadily declined at an average rate of about 2 percent per year, reaching 25.4 percent in 1985. Although the rate of decline has gradually diminished, it is likely that individual investors' ownership share of the equity market will fall below 20 percent before the end of the century. These statistics, based on official corporate shareholder registers, are deceptive, however. In order to maintain exchange

TABLE 3–1 Shareownership of Stock in Japan (all issues, all exchanges)

Financial Year	Individuals	Financial Institutions	Investment Trusts	Securities Houses	Corporations	National and Local Governments and Agencies	Foreigners
1949	69.1	9.9	—	12.6	5.6	2.8	—
1950	61.3	12.6	—	11.9	11.0	3.1	—
1951	57.0	13.0	5.2	9.2	13.8	1.8	—
1952	55.8	15.8	6.0	8.4	11.8	1.0	1.2
1953	53.9	16.3	6.7	7.3	13.5	0.7	1.7
1954	54.0	16.7	7.0	7.1	13.0	0.5	1.7
1955	53.1	19.5	4.1	7.9	13.2	0.4	1.8
1956	49.9	21.7	3.9	7.1	15.7	0.3	1.5
1957	50.1	21.4	4.7	5.7	16.3	0.2	1.5
1958	49.1	22.4	6.6	4.4	15.8	0.3	1.5
1959	47.8	21.7	7.6	3.7	17.5	0.2	1.5
1960	46.3	23.1	7.5	3.7	17.8	0.2	1.4
1961	46.7	21.4	8.6	2.8	18.7	0.2	1.7
1962	47.1	21.5	9.2	2.5	17.7	0.2	1.8
1963	46.7	21.4	9.5	2.2	17.9	0.2	2.1
1964	45.6	21.6	7.9	4.4	18.4	0.2	1.9
1965	44.8	23.4	5.6	5.8	18.4	0.2	1.8
1966	44.1	26.1	3.7	5.4	18.6	0.2	1.9
1967	42.3	28.2	2.4	4.4	20.5	0.3	1.9
1968	41.9	30.3	1.7	2.1	21.4	0.3	2.3
1969	41.1	30.7	1.2	1.4	22.0	0.3	3.3
1970	39.9	30.9	1.4	1.2	23.1	0.3	3.2
1971	37.2	32.6	1.3	1.5	23.6	0.2	3.6
1972	32.7	33.8	1.3	1.8	26.6	0.2	3.5
1973	32.7	33.9	1.2	1.5	27.5	0.2	2.9
1974	33.4	33.9	1.6	1.3	27.1	0.2	2.5
1975	33.5	34.5	1.6	1.4	26.3	0.2	2.6
1976	32.9	35.1	1.4	1.4	26.5	0.2	2.6
1977	32.0	35.9	2.0	1.5	26.2	0.2	2.3
1978	30.8	36.6	2.2	1.8	26.3	0.2	2.1
1979	30.4	36.9	1.9	2.0	26.1	0.2	2.5
1980	29.2	37.3	1.5	1.7	26.0	0.2	4.0
1981	28.4	37.3	1.3	1.7	26.3	0.2	4.6
1982	28.0	37.7	1.2	1.8	26.0	0.2	5.1
1983	26.8	38.0	1.0	1.8	25.9	0.2	6.3
1984	26.3	38.5	1.1	1.9	25.9	0.2	6.1
1985	25.4	39.3	1.4	2.1	25.6	0.2	6.0

SOURCE: Tokyo Stock Exchange

listing requirements, many medium- and small-capitalized companies fill their registers with the names of employees whose holdings are exaggerated. Thus, it is possible, although unverifiable, that individual ownership has already fallen below 20 percent.

In the Japanese stock market, far more than in other major world equity markets, it is important to consider the percentage size of individual share ownership because it represents most of the total market float (see Table 3–2). Stock investment trusts,

TABLE 3–2 Individual Investors'
Share of Total
Exchange Turnover

Year	Total Turnover (yen trillions)	Individual Investors' Share (percent)
1975	¥ 16.5	71.5
1980	¥ 36.5	59.2
1985	¥110.1	47.7
1986	n.a.	40.0*

*estimated
SOURCE: Yamaichi Research Institute

government agencies, domestic securities companies, and foreigners together hold less than 10 percent of total outstanding shares. The balance of the stock market consists of interlocking cross-shareholdings owned by financial institutions (such as life insurance companies or trust banks) and corporations. These holdings are seldom traded except as a short-term strategy to improve corporate financial statements at the end of the fiscal year. In such instances the issues are quickly repurchased.

Because they control roughly 75 percent of the genuine float, individual investors—and, by extension, the diverse psychosocial factors that motivate their market behavior—are often crucial determinants of stock market movements. Although a discussion of Japanese market psychology is beyond the scope of this book, it is worthwhile to briefly review the sources of information that assist individual investors in their buy and sell decisions. Indirectly, these sources can have a profound impact on market activity.

Japanese individual investors almost never undertake their own corporate research. Only the rare individual has examined a corporate financial report or investigated new product developments. Most Japanese individuals with an active interest in the equity market regard stocks in much the same way that some Americans or Europeans view horses. Tips from specialists (such as stock brokers or a favorite financial pundit), hints in the financial press, and personal inclination provide primary knowledge for investment decisions.

Many Japanese individuals rely exclusively on the advice of a single financial publication or a particular broker. Money is invested in a stock in the hope of quick profit with long-term investments quite rare. This fact contributes to the relatively high turnover of the Tokyo Stock market where individual investors, (holding 25.4 percent of total shares), accounted for 47.7 percent of trading volume on the first section of the TSE in 1985.

In seeking guidance for investments, Japanese individuals turn to two types of financial publications. In the vernacular these are termed **repotoya** (derived from the English "report" and the Japanese "ya" meaning shop or firm) and **shimbunya** (derived from the Japanese "shimbun" or newspaper and "ya" meaning shop or firm). Repotoya are companies that publish one or several stock market reports on a weekly (or sometimes biweekly) basis. Varying in quality and accuracy, the reports frequently take the form of newsletters designed to inform subscribers about market rumors and suspected corporate developments. Subscribers are small individual investors with little or no knowledge of equity investment. Although some of the publications produced by repotoya are legitimate, many are designed to exploit subscriber gullibility. A famous and extreme case of such exploitation was the *Toshi Journal.*

A monthly publication designed to provide its readers with stock market tips, the *Toshi Journal* also functioned as an investment advisor to its readers, inviting them to let it invest their money. When the publication went bankrupt in 1984, more than 10,000 individual Japanese investors lost a total of ¥350 billion (about $1.5 billion at 1984 exchange rates).

There are a handful of vernacular stock market dailies (*shimbun*) which provide stock market information for the Japanese investor (the *Kabushiki Shimbun* and the *Nihon Shoken Shimbun* are the most popular). The *Nihon Keizai Shimbun* ("Japan Economic Journal"), a national financial newspaper, is Japan's equivalent of *The Wall Street Journal* and has the distinction of being the biggest circulation daily business newspaper in the world. Stock market journalists, termed *kabushiki hyoronka* ("stock evaluators") write freelance articles for the newspapers and sometimes appear on television. Many of these self-proclaimed experts are alleged to accept payments from investor groups and others in exchange for promoting a particular stock. The employees of the securities firms (fund managers, economists, analysts) also write freelance articles but rarely, if ever, speak publicly. A few financial journalists have achieved notoriety and are followed avidly by individual investors in Japan.

THE "WEIGHT OF MONEY" AND STOCK MARKET DIRECTIONS

From September 2, 1985 to September 1, 1986, the Nikkei Stock Average rose 6,094.11 points or roughly 48 percent. During the same period, the yen appreciated by more than 35 percent. Those U.S. dollar investors obtaining returns equal to the index were able to reap profits of roughly 80 percent in dollar terms. Domestic investors, giddy from the unprecedented heights reached by share prices, forecast consistent, unimpeded growth for years to come. Margin buying reached record levels, with margin purchases representing more than half of daily sales volume.

While pessimists discussed the inevitability of a market crash, optimistic individual and institutional investors continued pouring funds into the market. A correction did occur with a drop of 17 percent (3,000) points between late August and mid-October 1986. The shipbuilding and steel industries fell the most with Nippon Kokan, for example, losing 48 percent. However, during a mild year-end rally in December, the market surpassed the August 20 peak of 18,936, reaching 18,982.96 at one point on December 19, as shown in Figure 3–3. The market closed 1986 at 18,701.30. Although the market reached new record highs in early 1987, many specialists continued to foresee a substantial market decline or a market crash in the near future.

The bull market of 1986 (and the subsequent shakeout in the late summer and fall) is alternatively enigmatic or easily explicable—the choice depending upon the world view of the analyst. A remarkable event in the history of the TSE occurred on March 22, 1986, and helps (or on the other hand, hinders) the attempt to provide an explanation. On that day in March, perhaps using the vernal equinox as a symbol, a TSE executive called a press conference. During the conference, the executive warned indi-

FIGURE 3–3 The Nikkei Stock Average in 1986

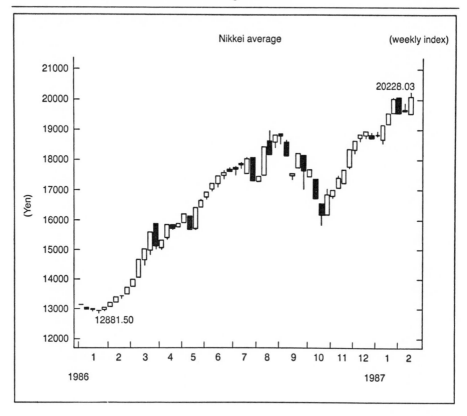

vidual investors to beware of impulsive equity investments. Traditional market volatility would make a shift in share prices likely in the near future. *Caveat emptor* the TSE cautioned; an unprecedented official warning from the administrators of the world's second largest stock exchange. What did this mean? Who is moving the market? And why? There are two complementary explanations.

The Weight of Money. The high Japanese savings rate (more than 20 percent of disposable personal income), windfall corporate earnings resulting from substantial oil price reductions, and vast tokkin funds have contributed to the formidable "weight" of funds seeking an investment medium.[20] Today, the weight of money is moving the market just as thermal currents in the atmosphere move a glider. The glider can glide for hours or days, rising higher and higher, but when the current of air (which, incidentally, is warmer than the surrounding air) disappears, the glider returns to the ground. Vast pools of institutional funds are buoying the market in the same way that heated currents of air lift a glider. And, just as a glider has no motor, the market itself has no fundamental reason of its own to remain aloft.

In late 1986, the average price/earnings ratio (PER) of all the stocks listed on the first section of the TSE was more than *triple* the average U.S. PER (see Chapter 4). Domestic institutional investors, by pouring *trillions* of yen of tokkin funds, fund trusts, and investment trusts (see Glossary and Chapter 9) into the market are keeping share prices artificially high. Simultaneously, individuals seeking a higher return for their savings during a time of record low interest rates, have turned to the equity market for solace and hope. If crude oil prices hold steady and the Bank of Japan cuts its discount rate in 1987 (to 2.5 percent or lower), the market could reach astounding heights— perhaps exceeding 25,000 before the end of 1987. Sooner or later, however, institutions will take their profits and go elsewhere. Individuals, seeing the market steadily decline, will cut their losses and go back to the banks which have always protected their liquidity while providing peace of mind. But until that day arrives, the market will rise and rise to the stratosphere. In any case, who can truly say that the higher the rise the harder the fall?

The Charts. Chartists are like chiropractors. Those who use their services swear to their efficacy, most others ignore them, and a few excoriate them as quacks. In Japan, where the stock market is less than efficient and cross-shareholding has reduced the number of shares available for trading by roughly 70 percent, charts bear a curious connection to reality. Perhaps microcharts of Japanese corporate share movements and

---

[20] Tokkin funds and kingaishin funds (fund trusts) reached an estimated aggregate total of ¥17.3 trillion ($110 billion) at the end of October 1986.

macrocharts of market movements are accurate prognosticators. Or, alternatively, the charts could be meaningful residues of psychological factors which actually do move the market. In any case, according to the charts, the Tokyo stock market has moved in a classical wave pattern with cyclical bull and bear phases. The current bull market (the fourth since 1950), with its remarkable ascent, rises like a tidal wave over Japan, promising an imminent crash. Although institutional investments may swell the market higher still, a collapse is inevitable. History repeats itself. Caveat emptor.

CHAPTER FOUR

The Stock Market: The Foreign Investor and Equity Analysis

OVERVIEW

Why should a North American or European investor select the Japanese equity market for overseas investment? The best and most obvious answer is one used by institutional investors for years: The Japanese stock market is sustained by a large domestic market and thus does not necessarily echo the bull and bear cycles in the United States and other countries. Therefore, a bear market precipitated by a recession in the United States can exist concurrently with an upturn in the Japanese market or in key sectors of the market. Alternatively, both American and Japanese markets could be bull markets with completely different sectors outperforming others in each case.

The Japanese stock market is so large that many sectors are oriented primarily toward servicing the domestic market and rise and fall largely as the result of domestic indicators, such as housing starts, interest rates, and the Japanese consumer price index. The individual foreign investor rarely considers this aspect of the market because attention is ordinarily focused on major issues such as the trade imbalance between Japan and the United States or Europe.

The Japanese dominate market share in many of the most common household and personal products: televisions, VCRs, watches, cameras, and calculators. As a result, the investor may consider only a narrow range of investment opportunities in Japan restricted to glamour companies (e.g., Sony) and glamour sectors (e.g., VCRs and computers) while overlooking domestic oriented investment opportunities that are less visible and unpublicized.

The former relationship of Japanese postwar economic dependency on the United States swiftly evolved into a highly interdependent financial market system among Western countries and Japan. This development necessitates a common standard for evaluating investment opportunities in global markets. This has been accelerated by demands made by foreign institutional investors who have convinced Japanese management and government that it must comply with more "international" reporting standards. Both large and small investors can benefit from this development as a growing number of Japanese companies issue financial statements in English.

The adage about the Japanese economy, "If the United States sneezes then Japan catches a cold," remains partially true for some export-oriented, high profile Japanese companies that strongly depend upon foreign markets for revenue, such as Sony. Yet, the conclusion that Japanese investment opportunities hinge upon the vagaries of the U.S. and other foreign markets, causes the investor to ignore a majority of investment opportunities. Because discrepancies in taxation and valuation still abound, the well-informed investor can secure gains missed by the more cautious investor.

Securities analysis is a nascent field in Japan, where institutional investors are only beginning to apply the analytical rigor long a characteristic of Western portfolio management (see Chapter 9). Individual investors in Japan (who accounted for roughly 40 percent of total sales volume in 1986) follow popular trends with virtually no regard for corporate fundamentals.

There are pronounced differences in attitude toward debt, profitability, diversification, the function of subsidiaries, and insider trading in the United States and Japan which serve to shape the investment environment. The Japanese market is dominated by investors who trade actively for speculative gain. The accounting method is more conservative and tends to understate earnings. Because there is no tax on capital gains (see Glossary), the market is speculative and can be volatile. On the other hand, foreign investor participation in the market is growing and foreign investment strategies, which differ from Japanese approaches, will increasingly affect Japanese views of investment style.

It is important to calculate U.S. and Japanese taxes levied against capital gains and dividends, as well as commissions for executing orders, before making an equity investment. It may be advantageous for the investor to consider mutual funds operated by Japanese and non-Japanese securities firms which invest in shares, bonds, or a combination of the two and which are oriented primarily or exclusively toward Japanese investment.

As a result of the difference in investment approaches between U.S. domestic investors and Japanese domestic investors, modern portfolio theory (a U.S. market model) is inapplicable to the Japanese stock market, where market efficiency is an equivocal and elusive phenomenon. Nonetheless, fundamental analysis of corporate financial statements and product developments can provide the soundest investment guidance for long-term investments in Japan. Today, the issue among foreign institutional investors is no longer "Should I consider investing in Japan" but "Should I increase or decrease my holdings until this particular business cycle ends." The following sections are written for the North American or European investor wishing to assess Japanese stocks.

HISTORY OF FOREIGN INVESTMENT

Prior to 1960, foreign investment in Japanese securities was prohibited. From 1960, when the stock market opened to restricted foreign investment, to 1970 when controls were relaxed, foreign purchases of Japanese stocks were negligible. U.S. residents were discouraged from purchasing foreign securities by the Interest Equalization Tax (repealed in 1973) which initially imposed an 18.75 percent tax on the purchase price of foreign shares. Beginning in the early 1970s, many foreign institutional investors, perceiving the promising growth potential of Japanese industry, invested heavily in blue chips listed on the first section of the Tokyo Stock Exchange. In 1970, 77 Japanese blue chip firms were available as American Depository Receipts (ADRs) of which 12 had secured SEC S–1 registration.

In August 1971, the U.S. government eliminated the gold standard (termed the **Nixon Shock** in Japan) and immediately thereafter, Japan allowed the yen to float in the international foreign exchange market. Resulting partially from yen speculation, foreign investment in the Japanese stock market increased considerably. This continued until the Ministry of Finance prohibited net increases in Japanese shareholdings in late 1972 in order to discourage further speculation. The ban remained in effect until the oil shock of late 1973 caused share prices to collapse. In 1980, following the new, free-in-principle foreign exchange law, foreign investment in the Japanese stock market increased considerably. Led by Middle Eastern funds given to capital management firms and followed by U.S. pension funds, foreign investment (primarily in blue chip equities) reached new highs. However, during most months of 1984, 1985, and 1986, foreign investors were *net sellers* of Japanese stock (see Table 4–1). Foreign ownership of Japanese stock rose from 1.4 percent in 1961 to 3.2 percent in 1970 to 6.5 percent at the end of 1985. However, foreigners accounted for 15 percent of all Tokyo Stock Exchange trading in 1985.

REGULATIONS

Under the foreign exchange law of 1980, a single foreign investor is permitted to own a maximum of 10 percent of a corporation's total equity as an "indirect investment." A non-Japanese investor intending to acquire a full 10 percent holding in a Japanese company must file prior notification of intent to buy with the Ministry of Finance. Foreign investors intending to purchase more than 10 percent of a company's stock are regarded as "direct" investors. Direct investment in Japanese corporations also requires prior notification of the Ministry of Finance. In addition, acquisition of more than 25 percent of a company's shares is subject to review by the Ministry of Finance in order to ascertain if national security would be imperiled by foreign ownership. In all cases, the Ministry has the power of veto.

THIRTEEN PITFALLS IN EVALUATING EQUITY INVESTMENT IN JAPAN

How can a foreign investor differentiate between desirable and undesirable equity investments in Japan? Even those investors

TABLE 4–1 Net Purchases of Stock
(¥ billions)

Period	Foreigners	Domestic Financial Institutions
1984		
Q1	−199	167
Q2	−876	337
Q3	−246	205
Q4	−261	278
1985		
Q1	74	250
Q2	−442	457
Q3	−269	298
Q4	−413	114
1986		
Q1	164	251
Q2	−565	776
Q3	−2,136	983

SOURCE: Tokyo Stock Exchange

with a good track record in evaluating equity investment in the United States or Europe may be misled by their very success in U.S. or European markets. Assumptions appropriate to the U.S. or other markets may not be appropriate to the Japanese market. Thus, what may be a poor investment in the United States or Europe could be a solid investment in Japan because of fundamental differences in accounting, taxation, and key financial institutions.

Investing in Japanese stocks requires modification of standard (American) principles of equity valuation; furthermore, the foreign investor must weigh additional costs in investing abroad such as taxes on overseas capital gain. The following thirteen *pitfalls* highlight key differences between the Japanese and U.S. markets and how they affect foreign investors. Bearing in mind these pitfalls, investors can reap handsome profits by investing in the Japanese stock market.

PITFALL #1: *Banks play a larger role in the capital structure of Japanese companies than their U.S. counterparts.*

Japanese banks have traditionally served short-term corporate financing needs to a greater extent than U.S. banks.

Short term debt continues to be favored by Japanese management as a means of acquiring additional capital and it is preferred to equity offerings. The average proportion of short-term debt to total liabilities (including equity) is in the 25 percent range as compared to about 4 percent in the United States.

In contrast to indirect financing, most Japanese corporations have 20 to 25 percent equity to total assets, far less than their North American or European counterparts. However, the equity to asset ratio of Japanese corporations has been increasing steadily since 1980 (and rapidly since 1984) as the result of increasing internal reserves. Growing investments in domestic and foreign capital markets have also contributed to the increase. According to a Bank of Japan survey of 620 large corporations, average equity to asset ratios in the manufacturing sector reached 29.8 percent at the end of March 1986, the highest level since 1962.[1] The ratio for nonmanufacturing corporations exceeded 15 percent for the first time ever, reaching 15.5 percent. Despite these increases and the deteriorating role of banks as sources of corporate funding (see Chapter 7), indirect financing is still the prevalent mode of fund raising in Japan.

Until the mid-1960s, it was the norm in Japan to offer shares at par to shareholders of record. Given the growing discrepancy between par price and market price (usually ¥50 par value per share for most old-line companies, or about $0.32 at current exchange rates), Japanese companies could not raise sufficient capital by issuing shares. During the past 20 years, this situation has changed and it has become more common for Japanese companies to raise capital through public equity offerings at market price. Nonetheless, debt financing through short-term bank loans still outweighs other means of obtaining capital in Japan. Unless this is fully understood, the foreign investor may be discouraged from investing in a company that appears to be perpetually awash in debt.

The current ratio, a standard ratio used by securities analysts to test financial stability (by determining how readily a company could cover its debts), assumes a balance of approximately 2:1 (current assets : current liabilities) as desirable for U.S. industries. This general rule of thumb varies from sector to

---

[1] As reported by the *Japan Economic Journal*, January 3–10, 1987, p. 2.

sector. Many Japanese companies, by comparison, appear to be dangerously leveraged (from the American perspective) because of their reliance on debt financing from banks. A comparable Japanese ratio may be 1:1, or even less, with current liabilities equaling or exceeding current assets. Japanese companies also have low market capitalization compared to their U.S. counterparts.

Debt often appears in some combination of short-term bank loans, short-term commercial paper, and long-term borrowing from credit banks. Widespread use of short-term debt makes the relationship between interest rates (set by the Bank of Japan) and corporate borrowing much closer than in the United States. Japanese corporations also frequently issue and accept trade payments in the form of 60-, 120-, and 180-day notes.

Corporate debt financing through loans is possible by tapping the vast reservoir of money made available by Japanese individual bank deposits. NCDs are particularly popular in Japan (see Chapter 8), with three-month certificates of deposit earning approximately 4.5 percent at the end of 1986. Japanese savings as a percentage of nominal GNP is the highest in the world: 17.5 percent in 1985, compared with 4.25 percent for the United States, and 12.25 percent in the United Kingdom. Stocks are viewed as speculative instruments for financial gain, with the majority of individuals preferring to place their money in savings accounts (demand and time deposits) which earn low interest but which are secure and are untaxed up to amounts of ¥3 million for each of three types of account (see Appendix II). The Japanese government has looked the other way with postal savings accounts, for example, and individuals have circumvented the ceiling restriction on postal savings by opening multiple accounts under different names (regulations, however, will soon change).

Because housewives in Japan traditionally manage the household income, household investment patterns will change as securities firms increase marketing efforts to convince housewives to invest a larger percentage of household assets in securities-related financial products (ranging from medium-term government bond funds and cash management accounts to Euromarket instruments). These and other changes in household financial management and stock investment will be gradual, however. For the foreign investor, such changes mean minor adjustments in individual investment patterns which do not alter significantly the equity investment climate in Japan.

As long as the Japanese remain avid savers, corporations will continue to engage in debt financing. Barring a significant change in taxation, banks will continue to tap into large pools of savings to finance industry, industry will continue to prefer debt financing to equity offerings, and the individual investor in Japan will continue to be motivated primarily by the prospect of speculative short-term gain.

Japanese companies prefer financing through debt rather than equity because debt financing through loans is less expensive than other types of financing and is easier to obtain. Japanese commercial banks can circumvent regulations limiting most lending to short-term loans. In the past, commercial banks converted short-term funds into long-term loans to corporations by purchasing five-year bank debentures from long-term credit banks. In addition, three long-term credit banks supply long-term loans directly to industry: the Industrial Bank of Japan, the Long-Term Credit Bank of Japan, and the Nippon Credit Bank (see Chapter 7).

PITFALL #2: *Japanese P/E ratios are higher than U.S. P/E ratios.*

Price/Earnings ratios (P/E ratios) are calculated as follows: P/E = Share Price/Earnings Per Share. The higher the earnings per share estimates, the lower the P/E ratio (PER). The price/earnings ratio, a method of calculating whether a stock is overpriced or underpriced, still is greatly relied upon by investors throughout the world. It has more weight in the United States, however, than in Japan.

The average P/E ratio of the 225 issues that constitute the Nikkei Stock Average stood at roughly 10 during the 1960s, rose to 20 during the 1970s and reached about 30 in 1985. By the end of 1986, the average P/E ratio had risen to roughly 50 (see Figure 4–1). At the top end of the P/E range are firms such as Koa (995 times earnings), All Nippon Airways (749 times earnings), and Mochida Pharmaceuticals (464 times earnings).[2] Trading in somewhat lower multiples are well-known electronics firms such

---

[2]The P/E ratios provided apply to prices on December 27, 1986—the last trading day of the year.

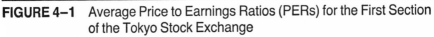

FIGURE 4–1 Average Price to Earnings Ratios (PERs) for the First Section of the Tokyo Stock Exchange

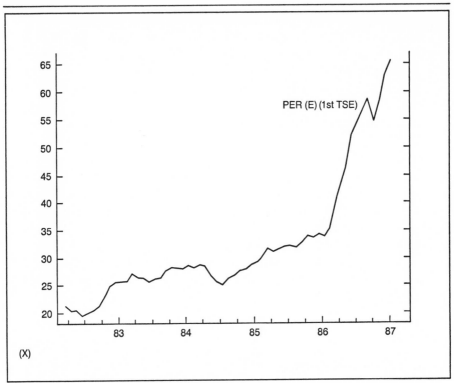

as Casio (54), Victor Company of Japan (70), and Pioneer (100). At the bottom of the range are firms such as Mitsubishi Oil (7 times earnings), Sumitomo Warehouse (14), and TDK (17). Japanese P/E ratios are usually higher than their U.S. counterparts and the range of PERs is far broader in Japan than in the United States or the United Kingdom (see Tables 4–2 and 4–3).

While the prices of Japanese shares have risen far beyond their book value, dividend yields have plummeted. In the 1960s, yields were 4 to 5 percent and declined to 2 to 3 percent in the 1970s. From 1980 to 1985, yields declined from 2 percent to 1 percent, dropping further to 0.69 percent at the end of 1986 (see Figure 4–2).

Taxation is one reason for the low yield of dividends in Japan. Capital gains procured by domestic institutional investors

TABLE 4–2	Comparative Price to Earnings Ratios for Three Countries* (banking)

Company	P/E
United Kingdom	
Barclays	6.8
Lloyds	6.0
Midland	8.6
United States	
Bank of New York	8.0
Citicorp	8.0
Chemical Bank	6.0
Morgan Guaranty	9.0
Japan	
Dai-Ichi Kangyo	74.7
Fuji	69.2
Industrial Bank of Japan	112.0
Sanwa	60.8
Sumitomo	74.5

*On January 6, 1987

SOURCES: *Financial Times, The Wall Street Journal, Japan Economic Journal.*

are taxed as a component of corporate taxes. However, for all good purposes, there is no capital gains tax for individuals. Individual investors *are* taxed on capital gains only if transactions with one broker exceed 50 per year or the individual buys (or sells) a minimum of 200,000 shares in a single company in a single transaction. (Although it is likely that a capital gains tax will be introduced in Japan in the near future, it will be difficult to enforce.) Dividends, however, are taxed as income. This encourages investors to neglect dividends as a source of income and seek capital gains through turnover instead. Thus, shareholder complaints regarding insufficient yield are unlikely. Traditionally, dividends are based on par value (e.g. 10 percent annual yield on a share of ¥50 par value) and seldom correlate with earnings.

A major reason for a discrepancy between Japanese and U.S. price/earnings ratios is that many Japanese P/Es are based upon nonconsolidated (parent) company earnings while their counterpart U.S. corporations calculate earnings on a consolidated

TABLE 4–3 Comparative Price to Earnings Ratios for Three Countries* (electronics)

Company	P/E
United Kingdom	
British Telecom	11.3
Cable & Wireless	17.1
Plessey	11.8
United States	
General Electric	17.0
IBM	13.0
ITT	23.0
Nynex	11.0
Japan	
Hitachi	32.9
NEC	52.0
Oki Electric	173.1
Pioneer	95.3
Sony	25.2

*On January 6, 1987

SOURCE: *Financial Times, The Wall Street Journal, Japan Economic Journal.*

basis. Financial statements in Japan are centered around the nonconsolidated (parent) company because this is the object of creditors' attention and financial statements are prepared largely for the benefit of the creditor, rather than the investor.

As a result, with the exception of consolidated financial statements issued for purposes of foreign financing, Japanese corporations historically have provided financial statements on a company-by-company basis only. All investments in affiliated and subsidiary companies were carried at cost in the financial statements of the investor. Japanese corporations included profits and losses on transactions between affiliated companies in the financial statements. Because subsidiary and affiliated entities were given the *appearance* of autonomy, parent corporations —for purposes of financial reporting—*allocated* profits within the group of companies. This procedure has enabled Japanese corporations to *create* profits for subsidiaries or affiliates.[3] With

---

[3]Thus, there have been many cases of bankrupt companies whose financial statements indicated consistent profit in the years preceding insolvency.

FIGURE 4–2 Average Dividend Yields of All Issues Listed on Tokyo Stock Exchange First Section

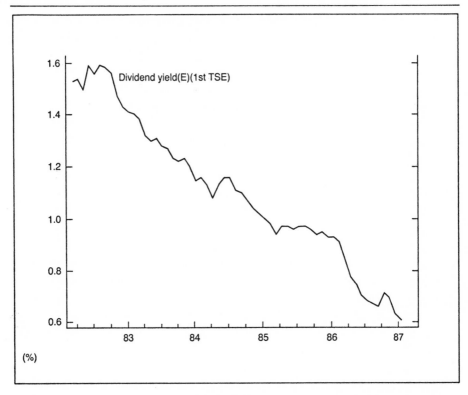

this in mind, it becomes clearer how the overseas subsidiaries of Big Four securities companies (discussed in Chapter 2) were in some cases far less profitable than financial statements suggested.

Consolidated financial statements have been required only since April 1977 and they *supplement* parent company statements rather than serving to summarize all parent company information along with consolidated information. Consolidated statements are frequently less detailed than parent company statements, and they are issued on a semiannual basis (rather than quarterly, like parent company statements). Also, there is

Such "profits" are often generated through the sale of portfolio holdings and other assets to affiliated companies.

a lag in making consolidated statements public—usually one month after parent company financial statements have been issued.

The equity method, one method of calculating earnings by subsidiaries, has been applied uniformly to companies only since April 1983. The equity method requires that earnings be consolidated with parent company earnings if the parent owns more than 20 percent but less than 50 percent of a company. Prior to the 1983 regulation, the majority of companies favored the cost method over the equity method, making it difficult for the investor accurately to calculate parent company earnings historically in cases in which the companies recently switched to the equity method.

Using the equity method to calculate earnings boosts overall nonconsolidated earnings. This means that earnings per share estimates (EPS) increase. Usually, the process of consolidating earnings boosts earnings per share estimates even higher, causing the PER to decline and thus making the investment more attractive. Investors in the United States seek American stocks with a high EPS and a low P/E. Thus, foreign investors considering Japanese stocks generally can rely on EPS and P/E figures *relative to other companies within the same sector*, but they should not be compared across the board with U.S. or other non-Japanese companies in the same sector.

Blue chip stocks of suitable investment grade for individual investors—stocks which show solid secular growth patterns—have low P/E ratios relative to other consolidated companies on the Tokyo Stock Exchange and usually are good long-term investments. A handful of these companies (see Appendix II) conform to SEC regulations for filing on the New York Stock Exchange. Since these companies use American Generally Accepted Accounting Principles (GAAP) instead of Japanese accounting principles, their PERs can be contrasted freely with American firms in the same sector.

If consolidated earnings boost the earnings per share and help lower the P/E ratio to levels somewhat more acceptable to foreign investors, why do Japanese companies not rely more on consolidated financial statements to woo foreign investors? Foreign investors prefer consolidated financial data to nonconsolidated because a parent company usually is both a major shareholder of subsidiaries and the *primary creditor or guarantor* of loans taken out by subsidiaries. So decisions made by the parent company affect consolidated subsidiaries, which are treated as part of the parent company by management. In fact, large export-oriented companies with relatively large quantities of shares held by foreign investors increasingly *are* making efforts to provide investors with consolidated financial data, but Japanese methods of consolidation still tend to understate the EPS, and thus increase the P/E ratio.

Japanese individual investors rarely review corporate financial statements and Japanese securities analysts give them far less attention than their professional counterparts in the United States, where fundamental stock analysis is preferred. The needs of Japanese creditors are different from the needs of the investor, and this is reflected in Japanese financial statements. For example, in Japan, subsidiaries are not liable to creditors for defaults on loans by the parent company and parent companies exercise little control over subsidiaries in determining dividend policy or in liquidating assets.

Declining individual ownership of total outstanding shares conjoined with growing market demand is also a factor in explaining the high (and rising) Japanese PERs. Individual ownership, as mentioned in Chapter 3, has declined from 69.1 percent when the stock exchanges were reopened to roughly 26 percent in early 1986. Simultaneously, institutional ownership now accounts for about 65 percent of all outstanding shares. A substantial portion of institutional ownership takes the form of **cross-shareholding** (see Glossary) and *shares that are instrumental in maintaining corporate relationships are not ordinarily sold.*

Concurrent with this change of equity ownership in Japan, equity investments have recently become increasingly popular for individual *and* institutional investors. Thus, while the float of corporate shares has declined, market demand has increased. Meanwhile, the ratio of new issues to total shares outstanding has declined. These factors have helped to drive up share prices. Higher share prices in Japan, of course, do not correlate with corporate profits and, in any case, Japanese corporate profits do not correlate with dividend yield. This has resulted in a peculiarly skewed equity landscape in which great market demand (which at times has exceeded supply) has competed for a decreasing supply of shares while an antiquated system of dividend calculation has remained unmodified.

There are other reasons why Japanese corporate earnings tend to be understated, resulting in higher P/E ratios than many foreign investors find comfortable (see Pitfall #3, below). Paul Aron, Vice Chairman of Daiwa Securities America, Inc., analyzed U.S./Japanese P/E ratio differentials between 1981 and 1984, and his tentative conclusions indicated that if Japanese stock analysis were readjusted to conform to American Generally Accepted Accounting Principles (GAAP), Japanese P/E ratios would decline sharply and closely approximate U.S. P/E ratios.[4]

In addition to methods of consolidation and accounting differences, some reasons include:

1. *Differing methods for calculating number of shares outstanding.* American analysts average the number of shares outstanding over a fiscal year to determine earnings per share; Japanese earnings per share (EPS) are calculated on the basis of number of shares outstanding at the time the financial report is issued.

2. *"Hidden" assets.* In Japanese corporations, land and securities are often understated on the balance sheet (see Pitfall #4). Thus, for example, city banks have enormous "hidden" assets in the form of share holdings. It has been estimated that actual net assets per share are four times higher than stated on the balance sheets.

When Aron wrote his report in October 1984, Japanese PERs were 15 percent higher than U.S. PERs. However, during the ensuing two years, Japanese PERs rose at a dramatically higher rate than U.S. PERs. As a result, the average PER of all issues listed on the first section of the TSE at the end of January 1987 was 56.25, while the average PER for the S&P 500 was roughly 18.5.

Thus, as a result of the ascent of Japanese PERs relative to U.S. PERs, Aron's argument, while not totally invalidated, is at-

---

[4]Paul Aron, "Japanese Price Earnings Multiples Revisited; Some Further but Still *Tentative Observations and Thoughts*," Paul Aron Report #27, Daiwa Securities America, Inc., October 19, 1984.

tenuated. If Japanese earnings are calculated on a U.S. basis, then the average PERs would indeed decline by 15 percent. If corporate earnings were calculated on a fully consolidated basis, then Japanese PERs would fall another 15 percent. However, even after these adjustments, Japanese PERs (at the end of 1986) would not be comparable to those in the United States or Europe.

Finally, P/E ratios tend to correlate inversely with interest rates so that when interest rates decline, P/E ratios increase and when interest rates increase, P/E ratios decline. During the calendar year of 1986, four interest rate cuts by the Bank of Japan brought the discount rate to a postwar low of 3 percent. This compares with a U.S. discount rate of 5.5 percent. Although no causality can be asserted between interest rates and PERs, low Japanese interest rates relative to the United States should be taken into account when assessing the price of Japanese shares.

When determining the P/E ratio of a Japanese company, the investor must examine the PER of the Japanese corporation on a historical basis and in comparison with other companies in the same sector, rather than simply compare it with a U.S. corporate counterpart. American or European assumptions about the measurement of earnings projections and P/E ratios can steer the foreign investor away from good investment prospects in the Japanese market.

Some analysts speculate that the PERs (and other valuation differentials) between Japanese corporations and their U.S. or European counterparts will be gradually reduced. This could be caused by the internationalization of Japan's financial markets generally and by the integration of the Tokyo stock market into broader global markets specifically. Foreign portfolio management techniques will be adopted by Japanese fund managers (see Chapter 9). The methods of security analysis used by foreign securities company branches in Tokyo will someday be mastered by the Big Four research institutes. Simultaneously, Japanese individual and institutional investors will diversify their equity investments internationally and will cultivate an appetite for lower multiple foreign issues. All of these factors could perhaps contribute in some way to a reduction in the unjustified differences in multiple levels between Japanese equities and those of other global stock markets.

Nonetheless, the Japanese stock market is only a market of stocks. Supply and demand factors will always play a vital role in determining the price of a stock. One result of the internationalization of Japan's financial markets will be a closing of ranks among the members of the keiretsu clubs. Cross-shareholding will be used as a Chinese wall to keep out the barbarian hordes. The float of shares traded on the stock exchanges will remain small. At the same time, Japanese investors will decide what they want and what they wish to discard on the basis of trends and fads which have no Western counterpart. The high price paid for NTT equity in 1986 and the concurrent exclusion of all foreign buyers provides but one demonstration of this. A stock is worth what the market will pay. If the Japanese market will give a kingdom for a horse then global valuation techniques and internationalization will have no bearing on that decision.

PITFALL #3: *Differences in accounting procedures between Japanese and U.S. corporations, such as the type of depreciation method reported, understate Japanese earnings estimates.*

This point is tied to Pitfall #2 because differences in accounting procedures are among the most important reasons Japanese P/E ratios are relatively high and earnings per share (EPS) estimates are relatively low (making investment less attractive).

Japanese financial reporting favors declining balance methods for gauging depreciation, while U.S. financial reports favor straight-line depreciation. Japanese tax laws do not allow companies to use different methods of depreciation for tax authorities and for shareholders. Consistent with Japanese preparation of financial statements for creditors, statements minimize income in order to reduce the tax burden. Intangible assets also are rapidly expensed, but these constitute a small part (less than 2 percent) of total fixed assets. Japanese depreciation methods understate earnings when compared with standard U.S. accounting principles (American GAAP). Declining balance methods of depreciation may especially affect earnings estimates for companies, particularly companies in fields where capital investment in plant and equipment is substantial and must be continuously upgraded. The investor with access to financial statements can get a better sense of corporate earnings by looking at the cash flow (net income plus depreciation minus dividends paid) than by considering net income alone.

Other accounting differences that understate earnings are: regulations in Japan requiring identical tax and stockholder reports, tougher regulations concerning corporate tax deductions, and Japanese law governing reserves. As mentioned briefly above, U.S. companies can issue reports to stockholders and to financial authorities that differ—the former maximizes earnings per share, while the latter minimizes taxable income. Japanese companies cannot do this. Also, tax deductions (deductions from taxable income) for entertainment are not allowed, although the cost of entertainment is often considerable. Finally, differences in calculations concerning corporate reserves understate earnings.

PITFALL #4:   *It is argued that because PERs have risen to unprecedented heights, "hidden assets" provide a key to evaluating the share value of many Japanese corporations. Although true, this argument can be misleading.*

The "hidden asset" theme in Japan rose to popular attention in 1984 and reached a peak of popular interest in early 1986. Hidden assets result from the particular treatment of corporate assets by the Japanese accounting system. In Japanese accounting, the value of property or shares acquired by a corporation is listed on the corporate balance sheet at the historic cost not the market price. This accounting practice is utilized regardless of the date of the original entry or the method of valuation.

The differential between historic cost and market price is most glaring in the case of real estate holdings, particularly urban property. The best known example in Japan is that of the Mitsubishi Estate Company which has extensive holdings of land and buildings in the Otemachi section of Central Tokyo, where land prices are among the highest in the world. Because most of the land holdings were valued at prices current during the American Occupation, the land holdings are booked at a small fraction of their current value. The hidden assets of Mitsubishi Estate Company are estimated to be roughly ¥12.5 trillion. Nevertheless, although share prices have risen significantly as a direct result of the hidden assets, the total market capitalization of the company is only about ¥3 trillion. In January 1987, Mitsubishi Estate traded at a price to earnings multiple of 140.

The record highs achieved by the Tokyo stock market in 1985–86 enabled many companies to have enormous unrealized capital gains. The vast majority of corporations listed on all of Japan's stock exchanges could derive hefty profits from the sale of their holdings of equities. The differential between the current market price of stock holdings and their purchase prices are often of exceptional proportions. Such corporations as Matsushita Electric Industrial, Tokio Marine & Fire Insurance, and Hitachi could reap capital gains of *more than* ¥2 trillion ($12.5 billion) if they sold their share holdings at current market prices. It is noteworthy that the possession of this exceptional unrealized wealth has given many corporations the confidence to take risks that would never before have been considered. Recent participation in **zaitek** (domestic and international financial arbitrage—see Glossary and Chapter 9) has, in part, been made possible by the unrealized capital gains that buttress corporate collateral and corporate daring.

Japanese corporations have vast land holdings as well as substantial equity holdings which are listed on the corporate books at historic cost. Therefore, such companies appear to be good buys for the investor. They may well be—*but* there is a *caveat*.

In the United States, a corporation, such as Mitsubishi Estate Company, having assets that greatly exceed total capitalization, would be a takeover target. Corporate acquisitions do occur in Japan (see Chapter 3) but *cross-shareholding renders many companies inaccessible to takeover bids.* The structure of the keiretsu is designed to prevent hostile acquisitions. If the majority of the shares of a company (such as Mitsubishi Estate Company) are held by keiretsu insiders, then even if a corporate raider were to acquire the total float of corporate shares, the raider would still not own enough. For this reason, a tender offer to acquire all of a company's securities is rarely feasible in Japan, where the total volume of freely traded stock is frequently in the 25 percent to 35 percent range.

Of course, there are companies in Japan with hidden assets which are not members of a group. These companies can be takeover targets. But, even in these cases, *hostile* takeovers leading to the liquidation of corporate assets in order to enrich shareholders are anathema in Japan. A foreign investor with a watertight strategy for taking over a Japanese "cash cow" or "asset cow" would still have to contend with regulatory authorities who would be likely to do all possible to thwart the acquisition.

The investor analyzing a company in terms of its book value and market price must carefully consider a number of questions.

1. Is it probable that, in the foreseeable future, the company could be acquired by another firm and liquidated? (The answer to this question will almost certainly be a categorical no.)
2. Could the company liquidate part, or all, of its hidden wealth without significantly damaging plant, equipment, or production? (The answer is frequently yes.)
3. If the answer to number (2) is affirmative, could land holdings be sold for urban development?

These questions can only be addressed on a company-by-company basis with careful research and insightful long-term projections.

The entire Japanese stock market can be viewed as a significant discount to asset value. Indeed, the majority of corporate share prices could be permanently readjusted upward because of revaluation resulting from a dramatic increase in corporate assets following the sale of "hidden assets." However, it is difficult for any investor, particularly a foreign investor, to anticipate such sales. The time may come when Japan's domestic development will exercise inexorable pressure on companies to sell land. But it will not be easy to foresee such moves. In order to capitalize on the "hidden asset" theme, the foreign investor must make long-term investments in the expectation that someday corporate holdings will be sold. Nonetheless, regardless of the degree of future corporate restructuring, corporate equity holdings, which are booked at historic price, will not be sold unless necessitated by severe cash flow problems. These cross-shareholdings are the keystone of the keiretsu structure which underlies part of Japanese corporate policy and corporate culture. For this reason, *an analysis of the majority of Japanese companies must include a major discount to assets.*

PITFALL #5: *Japanese company earnings and market price for stocks may be affected adversely by par price offerings or by the distribution of free shares.*

Roughly 100 to 300 companies each year raise money through equity share offerings on the Japanese market. In the past, these were almost always rights offerings or allotments to existing shareholders, with shares offered at par. Par price issues originated in a smaller, slower stock market and served as a means for companies with rising earnings to issue shares to existing shareholders in lieu of an increase in the per-share dividend. Stock offerings issued at par to stockholders[5] may be anywhere from one-third to as little as one-tenth of the market price of the stock.

Par price issues made economic sense before the mid-1960s, but have since fallen out of favor. Rapid economic growth in the economy in past decades created a growing gap between par prices for stocks and their market value. This, in turn, caused opponents to argue that shareholders could obtain par price shares in proportion to their holdings, receive the same per share dividend, and turn around and sell their shares for a profit at market price. As a result, during the past 15 years, market price issues have increased, along with "free market distribution," reducing the frequency of par price issues.

Free stock distributions may be preferred by Japanese management over cash dividends in periods of rising earnings in order to preserve cash and to increase investors' return. There also are accounting benefits. Free stock distribution enables a company to shift money from capital reserve accounts to common stock accounts. Free stocks are distributed, in theory, when the share price has been depressed by a low ex-rights price and is expected to rise again, increasing the value of stocks held by

---

[5]See **par value** in the Glossary.

shareholders. There is no guarantee, however, that this will occur.

PITFALL #6: *The financial stability of highly leveraged Japanese corporations is supported by cross-shareholding and other aspects of corporate groupings. This serves as a buffer against bankruptcy.*

Chapter 1 mentioned the prewar zaibatsu combines that dominated broad sectors of the Japanese economy. Such conglomerates as the Mitsui Group, the Mitsubishi Group, the Sumitomo Group, and the Yasuda Group were reincarnated after World War II in the form of keiretsu and member companies, and continue to work in concert although they are legally and financially independent. Some histories of Japan indicate that the prewar zaibatsu were shattered by American Occupation antimonopoly laws. However, while keiretsu are weaker than pre-World War II zaibatsu, they continue to be a dominant feature of the Japanese economic environment.

From the perspective of the investor, the size and financial clout of keiretsu conglomerates, coupled with cross-shareholding, insures the financial stability of any single corporate member despite seemingly dangerous amounts of short- and long-term debt on the balance sheet (particularly the former). Corporations frequently borrow from fellow keiretsu financial institutions so that there is minimal risk of having debts called in. As a result, large shareholders in a company may also double as creditors. The contemporary keiretsu conglomerate behaves in a way contrary to U.S. antitrust legislation, but it is perfectly legal and consistent with Japanese corporate trends during the past century.

Most large financial institutions in Japan are affiliated in some way with one of the industrial conglomerates, as are many medium and small corporations. Keiretsu control has ramifications throughout the Japanese economy and affects all financial and industrial concerns.

It is not always important for the investor to identify the group to which a company belongs and not all Japanese companies can be identified with a particular keiretsu network. It *is* important, however, for the investor to bear in mind that the financial dealings among members make seemingly dangerous levels of debt tolerable. Furthermore, Japanese companies tend to spin off or acquire a greater number of affiliates or partially owned subsidiaries than their U.S. counterparts, strengthening the financial credit and material supplies network among them.

PITFALL #7: *The relationship between interest rates (and other economic indicators) and the stock market in Japan does not mirror the relationship that exists in the U.S. economy.*

Banks have a unique relationship with many fellow keiretsu members because they simultaneously function as creditors and as shareholders. In this respect, banks (primarily private commercial banks but also the long-term credit banks) have a closer financial relationship with industry than is the case in the United States. Interest rates set by commercial banks affect the cost of short-term borrowing to industry, but interest rates per se do not affect the stock market in the same way that they do in the United States because equity investment by Japanese is not a direct alternative to other forms of investment or savings.

In the United States, discussion of the relationship between U.S. banks and the U.S. stock market invariably refers to the impact of interest rates (and other types of monetary policy established by the Federal Reserve Board) on price movements in the stock and bond markets. Similarly, the price of gold and other commodities has a direct effect on price movements in the stock and bond markets (and vice versa). The Japanese stock market is not as sensitive as the U.S. market to short-term interest rates because the market is made by individual investors who buy and sell stocks as a speculative venture (in which capital gains are untaxed), rather than as an investment *alternative* to savings accounts and other instruments affected by interest rates.

PITFALL #8: *Price movements in the U.S. market affect the Japanese market and vice versa.*

This point is linked to Pitfall #7, above. The Tokyo and New York stock markets are the two largest markets in the world. Not surprisingly, price movements in one affect price movements in the other. But to what extent?

Americans investing in Japan spread risk and increase opportunities for reward by investing in multiple markets instead of one. This point is particularly convincing when the growth rates of the two markets are compared. Nonetheless, the foreign investor must understand the extent to which economic indicators and price movements in one market affect the other because no large financial system operates without affecting, and being affected by, other systems.

Changes in interest rates and other indicators in one market affect price movements in the other, and the Tokyo market is indisputably more sensitive to U.S. indicators and price movements than the U.S. market is to Tokyo. There are several reasons for this. Japan is a capital exporting nation, with vast holdings of U.S. Treasury issues, as well as U.S. real estate and equity. Fluctuations in the U.S. market directly affect the value of Japanese investments. Also, many of the largest Japanese companies are dependent upon exports to the United States and other foreign markets, so the exchange rate, consumer price index, and other factors affect the price of Japanese stocks in Japan. Similarly, U.S. investors managing global funds shift money from one market to another and study Japanese economic indicators and stock price movements when evaluating investment. Investors on both sides must engage in a certain amount of second-guessing as they jockey for positions in a market which is constantly correcting itself as it adjusts to global investment patterns.

The reactions of Japanese and non-Japanese investors may be similar, but are not necessarily *simultaneous*. If Wall Street looks weak, Japanese investors may become net sellers in the United States and return to their domestic market, while American investors view Japanese stocks as relatively expensive and become net sellers. For example, in the first half of 1984, interest rates in the United States were high and the economy was expanding, which made foreign (Japanese and other) investment in the United States appealing. In August, when the rates began to fall, Japanese investors seeking higher interest rates in the U.S. market became less interested in investing in the United States and the capital outflow from Japan decreased. Diverted to domestic markets, some of the excess capital flowed into the stock market, driving up the Japanese market and helping it rebound from its lows in the first half of the year.

Although all equity market movements are interdependent, the key for the foreign investor is to be sensitive to those indicators and price movements in and outside Japan which invariably affect the Tokyo market.

PITFALL #9: *The yield (ratio of dividends to stock price) on Japanese common stock is extremely low by U.S. standards.*

Yields are calculated as follows:

Yield = Par value × Dividend rate/Market value

Most dividends in Japanese companies are paid out twice a year. Dividend size is based upon a percentage of the par value of a company's stock. Extra dividends commemorating the founding of the company (e.g., the fiftieth year of operations) are popular.

Why are dividends so small by U.S. standards? While capital gains, or gains brought about by the sale of a stock, are not taxed in Japan, dividends are. The 15 percent tax on dividends is deducted at source for both Japanese and foreign investors. This essential difference between Japanese and non-Japanese taxation on capital gains accounts for some of the volatility evident on the Japanese stock exchanges, where the individual motive for investment is largely speculative.

PITFALL #10: *ADR and common stock prices vary for each common stock and purchase of one must be weighed against the other with respect to marketability and taxation.*

The American Depository Receipt (ADR) is a negotiable instrument equivalent to a fixed number of shares of stock in a non-U.S. corporation. The receipts serve to certify that the shares they represent have been purchased and are being held by a custodian (usually the foreign branch of a U.S. bank). There are two types of ADRs:

1. *Sponsored ADRs* have been created by the company itself, which has agreed to conform to SEC reporting criteria. Only sponsored ADRs are traded on the New York Stock Exchange. At the end of March 1986, of the 56 foreign companies listed on the NYSE, 7 were sponsored Japanese ADRs.

2. *Unsponsored ADRs*, created by banks, are registered with the SEC. These ADRs are traded on NASDAQ and the OTC markets and are reported in the National Quotation service's pink sheets. More than 100 Japanese ADRs currently trade over the counter; while of the 260 foreign equities traded through NASDAQ, 17 were Japanese issues at the end of March 1986 (see Appendix II).

Liquidity varies among the various ADRs and the investor should ascertain the number of ADRs of a given stock that are outstanding and currently trading. The investor may or may not have the option of choosing between purchase of ADRs and common stock from the same company; the choice depends upon whether a company has ADRs available (Appendix II lists all Japanese ADRs at the end of March 1986) and whether both can be readily purchased by foreigners without restriction. Sometimes the investor has the luxury of choosing between purchase of common shares and ADRs and has the opportunity to select the less expensive of the two *when prices of ADRs deviate from the price of the underlying stock.*

Fluctuations in yen-dollar exchange rates affect the price of ADRs (and influence estimates for earnings per share). If the yen appreciates against the dollar, then the ADR price appreciates by the same percentage (assuming no change in price of stock in yen). Thus, an ADR priced at $14 would appreciate by 7 percent to $14.98 if the yen appreciated against the dollar by 7 percent. On the other hand, if the yen weakens, the value of the dollar-denominated ADR declines accordingly. Some companies, however, may benefit from a weaker yen (particularly export-oriented companies) and show improved earnings, driving up the price of the ADR.

Currency factors can occasionally cause the price of a Japanese company's U.S. securities to fluctuate independently of supply and demand factors. Theoretically, a U.S. investor can profit from share price appreciation on a Japanese ADR while the stock in Japan is falling. Thus, a rising yen can offset share price declines on the Tokyo Stock Exchange. For example, Sony Corporation closed 1986 at ¥3,450 (on December 27), *down* 13.75 percent from the closing price of the preceding year. Sony Corporation's ADRs, however, traded at $21 at the end of 1986 (compared to $19.50 at the end of 1985), *up* 7 percent.

The volume of ADRs traded, although growing, is much smaller than the volume of trading in common shares in Japan. Among the most active Japanese ADRs are Canon, Sony, Toyota, Hitachi, Honda Motor, and Fuji Photo Film. Because of active trading in the sponsored ADRs by U.S. pension funds, a number of ADR nominees have become, at various times, major shareholders in Japanese corporations. For example, at the end of 1984, Moxley & Co. was the biggest single shareholder of Honda Motors (with a 5 percent holding) and held more than 7 percent of Fuji Photo Film at the end of 1985.

For those ADRs traded in particularly small amounts, relatively minor transactions can have a disproportionate impact on the ADR price, regardless of the value of the underlying Japanese share price.

PITFALL #11: *Japanese individual and institutional investors have investment objectives that diverge from those of foreign investors, and this affects the investment climate in Japan.*

The investment objectives of individual and institutional investors in Japan are so different from foreign investors that they contributed to the so-called two-tier market in 1984-85. Individual Japanese investors, participating in the market largely for speculative reasons, drove up the price of shares in biotechnology and pharmaceuticals based upon rumors concerning prospective medical and scientific breakthroughs. Financial stocks, particularly banks (see Chapter 7), also became speculative plays. At the same time, foreign institutional investors were net sellers of blue chip stocks, precipitating Japanese investor disenchantment with blue chips. This illustrates how the investment patterns of one group can be imitated by the other, although individual investment objectives differ from the objectives of institutional investors.

Japanese individual investors buy and sell stocks and bonds for speculative reasons in an environment in which capital gains are untaxed. Although individual ownership accounted for only about 25 percent of outstanding shares in 1986, individuals accounted for 40 percent of trading volume. Foreign individual ownership was only 6.5 percent of outstanding shares, but accounted for a much higher percentage of trades executed among the largest brokerage firms.

Although Japanese institutional investors hold the majority of shares in the market, they prefer not to actively trade their shares. There are indications, however, that Japanese institutional investors are becoming more active in the market (see Chapter 9 for a detailed discussion). In 1984, for example, domestic institutions were net buyers and helped absorb the decline in the Nikkei Stock Average precipitated by foreign institutional net selling. The graying of Japan is creating ever larger pools of pension funds and increasing amounts of this liquidity will find its way into the stock market. At the same time, stock investment trusts (see Chapter 2) have become a major market influence.

As financial deregulation progresses, traditional patterns of institutional investor behavior will change. The maturation of the Japanese economy during the past decade has restricted lending opportunities while the assets of financial institutions have mushroomed. The full extent to which institutions will use these burgeoning funds to become more active *long-term* players in Japan's stock market is not yet clear. However, opportunities for institutional participation in the market are increasing. For example, "designated cash trusts" (tokkin—see Chapter 9) offer a tax benefit to institutional investors and have attracted considerable institutional investment in stocks and bonds, accounting for a very large portion of all institutional buying.

Institutional investors in Japan still rely heavily on equity investment to help cement business relationships. Banks, for example, are stockholders primarily in order to maintain a client base for loans. Bank investment in corporations has traditionally been preferred by industry because banks do not expect high cash dividends and rarely attempt to control or take over a company unless it is threatened by bankruptcy. Insurance companies also hold shares for goodwill to stabilize insurance, pension, and loan business.

Restrictions on capital gains from stockholdings (the Insurance Business Act) and the corporate tax (a basic tax rate on retained profits of 43.3 percent in 1984-86)[6] applied to realized capital gains discourage institutional selling. Unlike capital

---

[6]A new tax law will result in reduced corporate taxes beginning in 1987 (i.e. new rates will apply to books that corporations close after April 1, 1987). The basic corporate tax rate for retained profits will decline to 42 percent in

gains for individual investors, corporate capital gains are taxed. According to Yumi Kobayashi, a former security analyst at Paine Webber, the insurance industry in Japan estimated that taxes and trading commissions on equity were so high that a stock appreciating 30 percent during a six-month period was equivalent to a return from bond holdings. Japanese stocks have a low yield (see Pitfall #9 above) and insurance companies and banks prefer to generate revenue through lending and zaitek (see Chapter 9) rather than from stocks.

Finally, Japanese and non-Japanese investment patterns are shaped not only by attitudinal differences, but also by opportunities. For example, foreign investors are not allowed to buy stocks on margin (see Chapter 3) and consequently they can not buy and sell short. Japanese investors, on the other hand, can sell short by selling marginable stocks to others and subsequently buying them back at a lower price if the stock is expected to fall. The Japanese investor expecting a stock to rise will often buy short.

PITFALL #12: *The growing presence of foreign (primarily institutional) investors in the Tokyo stock market can affect the market.*

This point continues issues raised in Pitfall #11. During the past few years, foreign investors have become active traders in the Japanese stock market and currently hold about 6 percent of all listed shares. In early May 1984, for example, foreign institutional shareholders became heavy net sellers and this triggered a plunge in the Nikkei Stock Average, causing a 12 percent decline in less than one month. This and other examples of the interplay between the world's two largest equity markets point to the obvious: the concept of geographical diversification can have its limits. While it is useful to think of the Japanese market as a means of spreading risk and expanding rewards beyond options available in the United States, it would be incorrect to portray

---

fiscal 1987, to 40 percent in fiscal 1988, and 37.5 percent in fiscal 1989. Simultaneous with these reductions will be an increase in the basic tax rate on distributed profits which will cause the rate to rise in graduated increments from its 1986 level of 33.3 percent to 37.5 percent in fiscal 1989.

the Japanese market as operating independently of the United States and other world financial and political concerns.

It is noteworthy that, although foreign investors were net sellers during most quarters of 1984–86 (see Table 4–1), their trading activity had little overall market impact. Nonetheless, this does not preclude the possibility that foreign investment will have significant future influence on specific market sectors.

PITFALL #13: *The Japanese stock market is governed by less stringently enforced regulations than the U.S. market, causing some market manipulation.*

Ramping and cornering operations were discussed in Chapter 3. It is common for Japanese securities firms to publicly deny that they engage in a variety of tactics that would not be tolerated by the Securities and Exchange Commission in the United States. Although also illegal in Japan, these activities are tacitly ignored and thus, indirectly, condoned.

Price ramping, in which large brokerage firms (and others) push up stock prices by means of promotion, are not uncommon. Ramped stock prices usually decline after the campaign winds down and profit taking has subsided. The ramping of stock prices is a procedure consistent with the strong affiliation brokerage houses establish with Japanese corporations after serving as their lead underwriter for a number of years. If a brokerage house believes that the stock price of one of its clients is undervalued on the market, it may ramp up the price by promoting the stock and cornering as much of the market share as possible. If the number of outstanding shares is too great, or if other brokerage houses act to defeat this type of action, the campaign may fail. It is possible that ramping had a part to play in the rise of bank stocks (see Chapter 7).

The Big Four securities firms have allied themselves with commercial banks, insurance firms, subsidiary or affiliated brokerage firms, and other financial institutions in large financial networks, reinforced by cross-shareholding. Thus, although the Big Four appear to dominate a very large percentage of domestic buying and selling (see Chapter 2), the portion actually is higher because many of the medium and small brokerage houses are subsidiaries or affiliates of one of the Big Four (discussed in Chapter 2).

The foreign investor living outside Japan is not ordinarily in a position to recognize the symptoms of price manipulation when he is studying a particular potential equity investment. Japanese equity specialists, however, can often evaluate a rising issue by assessing its technical characteristics (a quick glance at the appropriate charts) and comparing this with the identities of the securities firms placing the majority of stock orders (by consulting the daily *teguchi* which details the net tradings of brokers). Such a deduction, followed by telephone calls to close associates, can permit a reasoned judgment that a stock is being ramped.

The foreign investor cannot—and should not attempt to—anticipate stock price manipulations. Instead, through the careful fundamental analysis of promising stocks, the foreign investor can select the best medium- or long-term equity investments available. By avoiding the pitfalls outlined above, and through sound fundamental analysis, the prudent U.S. or European investor can outperform Japanese professionals whose penchant for rumors and trends and whose neglect of critical financial data often lead to poor investment decisions.

SOURCES OF INFORMATION

There are a small number of English language periodicals that provide valuable information about the Japanese stock market for the foreign investor. *The Asian Wall Street Journal*, published by Dow Jones Company, provides good general coverage. The *Far Eastern Economic Review*, also owned by Dow Jones Company, offers weekly summaries of outstanding events in Japan's financial markets. The *Japan Economic Journal*, published by Nihon Keizai Shimbun Company, provides a weekly selection of articles which appeared in the *Nihon Keizai Shimbun* as well as a summary of weekly activity for all stocks on the first section of the TSE. The *Japan Stock Journal* provides more detailed and technical coverage of the stock market than the *Japan Economic Journal*. Reports on specific companies listed on the exchanges are available from all the brokerage firms. Many securities firms in Tokyo will give reports to individual investors on request.

CHAPTER FIVE

The Bond Market

OVERVIEW

In October 1985 a bond futures market opened in Tokyo, marking the first futures trading (excluding commodities) in Japan during the postwar era. In February 1986, the Japanese government began to issue six-month discount paper by public auction. In 1986 and 1987, guidelines for issuing unsecured bonds were relaxed, and five Japanese bond rating agencies were busy evaluating corporate bonds. In 1985 and 1986, a variety of banks were allowed to deal in government bonds.[1] While an auction system is used for selecting underwriters for 2- to 4-year bonds, the Ministry of Finance forms the syndicates for all 10-year issues. However, it is likely that in the near future long-term government bonds will be offered at auction. These and other deregulatory actions are slowly leading to the transformation of the tightly regulated government securities market into a market *relatively* free from government control.

The bond market in Japan is second in size only to the U.S. bond market. In January 1986, the total size of the bond market

---

[1]City, regional, long-term credit, trust and sogo banks, and the Norinchukin Bank were all authorized in April 1985 to sell long-term (10-year) government bonds. In October 1985 these institutions were permitted to sell medium-term (two- to four-year), interest-bearing government bonds and long-term government discount bonds.

exceeded ¥260 trillion ($1.6 trillion). Japan's market in government debt is also the second largest in the world. Compared with the active stock market, the bond market for private corporations is still quite small. Japanese government bonds constitute most of the debt market. At the end of January 1986, the outstanding amount of central government bonds totaled ¥133 trillion ($782 billion), roughly 52 percent of GNP and triple the 1975 level.

Trading volume in the Japanese government bond market is swiftly approaching the size of the market in U.S. Treasury issues. In the United States, total trading by bond dealers was an estimated $38 trillion in 1986 while the figure for Japan exceeded $27 trillion (¥4,500 trillion), double the 1985 level. The enormous trading volume in the Tokyo bond futures market (see below) was largely responsible for the massive increase in the volume of trading.

In contrast to government bonds, corporate bonds outstanding totaled ¥13 trillion ($53 billion), about 10 percent of outstanding government bonds. Furthermore, 75 percent of the corporate bonds were issued by utility companies. Total domestic straight bonds issued only by *private* corporations in fiscal 1985 equaled just ¥2.6 trillion ($16 billion). A full 9 percent of that amount was a government placement of Nippon Telegraph and Telephone Public Corporation (see Chapter 3) which was privatized in the spring of 1985.

The convertible bond market, of growing popularity in Japan, attracted 138 companies in 1985, which raised $10.3 billion in the domestic market. The market for bonds with warrants attached has also grown substantially as Japanese investors have come to appreciate their advantages. Indeed, many warrant issues have been oversubscribed. Some have been in such demand and short supply that they have been purchased at premiums over normal trade prices ("gray market" transactions), occasionally being fully sold prior to the subscription date.

HISTORY

During the years following the Second World War, the Japanese government, under the close supervision of the Occupation authorities, was encouraged to promote low interest rates in order to rebuild the industrial infrastructure. Conservative fiscal policies and the careful cultivation of balanced budget policies led to nearly two decades of surpluses.

Because most savings in the private sector consisted of bank deposits, lending by banks was the primary means of fulfilling corporate capital demand. At the same time, corporations relied on banks as the primary purchasers of their debt issues. However, because banks utilized most of their available funds to extend loans for the rebuilding of plant and equipment, the market for corporate bonds was constrained and the secondary market in corporate bonds was insignificant. As a result, banks used corporate bonds as collateral for the low interest financing they obtained from the Bank of Japan.

The tight monetary policy promoted by Central Bank officials during the 1950s enabled the primary bond market to grow rapidly. The Korean War stimulated corporate growth which in turn led to the creation of the **Kisaikai** (bond flotation committee—see Glossary) devoted to the monitoring of issuers and issues.

Composed predominantly of banks, for more than 30 years the Kisaikai has determined the issuing conditions of straight corporate bonds. Preference has traditionally been given to the corporate issues of special industries (steel, gas, electric power). Although these industries no longer require special cultivation, the mandate of the Kisaikai has not been altered. Coupons are fixed by the Kisaikai and are linked to coupons on long-term government bonds, effectively preventing corporate bonds from competing with government bonds.

The recession and near collapse of the stock market (see Chapter 3) in 1965, led to the abandonment of the balanced budget policy and the first issuance of government bonds in the postwar era. Virtually the entire issue was purchased by financial institutions and later transferred to the Bank of Japan where it was held to maturity.

During the period 1965–1974, small volumes of government bonds were issued annually. Not until the recession of 1975 (largely a result of the oil crisis) did the issuance of debt become a major means of government financing.

In 1977 financial institutions were permitted to sell government bonds in the secondary market. At the same time, the market in **gensaki** (repurchase transactions discussed in Chapter

8), which had existed in an incipient form since 1949, grew rapidly. The creation of the gensaki market expanded the domestic money market which had previously been confined to the two interbank markets, the discount market, and call market (see Chapter 8). By the early 1980s, the secondary bond market was fully developed.

The Japanese bond market is comprised of three types of bonds as well as several kinds of recently developed foreign currency bonds. Each type of bond and its market are discussed below.

SECURED OR UNSECURED?

From the issuance of the first corporate bonds during the Meiji regime for more than 50 years, Japanese bonds were unsecured. A plethora of bankruptcies during the Depression years led to a governmental decision in 1933 to make the collateralization of all corporate bonds mandatory.

The collateralization principle has been rigidly enforced by the authority of the Kisaikai. Kisaikai protection of the principle of securing bonds results from an important vested interest. Most of the members of the Kisaikai are banks that administer bond collateral. In their role of **commissioned banks** (see Glossary), they perform trustee services and fulfill other, peripheral, functions for a fee. The commissions derived from this administration are an important source of earnings. The requirement that Japanese issuers could only sell secured bonds impeded the opening of the Samurai bond market in 1979 and the Euroyen bond market in 1984.

The Kisaikai continues to meet on a monthly basis and has retained its authority to oversee the queue of bond issuers and approve issuing terms and amounts. Yet, the Kisaikai's anachronistic character and failure to adjust to contemporary financial conditions are tolling its death knell. The **Keidanren** (Federation of Economic Organizations) has discussed alternatives to the Kisaikai and eventually this product of the era of scarce capital may fade away.

Regardless of the Kisaikai's fate, the near future will see the transfer of decision-making authority regarding the issuing terms of corporate bonds from the commissioned banks to the issuing firms and securities firms themselves. Foreign pressure will force a change in the allocation of the underwriting syndicate share of government long-term bonds. Because any major restructuring of syndicate shares would disrupt the embedded system, it is probable that an auction system for long-term government bonds will be instituted as a resolution to the problem of equitable syndicate allocations. This, in turn, would render obsolete many Kisaikai functions.

A gradual move from indirect to direct financing in the late 1970s led the Big Four securities companies to pressure the Ministry of Finance to alter the collateral requirements of major corporations. It was argued that collateral requirements were particularly onerous for construction companies, wholesalers, and trading companies, enterprises that do not require substantial fixed assets. The Ministry of Finance conceded this point and offered a tough compromise which permitted high quality foreign issuers as well as 17 domestic blue chip firms meeting strict financial criteria to issue bonds without collateral. The banks (which faced the loss of commissions for unsecured bonds) subsequently blocked the issuing of straight bonds without collateral by leaving the issuing rules incomplete.

In 1979, Sears, Roebuck and Co. floated an unsecured five-year Samurai bond. Later the same year, Matsushita Electric Industrial Company floated an unsecured ¥50 billion convertible bond issue in the domestic market. Three years elapsed before another Japanese company (Nissan Motors) did the same. Because the Kisaikai does not control the convertible bond market, convertibles (secured and unsecured) surpassed straight corporate bonds in the 1980s as the primary vehicle for domestically issued private sector debt.

In 1984, a relaxation of issuing rules for bonds, including permission for foreign corporations to issue Euroyen bonds (which are *unsecured*), led to a modification of requirements for unsecured straight bond issues. As Japanese corporations became eligible to raise funds in the Euroyen markets, domestic collateral requirements were rendered pointless. In early 1985, TDK (the largest magnetic tape manufacturer in Japan) floated a ¥10 billion six-year unsecured straight bond. This was the first unsecured straight bond issued in Japan in 50 years.

Currently, about 70 Japanese blue chip corporations are allowed to issue unsecured debentures and roughly 180 can issue unsecured convertible debentures. In order to revivify the domestic bond market, in January 1987 the Ministry of Finance announced a relaxation in issuing requirements and an increase in the number of companies permitted to issue unsecured debt at home.[2] In April 1987, the number of companies allowed to issue straight unsecured bonds will more than double to 170 and the number eligible to issue convertible bonds will reach 330. In addition, beginning in 1987, regional banks will be allowed to issue domestic convertible debentures.[3]

It is likely that during the next several years the basic collateralization requirements will be further relaxed or abolished, permitting domestic firms to *freely* float unsecured bonds. As a direct result, corporations (and perhaps commercial banks) which would have been disqualified as domestic straight bond issuers under current regulations will be allowed to issue bonds *if* they obtain an adequate rating from a rating organization. Thus, small-capitalized companies, without a stock exchange listing, would become eligible to issue debt. This, in turn, promises a bright future for a small group of young upstarts, Japan's new bond rating agencies.

Because all Japanese bonds since the prewar era were secured, rating agencies were unnecessary. Japanese underwriters rated corporate bonds in four classes determined exclusively by the financial ratios of the issuing corporations. These ratings did not correspond in method or meaning to the categories traditionally used by Moody's and Standard & Poor's. The absence of impartial rating agencies made it difficult for Japan to adopt an unsecured system and at the same time protect individual investors accustomed to a market in which marketable bonds were fully collateralized.

In 1979, the Japan Bond Research Institute (JBRI) of the Nihon Keizai Shimbun Co. began providing ratings which paralleled in style and technique the Standard and Poor's system. JBRI currently rates all outstanding convertible bond issues

---

[2] In 1986 a company intending to issue straight unsecured bonds was required to have minimum net assets of ¥110 billion. In April 1987 this will be reduced by half. Those companies not meeting the minimum net asset requirement can qualify by obtaining an AA rating (from a qualified agency).

[3] Commercial banks have been authorized to issue convertible bonds in the Euromarkets (see Chapter 6) since 1985. However, the Ministry of Finance decided to permit regional banks to raise funds through the issuance of *domestic* convertible bonds beginning in 1987 (see Chapter 8). It is probable that city banks will also receive authorization to issue these securities.

(roughly 400), all Samurai bonds, and some Euroyen bonds. In 1981, Mikuni's Credit Rating Company was established by a prescient entrepreneur (and a staff consisting largely of female college graduates). Within a short time, Mikuni's was providing ratings of virtually all unsecured convertible issues in Japan. In 1985 and 1986, three additional bond rating organizations were established: the Japan Credit Rating Agency, Ltd. (JCR), Nippon Investors Service, Inc. (NIS), and Moody's Japan K.K. (a subsidiary of Moody's Investors Service, Inc.).

THE PRIMARY MARKET

Article 65 of the Securities and Exchange Law stipulates that institutions other than securities companies (e.g. trust companies, banks, etc.) are prohibited from engaging in securities activities. There is a singular exception, however. Banks and trust companies *are* permitted to participate in the underwriting of government bonds (known as public bonds in Japan—see below). Public bonds are ordinarily underwritten on standby commitment by syndicates comprised of various financial institutions. Corporate bonds, on the other hand, are sold exclusively by syndicates of securities companies on a firm commitment basis. Bank debentures are usually sold by the issuing institution directly to investors.

Public Bonds

The Japanese government, in order to finance a growing budget deficit, has become the primary borrower of funds in Japan's debt market. The term, *public bonds*, subsumes central government bonds, municipal bonds, and public agency bonds (which are issued by public corporations). There are two types of central government bonds:

1. *Revenue bonds* (also termed *deficit financing bonds*) are issued by the Ministry of Finance and, because they must be authorized by the Diet, they are sometimes referred to as authorized bonds. The government expects to discontinue the use of these bonds by fiscal 1991 and will reduce its dependence on them during the next several years.
2. *Construction bonds*, also issued by the Ministry of Finance, do not require consideration by the Diet.

Prior to 1975, government bonds were issued as long-term (7- to 10-year) interest-bearing instruments which were subscribed to by syndicates encompassing all of Japan's financial institutions and often sold to the Bank of Japan one year after issue. Each member of the syndicate was (and continues to be) assigned a fixed underwriting share in accordance with a formula based in part on the institution's assets. The purchase of the bonds was obligatory. In sharp contrast to the U.S. market where bond prices are determined at auction, the terms and conditions of the Japanese public bond issues were strictly assigned by the government. Syndicate members, considered to be bound by patriotism, were required to buy the bonds regardless of their below market interest rates.

During the past decade, the growing deficit has induced two major changes:

1. The Bank of Japan can no longer afford to buy the bulk of government debt issues. As a result, the city banks, which underwrite roughly 45 percent of long-term government bonds, have been obliged to keep the issues to maturity or trade them.

2. At the same time, the government has been forced to offer more competitive yields to maturity. The coupon rate on long-term government bonds is intrinsic to Japan's interest rate structure and is inviolable. However, during the 1980s, through the negotiation of issue prices, financial institutions, particularly the city banks, have demanded and received somewhat more competitive pricing of long-term government issues.

In addition, midterm government bonds are now sold at auction to those firms that have current accounts with the Bank of Japan and are members of the government bond underwriting syndicate. Only two foreign securities firms, Merrill Lynch and Salomon Brothers, currently qualify to have accounts at the Bank of Japan. In 1987, a current account at the central bank will no longer be required. Thus, at least 20 foreign securities companies should be eligible to participate in midterm government bond auctions beginning in 1987.

In recent years, a variety of types of government bonds have been offered. These include 15-year floating interest rate bonds tailored to the investment needs of the trust banks, medium-term (two-, three-, and four-year) interest-bearing bonds which have been issued since 1978, and medium-term (five years only) discount bonds. The first auction of bonds with maturities of less than one year occurred in February 1986. In October 1986, a ¥500 million issue of a 20-year national government bond was issued. In 1987, four issuances of 20-year national bonds, totalling ¥2 trillion, will be floated. A substantial portion of medium-term bonds are underwritten by securities companies and are sold to the general public. In addition, 60-day government bills, intended to bridge revenue shortfalls, are also issued when needed and are purchased almost entirely by the central bank.

Foreign companies have been severely curtailed in their participation in long-term government bond underwriting. Foreign banks have been limited to a share of 0.01 percent and foreign securities companies have been allowed a generous 0.07 percent. By contrast, domestic securities companies are allowed to underwrite a share about 225 times larger than their foreign competitors. Following the 1986 designation of Nomura and Daiwa as primary dealers in U.S. Treasury issues and accompanying U.S. congressional demands for reciprocity, the Ministry of Finance agreed to increase the underwriting share of foreign institutions.

The large government deficits that began in 1975 were funded with 10-year public bonds. Thus, beginning in 1985, vast numbers of these bonds reached maturity. Annual turnover of government bonds in 1985 exceeded ¥400 trillion, while the outstanding balance of government bonds exceeded ¥120 trillion in late 1985. The outstanding balance was expected to reach ¥142 trillion yen by March 31, 1987. Furthermore, mass redemption of government bonds currently in circulation will reach a peak in May 1988. In that month, for example, the average *daily* amount redeemed will be more than ¥3.6 trillion.

In fiscal year 1986, an estimated ¥22 trillion of national government bonds were issued, of which roughly half were rollovers. In order to successfully refinance its debt, the Japanese government was forced to consider some liberalization of regulations restricting bond sales. As a result, a new market in short-term securities was approved by the Ministry of Finance in 1981 (and began in 1985) and a government bond futures market was opened in late 1985 (see below).

There were other critical developments. The Banking Act and the Securities and Exchange Act were revised in 1981 in order to permit banks to deal in and sell public bonds (beginning in 1984). This was the first of many actions by the Ministry of Finance that blurred the distinction between banks and securities firms. In June 1984, as a result of the revisions, the city banks, long-term credit banks, and trust banks began to deal in government bonds. In 1986, these banks were joined by regional banks, sogo banks, credit associations, and foreign banks.

Beginning in 1984, the medium-term government bond funds sold by securities firms since 1980 were permitted to operate almost precisely as savings accounts. The funds, which offer interest rates significantly above ordinary savings accounts, require a minimum deposit of ¥100,000 and are managed as mutual funds. However, once established, the funds function as savings accounts and can be fully accessed through automated teller machines. In this way, medium-term government bond funds were used as an agent in the erosion of Article 65 (see Chapter 2), which separates the activities of banks and securities firms.

Additional deregulatory measures regarding government bonds further weakened the demarcation between banks and brokerage houses in 1986. Securities firms were permitted by the Ministry of Finance to include short-term government notes in their investment trusts. In addition, all financial institutions were allowed to offer an expanded range of new products, combining ordinary accounts and medium-term government bonds.

Corporate Bonds

Domestic Japanese corporate bonds fall into a simple classification:

    I.   Straight bonds.
        a.   Issued by electric power supply companies.
        b.   Issued by other industries.
   II.   Convertible bonds.
  III.   Bonds with warrants attached.

Straight bonds, convertibles, and bonds with warrants are issued domestically as yen-denominated instruments and they are issued overseas as yen- or foreign-currency-denominated instruments. The following discussion provides brief summary descriptions of each domestic category.

Straight Bonds. The Ministry of Finance has set forth rigid guidelines specifying the minimum corporate requirements and minimum issuing requirements for corporate bonds. Key among them is that *minimum net corporate assets* must exceed ¥6 billion. Under the *month end issuance system*, bonds can only be floated at the specified time. Lead managers for corporate issues are predetermined in accordance with a special *lead manager rotating system* designed to assure each of the Big Four securities firms an appropriate share of underwriting business.

The nine electric power supply companies receive preferential regulatory treatment from the government because they are public utilities. Roughly 75 percent of domestic straight bond issues are electric power bonds. While debt issued by the electric utilities is sold exclusively in the domestic market, other industrial bonds are sold both domestically and internationally (in the Eurobond market—see Chapter 6).

As the size of public bond issues grew during the 1980s, effective interest rates rose, thus pressuring private corporations to seek cheaper sources of funds through other instruments and in other markets. The domestic market for corporate bonds has been in decline since 1981. In 1985, 80 percent of all industrial straight bond issues were sold outside Japan. The ceiling for corporate bond issues, specified by the Commercial Code, is the total of a corporation's capital and reserves or the value of outstanding net assets in the latest balance sheet, whichever is lower.

In fiscal year 1975, all straight corporate bond issues in Japan totaled ¥1.5 trillion. A decade later, in fiscal 1985, corporate bond issues totaled ¥900 billion of which ¥872.5 billion was accounted for by electric power firms and Nippon Telegraph and Telephone Corporation (NTT). The market for straight corporate bonds was bled by the Euroyen market which offered a far less regulated and more profitable environment. The future—if there is one—for Japan's market in *privately* issued straight bonds is now in the hands of the regulatory authorities. Unless the issuing system is fully deregulated the market will have a pauper's grave.

Convertible Bonds. Convertible bonds are bonds convertible to a fixed number of equity shares in the same corporation in accordance with the terms of the issue. Because of the conversion option, convertible bonds offer coupon rates considerably lower than straight bonds. In Japan this differential is usually about 3 percent. In nearly all cases, the issuers of the convertibles permit bondholders to convert the bonds into stock from two months from the date of issuance of the bond until the day before the redemption date.

The conversion price (the effective price paid for the stock when conversion occurs) is designated by the issuer and is based on the market price of the issuing company's stock at the time of the issue. An adjustment is usually made in order to protect bondholders from dilution through stock splits, gratis issues, stock dividends, or the sale of stock at a lower than market price.

In Japan, unlike the United States, issuing conditions in the convertible bond market are not decided by mutual discussion between issuer and underwriter. The benchmark interest rate on convertibles is not tied to government bonds. As a result, in accordance with market conditions, convertible bonds in Japan can have lower interest rates than government bonds.

If the price of a convertible bond and the value of the underlying common stock are equal, then the bond and stock are at parity. Parity price is determined by the formula:

Parity price = Stock price/Conversion price x 100

A premium resulting from a variety of factors (differentials between yields of the convertible and stock, peculiarities of the supply and demand situation in the convertible market and the stock market, as well as the differential between the conversion price and the stock price) is calculated according to the following formula:

$$\text{Premium} = (\text{Market price} - \text{Parity price})/(\text{Parity price}) \times 100$$
$$= (\text{Market price}/\text{Parity price} - 1) \times 100$$

A *premium spread* exists if the rate is above 0 and a *discount spread* occurs if the rate is below 0. The value of a convertible bond is determined in accordance with the *theoretical stock price*, which is simply the product of the convertible's market price and conversion price divided by 100:

$$\text{Theoretical stock price} = \frac{\text{Market price} \times \text{Conversion price}}{100}$$

Japanese convertible bonds currently have maturities of 6, 8, and 10 years, with the vast majority having redemption periods of 6 years. The bonds are normally issued in denominations of ¥100,000, ¥500,000, and ¥1,000,000. At the end of 1985, the total value of the domestic convertible bond market was roughly $33 billion (¥5.251 trillion) and represented a sizable share of the total sales value of the Tokyo Stock Exchange.

All convertible bond transactions under ¥30 million are required to take place in the stock exchange; larger transactions need not be traded on an exchange, although in practice nearly all are. Domestic convertible bond issues can be unsecured with floating liens or fully unsecured.

Issuers of convertible bonds (as for straight bonds) must have net assets exceeding ¥6 billion. Furthermore, the total issue amount cannot constitute more than an increase of 20 percent of all outstanding shares at the time of issue.

Trust banks, seeking investment diversification for their **kingaishin** funds (see Glossary and Chapter 9), were the biggest investors in the convertibles in 1985. At the end of 1986, 156 companies listed 159 convertible bonds on the Tokyo Stock Exchange.

In 1985–86, the trading of convertible bonds in the gray market was sometimes so intense that issues sold out before their listing date on the stock exchange. Stock exchange listing of convertible bonds usually requires 20 days from payment date following the subscription period. Many convertible bonds traded over-the-counter for premiums of 30 to 50 percent during the interim preceding listing. Determined to discourage this practice, the Tokyo Stock Exchange issued rules in December 1986 prohibiting the conclusion of buy and sell contracts before the close of subscription. At the same time, issuers were encouraged to reduce the interval between issuance and listing.

From 1975 to 1983, the amount of foreign-currency-denominated convertible bonds issued in the Euromarket far exceeded the amount of domestic convertibles issued. From 1983 to 1985, this relationship turned around as the result of the growing domestic popularity of the instrument and interest rate differentials between Japan and Switzerland (the major market for Japanese convertibles) as well as other economies.

The eligibility requirements for the issuance of overseas convertibles are virtually the same as the requirements for domestic issues. Overseas issues are usually unsecured and unguaranteed. Unlike domestic issues, which bear coupon rates determined by formula, the coupon rates for overseas issues fluctuate in accordance with supply and demand.

Bonds with Warrants Attached. A warrant bond is a corporate debt security that gives its holders the right to buy the issuer's common stock at a future date at a specified price. Although the warrants themselves resemble rights, they differ from rights because they have no value when issued and have a far longer life (see the discussion of detached warrants in Chapter 3). Because of the character of the Tokyo stock market, equity warrant bonds often amplify stock price movements and enhance volatility.

A 1981 amendment to the Commercial Code permitted the issuance of bonds with warrants. The need to hedge foreign exchange risk was a crucial factor influencing the passage of the amendment. In 1986, the Ministry of Finance abolished restrictions on the domestic issuance of corporate bonds with detachable warrants. In addition, investment trusts were permitted to invest a maximum of 20 percent of net assets in warrant bonds (life insurance companies are likely to receive similar authorization in 1987).

There are two types of bonds with warrants:

1. Domestic and yen-denominated. (Prior to 1986, all domestic bonds with warrants had nondetachable rights.)
2. Overseas and foreign-currency-denominated. Foreign issues of bonds with warrants can be either nondetachable or detachable, although, in practice, all are detachable.

Minimum government requirements for the issuance of bonds with warrants are much the same as the requirements that apply to straight corporate bonds and convertibles. The issuer's net assets must exceed ¥6 billion. The total issue of bonds with warrants cannot exceed a 20 percent increase of the total number of outstanding shares at the time of issue.

The usual exercise price for warrants is 2.5 percent higher than the average closing price during the preceding six days. Ordinarily, a cash payment is made for exercising the warrant. Occasionally, in the domestic market, a substitute corporate bond payment is made. For example, Sankyo Electric Company and Daei, Inc., issuers of the first warrant bonds traded in the Tokyo Stock Exchange, will accept payment for new shares with the relative bond at issuing price. Thus, the bond can be exchanged for new shares just as in the conversion of convertible bonds.

Financial Debentures

During the period of postwar reconstruction, the three long-term credit banks (the Industrial Bank of Japan, the Long-Term Credit Bank of Japan, and the Nippon Credit Bank) as well as the Norinchukin Bank (Central Cooperative Bank for Agriculture and Forestry), the Shoko Chukin Bank (Central Bank for Commercial and Industrial Cooperatives), and the Bank of Tokyo, were permitted to obtain funding through the issuance of medium- and long-term debentures at rates slightly above public bond yields.

Through the issuance of these financial debentures, the five banks used their leverage to extend medium- and long-term credit to a wide range of businesses requiring high risk loans in the 1950s and early 1960s. Under the aegis of the "priority production policy," the government emphasized the development of vital sectors (steel, fertilizer, and so forth) in order to promote reconstruction. Thus, the funds raised through the debentures were channeled directly into the industrial sector, on a mortgage basis, for the purpose of rebuilding plant and equipment.

Today, the long-term credit banks issue five-year coupon-bearing financial debentures and one-year discount debentures. Licensed as institutions providing specialized long-term lending, these banks are restricted from taking deposits and depend upon the debentures as a primary means of raising funds.

The debentures are sold directly by the issuers, rendering underwriting syndicates unnecessary. In accordance with tradition, the Big Four securities companies sell 5 percent of those debentures bearing coupons and about half of all discount debentures.

Yen-Denominated Foreign Bonds: Samurai and Shibosai

Prior to 1970, yen-denominated bonds could only be issued by Japanese institutions. In 1970, the Ministry of Finance authorized the purchase of foreign securities by residents and, at the end of that year, the Asian Development Bank (ADB) sold a ¥6 billion issue (lead managed by Nomura) with a seven-year maturity in the Japanese public bond market. The introduction of this type of yen-denominated public bond, issued by a foreign institution, was a milestone in the history of Japan's capital markets. The new nonresident yen bonds were termed **Samurai bonds** and were modeled after American Yankee bonds.

The Asian Development Bank (heavily subsidized by the Japanese government) was a symbol of Japan's foreign aid efforts within the Pacific Basin Region. Thus, it was hoped in 1970 that the first Samurai bond would be a precursor of increased Japanese participation in foreign economic aid. The financial press in Japan editorialized that the nation had come of age and its economic aid to the Third World would soon be commensurate with its foreign reserves and burgeoning affluence. This was not the case. Instead, the ADB issue proved to be a harbinger of the emergence of a new capital market and not a shift in ideology or world view.

The ADB Samurai issue was followed by a number of yen-denominated foreign issued public bonds floated by supranational institutions and sovereign entities. In 1977, private placements by foreign borrowers, termed **Shibosai bonds**, proved their popularity. Throughout the past decade, the Shibosai or private placement has been characterized by issues smaller than Samurais, floated by less creditworthy institutions at higher coupons.

The Shibosai bonds were often lead managed by banks and bore a striking resemblance to bank loans. The private placements could not be traded for two years and the arranger would often assume a 30 percent share of the issue. Samurai issues have outnumbered Shibosai by a minimum of 3 to 1. The number of Samurai and Shibosai issues have increased steadily with the exception of interruptions caused by the two oil crises. Lead underwriters for the foreign issued bonds are currently limited to securities firms, long-term credit banks, and city banks. Foreign underwriters are permitted to participate in the issues but are limited to 5 percent of the issue amount.

Under current (1986) guidelines, any foreign entity with an A or better credit rating can issue debt in the Samurai or Shibosai markets (included in this category are unrated entities which provide a guaranty from an A-rated guarantor). In addition, corporations with ratings below A can issue bonds in this market *if* they fulfill certain minimum financial requirements, including a shareholders' equity ratio of 30. Although the shareholders' equity ratio must be satisfied by *all* issuers, companies with net assets above ¥300 billion need fulfill just two of the four ratios listed in Table 5–1. Companies having net assets between ¥110 billion and ¥299 billion must fulfill three of the four ratios. These requirements have been perceived by actual and potential foreign issuers as excessively demanding. While most issuers have had to maintain an equity-to-asset ratio of 30 percent, some blue chip corporations have been asked by the Ministry of Finance to maintain net assets above $2.5 billion (¥400 billion).

In 1987, the minimum balance sheet requirements listed in Table 5–1 will be significantly modified. Foreign issuers with double A and higher ratings will be allowed to float yen bonds without meeting minimum levels of equity-to-asset ratios and net assets. Those issuers with a single A rating and net assets of

TABLE 5-1 Qualification Standards for Samurai and Shibosai Bond Issues by Nonresident Private Sector Companies in 1986

Minimal Financial Criteria	Requirements*	
Net asset size (¥ billions)	300–600	150–300
Net assets/total assets (%)	40 or more	45 or more
1. Long-term debt/capitalization	35%	40%
2. Profit before interest/total assets	8%	8.5%
3. Interest coverage ratio (X)	3	3.5
4. Long-term debt/cash flow ratio	2/4	3/4

*A-rated companies with net assets exceeding ¥600 billion need not meet these requirements. Companies with net assets less than ¥150 billion are considered on a case-by-case basis.

more than \$1.5 billion will also be exempted from fulfilling the requirements. The ratings must be provided by one of five agencies approved by the Ministry of Finance.[4]

Interest rates for Samurai and Shibosai placements are based upon the prevailing long-term prime rate adjusted to the creditworthiness of the issuer. Samurai bonds were first listed on the Tokyo Exchange in 1973. Despite the listings, most transactions occur in the over-the-counter market (see below). Shibosai bonds have little liquidity and are sold on a limited basis to institutions and other groups.

Maturities of 5, 7, or 10 years are common and redemption until recently was mandatory. Thus, Samurai issues with maturities longer than 5 years contained mandatory redemption provisions requiring that 10 percent of the principal amount of a 10-year issue be redeemed annually beginning in the sixth year. This resulted in an average life of 9 years for a 10-year issue. In 1985, the World Bank issued a 10-year bond with a bullet maturity. Currently, private corporations with net assets above ¥110 billion are permitted to issue bullet maturities of up to 12 years.

In 1984, liberalization measures introduced by the Ministry of Finance increased the attractiveness of the Samurai and Shibosai markets for foreign investors. In 1986, the "no return

---

[4]Moody's Investors Service, Inc., Standard & Poor's Corporation, Japan Bond Research Institute, Nippon Investors Service, Inc., and Japan Credit Rating Agency, Ltd.

rule," which prohibited issuers of Samurai bonds from later issuing Shibosai bonds, was eliminated despite the objections of the Big Four securities firms. Although the Big Four had cornered the underwriting market for Samurai issues, they competed with banks which were authorized to lead manage private placements. This relaxation of requirements was motivated by apprehensions that the Samurai market would be replaced by the Eurobond market (see Chapter 6) which was offering better overall issuing conditions.

During the summer of 1986, a strong yen conjoined with low interest rates motivated sovereign borrowers to redeem their Samurai bonds and raise capital in the more attractive Euroyen market where Euroyen issues were yielding 50 basis points more than Samurais. Finland, Sweden, Thailand, and Australia redeemed bonds with coupon rates of 7.8 to 9.2 percent. A series of additional redemptions, prompted by similar reasoning, followed. When the dust settled at the end of 1986, 22 issuers had redeemed Samurai bonds ahead of schedule. The majority of these issuers substituted cheaper Euroyen bonds for their redeemed Samurais.

As a result of these redemptions (and under pressure from the government), the Big Four securities firms began to actively support a secondary market for small investors in Samurai bonds (see below). This, in turn, facilitated market access by individual investors. At the same time, the Ministry of Finance authorized life insurance companies to coarrange private placements of Samurai bonds. In late 1986, the Ministry of Finance announced a relaxation of balance sheet requirements for issuers.

As of late 1986, none of the government's actions had succeeded in rescuing the foundering Samurai market. During the first nine months of 1986, Samurai bond issues totaled ¥500 billion ($2.9 billion)—a substantial decline from the ¥1.115 trillion of total Samurai issues in fiscal 1985.[5] By contrast, Euroyen bond issues by non-Japanese issuers reached ¥2.331 trillion during the first nine months of 1986 (far surpassing the ¥1.446

---

[5]During 1986, 21 new Samurai bonds were issued, compared with 35 new Samurai issues in 1985.

trillion for all of fiscal 1985). Thus, Euroyen issues outnumbered Samurai issues by more than six to one.

In order to revive the Samurai market, the Tokyo Stock Exchange, in late 1986, proposed increasing the length of trading sessions for large-lot Samurai issues from 30 minutes to two hours per day. Several other changes, including the installation of new telephone lines connecting the exchange and major market markers, were also proposed. Nonetheless, it is unlikely that any of these cosmetic improvements will alter the morbidity of the Samurai market. The market's lack of liquidity (resulting directly from its lackluster performance in comparison with the Euroyen bond market) and unavoidable settlement delays will not be counterbalanced by these measures. Thus, investors seeking yen-denominated issues in 1987 will most likely turn to the market in Euroyen or to Japanese government debt.

Foreign-Currency-Denominated
Foreign Bonds (Shogun Bonds)

The first foreign-currency-denominated bonds (**Shogun bonds**) were issued in 1972 as private placements. From 1972 to 1974, 55 issues were offered by nonresident borrowers and were bought by Japanese financial institutions, primarily banks. The bonds were purchased with foreign currency borrowed from overseas branches of the purchasing institutions. The first oil crisis undermined the market in these bonds. The sudden rise in short-term interest rates caused institutions that had borrowed funds in the short-term money market to suffer substantial losses.

The Shogun market was revivified in the late 1970s with four public U.S. dollar bond issues floated by European entities. The issues were for $100 million dollars each, with maturities of 10 or 12 years, and coupons ranging from 9 percent to 10.75 percent. Japanese corporations utilized the resurrected Shogun market as a tool for recycling surplus funds earned through exports.

Unlike Samurai bonds which were handled by domestic underwriters and subscribed to by domestic investors, the four Shogun issues in 1978–79 were underwritten and purchased by non-Japanese as well as Japanese institutions. Roughly 80 percent of these Shogun issues were offered in the domestic market by Japanese underwriters, while the balance was placed by foreign syndicates in European markets. Also unlike Samurai bonds, the Shogun bonds were issued in Europe and were listed on the Luxembourg Stock Exchange. In addition, there were no participating Japanese commissioned banks, foreign banks functioning as fiscal agents for all of the issues.

The third incarnation of the Shogun bond market began in June 1985 with a $300 million World Bank issue having a 10-year maturity and a 10.5 percent coupon. This was followed by seven additional Shogun bonds in 1985, the majority denominated in U.S. dollars, with one European Currency Unit (ECU) and one Australian dollar issue. Shogun issues from June 1985 to the end of September 1986 totaled only ¥240 billion ($1.5 billion).

Currently, Shogun bonds are distributed through Japanese underwriting syndicates with foreign underwriters limited to 5 percent of the total issue amount. The Shogun issues are normally listed on the Tokyo Stock Exchange, and Japanese commissioned banks act as fiscal agents. Maturities range from 5 to 10 years and there are no specific guidelines regarding acceptable currencies. Private placement of the issues is prohibited. Acceptable balance sheet fundamentals mirror those applicable to Samurai issues. The relaxation of minimum net assets and equity to asset ratios which will apply to Samurai bonds in 1987 will thus also be applicable to Shogun issues. In addition, the period between registration and the issuing of the bonds will be reduced from the current 30 days to 15 days. The Ministry of Finance expects these measures to stimulate the lagging market in Shogun issues.

In late 1986, the Big Four requested that the Ministry of Finance establish a clearing system in the domestic bond market. It is hoped that such a clearing system (similar to Cedel or Euroclear) will help to remedy the negligible liquidity of the Shogun bond market by encouraging active trading by foreign investors. Because growth of the Shogun market has been stunted by the absence of investor interest, it is likely that a clearing system will be established in early 1988.

TYPICAL TERMS AND CONDITIONS FOR A SAMURAI OR SHIBOSAI BOND ISSUE

Issue amount:	¥10 billion to ¥60 billion.
Maturity:	7 to 15 years.
Coupon and Price:	Interest payable semiannually varying from 0.1 percent to 0.3 percent of the long-term prime rate.
Underwriting commission:	1 to 1.6 percent (lower rate for Shibosai bonds).
Withholding tax:	Exempt. (Principal, interest, and premium, if any, payable without deduction in the issuer's country.)
Governing law:	Japanese law.
Negative pledges:	Negative pledges as well as pari passu, restriction of sale and lease-back transactions, cross default, and certain other restrictions ordinarily apply to corporate issuers.
Listing:	Tokyo Stock Exchange (for Samurai issues).
Denomination:	Bearer bonds of ¥1,000,000 and ¥100,000.
Lead manager or arranger:	One of the major securities firms, a long-term credit bank, or a city bank.
Underwriting fee:	1.5 percent (7 years or less). 1.6 percent (7–15 years). 1.75 percent (more than 15 years).
Commissioned company fee:	0.09 percent (supranational entity). 0.135 percent (sovereign entity). 0.23 percent (private corporation).
Recording fee:	0.08 percent.
Listing fee:	¥1,300,000.
Issuer's legal counsel:	¥8,000,000.
Miscellaneous costs:	¥20,000,000.
Recurring expenses:	0.05 percent of the average bonds outstanding. (Commissioned company annual fee—applicable to private corporations only.) 0.2 percent of the principal amount redeemed (commission for handling redemption of principal). 0.30 percent of the interest paid (interest payment commission).

THE SECONDARY MARKET

The Over-the-Counter (OTC) Market

Nearly all (94 percent in fiscal year 1985) secondary bond market trading occurs in the OTC market and nearly all (95.6 percent in fiscal 1985) trading in the OTC market is in national government debt. Trading in government bonds dominates trading volume; the average turnover in the first half of fiscal 1986 was 13.6 times (all other bonds traded 1.36 times). Thus, the secondary market is virtually subsumed by the market in government issues.

The secondary market was not always dominated by government issues. Ten years ago, secondary dealing in government bonds constituted a minuscule 4.6 percent of total secondary market trading volume. In 1977, the Ministry of Finance authorized banks to liquidate their government bond holdings one year after issuance. By 1980, 60 percent of all secondary trading was represented by long-term government bond issues.

In addition to the small number of bellwether bonds, a range of other public bonds, including gensaki, are also traded in the secondary market.[6] However, because liquidity is the key to demand, national bonds tend to dominate the field. The entry of banks and other financial institutions to the bond-dealing profession (in 1984 and 1985) increased bond liquidity and, in turn, led to an increase in the size of the secondary market. In 1985, ¥2,404 trillion ($13.5 trillion) in government bonds were traded, four times the amount traded in 1984 and a 15-fold increase over 1980.

In an effort to save Samurai issues from the seductive embrace of the Euroyen market, the Big Four securities firms began to trade Samurai bonds in the secondary market in the summer of 1986. For the first time since Samurai issues were in-

---

[6]**Gensaki** (bond repurchase agreements) represent an important segment of the secondary market in government issues. Long-term government bond gensaki transactions account for a large portion of all secondary government bond transactions. Although gensaki transactions bear a formal resemblance to bond transactions, they function as short-term money market instruments (using bonds as collateral) and are discussed in Chapter 8, which is devoted to money markets.

TYPICAL TERMS AND CONDITIONS FOR A SHOGUN ISSUE

Issue Amount:	U.S. $100 million to $300 million (or the approximate equivalent).
Maturity:	5 to 10 years.
Coupon:	In accordance with market conditions.
Issue Price:	Market conditions.
Redemption:	Noncallable (bullet).
Form of Bonds:	Bearer bonds with coupons attached (for private corporate issuers) or registered bonds (for agencies and municipal issuers).
Taxation:	No withholding tax imposed in issuer's country.
Listing:	Tokyo Stock Exchange.
Syndication:	Japanese and licensed foreign underwriters.
Governing law:	Law of Japan.
All-in cost:	Subject to market conditions (usually 10 to 20 basis points below U.S. Treasury issues).
Interest-rate swaps:	U.S. dollar fixed-rate funds can be swapped to U.S. dollar floating rate funds.
Currency swaps:	No guidelines.
Underwriting fee:	Same as Samurai issues.
Commissioned company fee:	0.7 percent (supranational entities). 0.1 percent (sovereign entities). 0.16 percent (private corporations).
Recording fee:	0.08 percent of bonds recorded.
Listing fee:	¥1,300,000.
Miscellaneous expenses:	¥20,000,000.
Legal counsel:	¥8,000,000.
Recurring expenses:	0.3 percent of outstanding amount (annual fee to commissioned company). 0.15 percent of interest paid (interest payment commission). 0.1 percent of principal amount redeemed (commission for handling the redemption of principal).

troduced, bid and offer prices were posted twice daily. Although the Big Four monopolized the authority to make a market in Samurai bonds, a range of financial institutions is permitted to deal in government issues.[7]

The Big Four securities firms function as brokers and dealers in the secondary market. They execute their OTC trades through the Japan Bond Trading Co. (Nihon Sogo Shoken), referred to as the "brokers' broker." Prices quoted are determined by assessing the customer, the transaction size, the price quotations of competitors, and the available inventory of the ordered issue.

The Japan Securities Dealers Association publishes a daily list of the most heavily traded issues and their average bid and asked prices. The Association also provides a weekly list of representative issues and their bid and asked prices.

The Exchanges

The bulk of convertible bonds and bonds with warrants are traded on the formal bond exchanges which are adjuncts of the Tokyo, Osaka, and Nagoya stock exchanges. Only about 6 percent of total bond trading in 1985 occurred on these exchanges.

Trading hours for convertible bonds, bonds with warrants, and large transactions (more than ¥10 million) of government bonds coincide with the hours for normal stock exchange trading (see Chapter 3). Small transactions are traded only during the afternoon session.

Large-lot trading of government bonds is conducted according to the zaraba or auction method described in Chapter 3. The itayose method is usually used for all smaller transactions in government issues.

THE BOND FUTURES MARKET

In the 1920s, speculation in Japan's stock exchanges was at least as popular as it is today. Speculators in the prewar era, however, enjoyed the added diversion of futures markets. Fu-

---

[7]These include second-tier securities firms, the city banks, the long-term credit banks, trust banks, regional banks, and the Norinchukin Bank.

tures were written against a variety of domestic bonds as well as French Government bonds.

A futures market is a marketplace where contracts for the future delivery of financial instruments (or commodities) are traded in accordance with established regulations. A bond futures contract is a transferable agreement to buy or sell bonds at a specified time and at an agreed-upon price. Futures contracts resemble shares of stock in the sense that each contract is identical in its provisions for quantity and grade. An individual wishing to buy or sell a contract can only do so through a broker and *must* maintain a margin account. Gains or losses in the value of an outstanding contract are calculated daily in the margin account resulting in "variation margins," which have their own interest income and expenses. One of the attributes of a futures contract is that positions are usually sold before the maturity of the contract. As a result, actual deliveries are rarely transacted.

The trading of bond-linked futures contracts in Japan was prohibited by the Occupation when the stock exchanges were reopened in 1949. More than 30 years elapsed until, on October 19, 1985, a market in government bond futures was opened on the Tokyo Stock Exchange.

In 1984, faced with the mass redemption of government bonds beginning in fiscal 1985, the regulatory authorities fully recognized the need to promote trading in government debt. Thus, the Ministry of Finance was forced by the steady growth of new issues and the outstanding balance of government securities to be particularly receptive to limited financial innovation.

Other factors reinforced the decision to establish the new market. Central among them was the creation in September 1984 of a bond futures market in Singapore which promised to become a link in an emerging international futures network. It would only be a matter of a short time, proponents argued, before established markets in London, Toronto, Sydney, Chicago, and New York (and four additional U.S. cities) would be linked with Singapore (and a proposed market in Hong Kong). If Japan did not act immediately it could be left on the sidelines.

Along with these strong incentives to consider bond futures trading, the Ministry of Finance was swayed by an equally formidable consideration. The gradual deregulation of deposit interest rates (see Appendix I) promised to increase the costs of financing government debt. A bond futures market would provide a hedge against fluctuations in interest rates. At the same time, such a market would give Japan's financial institutions the opportunity to hedge against losses resulting from declines in long-term government bond prices in the securities markets.

Finally, and perhaps not insignificantly, the 1984 "yen-dollar accord" provided for the creation of a futures market. Soon after the signing of the accord, the Ministry of Finance requested a report from the Securities and Exchange Council (an advisory body to the Minister of Finance) regarding the effects of futures trading on monetary policy. The report was delivered in late 1984. Shortly afterward, a bill for an amendment to the Securities and Exchange Law which would establish a new bond futures market—in which membership would include institutions other than securities firms—was submitted to the Diet and approved.

Located in a basement several levels below the main floor of the Tokyo Stock Exchange, the Japanese government bond futures market is the only recognized futures exchange (with the sole exception of Bermuda-based Intex) in which trading occurs away from the floor. Because the futures market was made a special affiliated body of the Tokyo Stock Exchange, the saitori (see Chapter 3) were given their traditional role of matching buy and sell orders. Brokers receiving orders or trading on their own account telephone the order to a saitori who uses a computer terminal to match orders. It is expected that the futures market will be completely computerized by the spring of 1988, rendering the saitori and their telephones obsolete.

Trading hours for the futures contracts are the same that apply to equity trading on the TSE: 9:00 A.M. to 11:00 A.M. and 1:00 P.M. to 3:00 P.M. This short trading period (based on Tokyo time) contrasts sharply with the more than nine hours per day (8:00 A.M. to 5:20 P.M.) that bonds are traded by brokers in the Tokyo spot market.

Although the Chicago Mercantile Exchange served first as a special subject of study and finally as a model, the Tokyo futures market was designed on an institutional rather than an individual scale. Individual members were excluded and an initial 141 corporate participants (consisting of the [then] 83 members and

13 special members of the TSE, 37 banks, and 8 foreign broker-age firms with Tokyo branches) were invited to join. In the sum-mer of 1986, an additional 45 participants were designated. At about the same time, the U.S. Securities and Exchange Commis-sion allowed resident U.S. investors to trade in Japanese bond futures. Thus, U.S. residents are permitted to open bond futures accounts with Japanese brokerage firms and trade the market.

The government bond contracts are based on price indices for fictitious issues of bonds. All of the contracts are for ¥100 mil-lion face value of 6 percent Japanese Government 10-year bonds. Actually, a variety of coupons on long-term government bonds that mature in 7 to 10 years are deliverable for the con-tract.

Before trading in the contract begins, the Exchange indi-cates the particular issues (and their conversion rates) that are deliverable for each contract. Consequently, each eligible con-tract has a different value (which is determined by the coupon and maturity). The value of a bond with a coupon other than 6 percent is equated to the futures final settlement price by means of a "conversion factor." Tables listing conversion factors for every combination of coupon and maturity are provided by the Exchange and by brokerage firms.

The futures price is quoted as a percentage of par with the smallest unit expressed in terms of 1 percent of ¥1. Each con-tract is an agreement to take delivery (a long position) or make delivery (a short position) on the 20th day of March, June, Sep-tember, or December. The agreement involves a commitment by both parties to pay losses or receive profits on a daily basis as long as the position remains open. The longest contract is for 15 months. The futures positions are "marked to the market" (ad-justed) daily in order to show gains and losses.

The bond futures market enables institutional investors hold-ing substantial quantities of long-term government bonds to hedge against interest rate fluctuations. Because margin re-quirements are low (3 percent of which only 1 percent need be in cash) and there is no securities transaction tax (unless physical delivery of the bonds is taken), investors have the opportunity to make windfall profits by buying or selling the market.

The autumn of 1985 saw an inauspicious beginning for the new market. Four weeks before bond futures trading was scheduled to begin, the Group of Five (the United States, Japan, the United Kingdom, France, and West Germany) agreed to lower the value of the U.S. dollar while maintaining or increasing interest rate levels in the other four nations. As a consequence, the Bank of Japan intervened to raise interest rates, thus closing the gap between Japanese public bond rates and U.S. Treasury bonds.

The Japanese government bond market was devastated, experiencing its biggest drop in two decades. As interest rates rose, the price of 10-year Japanese government bonds plummeted by 8 percent in less than one month. The Big Four securities houses (particularly Yamaichi)—which had purchased substantial positions to "celebrate" the opening of the new market—suffered enormous trading losses, and at least one bond dealer jumped out of his office window in despair.

The Bank of Japan followed its credit tightening policy of late 1985 with successive cuts in the discount rate during 1986. As a result of this and other factors (such as the "weight of money" available for investment), the bond futures market fully recovered. Indeed, so complete was the recovery that in March 1986, volume reached 26,725 contracts per day, representing ¥2.672 trillion yen (more than $16 billion) trading value. Less than five months later, the number of contracts more than tripled, making the long-term government bond the most actively traded coupon futures contract in the world. As a result, two-way volume in 1986 reached ¥1,870 trillion, roughly 10 percent higher than the volume of trading of U.S. long-term government bond futures on the Chicago Board of Trade.

The Big Four securities firms, which maintain a dominant presence in the securities markets (see Chapter 2), have accounted for about 40 percent of all trading in the government bond futures market. (Although it is not known how much of this trading is for their own account, it is generally believed that commission trading represents only about 15 percent of the total.) Of the remainder of the trading, a substantial share is handled by a U.S. investment bank—Salomon Brothers. The leader of the U.S. Treasury market, Salomon Brothers was one of the first foreign firms to establish a presence in the Japanese bond market (see Chapter 2). This, combined with its extensive experience in the U.S. bond futures market, made it a natural leader in

SUMMARY OF JAPANESE GOVERNMENT BOND FUTURES CONTRACT SPECIFICATIONS

Contract Size:	¥100 million face value government bonds.
Coupon:	Nominal 6 percent.
Price Quotation:	In percentage of par in minimum increments of ¥0.01 with a per contract value of ¥10,000 for each ¥0.01 increase or decrease.
Maturity:	10 years.
Contract Months:	March, June, September, December.
Trading Hours (Tokyo time):	9:00 A.M. to 11:00 A.M. 1:00 P.M. to 3:00 P.M.
Minimum Price Fluctuation:	¥1.00 per day subject to change by the Exchange should trading require an expanded limit. (A limit move has a contract value of ¥1 million.)
Last Trading Day:	Ninth business day prior to the delivery date.
Delivery Day:	The 20th (or the immediately following business day if the 20th is a holiday).
Settlement:	Equal to the futures price times a conversion factor, where the conversion factor is based on the price at which a deliverable bond would yield 6 percent.
Deliverable Bonds:	Any listed Japanese long-term government bond that matures seven years after the delivery date. The Exchange specifies which issues are deliverable for each contract.
Cheapest to Deliver:	The seller can select any deliverable issue to deliver, and prices among deliverable bonds vary. Buyer must specify "cheapest to deliver" when delivery is made.
Types of Deliverable Bonds:	Taxable institutions and individuals must deliver registered and bearer bonds. Tax exempt institutions must deliver registered bonds or bonds issued through the Bank of Japan book entry system. (Less than one percent of bond futures contracts run to delivery.)

| Cash Settlement: | If a futures contract is liquidated by offsetting a short or long position, the cash settlement procedures require four business days. |

Japan's new futures market. Depth of experience and expertise enabled the foreign firm to outpace all domestic players except two of the Big Four securities firms. Most of the remainder of the trading is conducted by special participants (primarily bank dealers prohibited from acting as brokers) with about 4 percent of contracts traded by corporate investors and roughly 0.6 percent transacted by domestic individual investors. Life and nonlife insurance companies and investment trusts have rarely participated in the market, while overseas investors have accounted for less than 1 percent of all transactions.

Although short-term transactions by professional dealers account for most of the activity in the futures market, other types of activity do occur and are likely to become more prevalent. Only a handful of Japanese fund managers have used the bond futures market to hedge their portfolios. However, as professional portfolio managers develop a better understanding of the new market, it is probable that they will seek the benefits derived from hedging with futures contracts. Arbitrage opportunities between futures market prices and spot market prices for government bonds other than the currently traded bellwether bond also occur and are likely to be exploited.

Although a timetable has not been proposed, it is generally expected that short-term government bond and treasury bill contracts will be listed on the futures market by 1988. The trading of yen bond futures on the London International Financial Futures Exchange (LIFFE) is expected in the spring of 1987 and will be followed by trading in an interchangeable contract on the Chicago Board of Trade by 1988.[8] This will establish an interna-

---

[8] At the time of writing, these contracts have neither been announced nor designed. The Japanese withholding tax is likely to be an obstacle in the creation of overseas Japanese government bond futures. A successfully devised contract will have to be based on the assumption that physical delivery will include full interest accrued to the bond. Without this assumption, pricing of the bonds would be difficult and would result in investor confusion.

SUMMARY OF MARGIN REQUIREMENTS AND COMMISSION SCALES

Initial Margin:	3 percent of face value, of which at least 1 percent must be cash and the balance securities. Minimum initial margin is ¥6 million.
Maintenance Margin:	The margin account must be maintained at 3 percent of contract face value. Any account that falls below the 3 percent margin minimum will receive a margin call. All margin calls must be met with cash. A margin call which is not met within three days will be closed out by the broker.
Marked to the Market:	Accounts are marked to the market at the end of each trading day. (This means that each account is charged with a profit or loss based on the difference between the entry price and the current day's settlement price.)
Securities Transaction Tax:	None if no delivery. 10 to 20 percent if physical delivery is taken. (There are differences between registered and bearer bonds. In addition, residents of different countries are taxed at different rates. The investor planning to take delivery must investigate the tax situation in advance of purchase.)
Roundturn Commission:	A one-time fee is charged whenever a position is liquidated. The maximum commission is ¥0.06 per ¥100.0 face value.
Commission Schedule:	As per Table 5–2.

TABLE 5–2 Commission Schedule for Long-Term Government Bond Futures Contracts*

Face Value (millions of ¥)	Commission (per ¥100)	Roundturn (millions of ¥)
100	0.06	0.06
200	0.06	0.12
300	0.06	0.18
400	0.06	0.24
500	0.06	0.30
1,000	0.06	0.60
2,000	0.05	1.00
3,000	0.0467	1.400
5,000	0.044	2.200
10,000	0.032	3.200

*December 1986

tional linkage connecting London, Chicago, and Tokyo. The forecast computerization of the market in 1988 should result in 24-hour trading. All of these factors will cause an increase in the market's trading volume. That, in turn, will give the new futures market an even bigger role in the bond market as a whole.

CHAPTER SIX

The Euroyen Bond Market

THE BIRTH OF OFFSHORE SECURITIES

Euromarkets are made possible by the existence of expatriated money termed Eurocurrency. The free convertibility of major currencies, which began in 1958, led to the formation of stateless residues of capital in Europe, particularly London. The Eurodollar capital market (the first of the Eurocurrency markets) was spawned by an expression of U.S. protectionism—the Interest Equalization Tax (IET) of 1963.[1]

The IET, which effectively placed a tariff on the importation of foreign securities into the United States, was designed to protect U.S. domestic interest rate structures from international encroachment while, at the same time, to reduce excess capital outflows. Chronic U.S. balance of payments deficits triggered the need to contain capital outflows through the IET. Five years after the birth of the IET, in 1968, mandatory investment controls reinforced a growing demand for Eurodollars by the overseas offices of U.S. corporations. As a result, international dollar-denominated money markets and capital markets grew rapidly in Europe. Unlike the closely regulated money markets of the United States, the new Euromarket was free of capital controls.

In the early 1960s, the availability of Eurocurrencies led to

---

[1] The IET was repealed in 1973.

the rapid development of Eurobonds. Eurobonds are debt securities issued by a borrower outside its country of residence and thus outside the country of the currency in which the bond is denominated. A Eurobond, then, is an international security *par excellence* and can be purchased by an investor of any nationality. Usually listed on the stock exchanges of London and Luxembourg and ordinarily sold over-the-counter in the world's major capital markets, Eurobonds are syndicated by groups of international banks. The majority of the banks involved in the Eurobond market are based in London and most issues are traded over the telephone and telex. Because Eurobonds are traded in an external market, they transcend capital restrictions. They are particularly susceptible to foreign exchange risk. These stateless bonds are the direct antecedents of the 24-hour global securities market which was in its incipient stage in 1986.

Dollar deposits in the two major Asian offshore banking centers, Singapore and Hong Kong, led to the emergence of an Asia dollar market which constituted a smaller scale parallel of the Eurodollar market. In the 1980s, dollar-denominated and yen-denominated instruments—particularly Asia dollar bonds and Asia yen bonds—were underwritten by Japanese securities firms for domestic and ASEAN (Association of Southeast Asian Nations) borrowers. As a result, bonds denominated in Asia currency have competed with the Samurai and Euroyen bond markets for Japanese institutional investor business.

The establishment of offshore banking in Tokyo in November 1986 (see Chapter 7) promises competition for the Euromarket and the Asia market *when* the tax structure is made competitive with other offshore banking centers. In the late 1980s, the Asia bond market (including Tokyo, Hong Kong, and Singapore) will probably develop further as one component of a global system in which debt denominated in offshore currencies will be routinely traded and swapped by the world's financial institutions and sovereign entities. Ultimately, distinctions between Euromarket and Asia market instruments will become incidental. Meanwhile, however, the Asia bond market is a small and insignificant zone of issuance and will not be discussed further in this book.

During the more than two decades of their existence, Eurobonds have provided borrowers with highly competitive sources of financing. At the same time, they have given affluent individual investors outstanding yields which can be concealed from tax authorities behind the anonymity of the bearer instrument. The caricature of the stereotypical investor has been the Belgian dentist, seeking high, tax-efficient returns on his considerable earnings. In 1985, according to the *International Finance Review*, the Belgian dentist had a new companion, in many ways his direct opposite: Mrs. Watanabe, the Japanese "wealthy middle class housewife who, with traditional Japanese conservatism, seeks to invest her savings, and sometimes the family housekeeping budget."[2] In 1985–86, Mrs. Watanabe and Japanese institutions were major investors in the Eurobond market.

By the 1980s, the Eurobond market had become, in terms of trading volume (more than $13 billion per day in 1986), the second biggest capital market in the world after the U.S. bond market. In terms of debt outstanding, the Eurobond market had grown to be the world's third largest securities market, trailing only the United States and Japan. Most of the funds raised in the Eurobond market have been through Eurodollar instruments, followed by Eurodeutsche mark bonds and Euroyen bonds. In 1986, the yen surpassed the deutsche mark as the second largest currency of issue, with a total of 160 Euroyen bond issues worth ¥2.9 trillion ($18.7 billion), almost double the amount of the preceding year (see Table 6–1).

EUROYEN BONDS

The first Eurobond issue denominated in yen was not floated until 1977, more than a decade after the emergence of the Eurobond market. A ¥10 billion issue offered by the European Investment Bank and lead managed by Daiwa, it was one of a handful of issues (worth ¥420 billion) during the period 1977–83. Domestic entities were prohibited from issuing Euroyen instruments. Nonetheless, in 1980 the supermarket chain, Ito Yokado, privately placed a ¥5 billion issue with the government of Kuwait. This private placement was followed by four additional private placements with OPEC treasuries.

Until 1984, supranational, sovereign, and public issuers were alone permitted by Japan's Ministry of Finance to raise

---

[2]See *International Finance Review*, December 21, 1985.

TABLE 6–1 1986 Eurobond Issues by Currency

Rank	Currency	Number of Issues	Total ($ mn)
1	U.S. dollar	827	114,309
2	Yen	160	18,666
3	Deutsche mark	179	17,155
4	Sterling	79	10,548
5	ECU	81	6,870
6	Canadian dollar	87	5,227
7	French franc	46	3,500
8	Australian dollar	91	3,077
9	Florin	23	1,372
10	Danish kroner	27	1,000

SOURCE: Nomura Research Institute

yen funds in Europe.[3] Beginning in December 1984, the Japanese government allowed foreign private corporations rated A or better (*and* fulfilling the same financial ratios applicable to Samurai bonds—see Chapter 5) to issue straight yen bonds in the Euromarkets. The eligibility requirements applicable to domestic entities mirrored the criteria necessary for the issuance of unsecured bonds in Japan. Following this regulatory relaxation, the key restrictions imposed on Eurobond offerings included fixed interest rates, a 180-day "seasoning" period, and minimum maturities of five years.

During the last month of 1984—the first month of the new Eurobond deregulation—10 issues were signed (more than in all of 1983), including the first Euroyen bond offered by a corporate entity (Dow Chemical). A total of 30 domestic corporations (including the electric power companies and state-owned institutions) were also authorized to issue straight Euroyen bonds or bonds with warrants. An additional 78 private Japanese companies, allowed to issue unsecured debt in the domestic market, were also given permission to issue convertible Euroyen bonds.

While Euroyen bonds issued by nonresident entities are tax exempt (in contrast to nonresident investment in Japanese government bonds where a 20 percent withholding tax is levied), a

---

[3]The Ministry of Finance has firmly asserted its power to authorize all yen-denominated instruments issued outside Japan.

withholding tax is applied to the interest paid on Euroyen issues by Japanese corporations. Nonetheless, in 1985, Japanese corporations borrowed more money in the Euromarket than in the domestic bond market.

The Japanese government further liberalized the issuing regulations for Euroyen bonds in April 1985, permitting dual currency bonds denominated in yen, zero coupon bonds, deep discount bonds, and floating rate notes. The new dual currency issues, carrying a yen coupon roughly 150 to 200 basis points higher than straight yen bonds and redeemable in dollars, were ordinarily swapped into fixed-rate dollar obligations at the spot rate.[4] In such issues, the borrower swaps the yen interest while the principal is paid in dollars. Theoretically, the dual currency issues can be viewed as dollar obligations by borrowers and as yen securities by investors.

Dual currency bonds are issued in yen and bear a yen coupon. Redemption of the bonds is in U.S. dollars or another major currency. Thus, dual currency bonds involve the *investor* in a forward foreign exchange transaction. The investor is compensated in two ways for assuming currency risk:

1. *Coupon.* Dual currency issues offer the benefit of yen income at a coupon rate higher than that available for straight yen bonds.
2. *Redemption.* The investor is given a redemption amount which includes a premium above the dollar value of the issue amount (based on the spot rate prevailing at the time of issue). Currently, the redemption amount is based on a rate of exchange that assumes a stronger yen against the dollar.

On the opposite side of the transaction, *borrowers* obtain relatively low-cost financing devoid of exchange risk. The proceeds of a dual currency issue are converted to the desired currency (usually dollars) at the spot rate. Coupon payments are converted to the issuer's chosen currency (usually dollars) at a forward rate which is fixed for the life of the bond. Although redemption is determined in the issuer's currency at a premium,

---

[4] By swapping the yen obligations into fixed-rate obligations in a major currency, the issuer can secure a relatively low final cost *if* the redemption amount (denominated in U.S. dollars or another currency) is calculated by a fixed exchange rate which is below the market rate in the forward exchange market.

the total cost to the borrower is often competitive with alternative financing vehicles.

By early 1986, an estimated ¥1 trillion in convertible bonds and warrant bonds were issued by Japanese companies on the Euromarket.[5] In 1985, Japanese corporations issued 64 percent of all convertible bonds and 80 percent of all bonds-with-warrants in the Euromarket. Japanese borrower interest in convertible bonds evaporated in 1986, although preference for bonds-plus-warrants remained strong. In 1986, Japanese investors were allowed, for the first time, to buy warrants while at the same time Japanese corporations were permitted to issue yen warrants in their home market independently of the attached debt.

About 90 percent of all Euroyen bonds in 1985–86 were floated by foreign borrowers and the vast majority were swapped into fixed-rate dollar obligations. Nearly half of the issues were dual currency bonds (see Figure 6–1). Because the placement of dual currency bonds is only possible in Japan, the dual currency issues currently promise a substantial flow back to Japan.

The arbitrage opportunity between Euroyen bond rates and Japan's long-term prime rate has been at the heart of the Euroyen bond market. Thus, the entire Euroyen market (like the Australian dollar, New Zealand dollar, and ECU Euromarkets) is based on the profitability of swaps. In the typical Euroyen swap, a borrower, having floated a Euroyen bond issue, will give its newly acquired yen debt to a Japanese bank which will convey to the borrower the yen it needs to make coupon payments. The bank, in turn, will borrow Eurodollars (or another agreed-upon currency) at the London Interbank Offered Rate (LIBOR) and forward the newly obtained dollar debt to the sovereign borrower. The borrower is obligated to make the dollar interest payments at an agreed-upon *discount* to LIBOR. In this way, the borrower has swapped fixed rate yen debt for floating rate dollar debt at a rate cheaper than could otherwise have been obtained.

Meanwhile, the Japanese bank has suffered an ongoing loss equal to the discount to LIBOR that has been negotiated with its

---

[5]It is noteworthy that convertible bond conversions and the exercising of warrants was one significant source of foreign selling on the Japanese stock market in 1985–86. Thus, while foreign investors were enthusiastic buyers of Japanese convertible issues in the Euromarket, they converted and sold the bulk of their purchases.

FIGURE 6–1 Breakdown of Euroyen Bonds by Types of Issue (1985)

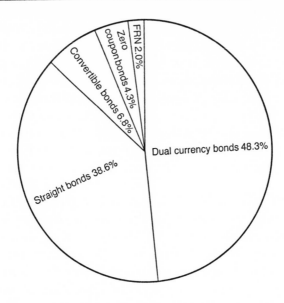

partner. Ideally, this is a paper loss which is counterbalanced by interest the bank obtains by lending the yen it has secured from the swap to Japanese corporations at the prevalent domestic long-term prime rate. In 1986, this rate was usually higher than the coupon rates on Euroyen bonds. However, volatility in the Eurobond market generally and in the Euroyen bond market specifically has caused fluctuations in the size of the arbitrage spread. As a result, many Japanese banks have suffered losses in their swap deals with borrowers in the Euromarket when the spread has disappeared.

Nonetheless, the banks have been motivated to act as partners in unprofitable swap deals in order to cultivate relationships with borrowers and especially with firms lead managing bond issues. The Big Four securities firms, for example, have rewarded those banks conducting swaps for their clients by providing colead management opportunities. These opportunities can yield additional revenue and, more importantly, generate prestige in the international sector.

The majority of Japanese banks are willing to exchange the profitability of a deal for the status resulting from active participation in a new international market. Thus, for example, in April 1986, the Long-Term Credit Bank of Japan (LTCB) syndicated a $200 million Eurobond issue for PepsiCo, Inc. Through the bank, PepsiCo swapped its fixed rate obligation of 7.3 percent for a floating rate obligation costing 7.05 percent. LTCB considered it worthwhile to incur a loss in this way in order to procure a share of the emerging market and the publicity of lead managing a prestigious issue.

It is important to note that the existence of arbitrage opportunities between Euroyen bonds and domestic corporate bonds for Japanese issuers promotes the independence of domestic bond issue terms from the long-term prime rate. This means that without parallel deregulation of domestic issuing criteria, the demand for long-term prime rate borrowing in Japan will progressively deteriorate. Thus, the more substantial the available arbitrage, the greater the pressure on the Ministry of Finance to relax domestic corporate bond issuing standards. In this way, the development of the Euroyen bond market has assured the inevitability of the gradual liberalization of domestic interest rate control (see Appendix I).

Similarly, the Euroyen bond market has placed pressure on the government to protect the Samurai and Shogun markets. Without yields and ease of issuance comparable to the Euromarket, the domestic market in foreign bonds (denominated in yen or foreign currency) will fall into desuetude. In 1986, steps were taken to assure the development of a secondary market in Samurai issues. More dramatic actions will be required in the late 1980s to revivify a market which, still in its infancy, has become obsolete.

The swap-driven character of the Euroyen bond market has assured that the majority of the issues by nonresidents are converted into other currencies, primarily U.S. dollars. During 1985–86, few borrowers were inclined to hold yen liabilities. This is not surprising. Only a small part of Japanese trade is financed in yen with the result that few borrowers require yen funding. Because the yen constitutes a tiny portion of world currency reserves and a small part of global lending, it has not assumed a significant role in international banking.[6] As a direct

---

[6]This contrasts sharply with the preeminent role of Japanese banks in international lending (see Chapter 7).

result, the Euromarkets in such yen-denominated floating rate debt instruments as floating rate notes (FRNs) and negotiable certificates of deposit (NCDs) have been negligible. An estimated 90 percent of all Euroyen issues have been swapped, representing 28.3 percent of all swaps executed in 1985.[7]

Beginning in April 1986, additional relaxation of regulatory constraints were introduced for resident and nonresident borrowers. For the first time, Japanese rating agencies were recognized as acceptable evaluators for any issuer. Issuing standards were simplified, rendering all single A or better rated companies eligible to tap the market.

In addition, with the exception of dual currency bonds, restriction on the flowback of the paper (the seasoning rule) was reduced to 90 days from 180 days in order to stimulate the development of the secondary market which had lagged behind the development of the primary market. The seasoning rules, which impede market liquidity, have been strongly opposed by the Big Four. Indeed, the securities companies have informally asked the Ministry of Finance to reduce the period to 30 days or to eliminate the transfer delay entirely.

Seasoning rules, however, have seldom been taken seriously by Japanese institutions and are often neglected or bypassed by means of postdated purchase agreements. Thus, although the Ministry of Finance may wince, **sushi bonds** (foreign currency Eurobonds—see Glossary) are domestically produced boomerangs, returning rapidly to the homeland of their issuers. Other types of Euroyen bonds move more slowly but, like trout preparing to spawn, will return to the birthplace of the yen.

The market was liberalized a little more when, in June 1986, the headquarters of foreign commercial banks with Tokyo branches were authorized to float long-term Euroyen bonds. Subsequently, the three long-term credit banks and the Bank of Tokyo were permitted to issue Euroyen bonds. It is likely that the market will be opened to the city banks in 1987 or 1988.

It is expected that a Euroyen commercial paper (CP) market will be established in April 1987. Although issuers of the new Euroyen CP initially will be confined to nonresident corpora-

---

[7]Estimated by the Nomura Research Institute.

tions, Japanese corporations probably will be authorized to issue yen IOUs in Europe one year later. Meanwhile, the Ministry of Finance will be faced with the thorny problem of determining whether the overseas *branches* of Japanese banks should be allowed to underwrite the short-term yen-denominated unsecured notes in foreign markets. The government has already decided to permit overseas *securities subsidiaries* of Japanese banks to underwrite commercial paper in the Euromarket and the British sterling market. Thus, it is probable that securities subsidiaries of the banks will also obtain authorization to underwrite Euroyen commercial paper by 1988.

In just 18 months, from the liberalization of the Euroyen bond market in December 1984 to the end of June 1986, U.S. corporations alone issued more than $7 billion worth of Euroyen bonds which were swapped into U.S. dollars. The World Bank borrowed a total of ¥190 billion in a series of nine issues. Thus, a major market grew to maturity as the direct result of the Yen-Dollar Accord of 1984. Euroyen bond issues in 1986 totalled ¥2.9 trillion ($18 billion), representing an increase of more than 1.8 times over 1985.

Several significant considerations have supported the appeal of Euroyen bonds for nonresident issuers and borrowers. Euroyen bond returns have been superior to the returns of Japanese government bonds. The yield gap between Euroyen bonds and Japanese public bonds (largely resulting from a frequent lag between Euroyen bond rates and Japan's discount and money market rates) has been one source of attraction for investors.[8] For the borrower, not only was the all-in cost of a Euroyen bond issue less than the cost of a Samurai, but also the paperwork necessary was far simpler. As a result, any issuer could go to the Euromarket, select a lead underwriter, establish the terms, and enter the market immediately. By contrast, in Tokyo, roughly eight weeks are needed to fulfill necessary requirements. These differences, however, are likely to change as the result of government efforts to revive the decaying market in Samurai, Shibosai (private placements), and Shogun bonds (see Chapter 5) as well as domestic corporate issues.

---

[8] The gap was roughly 50 basis points at the end of 1986.

Japanese corporations have elected to sell more debt in the Euromarket than at home. Although this can be viewed as a symptom of the antiquated character of Japan's regulatory system, the problem cannot be resolved by the simple abolition of inhibiting standards. Because the deficit financing needs of the government have pressured regulators to keep interest rates low and competition from the private sector minimal, a system has emerged on which the government's budget needs depend. If Japan's interest rate structure were allowed to react freely to global market forces, then the Ministry of Finance would find itself paying a far higher price to rollover and finance Japan's massive debt. This prospect holds little appeal for Japan's bureaucrats who are accustomed to a political economy in which market forces, far from being free, have been in a perpetual state of house arrest.

In order to reduce the burgeoning number of Japanese companies fulfilling their financing needs in the Eurobond market, the Ministry of Finance will probably allow shelf registrations in 1987. At the time of writing, a corporation must provide the Ministry with detailed financial reports prior to issuing a bond. Shelf registration would permit a company to register for a specified period of time with the latitude to issue bonds at will during the approved period without additional clearance.[9] By eliminating delays caused by queuing and other administrative requirements, shelf registration will facilitate the issuance of domestic corporate bonds. However, shelf registration alone will not provide a sufficiently powerful impetus to motivate corporations to seek funds at home. The freedom of choice conjoined with a growing pragmatism will encourage Japan's corporations to seek the most competitive financing available in the international marketplace.

In late 1986, Japanese institutional investors began, for the first time, to display strong interest in *buying* Euroyen bonds. In December 1986, alone, the Big Four sold more than $4 billion (¥623 billion) of Euroyen bonds to domestic institutions and corporations. These sales in the over-the-counter market represented nearly double the comparable figure for Samurai bonds

---

[9] When shelf registration is introduced in Japan, participating companies will be required to make financial disclosures on a quarterly basis.

(¥321 billion). The new Tokyo secondary market in Euroyen issues was stimulated by the desire of small domestic institutional investors to avoid foreign exchange risk.

JAPANESE BOOKRUNNERS

The yen's exceptional strength against major currencies, particularly the dollar, in 1986, and Japan's record low interest rates motivated a broad range of international borrowers to turn to the Euroyen market. As a result, Euroyen bonds grew faster than any other sector of the Eurobond market, surpassing all issues other than dollars. In addition, Euroyen bonds provided a means for refinancing more expensive Samurai bonds issued in Tokyo in the early 1980s. Although the Euromarket has not been able to compete with the superior terms available to U.S. corporations in their home market, supranational and sovereign entities have turned to the Euromarket with increasing frequency. This trend is likely to continue throughout the late 1980s with growing numbers of Japanese institutions also seeking financing through Euroyen instruments.

Three of the Big Four securities firms ranked among the top 10 bookrunners in the Eurobond market league tables in 1986 (see Table 6–2), a sharp change from 1985 when only Nomura ranked among the top 10. Both Nomura Securities and Daiwa Securities surpassed such traditional leaders as Morgan Stanley and Salomon Brothers in the total value of their Eurobond bookrunning. Nomura's share of the market rose from 3.8 percent in 1985 to 8.1 percent in 1986. Nikko Securities rose from 25th to 10th place, ahead of Union Bank of Switzerland and Goldman Sachs. The long-term credit banks ranked among the top 20 bookrunners, with the Industrial Bank of Japan and the Long-Term Credit Bank of Japan vying with universal banks and investment banks for mandates. Together, the Big Four and the leading two long-term credit banks ran the books for 21.3 percent of all Eurobond offerings in 1986, more than double the figure for the preceding year.

Article 65 of the Securities and Exchange Act of 1948 is currently interpreted by the Ministry of Finance as extending to the lead management of bonds outside Japan. Consequently, Japanese city banks are limited to coleading issues and cannot

---

TABLE 6–2 1986 Top 20 Eurobond Lead Managers

Rank	Manager	Amount ($mn)	Market Share (percent)
1	Credit Suisse First Boston	19,182	10.8
2	Nomura Securities	14,803	8.1
3	Deutsche Bank	12,444	6.8
4	Morgan Guaranty	9,897	5.4
5	Daiwa Securities	8,963	4.9
6	Morgan Stanley	8,868	4.9
7	Salomon Brothers	8,235	4.5
8	Banque Paribas	7,002	3.8
9	Merrill Lynch	5,971	3.3
10	Nikko Securities	5,141	2.8
11	Union Bank of Switzerland	4,874	2.7
12	Yamaichi Securities	4,440	2.4
13	Shearson Lehman Brothers	4,137	2.3
14	Goldman Sachs	3,621	2.0
15	Societe Generale	3,109	1.7
16	Industrial Bank of Japan	3,034	1.7
17	Swiss Bank Corporation	2,886	1.6
18	S.G. Warburg	2,788	1.5
19	Commerzbank	2,713	1.5
20	Long-Term Credit Bank of Japan	2,553	1.4

SOURCE: Nomura Research Institute

vie with the Big Four or the long-term credit banks for bookrunning business.

The relaxation, by the Ministry of Finance, of Euroyen bond issuing rules resulted in 80 issues (amounting to roughly $7 billion) in 1985. Of these, 73 were managed or comanaged by Japanese institutions with non-Japanese institutions securing a minuscule portion of the mandates. In 1985, the two market leaders, Nomura and Daiwa, together won roughly 60 percent of all mandates for Euroyen issues. In 1986, Nomura alone lead managed roughly half of the Euroyen bond issues for North American corporations. The Big Four collectively monopolized the lead management not only of Euroyen issues but also of all issues, regardless of currency, floated in Europe for Japanese corporations or institutions during the period 1985–86.

Because the vast majority of the 1985–86 market in Eurobonds with warrants were Japanese corporate issues, Japanese underwriters dominated this market sector. As a result, the Big

Four securities firms were the top four lead managers of bonds-plus-warrants in 1986, handling more than three-fifths of all issues.

The success of the Japanese bookrunners in the Euromarket is not the result of trading ability. The Big Four have not yet developed the trading skills characteristic of the leading U.S. and European banks. Indeed, not until recent market liberalization have such firms as Nikko and Yamaichi modernized their trading rooms. Instead, the Japanese domestic client base functions as a guarantee for the sales of securities underwritten in the Euromarket. Thus, the majority of the Eurobonds lead managed by Japanese institutions are placed in Japan, enabling the Big Four to maintain narrow margins on the basis of large sales volume. Record corporate profits (see Chapter 2) have enabled the securities firms to withstand underwriting losses resulting from decisions to procure market share at the expense of revenue.

The success of Japanese institutions as bookrunners in the Eurobond market in 1986 (and the likely continuation of their ascendancy) resulted from a number of factors:

1. *Systematic predatory pricing of issues* by Japanese Eurobond managers squeezed European and North American competition, thus increasing Japanese market share. In 1986, perhaps as a result, U.S. and European investment banks (such as Salomon and Credit Suisse-First Boston) sometimes refused to help Big Four firms syndicate and underwrite issues for major international firms. Japanese firms were infrequently invited to co-lead issues managed by non-Japanese institutions.

2. *Many syndications of Euroyen bond offerings were effectively private placements*, artificially priced below market levels. The long-term credit banks, for example, have managed offerings while giving no allotment of issues to comanagers. In this way, they have risen illicitly in the Euromarket league tables (which are determined on the basis of publicly traded issues).

3. *The growing frequency of swap arbitrage* (which has reduced the importance of relationships between borrowers and managers) gave Japanese bookrunners additional opportunities to win mandates. During 1985–86, Japanese institutions in the Eurodollar market ran the books for IBM Credit Corporation, General Electric Co., Exxon Corporation, American Express, and other comparable credits.

4. *The increasing number of Japanese borrowers* in the Eurobond market provided Japanese institutions with an indigenous and loyal client base. Although there have been many exceptions, Japanese borrowers generally prefer to award mandates to Japanese institutions as a means of maintaining existing relationships.

INNOVATION

An unexpected attribute of the Big Four, particularly Nomura and Daiwa, has been financial innovation in the Euromarket. Japan's financial institutions have not been renowned as the inventors of novel—let alone complex—instruments. Nevertheless, the opening of the Euroyen bond market signaled to Japan's securities companies that a new era of deregulation demanded the introduction of competitive investment vehicles. In October 1985, for example, Nomura introduced the "Heaven and Hell" $100 million Eurobond issue for IBM Credit Corporation. Chosen as "Deal of the Year" by *International Finance Review*, the issue involved three interest rate swaps as well as five currency swaps. The offering was designed to yield high premiums if the dollar were to rise significantly before maturity ("heaven") and, alternatively, a diminution of principal in the event of a major appreciation of the yen against the dollar ("hell").

Dual currency bonds, copied by Nomura from a Swiss franc prototype, constituted 48 percent of the Euroyen bond market in 1985. Yen and dollar bonds with principal repayment amounts linked to the spot yen/dollar exchange rate (or to the 30-year U.S. Treasury note yield) were also initiated by Nomura.

A *reverse dual currency bond* was first floated in the Euromarket in 1986 by Kawasaki Steel. This type of bond is purchased and redeemed in yen but has interest paid in dollars, allowing Japanese investors to take a foreign exchange position without incurring a foreign exchange risk. Simultaneously, the issue enables the borrower to obtain capital at a lower cost than a domestic issuance.

Sushi bonds, invented by Yamaichi, were devised to satisfy the particular portfolio needs of Japan's trust banks and insurance companies. The Ministry of Finance limits the proportion of foreign bonds that can be held in a portfolio (see Chapter 9). However, foreign currency bonds issued by domestic institutions are *not* classified as foreign bonds. Thus, a market developed in foreign-currency-denominated bonds issued by Japanese institutions in the Euromarket. Such issues, priced below U.S. Treasury securities but above Japanese public bonds, were purchased almost entirely by Japanese institutions in 1985–86.

Like sushi bonds, *deferred interest bonds* were devised by Japanese securities firms to suit the unique needs of Japanese institutional investors and borrowers. Deferred interest securities are five-year Eurobonds, currently issued in dollars, with interest deferred for the first three years. A Japanese investor can hold the bond as a long-term investment for three years. At the end of the third year, the investor can sell the bond at a premium based on the interest to be paid. In this way, the institutional investor secures a capital gain without interest revenue on a fixed income security.

One of the last Eurobonds floated in 1986 was the market's first *split dual currency issue*. Devised and led by Nomura, the ¥6 billion issue of Banca Nationale del Lavoro was entirely placed among Japanese investors. Priced at 101.5, the 10-year bond pays 4.7 percent for the first five years and 7.5 percent thereafter. Holders of each ¥100 million bond receive, on maturity, 60 percent of the proceeds in yen and $245,399 for the remainder, representing a ¥163 to the dollar exchange rate.

At the end of 1986, Daiwa launched the biggest Euroyen bond in the brief history of the market. Worth ¥130 billion ($812 million) and issued by Denmark, one of the heaviest borrowers in the Eurobond market, the bond represented an expansion of liquidity for the Euroyen bond market and the Eurobond market as a whole. The *"jumbo" Euroyen bond* was made both callable and putable after three years, effectively giving it a three-year life. Although not the first three-year Euroyen bond, the new issue promised to expand the opportunities for investors to buy three-year issues (which in 1986 traded at large premiums).

Japan's city and regional banks have strongly opposed the establishment of Euroyen bonds with maturities under five years. The commercial banks are convinced that securities with shorter maturities will lure customers away from their short-term borrowing. The long-term credit banks have also opposed the introduction of three- and four-year Euroyen bonds. They are persuaded that the flowback of medium-term Euroyen issues could offer significant competition for their debentures. Nonetheless, it is probable that, during the next several years, maturity floors imposed on Euroyen issues gradually will be abolished.

In 1986, a variety of hybrid products were developed by Japanese firms for the Eurodollar market. Nomura, for instance, introduced the *Stock Performance Exchange Linked Bond* (SPELBOND), which contains equity and fixed income components. While the coupon is fixed at 3 percent, the investor has the opportunity to profit from equity growth. Investors receive increased principal if the New York Stock Exchange Composite Index rises above 166. The amount received above par is based on the given value of the index when the instrument reaches maturity. Although the coupon yield is low, the equity portion does not involve a downside risk.

Of similar intricacy was an issue designed by the Long-Term Credit Bank of Japan for the Canadian branch of General Motors Acceptance Corporation (GMAC). The *dual currency Euroyen/Canadian issue* is a 10-year ¥10 billion bond yielding 8 percent in yen during the initial five years and 10.125 percent in Canadian dollars for the final five years. When the bond begins to pay interest in Canadian dollars, a put option can be exercised, offering a rate of ¥120.85 per Canadian dollar.

In October 1986, the Banque Nationale de Paris issued a *mixed dual currency bond*, designed by Nikko. Eighty percent of the bond was issued in yen, with the balance in New Zealand dollars, and it bore a 9 percent coupon payable in New Zealand dollars. Redeemable in *either* currency, this issue offered investors considerable flexibility at the time of redemption.

In addition to the variety of innovations discussed above, deregulation prompted the introduction of various new products outside the Euromarket. In the summer of 1985, the European Investment Bank offered an ECU 100 million Shogun bond issue with 80 percent placement in Japan and 20 percent placement in Europe, arranged by the Bank of Tokyo. In September 1985, the Asian Development Bank sold the first *yankee yen bonds*. Offered in the United States, this ¥35 billion issue was lead managed by Daiwa and First Boston.

In the near future, Japanese city and regional banks are likely to receive Ministry of Finance approval to lead manage Eurobond issues. Such authorization would constitute one additional step in the accelerated process of liberalization which began in 1984. One more stone will have been removed from the wall separating the functions of banks and securities companies. Meanwhile, Glass-Steagall, the Great Chinese Wall separating commercial banking from investment banking in the United States, will have become further dilapidated, with U.S. banks actively underwriting new issues behind the foil of their subsidiaries. Just as generals use foreign wars as a convenient means for testing new weapons and tactics, bureaucrats at the Ministry of Finance use foreign markets and foreign institutions as trial grounds for new financial innovations. Developments in the Euromarket will eventually be brought home to Tokyo.

The city banks have been pressuring the government to amend or abrogate Article 65. They have been forced to do so by a critical change in the structure of domestic corporate borrowing. During the 1980s, Japanese corporations have been moving systematically away from the indirect financing which has characterized corporate borrowing since the beginning of the Meiji Restoration. The sale of debt and, to a far lesser extent, the sale of equity, have been replacing the traditional corporate dependence on indirect sources of funds. As a result, the securities companies have reaped extraordinary profits. The city banks have coveted these rewards.

The major banks are the direct heirs to the prewar zaibatsu heritage. Sumitomo, Mitsubishi, Fuji, and others maintain a vast network of corporate relationships based on tradition and cross-shareholding. Their keiretsu relationships have the potential to procure underwriting business from the corporations with which they have maintained close ties for decades. Collectively, Japan's banks hold the largest block of liquidity in the free world. This financial power would enable them to absorb all of those issues which they underwrite and cannot profitably sell—or do not wish to sell. By underwriting and subsequently digesting convertible bond issues, the banks would ultimately increase ownership in the members of their keiretsu. Thus, the city banks are positioned to be underwriters *par excellence* in the domestic market.

Part II will survey Japan's banking industry and the money markets. The banks have recently begun using the Euroyen bond market as a training ground for anticipated inroads to be made in their home market. The increasing refinement of zaitek and the recent purchase by Sumitomo Bank of an interest in Goldman Sachs are only the beginning.

Banking and Money Markets

CHAPTER SEVEN

Banking

OVERVIEW

The indigenous Japanese banking system, like the financial system as a whole, is segmented into rigidly defined components. Commercial banks (13 big city banks and 64 smaller regional banks), long-term credit banks (3), trust banks (7), mutual loan and savings banks (69), as well as highly specialized financial institutions which have no direct counterparts in the West, together constitute a unique configuration of institutions. Monitored by the Ministry of Finance and the Bank of Japan, these organizations have been functionally limited and protected by the regulatory structure.

Like all groups of institutions in Japan, the various types of bank (and the individual constituents of each category) can be ranked hierarchically in accordance with a deeply embedded public view of their status and power. Japan's banking institutions can be crudely divided into two groups: national and local. National institutions maintain branches throughout the archipelago and long ago received government authorization to open overseas offices or branches. Local organizations are usually restricted to one or two prefectures and until very recently had virtually no participation in international business.

At the top of this hierarchy are the two biggest long-term credit banks with the Industrial Bank of Japan (IBJ) at the zenith. Great prestige is attached to loans received from the IBJ, and Japan's leading corporations are among its clients. The long-term credit banks are followed by the five biggest city banks, led by Sumitomo and followed by the two heirs to the unshakable zaibatsu heritage: Fuji and Mitsubishi. The trust banks fall below the city banks and, again, the familiar zaibatsu names (Mitsubishi, Sumitomo, Yasuda, Mitsui) are the most eminent.

The 64 regional banks, often based in small cities, confine their operations to local lending and do not function on a national basis. Below the regional banks are the 69 **sogo banks** which are termed "mutual savings and loan banks," by the government. Whereas the regional banks usually conduct business throughout a prefecture (or several prefectures), the sogo banks specialize their lending activities within a single metropolitan or rural sector. The sogo banks carry far less status (for borrowers and employees) than the regional banks. Beneath the sogo banks are the more than 450 credit associations or **shinkin banks (*shinyo kinko*)**, which range in size from the enormous Jonan Shinyo Kinko, with dozens of branches and deposits that exceed the assets of many sogo banks, to tiny credit units with only two or three branches and a handful of employees. The smallest banking units in Japan are the credit cooperatives (**shinyo kumiai**). The aggregate assets of the 480 credit cooperatives are far less than the assets of any one of the top city banks. Each credit cooperative is supported by small local businesses which provide it with deposits and are recipients of its loans.

Cutting across this classificatory scheme are three enormous institutions which act as the central banks for cooperatives and the credit associations. The biggest, the Norinchukin Bank, is the recipient of deposits from all the agricultural and fishery cooperatives in Japan. This has made it one of the 10 largest banks in the world. The Shoko Chukin Bank does much the same for small business cooperatives and the Zenshinren Bank is the terminus for the holdings of credit associations. Traditionally, these three giant specialists only accepted deposits and extended loans to their members. During the past decade, however, they have followed the nation into a growing participation in international financial networks. During the next 15 years, the three will either shed their provincialism or be eliminated as obsolete.

In Japan, the regulations that have promoted and protected financial segmentation are gradually being demolished. Before the end of this century, the system will be thoroughly transformed. At the time of writing, there are already clear indications that the commercial banks, for example, will be authorized to issue convertible bonds and to sell "housing loan mortgage investment trusts." These new freedoms would serve to undermine the protected province of the long-term credit banks (and the specialized institutions) which have taken for granted their unique right to issue long-term securities. Meanwhile, the long-term credit banks, faced with declining lending opportunities and shrinking spreads, are becoming investment banks. Thus, without specific legislation, the divisions separating the various types of bank will cease to exist and Japanese banks will be redefined.

Throughout most of Japan's history, capital has been in short supply. Banks, the traditional suppliers of capital, have been in relationships of superiority to corporations, the customary borrowers. In the 1970s, this relationship of superiority-inferiority, giver-receiver began to change. Many of the corporations that grew to enormous proportions in the postwar era (such as Sony, Matsushita Electrical, Nippon Gakki, or Shiseido) have had little need for indirect financing. Others have gradually moved away from the tight bonds that linked them with a single keiretsu bank. Many corporations borrow from banks for the sole purpose of maintaining a relationship which has historical value and could, given an unexpected change in economic fundamentals, be valuable again.

During the 1980s, the growth of the Euromarkets conjoined with domestic regulatory changes enabled corporations to issue debt in overseas markets at a cost far below bank loans. Thus, Japan became part of the global trend which has seen an increasing disintermediation of funds in favor of the securitization of debt.

The Big Four securities companies have made a concerted effort to encourage Japanese corporations to raise money in the Euromarkets. Motivated by the desire to seize a major share of Euromarket bookrunning (see Chapter 6), the securities companies were also driven by the desire to sever the ties between corporations and the city banks. The major city banks, in response, have been waging a war of their own. They are determined to demolish Article 65 (see Chapter 2) and use their domestic and international networks to participate *fully* in the securities industry. Indeed, the city banks are already planning to join the trust banks and foreign banks in the discount brokerage business.

Concurrent with these developments, falling domestic interest rates saw the return on government bonds in early 1987 reach the lowest level since the Russo-Japanese war of 1905. At the same time, the impending elimination of tax free savings accounts led to changes in the domestic deployment of investable funds. As a result, Japanese institutional and individual investors have moved away from savings accounts to the debentures of the long-term credit banks, to foreign-currency-denominated bonds, and to the equity markets. Of course, the traditional banking activity of raising funds through deposits and lending the funds at a healthy spread to corporations has not become defunct. However, the long-term future promises a reformulation of the term *banking* in Japanese finance and the emergence of new all-purpose Japanese banks resembling the universal banks of Switzerland and Germany.

COMMERCIAL BANKING

Structure and Stability

In 1986, 138 insolvent U.S. banks, 26 in Texas alone, were liquidated or merged with healthy institutions. This was not the first recent spate of record incidences of American banking insolvencies. In 1984 and 1985, the numbers of annual bank failures were also exceptional, and in 1987 more than 150 banks are expected to become insolvent. By contrast, Japan had one bank failure in 1986 (discussed below). The result of massive, long-term corruption, this was the first banking insolvency in Japan since World War II.[1] Japan's Deposit Insurance Corporation (DIC) has never been obliged to spend money. By contrast, in

---

[1] In 1978, a bank run nearly forced the Taiko Sogo Bank into insolvency. The bank was rescued, however, by a capital infusion from the city banks at the behest of the Bank of Japan. The Bank of Japan maintained the policy of intervention in the event of an imminent bank failure. This policy has been modified recently and banks have been informed that they can no longer expect central bank rescue in the event of a liquidity crisis. Simultaneously, the

1986 alone, the U.S. Federal Deposit Insurance Corporation (FDIC) paid $2.8 billion to reimburse depositors for lost funds.

The Japanese commercial banking system is historically and structurally different from its U.S. counterpart. The differences have resulted in a smaller number of banking institutions operating in a more regulated and protected financial environment. If bank failures are perceived as an indicator of pathology, then Japan's commercial banking system is healthier than the U.S. system. Proponents of open market competition, however, may interpret the situation in accordance with their own theories. Japanese regulators have been satisfied with the domestic banking structure and only recently and reluctantly have succumbed to the demands of deregulation.

Commercial banks in Japan are classified by the Bank of Japan into three distinct types: city banks, regional banks, and foreign banks. The city banks are big money center banks based in major cities and have traditionally functioned as the primary source of funds for Japanese industrial development. Included in this category is the Bank of Tokyo which is a "specialized foreign exchange bank." Regional banks, scattered throughout Japan, have not suffered from the chronic cash deficiencies of the city banks. As a result, they have been smaller borrowers from the central bank and have usually been lenders in the interbank market. Foreign banks, never major players in Japan's commercial banking world, have multiplied and expanded during the 1980s.

Although several of the big Japanese commercial banks have ancient antecedents, the five biggest banks (as commercial banks) are less than 100 years old. Dai Ichi (predecessor of Dai Ichi Kangyo) was founded in 1872 as the First National Bank. The big zaibatsu banks, Mitsui (1876), Yasuda (1880), Mitsubishi (1893), and Sumitomo (1895) all date from the late nineteenth century. In 1910, these five banks held 20 percent of the deposits of all commercial banks in Japan,[2] while the aggregate deposits of all the commercial banks represented 72.8 percent of

---

Deposit Insurance Corporation (DIC) has been given broader powers to arrange mergers. In addition, the DIC's protection of individual accounts was raised from ¥3 million to ¥10 million—about two-thirds the $100,000 of insurance protection guaranteed by the U.S. FDIC.

[2]Raymond W. Goldsmith, *The Financial Development of Japan, 1868–1977*, p. 49.

the nation's deposits.[3] During the course of the twentieth century, the weight of bank deposits gradually shifted from the commercial banks to the cooperatives and their central banks (Norinchukin and Shoko Chukin). By 1980, commercial banks and cooperatives held nearly equal shares of Japan's total deposits.[4]

Between 1930 and 1944, the Japanese government undertook a process of concentration in which it induced bank closings and mergers. From 700 commercial banks in 1931, the number declined to 400 in 1936, and fell below 200 in 1941. By the end of World War II, there were 72 commercial banks in Japan.[5] This process resulted in a massive strengthening of zaibatsu banking power which was later forced underground and weakened (but not obliterated) during the Occupation.

The city banks can be divided into two distinctive groups:

Old Keiretsu Banks. Sumitomo Bank, Mitsui Bank, and Mitsubishi Bank are the contemporary incarnations of the "Big Three" zaibatsu banks which virtually controlled Japanese industrial development prior to the second World War. Fuji Bank was the main bank of the smaller Yasuda zaibatsu. Dai-Ichi Kangyo Bank is a marginal member of this category. Dai-Ichi Bank was the main bank of the Dai-Ichi zaibatsu. In 1971, Dai-Ichi merged with the Kangyo Bank, a government financial institution for short-term lending for agricultural and real estate development.

New Keiretsu Banks. The bank mergers that were engineered by the wartime government resulted in the creation of a small number of large city-based banks. The biggest, Sanwa (which means triple *wa* or triple harmony), was formed in 1933 from the amalgamation of three banks. Similarly, Tokai Bank was the result of the merger of three banks in 1941. During the postwar period, these banks established relationships with corporations in zaibatsu-like arrangements of cross-shareholding —the bank-centered keiretsu.

---

[3]This figure includes bank debentures. See Eisuke Sakakibara and Yoriyuki Nagao, eds., *Study on the Tokyo Capital Markets*, p. 6.

[4]*Ibid.*

[5]Goldsmith, p. 119.

The new bank groups are not as cohesive as the old keiretsu networks because the relationships (based on interlinked cross-shareholding and unwritten obligation) among the group companies are recent and incidental creations. Whereas the members of an old keiretsu often share a zaibatsu name and have inherited a concatenation of commitments and interdependencies, the members of new bank groups share only a common relationship with a main bank and some stock ownership.

In 1986, although no longer as proportionately rich in assets as they once were, the contemporary versions of the zaibatsu banks continued to exercise exceptional power within Japan's corporate and financial establishment. Each of the former zaibatsu banks today directs the lion's share of its lending to keiretsu affiliates, particularly the trading companies. Many of these companies have accumulated substantial cash surpluses and no longer depend upon their main banks for funding. Instead, they borrow in order to maintain relationships and the banks in turn are forced to lend at cut-rates.

In Japan, banks traditionally have been the primary provider of industrial funds for plant and equipment. Indeed, Japanese banks were so powerful in the domestic market that prior to the first oil shock of 1973, Japan was referred to as the "Bankers' Kingdom."[6] Although this epithet has fallen by the wayside, today less than 23 percent of Japan's funds for capital investment are derived from the securities markets. In any case, if aggressive city banks such as Sumitomo and Fuji have their way, not only Japan but the entire industrial world will someday be *their* kingdom for all financial services, including investment banking.

City Banks

The city banks have their headquarters in major cities and use their networks of branch offices to conduct banking business throughout Japan. The 13 city banks include the 4 largest commercial banks in the world, while 4 other city banks rank among the world's 25 biggest banks (see Table 7–1).

The city banks rely far more on the interbank market for lending and deposit taking than do U.S. or European commer-

---

[6] Roy Hofheinz, Jr. and Kent E. Calder, *The East Asia Edge*, p. 127.

TABLE 7–1 Global Ranking of City Banks*

World Rank		Head-quarters	Deposits 9/30/85 ($ millions)
1	Dai-Ichi Kangyo Bank, Ltd.	Tokyo	124,646
2	Fuji Bank, Ltd.	Tokyo	109,736
3	Sumitomo Bank, Ltd.	Osaka	108,531
4	Mitsubishi Bank, Ltd.	Tokyo	102,813
6	Sanwa Bank, Ltd.	Osaka	99,051
18	Tokai Bank, Ltd.	Nagoya	73,969
20	Mitsui Bank, Ltd.	Tokyo	71,462
24	Bank of Tokyo, Ltd.	Tokyo	62,439
29	Taiyo Kobe Bank, Ltd.	Kobe	58,550
31	Daiwa Bank, Ltd.	Osaka	57,948
51	Kyowa Bank, Ltd.	Tokyo	39,167
55	Saitama Bank	Urawa	36,761
72	Hokkaido Takushoku Bank, Ltd.	Sapporo	28,262

---

*Ranked by deposits on September 30, 1985, by the *American Banker*, July 29, 1986, p. 54.

cial banks. As the result of successive cuts in the discount rate in 1986, the city banks significantly increased their funding from short-term instruments in the interbank and "open" markets. An estimated 70 percent of all funds raised during the first half of fiscal 1986 were derived from the money markets. The easy credit of 1986 led to a decrease in the cost of funding which exceeded cuts in lending rates. This in turn enabled the city banks to achieve record profits during the six months ending September 30, 1986. Combined operating profits for the 13 banks rose 42.4 percent from the preceding six months.

The city banks have recognized that the asset-based loan products which they have provided since the early Meiji era are rapidly becoming obsolete as a major source of income. As a result, they have begun to seek growth through innovations. New types of loans and new client bases are being developed. Skills in international operations, which had formerly been a minor segment of banking structure, are now regarded as the key to future survival. Transaction oriented activities, especially those that generate commissions, are viewed as potentially the most lucrative areas of commercial banking. All of the banks are expanding their foreign exchange operations and are training staff in affiliated securities companies for future securities dealing and sales.

TABLE 7–2 Banking International Assets and Liabilities by Nationality*

Nation	Assets ($ billions)	Liabilities ($ billions)
Japan	639.6	621.5
United States	580.3	545.6
France	221.0	207.8
United Kingdom	182.5	181.5
Germany	164.9	142.8

*As of September 30, 1985.
SOURCE: Bank for International Settlements.

Overseas Business and Acquisitions

International Lending. Although traditionally domestically oriented institutions, the city banks have been swiftly expanding their international business during the 1980s. In fiscal 1985, for example, the 13 banks exceeded U.S. and U.K. banking institutions in terms of the volume of international lending (see Table 7–2).[7] Indeed, Tokyo has replaced London as the leader in Eurocurrency *loan* transactions. As the result of the sharp appreciation of the yen which occurred between 1985 and 1986, the banks' reserves for overseas loan losses were drawn. Simultaneously, the city banks seized a major portion of the burgeoning domestic credit flows being intermediated in the international financial markets.

Global cross-border lending by banks rose steadily during 1986, largely as a result of increased lending in the interbank market by Japanese city banks. Although Japanese banks just barely surpassed the United States to become the world's leading international bankers in 1985 (see Table 7–2), in 1986 Japan's city banks established an unequivocal dominance. According to the Bank for International Settlements, foreign lending by Japanese banks reached $1.02 trillion at the end of September 1986, representing 31.6 percent of all international loans extended by banks in the major industrial countries. (By

---

[7]Statistics for Japan include the three long-term credit banks.

TABLE 7–3 Equity-to-Assets Ratios
of the Thirteen City Banks
(at the end of March 1986)

Institution	Equity-to-Assets Ratio
Dai-Ichi Kangyo Bank	2.04
Fuji Bank	2.56
Sumitomo Bank	2.62
Mitsubishi Bank	2.43
Sanwa Bank	2.26
Tokai Bank	2.09
Mitsui Bank	2.07
Taiyo Kobe Bank	2.02
Bank of Tokyo	2.57
Daiwa Bank	1.51
Kyowa Bank	2.02
Saitama Bank	2.31
Hokkaido Takushoku Bank	1.98

SOURCE: Ministry of Finance

contrast, the comparable statistics for the U.S. were $601 million and 18.6 percent, respectively.)

There are two reasons for emerging Japanese strength in international banking:

1. *High levels of liquidity in Japan*, resulting from the nation's enormous trade and current account surpluses, have helped the city banks to aggressively increase international lending activities.

2. *Relatively low equity-to-assets requirements* have enabled the city banks to provide cheap loans in the global markets. In this way, Japanese banks have been able to undercut other money center institutions. The average equity-to-asset ratio for the city banks was 2.19 percent at the end of March 1986 (see Table 7–3); this compares with ratios of 5 to 6 percent for U.S. banks. The 1954 Banking Act required a capital-to-asset ratio of 10 percent; however, this level was considered absurdly high by the banks and was ignored.

In 1986, the Ministry of Finance announced new guidelines requiring *all* banks to establish equity-to-asset ratios of 4 percent or more by 1989.[8] The across-the-board improvement in capital adequacy ratios will be easily achieved through the sale of recently authorized *new* products (such as mortgage trusts, subordinated notes, and convertible bonds) and the inevitable decrease in corporate lending. Thus, as an indirect result of forced improvements in capital adequacy, banks have been authorized to sell types of securities that a short time ago would have been rendered taboo by Article 65.

Overseas Branches and Subsidiaries. During the early 1980s, the five major city banks and the Bank of Tokyo invested substantially in the expansion of their overseas retail banking operations. Dai-Ichi Kangyo, for example, spent billions of yen to invest in portions of banks in the United Kingdom, Hong Kong, Singapore, and Australia. The Bank of Tokyo has major branches in Australia (unprofitable) and Canada (profitable) as well as better known operations in North America and Europe. All of the major city banks set up international financial subsidiaries in London and Switzerland in order to participate fully in the Euromarkets. Meanwhile, a handful of Japanese banking institutions have made major purchases in the United States and Europe. These investments are briefly surveyed below.

Nearly all Japanese commercial banks with operations in the United States have used California as their home state (see Table 7–4). This is to be expected. Although New York is North America's center for international banking, Japan is California's biggest trading partner. California imports about $27 billion of goods from Japan annually while Japan imports roughly $7 billion per year (including $1 billion of agricultural products) from California. By far the richest state in the United States, California, if it were an independent nation, would have the seventh largest economy in the world. Japanese banks in California serve the more than 1,000 Japanese corporations with California subsidiaries as well as the state's substantial

---

[8]The denominator in the calculation of the ratio of shareholders' equity to assets was changed by the Ministry of Finance from total assets to deposits plus CDs. Beginning in fiscal 1987, the overseas branches of the city banks will be required to maintain equity-to-asset ratios of 6 percent.

TABLE 7–4 Japanese Affiliated Banks in California*

Bank	Assets* ($ millions)
California First Bank	5,002
Sumitomo Bank of California	2,752
Mitsui Manufacturers Bank	1,780
Golden State Sanwa Bank	1,405
Mitsubishi Bank of California	909
Tokai Bank of California	401
Dai-Ichi Kangyo Bank of California	202
Kyowa Bank of California	89

*December 31, 1984.
SOURCE: Nihon Keizai Shimbun

Japanese population. At the same time, they have the potential to become increasingly involved in the state's massive trade with Japan.

Five of the 11 largest California banks are Japanese owned. For example, California First Bank is owned by the Bank of Tokyo. Similarly, BanCal Tri-State Corporation, the parent company of the Bank of California, the state's oldest bank, was purchased by Mitsubishi Bank in 1983 at a cost of $282 million. With branches in Oregon and Washington, as well as a representative office in Taiwan, BanCal served to broaden Mitsubishi's international banking operations.

In 1986, Sanwa Bank, the fifth largest bank in Japan and the sixth largest bank in the world, bought Lloyds Bank California (a unit of London-based Lloyds Bank (PLC) for $263 million. The acquisition was merged with Sanwa's California bank, Golden State Sanwa Bank, making it the sixth largest bank in California. This was not Sanwa's first U.S. acquisition. In 1985, the bank bought Continental Illinois's leasing subsidiary, the 13th largest leasing unit in the United States, for $50 million. Now the major component of Sanwa Business Credit Corporation, this was the first Japanese purchase of a U.S. leasing operation.

The biggest spender in the American financial market is Fuji bank which, in 1984, outbid Security Pacific National Bank and paid $425 million for two finance subsidiaries of Walter E.

Heller International.[9] In this way, Fuji hoped to provide a majority of Japanese corporations in the United States with leasing and factoring services. At the time of purchase, the two units had aggregate nonperforming debts of $400 million. In 1986, Fuji Bank added $300 million in equity to Heller International Corporation, bringing its total investment to $725 million.

Two years after Fuji Bank's initial investment, Sumitomo, which had been approached by Heller International and turned down the overture to buy the expensive units, invested $500 million in a 12.5 percent share of the prestigious New York investment bank, Goldman Sachs. Sumitomo's bid to enter the ranks of international investment banking is discussed in the section below.

Purchases such as these, which received little publicity in the U.S. press, were just a segment of a general Japanese international banking strategy to establish a network of retail banking and other services in the United States. Although U.S. money center banks are easy to buy, Japan's city banks have generally found them far too expensive and there have been few purchases. Furthermore, many of the acquisitions have resulted in unanticipated problems. For example, the Mitsubishi-owned Bank of California lost money in 1984 and only marginally moved into the black the following year as the result of write-offs. Similarly, Fuji Bank has experienced substantial losses in its Walter Heller subsidiaries and is not likely to make the units more than marginally profitable for several years.[10] It is noteworthy that Sumitomo Bank, perhaps Japan's most farsighted banking institution, has not purchased a U.S. commercial bank or bank affiliate.

While buying U.S. institutions, the leading city banks have set up overseas subsidiaries to participate in the Euromarket

---

[9] Heller International Corporation (a holding company created by Fuji bank) acquired Walter E. Heller & Co. (renamed Heller Financial Inc.) and Walter E. Heller Overseas Corporation from Chicago-based Walter E. Heller International in January 1984. Heller Financial Inc. is the core unit and handles U.S. domestic commercial banking business under the management of the Fuji Bank–controlled holding company (Heller International Corp.).

[10] The net loss in 1984 was $182 million and the net loss in 1985 was $32 million.

and generate profits from zaitek (see Chapter 9). Fuji Bank, for instance, created Fuji International Finance in London which is devoted to Euromarket trading, Fuji Bank (Schweiz) to cover the Swiss capital markets, and Hong Kong-based Fuji International Finance to participate in Pacific Basin markets. Like the trading companies and some other blue chip corporations, Fuji is now scouting the world for opportunities to produce revenue from arbitrage.

While U.S. banks were intensely involved in buying London stockbrokers in anticipation of Big Bang (October 27, 1986), no Japanese banks made a move in that acquisition area. Not surprisingly, the Ministry of Finance issued a warning forbidding domestic banks from making such a direct and blatant entry into full-scale brokerage activities. Nevertheless, although Article 65 prohibits banks from participating in the securities industry, it does not apply to the overseas activities of banking institutions. Therefore, the major city banks have used their overseas subsidiaries as one means to learn about the securities business while simultaneously participating in and profiting from as wide a variety of undertakings as possible. This is what social anthropologists term *participant observation.* No Japanese bank has observed and participated in "nonbanking" business more than Sumitomo. For this reason, Sumitomo's strategies are discussed in detail below.

The Case of Sumitomo Bank

In June 1976, the Canadian refinery, Newfoundland Refining Company, declared bankruptcy. This event distressed executives at Ataka America, the U.S. subsidiary of Ataka & Co., Japan's tenth largest trading firm (**sogo shosha**). The occurrence also disturbed Shozo Hotta, president of Sumitomo Bank, and, at that time, one of the most influential figures in Japan's financial world.

Ataka & Co. had provided the Canadian refinery with nearly $1 billion of financing. By the time the dust had settled, uncollectible funds totalled $800 million. Although Ataka was merged with C. Itoh & Co. (Japan's fourth largest trading firm) in October 1977, Sumitomo, Ataka's main bank, was obliged to absorb the entire loss. Before the debacle, Sumitomo was the biggest and most profitable bank in Japan; afterward, it was the eighth largest bank—and far from the most profitable.

It is easy to note a superficial parallel between Sumitomo's plight and the severe losses and subsequent indebtedness that caused Yamaichi Securities Company to plunge from first to fourth place in the Japanese securities industry in 1965 (see Chapter 3). Sumitomo, however, unlike Yamaichi, spurned conservative policies and concentrated instead on profitability. A decade after the Ataka incident, Sumitomo had risen to third place among Japan's banks and for seven years had been the nation's most profitable banking institution. Indeed, Sumitomo Bank was the most profitable financial institution in Japan in 1979–83, until Nomura Securities Company seized the distinction in 1984.

Osaka-based Sumitomo Bank has long been the most tightly run of Japan's 13 city banks. After the end of the Occupation, Sumitomo organized a very close regrouping of its prewar zaibatsu, which in turn rendered the Sumitomo keiretsu more cohesive in the maintenance of relationships than any other keiretsu in Japan. As the "main bank" for such monolithic corporations as Sumitomo Chemical, Sumitomo Heavy Industries, Sumitomo Metal Industries, and Nippon Electric, as well as two dozen additional keiretsu firms, Sumitomo Bank became the most powerful banking institution in Asia during the postwar era.

An Osaka tradition, at least as old as the pretwentieth century Big Ten money lenders, has made Osaka financial institutions bluntly bottom-line oriented. Thus, Osaka bears a relationship to Tokyo that is somewhat analogous to Edinburgh's relationship to London. Sumitomo is generally regarded to be a typical Osaka firm, despite its wide Tokyo base of operations. In Tokyo banking, it is considered tactless to discuss business relationships in terms of profit and loss. Because relationships among entities are perceived as permanent, they are considered to transcend the more transient and mundane problems of changing financial conditions. Osaka institutions, unlike their Tokyo brethren, sometimes prefer the loss of a relationship to the loss of funds. Thus, it is not startling to observe that Sumitomo Bank has assessed, with considerable admiration, the ascendancy of New York-based Citicorp.

Ultimately, Sumitomo intends to mimic the successes of Citicorp, the parent holding company of Citibank, which is North America's biggest and most profitable banking institution. Citicorp has provided Sumitomo with an example which it has been striving to emulate. Becoming a global bank, transcending national frontiers, and offering the widest conceivable range of financial products to the broadest possible client base is Sumitomo's singular aspiration. Motivated by this goal, Sumitomo has spent years attempting to chip away at the stones supporting Article 65.

While lobbying at home with the Ministry of Finance, the Bank has attempted to build acquisitions into the giant lever that Archimedes once requested. Three unusual investments, a Swiss bank, a domestic mutual savings bank, and a partnership with a U.S. investment bank serve to illustrate Sumitomo's wide-ranging attempt to seek strength through acquisition and diversification. Each of these ventures is discussed briefly below.

Banca del Gottardo. In July 1984, Sumitomo bought a 52.7 percent interest in Banca del Gottardo from the liquidators of Banco Ambrosiano's Luxembourg subsidiary (the Swiss bank was a big fragment of Banco Ambrosiano's crumbling financial empire). The price tag ($144 million) for the Lugano-based bank was the highest ever paid for a European corporate acquisition by a Japanese company.

By means of a judicious and diplomatic management style, Sumitomo succeeded in retaining Banca del Gottardo's staff. The number of Japanese directors and managers assigned to the acquisition was kept to a minimum and their roles constrained. The Swiss bank was allowed to retain considerable independence. Sumitomo carefully positioned the Swiss bank between Zug-based Sumitomo Finance International on the one hand and Sumitomo's Tokyo-based international banking department on the other hand. Between 1984 and 1986, Banca del Gottardo rose from being one of the smaller Swiss banks (ranked about 20th) to the bottom of the top ten. In Euroyen bond underwriting, the bank rates fourth in Switzerland, after the Big Three Swiss banks.

By convincing the Ministry of Finance that its 52 percent ownership in Banca del Gottardo does not make the bank a domestic financial institution, the Sumitomo-controlled bank has set up a representative office in Tokyo which is classified as a foreign (Swiss) bank. Banca del Gottardo is a member of the permanent syndicates in the Swiss underwriting market and has lead managed many issues floated by Japanese firms in the Euromarket. Under Sumitomo's auspices, the Swiss bank has become increasingly involved in underwriting Japanese corporate business, a legitimate banking activity in Switzerland (where universal banking laws prevail) but one which is proscribed by Article 65 in Japan. In this way, Sumitomo wants to become increasingly involved in domestic underwriting activities.

Heiwa Sogo Bank. Heiwa Sogo Bank was the seventh largest sogo bank (mutual savings and loan institution) in Japan and ranked 264th among the world's top 500 banks at the end of September 1985 (see Table 7–11). The bank's 101 branches, many located near train stations, were open unusually long hours (until 7:00 P.M.) and attracted blue collar deposits. Throughout most of its existence it was a one-man bank, directed and manipulated by its founder, Eizo Komiyama, who died in 1979.

During a government investigation, which began after Komiyama's death and culminated in the closing of the institution seven years later, a complex web of inside fraud was uncovered. The machinations of bank employees included the creation of dummy corporations which accepted bank loans without collateral, unbooked "loans," as well as hefty political contributions. That the Ministry of Finance began examining Heiwa Sogo in 1979 and yet announced no problems with the institution could perhaps correlate with these contributions. When the story broke in 1986, Heiwa Sogo promised to be Japan's first bank failure in half a century and its biggest banking scandal.

No sooner had the Ministry of Finance prepared a list of possible merger partners for Heiwa Sogo than Sumitomo volunteered to absorb the insolvent institution. In so doing, it precluded its idol, Citicorp, from pursuing strong acquisitive designs of its own and beat all other city banks to the mark. Indeed, *before* the news regarding Heiwa's insolvency had become public, Sumitomo Bank had already acquired (through its subsidiaries) 34 percent of Heiwa Sogo stock. Sumitomo had four vested interests in acquiring Heiwa Sogo:

1. *Branch network.* A bank must receive special Ministry of Finance authorization to open new bank branches in Japan (with seldom more than one branch per bank per year approved). Such permission, never easily obtained, is contingent upon a host of qualifying factors. Prior to the merger, Sumitomo Bank had 241 branches in Japan. By adding most of the 101 Heiwa Sogo branches to its existing network, the Bank would have more branches than any other city bank in Japan with the exception of Dai-Ichi Kangyo Bank (356 branches) and Taiyo Kobe Bank (353). In addition, many Heiwa Sogo branches are located in areas where Sumitomo has traditionally been weakly represented (such as adjacent to Tokyo railroad stations). Thus, the merger enabled Sumitomo to leapfrog over regulatory constraints and instantly strengthen its Tokyo branch network.

2. *Deposits.* By adding Heiwa Sogo deposits to its own, Sumitomo would have ¥23.56 trillion yen,[11] making it the second largest commercial bank in Japan (and in the world), trailing Dai-Ichi Kangyo Bank by just ¥3 trillion ($18.7 billion). Heiwa Sogo holds many small passbook deposit accounts which, because of the decline in indirect financing, have become a vital source of income for Japan's city banks. Furthermore, the vast majority of the Heiwa Sogo accounts are those to which salary payments are directly deposited by employers.

3. *Clients.* Sumitomo Bank, like the other great zaibatsu bank, Mitsubishi, is a premier lender to large capitalized blue chip domestic companies. For a variety of reasons (discussed elsewhere) lending to big companies has been in decline while lending to small- and medium-capital-

---

[11] Using asset figures for September 30, 1985, derived from the *American Banker*, July 29, 1986, p. 54.

ized firms has become increasingly vital to banking profitability. Loans to small- and medium-capitalized companies represented more than 50 percent of the total lending by city banks in 1986. These loans have margins of from 50 to 100 basis points higher than the loans to major corporations. Since its creation, during the period of postwar recovery, Heiwa Sogo had specialized in small business lending. The insolvent bank's clients will provide a valuable source of income for Sumitomo and will make the city bank one of the major lenders in Japan to small businesses.

4. *Securities business.* Meiko Securities Company, an affiliate (see Chapter 2) of Sumitomo Bank, can buy (with loans extended by the bank) some of the Heiwa branches that are redundant to Sumitomo business. In this way, Sumitomo can promote its interests in the securities industry by expanding Meiko's retail operations in the Tokyo metropolitan area.

In March 1986, Sumitomo Bank signed a merger agreement with Heiwa Sogo to become effective October 1, 1986. The terms of the agreement, which have not been made public, involve an exchange of equity which give the merger a paper cost rumored to be ¥100 billion.

Sumitomo was regarded by the government as a white knight slaying disaster during Japan's first banking crisis of modern times. The Bank of Japan promised to provide emergency loans at the official discount rate. The Ministry of Finance agreed to permit all former Heiwa Sogo branches to continue closing at the late hour of 7 P.M., although other banks are required to maintain normal banking hours (closing at 3 P.M.).

Meanwhile, the white knight will be obliged to shoulder the burden of nearly all of the Heiwa Sogo uncollectible loans, estimated at ¥170 billion ($1.1 billion). At first glance, this may seem to be a high price to pay for some branches and clients or an extra ¥1.255 trillion in deposits. However, the price tag involves an unmarked discount. The Ministry of Finance authorized Sumitomo to sell all Heiwa branches sharing business areas with existing Sumitomo branches. During 1987–88, Sumitomo Bank will sell about 20 Heiwa Sogo branches which will yield an éstimated revenue of at least ¥100 billion ($625 million). This will effectively reduce total acquisition costs.

Goldman Sachs and Co. At the time of writing, Sumitomo's purchase of a one-eighth interest in privately held Goldman Sachs and Co. stands as the most daring effort by a Japanese bank to share in the profits of global investment banking. With the official expectation of becoming a limited (nonvoting) partner in Goldman Sachs, Sumitomo arranged to exchange $500 million for a maximum 12.5 percent share of the Wall Street firm's pretax income from the end of 1988.

The U.S. Glass-Steagall Act, along with the Bank Holding Company Act, established the still rigid separation between commercial and investment banking in the United States. This forced Sumitomo to insist upon its limited involvement with Goldman. At the same time, Article 65 prohibits Japanese banks from owning more than 5 percent of a domestic securities company. Because Goldman Sachs is a member of the Tokyo Stock Exchange (see Chapter 2), the size of the Sumitomo stake was of particular concern to the Ministry of Finance in Tokyo. By insisting that it would be only a silent partner, merely sharing in profits, Sumitomo hoped to forestall Japanese and U.S. government opposition to the deal. In November 1986, the U.S. Federal Reserve Board provided only a conditional approval of the tie-up. The Fed's authorization set a 24.9 percent limit on Sumitomo's combined present and future investments in the U.S. investment bank, and prohibited any Sumitomo acquisition of equity in Goldman Sachs affiliates. These conditions took Sumitomo by surprise and forced the bank to abandon plans to set up a London joint venture with Goldman.[12]

From the perspective of Goldman Sachs, the deal with Sumitomo was a superb method of raising capital without going public. After all, despite its ownership, Sumitomo will have no voting rights and no representation on the Goldman Sachs management committee. The U.S. firm will benefit immediately

---

[12]Sumitomo Bank had planned to convert the London branch of Sumitomo International Finance AG (the Zug-based securities unit of Sumitomo) into a joint venture company owned equally by Goldman Sachs and Sumitomo Bank.

from the substantial cash infusion and is expected to build up greater securities trading positions and finance new activities in the Euromarket and Tokyo. Meanwhile, Sumitomo will direct Japanese corporate business to Goldman. In three to five years, when city banks are authorized to manage pension funds, Sumitomo will probably channel substantial assets to Goldman Sachs for management.

How Sumitomo will benefit from its deal with Goldman Sachs is unclear. It is possible that the exceptional profitability of Goldman Sachs will reward Sumitomo handsomely, providing a better annual return than could be obtained from U.S. Treasury investments. Of course, Sumitomo hopes to compete more successfully with the Big Four and the Industrial Bank of Japan in the U.S. Treasury market and Goldman could be of considerable assistance. Also of importance will be Sumitomo's opportunity to learn the investment banking business from a leader of the field. This will be a far more valuable source of training than seconding bank employees to affiliated third-tier securities firms,[13] such as Meiko Securities Company. Nonetheless, $500 million is a high price to pay for education. In any case, Sumitomo had already created (in 1985) a joint venture with Bankers Trust to establish an investment advisory company which would provide training for Sumitomo employees.

None of the discernible advantages serve to justify the risk of investing a massive block of capital in a tie-up venture that precludes control. It is most likely, therefore, that Sumitomo is building a road for a vehicle that has not yet been invented. There can be little doubt that the Bank had intended to eventually increase its stake in Goldman with, pehaps, the long-term intention of merging the U.S. firm with Sumitomo's international banking organization. This plan required the demise of Glass-Steagall and the development of universal banking in the United States. A future vision of this magnitude cannot be damaged by short-term regulatory interference. Meanwhile, Goldman Sachs has the option of dissolving the partnership after 10 years.

Through acquisition (Banca del Gottardo), merger (Heiwa

---

[13]Sumitomo cannot send trainees to Goldman Sachs without specific Fed authorization.

Sogo), and limited partnership (Goldman Sachs), Sumitomo Bank has attempted to magnify its domestic and international base of operations. By challenging Dai-Ichi Kangyo as Japan's biggest deposit-taking institution, Sumitomo has demonstrated the ambition to become the world's biggest retail banker. By investing in Goldman Sachs, Sumitomo has made a major commitment to merchant banking as well. The purchase of the Swiss universal bank demonstrates Sumitomo's determination to be on the leading edge of the securitization of international banking. Indeed, each of the three deals discussed above served to expand Sumitomo's potential to engage in the securities industry.

No Japanese institution, not even Nomura Securities Company, has developed such a comprehensive strategy for the realization of a vision. Sumitomo envisions itself as the world's biggest and most successful all-service financial institution. Certain that restrictive laws will be repealed, Sumitomo is planning now for the legal and institutional changes that will occur in the 1990s.

City Bank Share Price Manipulation?

The mysterious rise in the share prices of the big five city banks provides an outstanding example of the unpredictably sudden jumps in share prices that can occur with the collusion of securities firms and their brokers (see Chapter 3). For many years, all of the city bank stocks were thinly traded and their prices remained within a narrow zone. In December 1983, most bank shares were valued in the ¥500 range. However, by March 30, 1984, the share prices of the top five city banks had risen by at least 100 percent: Sumitomo was the highest at ¥1,220, followed by Fuji Bank at ¥994, Mitsubishi Bank at ¥930, Sanwa Bank at ¥926, and Dai-Ichi Kangyo Bank at ¥865. This share price scale almost exactly mirrored the pattern of the banks' comparative profitability.

One obvious and direct effect of the share price growth was a sharp rise in the banks' capitalization. This rendered the bank shares eligible for margin trading, which in turn increased speculative buying, ultimately boosting the share prices higher.

In July and August 1985, Sumitomo Bank shares reached a

FIGURE 7–1   The Rise of Sumitomo Bank Share Price

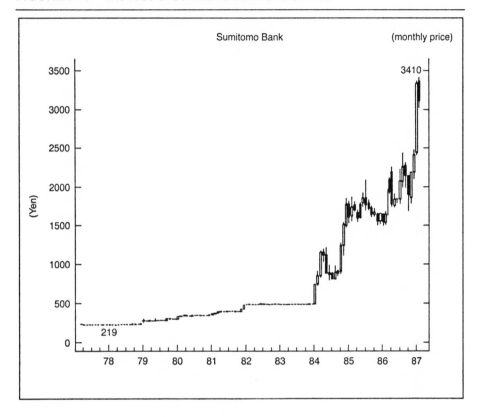

high for the year of ¥2,150, Dai-Ichi Kangyo rose to ¥1,900, Fuji Bank peaked at ¥1,850, Mitsubishi Bank at ¥1,800, and Sanwa Bank at ¥1,720—triple to quadruple the stable range that had prevailed for many years. By early 1987, Sumitomo shares were priced at ¥3,000 (a sixfold increase over the 1983 share price), representing a PER of 85.3 (see Figure 7–1), while Dai-Ichi Kangyo Bank shares were ¥2,510, resulting in a price-to-earnings multiple of 89.4

Several theories account for the rise. According to one version, summarized in a December 1984 article in the *Nihon Keizai Shimbun*, Nomura Securities Company informed Sumitomo Bank that its shares were underpriced and should be permitted to rise with market demand. Sumitomo authorities agreed and Nomura brokers began to promote sale of the shares. The value of Sumitomo rose from ¥500 in December 1983 to ¥1,220 within three months. During late 1985 and the first half of 1986, the share price remained in a stable trading zone of ¥1,550 – ¥1,750. At the same time, the prices of other major bank shares also rose dramatically as the Big Four securities firms used promotional hype to drive up sales.

Another version of the bank share phenomenon suggests that the Bank of Japan is responsible. According to this view, the Central Bank stated that the city banks were undercapitalized. The city banks responded in concord by raising capital in the equity market—not at first through an issue of new shares but rather through the marketing efforts of securities firms.

During 1984, bank stocks were in such demand that few portfolio managers (in Japan or abroad) were able to buy enough of them. As a direct result, the majority of capital management firms maintaining portfolios of Japanese equities significantly underperformed the Nikkei Stock Average in 1984 (see Figure 7–2). Meanwhile, the price earnings ratios of the city banks had risen to 45 to 60 times earnings.

It is interesting to note that primary offerings at market prices, initiated by Dai-Ichi Kangyo Bank, followed the increases in share values. The money raised through these stock offerings enabled the major banks to finance new systemwide computerization facilities costing each institution roughly ¥40 to ¥50 billion and also were employed to pay for costly overseas acquisitions.

Although the cause of the exceptional increase in the price of bank share stocks in 1984–85 remains an enigma, there can be no question that the Big Four securities firms aided and abetted the debacle through strategic planning, sales, and promotion. Whether the banks themselves, led by Sumitomo, initiated the maneuver in order to raise capital is unclear and will remain so.

The Bank of Tokyo

The Bank of Tokyo differs from the other city banks and in many respects it is not a city bank at all. However, it is classified as a city bank by the Bank of Japan and is generally regarded as a leading player in the commercial banking sector. The bank has the distinction of being the only major financial institution in

FIGURE 7–2   Bank Stock Price Index and Trading Volume

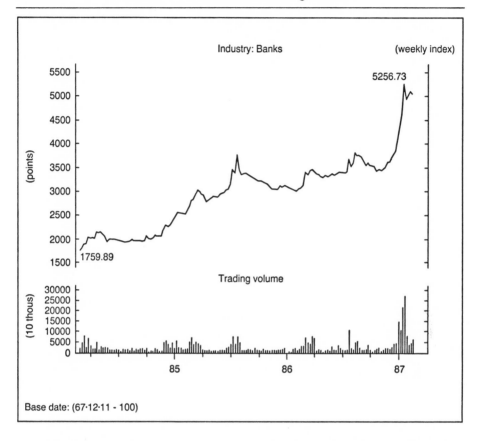

Japan that was not based on a Western model. Thus the close relationship between the bank and the government can be perceived as an indigenous and concrete expression of real relationships between Japan's financial and political worlds.

Formerly the Yokohama Specie Bank, the institution possessed a government monopoly on all foreign exchange trading from the beginning of the Meiji era until the end of World War II. Today the 17th largest bank in Japan and the 24th largest bank in the world, the Bank of Tokyo specializes in foreign trade financing and foreign exchange transactions. The bank earns more than 60 percent of its income from international financing through its extensive overseas branches and representative offices.

During the financial reorganization that occurred under the Occupation, the Yokohama Specie Bank was renamed the Bank of Tokyo and was converted from a government to a private sector institution. Nonetheless, the connections between the government and the bank remained unusually close and a disproportionately large percentage of government foreign reserves is still deposited there. Often the Bank of Japan intervenes in foreign exchange markets through the Bank of Tokyo. The Bank of Tokyo, in turn, uses its foreign branch network (roughly four times larger than any other city bank) to provide the government with vital financial intelligence.

Yusuke Kashiwagi (son of the former president of the Yokohama Specie Bank) was Vice Minister of Finance for International Affairs before becoming president and, subsequently, chairman of the Bank of Tokyo. It is interesting to note that Kashiwagi was instrumental in persuading the Ministry of Finance to establish an offshore banking market in Japan (see below). The intimate relationship between the Bank of Tokyo and the Ministry of Finance is illustrative of the tenuous demarcation between Japan's public and private sectors.

For many years, relying on its historical role and outstanding expertise, the Bank of Tokyo was the leading foreign exchange trader in Japan. In addition, the bank was the top lead manager of syndicated loans in 1985, acting as lead manager in 89 credits worth roughly $30 billion. During the first nine months of 1986, the bank lead managed 59, or 22.3 percent, of the 265 foreign currency bonds floated by domestic corporations. However, the ongoing deregulation of the Japanese financial markets has resulted in the steady erosion of the bank's preeminence and profits. In June 1986, the bank lost its AAA credit rating (reduced to AA1) from Moody's, the American credit rating agency. Although the primary reason for the credit change was the bank's loan portfolio, Moody's pointed out that the bank's limited relationships with small- and medium-sized domestic corporations constrained its future domestic business opportunities. Meanwhile, the bank's formerly unique specialization in trade financing is disappearing in the shadow of enormous domestic competition.

In order to expand domestic business, the Bank of Tokyo tied up with the Norinchukin Bank in 1985. In a comprehensive arrangement which involves cooperation in most areas of funding and client relationships, the banks claim that a complementary exchange of resources will make them more competitive with the city banks. In 1987, the Bank of Tokyo opened a wholly owned securities subsidiary in New York. Designed to specialize in trading U.S. Treasury issues, the new company, Bank of Tokyo Securities Inc., is intended to meet competition from the Big Four securities companies and the New York subsidiaries of the city banks.

Regional Banks

There are 64 regional banks in Japan, all devoted to domestic banking; 80 percent of these banks rank among the world's top 500. Nearly all are authorized foreign exchange banks. The large number of regional banks with their high levels of deposits makes them the second largest single type of banking institution in Japan, following the city banks and representing a little less than one-fourth of the entire banking sector's assets. At the end of March 1986, the 64 regional banks held deposits (including NCDs) of ¥96.797 trillion, about half the total deposits of the city banks (¥202.067 trillion—see Table 7–5).

The Bank of Yokohama, the Bank of Shizuoka, and the Hokuriku Bank maintain branches or representative offices outside Japan in order to service their domestic clients' overseas operations. However, the majority of the regional banks engage in very little international business. This domestic focus is now changing. The Bank of Yokohama, the biggest regional bank, already has 12 overseas representative offices in addition to 3 branches, several subsidiaries, and an investment bank based overseas. In Japan, the big always lead the way for the small. Beginning in 1983, more than 40 of the regional banks participated in several syndicated yen loans to the World Bank—lead managed by the Bank of Yokohama, of course. The establishment of a Tokyo Offshore Banking market in late 1986 promises to give the regional banks new opportunities to make headway in international, multicurrency banking business.

Unable to compete with the city banks' iron grip on blue chip

---

TABLE 7–5 World Rank and Assets of
Japan's Top 25 Regional Banks

World Rank		Assets* ($ millions)
71	Bank of Yokohama	28,476
96	Hokuriku Bank, Ltd.	18,191
101	Chiba Bank, Ltd.	17,006
107	Joyo Bank, Ltd.	16,303
108	Shizuoka Bank, Ltd.	16,167
114	Ashikaga Bank, Ltd.	15,193
120	Bank of Fukuoka, Ltd.	13,795
133	Bank of Hiroshima, Ltd.	12,542
135	Hachi juni Bank, Ltd.	12,399
149	Gunma Bank, Ltd.	11,160
160	Yamaguchi Bank, Ltd.	9,768
170	Chugoku Bank, Ltd.	9,099
171	Shichi jushichi Bank, Ltd.	9,015
177	Hokkaido Bank, Ltd.	8,753
180	Bank of Kyoto, Ltd.	8,665
181	Iyo Bank, Ltd.	8,651
185	Nanto Bank, Ltd.	8,421
186	Juroku Bank, Ltd.	8,403
191	Hyakujushi Bank, Ltd.	8,212
192	Daishi Bank, Ltd.	8,185
201	Shiga Bank, Ltd.	8,019
206	Suruga Bank, Ltd.	7,615
224	Hyakugo Bank, Ltd.	6,863
228	Kiyo Bank, Ltd.	6,699
232	Hokkoku Bank, Ltd.	6,497

---

*Ranked by deposits as of September 30, 1985, by
the *American Banker*, July 29, 1986, p. 54.

corporate lending, the regional banks specialize in lending to small local businesses and small- to medium-capitalized companies. Since late 1980, all of the automated cash machines (ATMs) provided by the local banks have been linked, resulting in a single national network.

Several of the regional banks, particularly the Bank of Yokohama, are almost as large as the smallest city banks. The Bank of Yokohama is a major lender to large corporations in the Yokohama region and could properly be classified as a city bank.

Unlike the city banks which are perpetually overloaded and

cash deficient, most of the regional banks are awash with deposits provided by individual depositors. As a result, the local banks are major providers of funds in the money markets. Many of those regional banks located in rural areas, however, have been suffering since the late 1970s from a growing loss of depositors resulting from high levels of rural to urban migration, which is concentrating a growing proportion of the total Japanese population in cities. Beginning in 1987, regional banks will be authorized to issue convertible debentures. The convertibles will supplement equity offerings and the issuance of overseas convertible bonds (allowed since 1985) as methods for fund raising.

Foreign Banks (Nontrust)

Prior to World War II, there were eight foreign banks operating full-service branches in Tokyo. During the initial years of the Occupation, these banks reopened and remained the only foreign banking institutions in Japan. Between 1950 and 1968, eight additional foreign banks established branches in Japan. Because the Ministry of Finance rejected nearly all applications from banks in North America and Europe, the foreign bank branches which appeared in Tokyo during the postwar period were primarily from the less-developed countries of Asia (Korea, India, Singapore, Thailand).

In 1968, yielding to strong international pressure, the Japanese government began to approve branch license applications from banks based in the industrialized nations. During the ensuing decade, 34 foreign banks joined the 16 already present in Tokyo. Nonetheless, the operations of the 50 foreign banks were severely constrained by special regulations which limited the types of business foreign bankers could conduct and the number of branches foreign banks could maintain (usually only one was permitted). Because foreign banks were not allowed to advertise, they could not compete with the domestic banks for deposits.

At the end of December 1986, there were 79 foreign commercial banks in Japan with a total of 113 branches. An additional 124 foreign banks maintained representative offices in Tokyo.

In early 1987, Merrill Lynch was granted a license to establish a bank (see Chapter 2). It will be the first securities firm to operate a banking subsidiary in Japan. The foreign banks constitute roughly 3 percent of the Japanese banking industry in terms of assets.

Most of the foreign banks in Japan have derived the bulk of their income from foreign exchange business. The lending business for the foreign banks has not been good and is not likely to improve significantly. As Table 7–6 indicates, foreign banks' share of domestic lending has been declining. The return on assets for most of the foreign banks has been plummeting for a decade and is now quite low. The average net return on assets for foreign banks in fiscal 1984, for example, was 0.11 percent.

This sad state of affairs was not always the case. During the halcyon years of the 1970s, the smaller number of foreign banks, led by the three biggest American institutions (Bank of America, First National City Bank of New York, and Chase Manhattan) shared a large demand for **impact loans** and a modest but profitable demand for yen loans. The high cost of oil and corporate expansion of plant and equipment to meet new production goals sent a horde of corporate borrowers to foreign institutions. The city banks, unable to provide foreign currency loans, often introduced their own clients to the foreign banks.

Foreign banks in Japan cannot easily procure long-term yen funding. Limited by regulations to accepting time deposits with maximum two-year maturities bearing interest rates determined by the government, the foreign banks are unable to develop a low cost deposit base for lending operations. Unlike the city banks which maintain hundreds of branches, nondomestic banks are severely constrained in their search for deposits. As a result, the foreign banks have been forced to develop a greater dependence on the interbank markets than their domestic colleagues.

In the 1970s, any domestic corporation seeking a foreign currency loan ("impact loan") was obliged to turn to the foreign banks in Tokyo. At this time, some of the major American and European banks derived 40 percent of their income from impact loans. Thus, the lending opportunities of foreign banks were seriously impaired by the revised foreign exchange law imple-

TABLE 7–6 Foreign Banks' Share of Domestic
Deposits and Loans

	Deposits and CDs			Loans		
	All Banks (A)	Foreign Banks (B)	B/A (%)	All Banks (C)	Foreign Banks (D)	D/C (%)
1975	96,385	1,015	1.05	89,507	2,740	3.06
1980	152,063	1,441	0.95	132,429	4,331	3.27
1981	167,636	1,829	1.09	145,231	5,075	3.49
1982	184,565	2,086	1.13	161,820	5,668	3.50
1983	197,346	1,955	0.99	178,764	6,125	3.43
1984	217,335	2,121	0.98	203,131	6,906	3.40
1985	235,407	2,465	1.05	226,641	6,159	2.72

SOURCE: *Japan Economic Journal*, November 29, 1986.

mented in 1980. This resulted in the abolition of restrictions on impact loans and the conversion of foreign currencies to yen. As a direct consequence, the foreign banks' market share of the impact loan sector declined from 60 percent in fiscal 1982 to 18.6 percent in fiscal 1984. The differential was taken by domestic competitors.

Prior to the deregulation, foreign banks could exploit their unrestricted opportunities to buy yen while their indigenous competitors were limited by strict quotas. Currently, domestic banks can freely procure foreign currencies. This equality with foreign banks conjoined with superior access to long-term funds enables domestic banks to offer cheaper loans than the foreign banks (which must often add the cost of raising yen funds in the call and bill-discount markets to their rates).

Many Japanese corporations are floating on a sea of liquidity and have no thirst for indirect funds. Zaitek at home and abroad often provides more money than many businesses can spend. Indeed, the corporate treasuries of several big corporations such as Toyota and Matsushita are virtually private banks. In this environment, it is not surprising to discover that the business of lending to corporations has been constricted. Even the biggest city banks have been obliged to provide clients with uncollateralized (and often unguaranteed) loans.

Faced with severe competition and inadequate access to

long-term funds, foreign banks, many with only shallow relationships with Japanese corporate society, have in the past participated in the grey area of providing financing to disguised
hoodlums, the **sarakin** (see Glossary). Yet even this questionable activity did little to significantly boost their lending opportunities.

The provision of international financial intelligence has
been one vital service the foreign banks have given to domestic
corporations. Growing numbers of Japanese companies have become involved in international business while, at the same time,
traditional exporters have increased their participation in overseas trade. Foreign banks quickly recognized the key role they
could play as superior suppliers of economic and trade data. As a
result, Japanese corporations have maintained relationships
with foreign banks that would otherwise have been terminated.

At the end of September 1986, the outstanding balance of
yen loans by foreign banks in Japan was ¥4.8 trillion, representing a decline of 6.9 percent from the preceding year. During
fiscal year 1985, lending decreased by 17.5 percent. The decline
in lending is an ongoing process, resulting from mounting difficulties in securing borrowers. Competition from aggressive city
banks which are determined to increase their lending to small-
and medium-sized businesses has eroded the opportunities of the
foreign banks to procure new business.

In 1985, one foreign bank threw in the towel. As the result
of consistently poor earnings, Marine Midland closed its Tokyo
branch and withdrew Crocker National Bank (which it owned).
American Express International Banking Corporation, prohibited by Article 65 from maintaining a banking branch and a
wholly owned securities branch, decided to close its Tokyo consumer credit operation. Although banking had been profitable,
Shearson Lehman concluded that securities business would be
far more lucrative than banking.

While a few foreign banks were abandoning ship, at least 20
percent of the foreign banks in Tokyo were discretely searching
for an acquisition target. Many foreign bankers in Japan are
persuaded that it is necessary to buy the retail deposits that
they cannot obtain through domestic marketing. Because Nomura was granted a banking license from the Bank of England
and with Daiwa became a primary dealer in the United States

(see Chapter 2), many believe that the Ministry of Finance is prepared to approve foreign purchase of a regional or sogo (mutual loan and savings) bank. Although a foreign takeover of a local bank would pose unique technical and managerial problems, aggressive foreign banks (such as Citicorp) are certain that the benefits far outweigh the risks.

Faced with the bleak future of lending, foreign banks have turned to other banking areas in their search for profit. As a result, the foreign exchange, bond, and swap markets are being groomed to be major profit centers in the Tokyo-based operations of the foreign banks. The leading foreign banks in Tokyo doubled and trebled their profits in these areas during fiscal 1985, while simultaneously lending activities were involuntarily curtailed. In fiscal 1985, the aggregate net income of 77 foreign banks totaled ¥30.4 billion, double the level of the preceding year. This was the first instance since 1981 that foreign banks as a group achieved an increase in profits. However, it remains to be seen whether or not foreign institutions can maintain profitability when the yen exchange rates and domestic discount rates finally stabilize. Meanwhile, city banks such as Sumitomo are gearing up to compete with the foreign banks in all areas of trading.

LONG-TERM BANKS

Long-Term Credit Banks

Created as tools for industrialization, the three long-term credit banks became a vital part of the postwar reconstruction. During the 1950s and 1960s, the three banks provided industries with vital long-term (five- to seven-year) financing at the long-term prime interest rate.[14] Just as 50 years earlier the Meiji regime had promoted the development of strategic industries, during the postwar period key industries targeted by the government were given preference by the banks.

---

[14] The long-term prime rate is a fixed interest rate set through mutual agreement by the three long-term credit banks, the trust banks, and major city banks in consultation with the Ministry of Finance and the Bank of Japan.

After the war, the government perceived the three long-term credit banks as special entities existing for the sole purpose of financing economic development. For this reason, the three banks were not intended to compete with the city banks. Whereas the city banks depended upon a broad base of deposits to fund the issuance of medium- and short-term loans, the long-term credit banks raised assets by selling bank debentures. The long-term credit banks were prohibited from accepting deposits other than the deposits of their borrowers. In this way the short-term lending of the city and regional banks was segmented from the long-term lending of the credit banks. As a result, the city banks maintain an average of about 210 branches per bank, while, by contrast, the long-term credit banks have an average of just 19 branches per bank.

Because they had a special statutory right to issue debentures (see Chapter 5), the long-term credit banks functioned like ersatz capital markets in an environment with underdeveloped demand for primary issues of equity and debt. The banks provided corporations with vital funding during a period of severe liquidity shortages. Today, in an era of cash surplus, the institutions are functionally superfluous and many of their traditional clients (steel, shipping, shipbuilding) are racing toward obsolescence. Some bank officials privately speculate that the long-term credit banks will be structurally modified through regulatory amendments.

The Industrial Bank of Japan (IBJ) is the oldest and biggest of the three long-term credit banks. Founded in 1895, the institution is the tenth largest bank in the world in terms of deposits (see Table 7–7). IBJ was originally a government entity intended to fund Japan's early industrial development and was subsequently used to finance the Pacific War. Prior to the War, IBJ was the largest single buyer of government bonds and held the bonds to maturity. Today, the institution continues to be the largest underwriter of government debt.

Although IBJ was privatized during the Occupation, like the Bank of Tokyo, its close government ties were disguised rather than eliminated. During the "descent from heaven" (**amakudari**—see Glossary), many officials from the Ministry of Finance and the Bank of Japan accepted positions at the long-term

TABLE 7–7 Long-Term Credit Banks: World Rank, Assets,
Share of Domestic Lending

World Rank*		Assets ($ millions)	Share of Loans Outstanding† (percent)
10	Industrial Bank of Japan	89,741	5.9
23	Long-Term Credit Bank of Japan	68,159	5.9
44	Nippon Credit Bank	43,425	2.8

*Ranked by assets as of September 30, 1985 by the *American Banker*, July 29, 1986, p. 54.

†To the companies listed on both sections of the Tokyo Stock Exchange as of March 1985.

credit banks. Because the distinction between the public and private sectors is not always as clear in Japan as it is in the West, it is neither accurate nor meaningful to describe the three long-term credit banks as private institutions. Their ties with the government are so close that in many respects they resemble auxiliary components of the Ministry of Finance.

IBJ has a long tradition of seconding employees to other institutions. In the 1960s, for example, many top IBJ executives, at government instigation, took positions at the competing long-term credit banks in order to assist them with development and strategy. During the securities crisis of 1965 (see Chapter 3), IBJ officers replaced the presidents of Yamaichi, Nikko, and Daiwa securities companies. Currently, IBJ employees fill the board rooms of leading industrial corporations and financial institutions.

IBJ is currently the only bank in Japan with a triple A rating from Standard & Poor's. Because it is Japan's preeminent lender of funds, companies derive status by virtue of procuring loans from the bank. The institution is the lead banker of at least 90 percent of Japan's top 200 corporations. Together, the three long-term credit banks account for nearly 15 percent of all loans outstanding to the companies listed on the Tokyo Stock Exchange.

The decline in the demand for long-term loans and the increasingly narrow spreads have motivated the two largest banks to seek a growing portion of revenue from international business. In 1986, for example, IBJ ranked among the 20 top underwriters of Eurobond issues (see Table 6–2). The bank is second to none as the leader of syndicated yen loans for nonresident firms. IBJ's purchase of J. Henry Schroder Bank (see Chapter 2), is illustrative of its determination to transcend its traditional role as a domestic supplier of long-term funds for industrial development.

The Long-Term Credit Bank of Japan (LTCB), like IBJ, is now in the process of redefining its business objectives and ultimately its entire structure. LTCB's purchase of a 20 percent equity share in the U.S. firm, Peers, a specialist broker in the field of mergers and acquisitions, is one example of the credit bank's direct move into the sphere of investment banking. Thus, LTCB is actively engaged in locating U.S. corporate acquisitions for its Japanese clients.

Trust Banks

At the turn of the century and during the subsequent two decades, there were hundreds of trust companies operating in Japan. In 1923, the Trust Law and the Trust Business Law were promulgated in order to control an industry in which widespread manipulation of funds had run rampant. Between 1923 and the end of the War, the number of trust companies fluctuated between 5 and 35. In 1948, trust companies were authorized by the government to participate in commercial banking activities.

The Ministry of Finance established a separate nonpermeable category of trust banking in 1960. This led to the excision of trust bank departments from financial institutions and the creation of newly segmented trust banks. Several of the smaller trust banks were created through the mergers of different trust departments. For example, Toyko Trust was the product of a merger between the Nomura Securities trust division and the Sanwa Bank trust division. In a move which would have been swiftly quashed in the United States but which was viable in Japan's unusual bureaucratic structure, Osaka-based Daiwa bank refused to abide by the government's demands and successfully retained its trust banking department. Two of the smallest regional banks, Bank of the Ryukuus and the Okinawa Bank,

TABLE 7–8   Japan's Seven Domestic
Trust Banks

World Rank*		Net Assets† ($ millions)
21	Mitsubishi Trust & Banking	71,072
22	Sumitomo Trust & Banking	70,333
25	Mitsui Trust & Banking	62,261
35	Yasuda Trust & Banking	53,582
45	Toyo Trust & Banking	43,335
74	Chuo Trust & Banking	26,084
161	Nippon Trust & Banking	9,742

*Ranked by assets as of September 30, 1985 by the *American Banker*, July 29, 1986, p. 54.
†At September 30, 1985.

also maintain trust divisions but these represent an insignificant portion of Japan's total trust banking activities.

There are currently seven trust banks in Japan, supplemented by the trust department of the one city bank (Daiwa) which is authorized to offer trust banking services. The banks operate under the provisions of banking laws that permit the parallel management of savings bank and trust bank operations. As a result, each of the trust banks is a commercial bank as well as a trust bank. Time deposits, taking the form of **negotiable loan trust certificates** (see Glossary) constitute a vital source of funds for the trust banks. Like the debentures issued by the long-term credit banks, these trust certificates have traditionally enabled the trust banks to raise long-term funds. Because of structural changes in financing and flows of funds throughout the Japanese financial system, the trust banks, like the city banks, have increased their dependence on the money markets during the 1980s.

At the end of September 1985, the trust institutions held combined assets representing about 15 percent (¥60 trillion) of total banking assets in Japan. The largest trust bank, Mitsubishi, is the 10th largest bank in Japan and ranks 21st in the world in terms of assets (see Table 7–8).

For many years Mitsubishi Trust has quietly supported Nippon Trust with large subsidies. This has rendered Nippon Trust

---

TABLE 7–9   The Nine Foreign Trust Banks in Japan

Institutions	Net Assets* (billions of yen)	Date of Establishment
Morgan Trust & Banking	40	October 1985
Nippon Bankers Trust	160	October 1985
Chase Manhattan Trust & Banking	20	November 1985
Cititrust	25	March 1986
Manufacturers Hanover Trust	10	April 1986
Chemical Trust & Banking	40	April 1986
Union Bank of Switzerland Trust & Banking	10	May 1986
Credit Suisse Trust & Banking	40	May 1986
Barclays Trust & Banking	30	May 1986

---

*At September 30, 1986.

a virtual affiliate of Mitsubishi, rather than an independent institution. Because Nippon Trust could not survive without Mitsubishi assistance, it is likely that, as trust banking is deregulated and competition increases, the small unprofitable institution will merge with its massive benefactor.

The trust banks specialize in asset-management activities, including, but not limited to, pension fund management (see Chapter 9). Unambiguous statistics are not available, but it appears likely that pension fund management is the most profitable sector of the trust banking industry in Japan. Although trust banks have been responsible for all of the actuarial and administrative aspects of the pension funds they handle, the high fees they receive provide a sizable proportion of total revenue.

During the six-month period ending September 1986, the 5 biggest trust banks ranked among the top 20 financial institutions in Japan in terms of pretax recurring profits. During this period, while the profit shares of the total financial industry procured by city and regional banks decreased, the shares of the trust banks increased significantly. The combined profits of the seven trust banking institutions increased by 26.9 percent from the preceding six-month period. As a result, the trust banks' profit share among all the banks and securities companies in Japan increased to 11.3 percent, a rise of 5 percent over the six-

TABLE 7–10   Funds Managed by Foreign Trust Banks*
(in ¥ billions)

Institutions	Tokkin	Kingaishin	Pension
Morgan Trust	0	40	1
Nippon Bankers Trust	227	18	9
Chase Manhattan Trust	26	2	0
Cititrust	33	27	0
Manufacturers Hanover	16	1	0
Chemical Trust	38	27	0
Union Bank of Switzerland	1	9	0
Credit Suisse	38	20	0
Barclays Trust	23	20	0

*At end of December 1986.
SOURCE: Yamaichi Research Institute.

month period that ended in March 1986. The outstanding performance of the trust banks was the result of growing interest rate spreads on loan trusts as well as commissions derived from the management of specified money in trusts (kingaishin funds).

In July 1985, nine foreign banks received authorization from the Ministry of Finance to enter the trust banking industry. Just as domestic trust banks are required to operate as wholly autonomous banking institutions, so also the foreign banks were obliged to set up separate trust banking entities (rather than simply create trust departments within their existing Tokyo branches). During late 1985 and 1986, all nine foreign banks opened trust banks in Tokyo (see Table 7–9).

Although faced with high start-up costs and expensive overhead, each of the banks considered trust banking operations to be potentially lucrative. The fees derived from managing the growing pool of Japanese pension funds were the primary attraction. However, in early 1987 the Ministry of Health and Welfare excluded foreign banks (to their dismay) from the management of its pension funds. The Ministry argued that the foreign institutions had not yet acquired sufficient experience in the Japanese market to qualify them as pension fund managers. As this book goes to press, only two of the foreign trust banks (see Table 7–10) have procured Japanese pension fund accounts.

During their first year of operation in Japan, the foreign trust banks procured small volumes of tokkin and kingaishin funds for management (see Table 7–10). However, with the exception of Nippon Bankers Trust (which accounted for about 44 percent of all funds accumulated by the nine foreign trust banks), the trust banks lost money in 1986 and are not likely to become profitable for at least three more years.

SPECIALIZED BANKS

Sogo Banks

The sogo are mutual loan and savings banks regulated through a Sogo Bank Law promulgated in 1951. The banks are colloquially known as "sandwiched banks" because they are "sandwiched" between the commercial banks on the one hand and the credit associations and cooperatives on the other hand. The primary source of funds of the sogo banks has been deposits and installment savings. The installment savings vehicle, unique to the sogo, involves depositors in a contract obliging them to make fixed deposits for a fixed period in exchange for specified borrowing privileges. During past periods of cash shortages, installment savings were extremely popular and the sogo thrived. Today, installment savings has become an antiquated institution little needed in Japan's diversified and thriving economy.

The largest of the 69 sogo banks, which are based in major cities, are bigger than the smaller regional banks (see Table 7–11). The sogo have specialized in lending to small businesses located in their local areas. As the deregulation of the financial markets increases the opportunities of medium and small businesses to raise funds through domestic zaitek operations, the demand for sogo-supplied loans will progressively diminish. Growing numbers of businesses already have been terminating their dealing relationships with local sogo. Simultaneously, city and regional banks, faced with declining demand for *their* lending, have been encroaching on traditional sogo territory.

Many of the small sogo, faced with decreasing client demand for loans and diminishing deposits, have been gradually selling their branches. It is expected that during the 1990s some of the sogo will be forced into mergers either with other sogo or, as in the case of Heiwa, with commercial banks. A foreign purchase of a sogo institution is also a distinct possibility.

TABLE 7–11   The Ten Largest Sogo Banks

World Rank*		Headquarters	Net Assets† ($ millions)
162	Nishi-Nippon Sogo Bank	Fukuoka	9,714
205	Tokyo Sogo Bank	Tokyo	7,799
209	Hyogo Sogo Bank	Kobe	7,594
233	Kinki Sogo Bank	Osaka	6,456
252	Nagoya Sogo Bank	Nagoya	6,038
254	Fukuoka Sogo Bank	Fukuoka	5,959
[264	Heiwa Sogo Bank‡	Tokyo	5,818]
274	Kofuku Sogo Bank	Osaka	5,564
282	Fukutoku Sogo Bank	Osaka	5,462
307	Chuo Sogo Bank	Nagoya	4,960
329	Hiroshima Sogo Bank	Hiroshima	4,610

*Ranked by assets as of September 30, 1985 by the *American Banker*, July 29, 1986, p. 54.

†At September 30, 1985.

‡Merged with Sumitomo Bank (October 1986) and included only for reference.

Zenshinren Bank

The Zenshinren Bank is the National Federation of Credit Associations. The 470 credit associations in Japan utilize the institution as a central bank. The considerable cash surpluses held by the credit associations are consolidated by the bank, making it the 23rd largest banking institution in Japan and 70th among the world's 500 top banks (see Table 7–12). The continuous cash

TABLE 7–12   World Rank and Assets of Three Specialized Cooperative Banks

World Rank*		Headquarters	Assets† ($ millions)
9	Norinchukin Bank	Tokyo	93,197
48	Shoko Chukin Bank	Tokyo	41,012
70	Zenshinren Bank	Tokyo	29,724

*Ranked by assets as of September 30, 1985 by the *American Banker*, July 29, 1986, p. 54.

†As of September 30, 1985.

surplus held by the bank is invested in government bonds and money market instruments.

Norinchukin Bank

The Norinchukin Bank is the Central Cooperative Bank for Agriculture and Forestry. The cooperative consists of three financial institutions (credit federations) which in turn consist of thousands of rural cooperatives. Each of the cooperatives is required to deposit about 70 percent of surplus funds in the appropriate federation. Each federation is similarly required to deposit a minimum 50 percent of surplus funds in the Norinchukin Bank.

The largest of the federations, the Credit Federation of Agricultural Cooperatives, is comprised of nearly 5,000 agricultural cooperatives (representing about six million agricultural workers) located in every farming village of every prefecture in Japan. The cooperatives are able to attract and hold individual accounts because they offer interest rates incrementally higher than those at commercial or sogo banks.[15]

The Norinchukin functions as a central bank for a large portion of the deposits originating in Japan's agricultural and fishing sectors. Because the bank is unique in this representation and especially because farmers hold considerable cash reserves derived from government subsidies, it represents a sizable portion of Japan's individual deposits. This has made it the sixth largest bank in Japan in terms of total deposits and the largest in terms of domestic deposits taken alone. As a result, the Norinchukin plays a major role in the money markets and the capital markets. The bank's cash surpluses are heavily invested in public bonds as well as such short-term instruments as NCDs. Norinchukin is one of the leading NCD traders in Japan's NCD market. In addition, at the end of fiscal 1985, the bank held more than ¥5 trillion ($33.3 billion) of national government bonds.

Like the long-term credit banks and unlike the commercial

---

[15] Demand deposits in the cooperatives offer interest rates 0.25 percent higher than commercial banks.

banks, the Norinchukin is able to issue debentures. The debentures are either one-year discount or five-year interest bearing issues. Deposits in the bank are received almost exclusively from the member institutions and the member institutions were traditionally the sole recipients of the bank's loans. This situation has changed considerably, and today the Norinchukin lends to a broad range of domestic borrowers.

Like other large Japanese institutional investors, the Norinchukin has been a major buyer of U.S. Treasury issues. At the end of the fiscal year 1985, the Norinchukin's portfolio of foreign-currency-denominated bonds exceeded ¥1.5 trillion ($9.7 billion), of which roughly half was invested in U.S. government debt. Norinchukin also holds a substantial volume of Samurai bonds as well as dollar floating rate notes (FRNs) and a variety of Euroyen issues.

The bank currently maintains a branch in New York City and a representative office in London. It is probable that during the course of the next decade, Norinchukin will follow the example of the long-term credit banks and seek increasingly to become an international institution offering diversified financial services.

Shoko Chukin Bank

Established in 1936 to assist small businesses to finance development, the Shoko Chukin Bank is "The Central Cooperative Bank for Commerce and Industry." Roughly two-thirds of the institution is owned by the government, with the balance held as shares by affiliated cooperative organizations. The Shoko Chukin functions as a central bank for more than 27,500 small business cooperatives.

Like the Norinchukin Bank, the Shoko Chukin has the statutory right to issue debentures. Lending is usually confined to affiliated organizations. Also like the Norinchukin, Shoko Chukin has opened representative offices in New York and London. Primarily concerned with fulfilling its clients' increased international business needs, the bank also hopes to cultivate linkages between small domestic businesses and overseas companies.

THE POSTAL SAVINGS SYSTEM

The postal savings system, a government financial institution, is not a bank and does not fall within the formal structure of Japan's financial markets. However, under the provisions of new laws and regulations, the postal savings system is in the early stages of a process that will transform it into a commercial bank. For this reason, the system will be discussed briefly below.

Classified as a service segment of the national postal system, post office savings are regulated by the Ministry of Posts and Telecommunications (MPT) and not the Ministry of Finance. Only individual savers are allowed to open accounts and a strict ceiling of ¥3 million is imposed. The post offices operate other enterprises associated with money, including money orders, postal transfers, postal annuities, and postal life insurance. Postal savings, administered as a distinct sector, consist of several basic types: ordinary deposits, time deposits, and installment savings. Time deposits in the form of savings certificates (**teigaku**—see Glossary) can be withdrawn after six months and offer interest rates superior to those offered by the commercial banks (which have long decried the competition).

Although it has been to the government's advantage to keep interest rates low (in order to finance budget deficits), the postal savings system has successfully maintained its superior rates for time deposits. Because a significant portion of total postal savings are derived from rural depositors, the ruling Liberal Democratic Party (heavily dependent upon rural voters) has long been loath to battle the MPT in order to bring postal rates in line with the banking sector.

Since it was established in 1875, the postal savings system has accepted time deposits from individual savers and provided annuities as well as life insurance. Because the thousands of post offices throughout Japan were able to provide these services, the postal savings system rapidly assumed significant proportions. In 1893, the system held 60 percent of the reported time deposits of all commercial banks.[16] By the end of 1944, the system had 193.8 million accounts[17]—far more than the total population of Japan.

---

[16] Goldsmith, p. 52.

[17] Ibid, p. 86.

Under the provisions of **maruyu** (see Glossary), Japanese individual savers have been allowed to establish a number of tax exempt accounts, including a ¥3 million ($19,500) postal savings account. The MPT has neither required identification for the opening of these accounts nor has it monitored the accounts in order to prevent the establishment of multiple maruyu within the system. As a result, Japanese savers open as many tax-exempt postal savings accounts as they desire. At the end of fiscal 1985 there were an estimated two accounts for every resident man, woman, and child.[18] Total deposits at the end of 1985 totalled ¥104.2 trillion ($685 billion), equivalent to nearly one-third of Japan's GNP and six times the total assets of Citicorp, the largest bank in North America.

At the end of 1986, a tax-reform package (at the time of writing, not yet approved by the Diet) promised to abolish the maruyu system. As the result of a bargain between the Ministry of Posts and Telecommunications and the government, MPT agreed not to oppose the elimination of tax-exempt savings and in return received a series of concessions. These concessions will gradually result in a restructuring of postal savings which will eventually produce a distinctive full-service banking institution. Four key privileges will contribute to these changes:

1. The right to sell government bonds to individuals over the counter at any post office. An initial ceiling of ¥1 trillion per annum will be imposed on the total postal system.
2. The right to extend loans to individual savers using government bonds as collateral.
3. The right to manage ¥2 trillion of its own deposits in a newly created Postal Savings Financial Deregulation Fund. The Fund will be increased by ¥500 billion annually until 1991.
4. The right to raise the maximum deposit from ¥3 million to ¥5 million.

In addition to these measures, the system will be granted increased interest rate returns from the Trust Fund Bureau.

During the course of the next decade, these new privileges

---

[18]The Ministry of Posts and Telecommunications does not release information regarding the precise number of savings accounts.

will be expanded and refined. It is probable that as the postal savings system becomes a postal savings *bank*, a variety of new instruments will be authorized. At the same time, the postal savings system will expand its ATM (automated teller machine) network which currently consists of more than 10,000 machines. In addition, while the post offices currently offer many types of credit card in partnership with businesses and consumer finance companies, they are likely to issue their own cards sometime in the not too distant future.

Because more than 19,000 of Japan's 23,673 post offices provide banking facilities, the postal system as a bank will have more branches than any financial institution the world has ever seen. By comparison, Citicorp maintains 2,990 branches and France's enormous Credit Agricole has 10,620. Thus, a sleeping behemoth promises severe competition for all banking institutions in Japan.

Simultaneous with the transmogrification of the sprawling postal savings network, there will occur a drastic decline in new deposits conjoined with massive disintermediation of ordinary and time deposits from the post offices. This will be part of the general trend in which funds are moving from deposits to higher yielding instruments provided by the securities markets. Consequently, the new Postal Savings Bank which will emerge in the medium-term future will most likely be of proportions similar to the five major city banks.

It is noteworthy that a portion of the tens of trillions of yen likely to flow out of the post offices will inevitably find its way to the equity market. This liquidity, combined with disintermediation from the entire banking system as well as vast corporate surpluses, will contribute to the sustenance of a bull market standing upon earnings multiples (see Chapter 4) so high that they are devoid of meaning.

THE TOKYO FOREIGN EXCHANGE MARKET

The Tokyo foreign exchange market is an interbank market representing most foreign exchange transactions in Japan. The market technically subsumes the Tokyo dollar call market which is a money market discussed in Chapter 8.

The Tokyo foreign exchange market did not reopen during

the postwar period until the end of the Occupation. Trading was desultory until 1963 when the central bank began exchange equalization operations. Following the establishment of a floating exchange rate system in 1973, trading volume increased dramatically. The revised foreign exchange law which took effect at the end of 1980 further stimulated market activity.

The Tokyo foreign exchange market is a telephone market and, because of its time zone, it is the first of the world's foreign exchange markets to open each day. The only major market of its kind in the world to have fixed trading hours (from 9:00 A.M. to noon and 1:30 P.M. to 3:30 P.M.),[19] the Tokyo foreign exchange market was a minor segment of global foreign exchange trading until recently. Traders in Tokyo were obliged to place orders in foreign markets during off-trading periods. This obligated foreign exchange brokers to pay commissions to their counterparts in other markets. The ability of the Bank of Japan to smoothly intervene in the foreign exchange markets was also constrained by this limitation. As the result of promotion by the central bank and domestic financial institutions, the foreign exchange market became a 24-hour trading center on December 1, 1986.

Market rates are often quoted on a telegraphic basis regardless of bid and offer quotations. In addition to yen transactions, trading includes U.S. dollar spot, future, and swap transactions as well as cross-trading in Swiss francs, deutsche marks, pounds sterling, and a number of other currencies. The domestic participants in the market comprise all 231 authorized foreign exchange banks. In addition there are nine foreign exchange brokers, including five of the six Tanshi Companies (see Chapter 8), and four specialist foreign exchange companies.[20] Finally, the Bank of Japan, as the central bank and as the representative of the Ministry of Finance (which has responsibility for exchange equalization operations), is a major market participant.

In February 1985, the interbank market, permitting direct

---

[19]The market is closed Saturdays, Sundays, and bank holidays.

[20]In 1983, in anticipation of the opening of the foreign exchange market to dealing with brokers outside Japan, a number of joint ventures were created by the Tanshi. These included Tokyo Tanshi's purchase of a 47 percent interest in Tullett and Riley, a joint venture between Nippon AP and Astley and Pearce, and a 25 percent investment by Yamane Tanshi in Charles Fulton (Asia).

foreign exchange transactions (without brokerage), was liberalized. By raising the maximum trading unit from $1 million to $10 million, this deregulatory action facilitated market growth.

At about this time, many Japanese trading companies began trading in the foreign exchange markets for their own accounts. The most remarkable was Hanwa Co., a medium-sized Tokyo-based trading company, specializing in steel products. During fiscal year 1985, Hanwa posted pretax recurring profits of ¥14.2 billion of which ¥9.8 billion was attributed to profits derived from foreign exchange speculation.

In 1986 the total yen-dollar exchange volume on the Tokyo foreign exchange market exceeded $3 trillion, more than double the amount of the preceding year and triple the volume of 1983. Spot and swap trading together produced a daily yen-dollar trading volume of roughly $10 billion, making the Tokyo market the leading center in the world for yen-dollar transactions. This remarkably rapid development can be attributed to the dramatic growth in yen trading triggered by the historic Group of Five (G-5) meeting at New York's Plaza Hotel in September 1985. As the result of central bank interventions and depressed confidence in the dollar, the yen became the leading currency in the foreign exchange markets.

In late 1986, six companies together sometimes accounted for as much as half of the daily trading volume. Often placing daily orders of $500 million to $1 billion, the companies represented a sample of some of the institutions currently participating in the market: two trading companies (Hanwa and C. Itoh and Co.), one securities firm (Yamaichi), one trust bank (Mitsubishi), one long-term credit bank (Long-Term Credit Bank of Japan), and one private corporation (Sharp). Overall, city banks, foreign banks, and trust banks have been the biggest participants in the foreign exchange market.

THE TOKYO OFFSHORE BANKING MARKET

An offshore banking market can be circuitously, although accurately, defined as a banking market that exists offshore. The term *offshore* is one of the more peculiar constructs in the arcane worlds of banking and finance. Any financial organization, or part of an organization, that is legally domiciled outside a particular sovereign nation can be referred to as offshore from the nation's perspective. This means merely that the nation's rule of law does not apply to the offshore entity. The concept, however, is often carried further and denotes a financial sector within a sovereign nation's jurisdiction which is only partially subject to government regulation. In this way, offshore becomes a euphemism for special tax and regulatory protection.

Offshore banking markets are international financial trading accounts at commercial banks which are devoted to handling offshore trading in external currencies. In these special accounts, even the currency of the host nation is treated as an external monetary unit. Although domestic residents are prohibited market access, the overseas subsidiaries of domestic corporations are considered eligible depositors. Offshore banking is normally exempt from reserve requirements and interest rate regulations as well as all taxation. The U.S. International Banking Facility (IBF), established in 1981, is exempt from deposit insurance assessments. Thus, an offshore banking market is a domestic bank account treated as though it were foreign. It is a bookkeeping technique, an accounting sleight of hand.

The world's biggest offshore banking center (with total deposits of about $750 billion in December 1986) is based in London. Second largest is New York's International Banking Facility (IBF), roughly one-third the size of the London market. These markets are followed in size by the offshore markets of Singapore, Hong Kong, the Bahamas, and the Cayman Islands[21]—all less than half the size of New York's IBF.

Prior to late 1986, Tokyo never had an offshore banking market. From the perspective of the Bank of Japan, such a market would undermine monetary policy, ultimately weakening control of the money supply. From the vantage of the Ministry of Finance's Taxation Bureau, offshore banking, which by definition is tax exempt, would deprive the government of tax revenue. The Tokyo Metropolitan Government agreed. The International Finance Bureau at the Ministry of Finance long regarded

---

[21] The Bahamas and the Cayman Islands are technically not offshore banking centers. They are simply tax havens.

offshore banking as a contradiction in terms: banking is something to be regulated and an offshore market is unregulated. Finally, authorities in Hong Kong and Singapore looked with horror upon the prospect of a competing offshore banking facility located in East Asia. Tokyo offshore banking would have the potential to divert the flow of funds away from the banks of Hong Kong and Singapore.

The first official proposal for the establishment of a Tokyo-based offshore banking market was offered in 1982 by Takashi Hosomi, then vice minister of international finance. Not surprisingly, the proposal was rejected out of hand by the Ministry of Finance. In addition, the Bank of Japan was adamantly opposed to the creation of any institution that would have the potential to weaken its tools for intervention and control of the money supply. The concept was revived in early 1985 when the subject of "liberalization" and "internationalization" of financial markets started to become in vogue at the Ministry of Finance.

In the spring of 1985, an advisory committee of 21 senior business officials and economists chaired by Yusuke Kashiwagi (chairman of the Bank of Tokyo) recommended to the Ministry of Finance that offshore banking be established as soon as possible. The committee suggested that Euroyen loans of more than one-year maturity be deregulated for nonresident borrowers and also suggested that domestic financial institutions be allowed to issue medium-and long-term NCDs in the Euroyen market. Overall, the committee envisioned a broad internationalization of yen-denominated financial instruments, with a Tokyo offshore banking market acting as the trading center.

By this time, the European market in London was worth an estimated ¥8 trillion and promised the possibility of enormous growth in the wake of future regulatory changes. It was feared that if the International Banking Bureau did not move fast, Japan would lose the opportunity to compete with London as a center for transactions in the international yen. Indeed, there was a danger that Japan would forfeit the historical moment and *never* become a center for international finance on a par with London or New York. Only with the existence of an offshore banking market in Japan, offering Eurocurrency transactions, could the yen someday become a fully international currency.

Facing the need to internationalize on the one hand and powerful pressures from the Tax Bureau and the Bank of Japan to maintain the status quo on the other, the International Banking Bureau arrived at a typically Japanese solution to the dilemma. It deliberated for a year. Then it announced the creation of the Japan Offshore Market (JOM) with a handful of weighty *provisos*:

1. The new market will not be exempt from local (prefectural) taxes.
2. It will not be exempt from stamp duties.
3. The rate of corporate taxation on interest income will be higher than the ordinary rate.
4. The new market must be quarantined from domestic money markets. The net inflow of funds from the offshore market to domestic accounts will be limited to a 5 percent balance on a daily basis. In the event that the net flow exceeds 5 percent, the full withholding tax must be imposed upon the total amount involved in the transaction.
5. Like the American IBF, individuals will be banned from market participation. However, unlike other offshore banking markets, securities transactions will also be prohibited and securities companies will be excluded from market involvement. Securities floated by nonresidents cannot be used as the basis for issuing money market instruments.
6. Accounts in the market cannot be used as the basis for the issuance of NCDs (negotiable certificates of deposit).
7. The minimum size of deposits will be ¥100 million, (about four times the deposit minimum for New York's IBF).

These severe restrictions gratified the Taxation Bureau (which had only compromised on the issue of withholding tax), pleased the Tokyo Metropolitan Government (which would receive full local taxes), disappointed the local banking community, and relieved Hong Kong and Singapore of short-term anxieties. The Bank of Japan, pragmatically recognizing the implacable existence of a Euroyen market which it cannot adequately control, perceived that it would be preferable to have Euroyen trading based in Tokyo (where operations can be scrutinized) rather than in distant London.

Optimists at the Ministry of Finance announced that the new facility would achieve total deposits of $85 billion soon after its opening. Bigger optimists suggested that eventually the Tokyo interbank offered rate (TIBOR) would replace the London interbank offered rate (LIBOR) as the standard interest rate for international yen transactions.

In late 1986, the Ministry of Finance issued licenses to 112 domestic financial institutions and 69 licenses to foreign banks with branches in Tokyo. Ten foreign banks (one-eighth of all the foreign banks with branches in Japan) did not deign to apply for licenses. These included universal banks (such as Deutsche Bank and Credit Suisse), the leading Hong Kong bank (Hong Kong and Shanghai Banking Corporation), and U.S. banks (such as Security Pacific and Irving Trust). Nonetheless, some foreign banks viewed the offshore market as a device to facilitate procurement and management of short-term yen assets. Most of the 69 that obtained licenses did so in order to be properly positioned when the market becomes more open.

While foreign banks were only marginally enthusiastic about the new facility, Japan's regional banks were elated. Unable to afford overseas branch networks, the regional banks welcomed the opportunity to offer their clients international financial services directly from Tokyo. The offshore banking market would provide these institutions with their first access to Euro-yen funds. At the same time, the regional banks would be able to bypass the restricted interbank market and instead borrow foreign currency from all available sources.

The city banks, trust banks, and long-term credit banks—with foreign subsidiaries already in place—were also pleased. These institutions could expand international banking business while simultaneously *reducing* overseas operating costs by assigning Tokyo employees to the offshore market. More importantly, the banks would have the opportunity to reduce their reserve requirements by transferring foreign assets from domestic accounts to accounts in the new offshore market.

Central banks dislike offshore banks and external currency because, by reducing reserve requirements, they vitiate a major tool of monetary policy. For example, during several periods of tight money in the United States in the 1960s, Federal Reserve policies were totally subverted by Eurodollar transactions. U.S. banks at that time borrowed vast volumes of Eurodollars from their overseas branches in order to counteract the lending ability which the Fed was attempting to deplete. Officials at the Bank of Japan, well aware of the dangers to the implementation of monetary policy, have carefully studied the impact of external currencies and offshore banking on the monetary policies of other nations. For this reason, the central bank has been bitterly opposed to the establishment of an offshore banking facility in Japan.

In order to prevent domestic banks from transferring domestic assets to the offshore market via their overseas subsidiaries, the government reduced the new facility's prospects for growth. Because flows of funds from the offshore facility into Japan are rigidly controlled, the market could not gain sufficient initial momentum to grow to the full proportions that its role merited. This restraint was compounded by restrictions on the inflow of funds that severely curtailed transfers from ordinary domestic accounts to the offshore banking market. As a result of these restrictions, the Tokyo Offshore Banking Market was not permitted to become a fully functioning market and is instead a facility for accepting deposits rather than a marketplace for raising funds and trading instruments.

The Tokyo offshore banking market opened on December 1, 1986. On that day, the Long-Term Credit Bank of Japan transferred virtually all of its foreign currency transactions—$11 billion—to the new market. Other banks shifted an aggregate total of $44 billion into the facility. This $55 billion opening day, with nearly all deposits denominated in U.S. dollars, surpassed the IBF's first day of business in New York. During the market's initial week of operation, a total of 112 domestic banks and 69 foreign banks established special offshore trading accounts.

The regional and sogo banks immediately began to use the offshore market as a means to expand their foreign currency lending activities. During the market's first month of operation, for example, a syndicate of 16 regional banks extended a 10-year,

$350 million loan to Thailand. In early 1987, in a rare collaboration, 5 sogo banks joined 17 regional banks to form a syndicate for an eight-year, $350 million loan to Indonesia.

The banking community (particularly foreign bankers) forecast that an offshore market shackled by local tax requirements would not grow. Subsequent growth, although not exceptional, far surpassed the bankers' bleak expectations. At the end of its first month, the offshore banking market maintained total outstanding assets of $93.7 billion, 75 percent of which was deposited by the overseas branches of the city banks. These funds were denominated in dollars and were deployed exclusively for arbitrage operations. Nearly 19 percent of the total assets in the offshore market were deposits or call money and the remainder were loans. It is likely that the Japan Offshore Market will quickly grow to proportions far greater than the offshore banking markets of Singapore and Hong Kong.

After its first month of operation, 22 percent (¥3.13 trillion) of the new offshore market's total assets were denominated in yen. Although this amount is less than 3 percent of the total size of the London offshore banking market, the modest sum brought the dreams of challenging London as the center for Euroyen transactions a little nearer to realization.

CHAPTER EIGHT

Money Markets

OVERVIEW

A money market is a market in high-quality, low-risk securities. The market is comprised of the institutions that trade the instruments on a short-term basis at prevailing interest rates. In the absence of formal exchanges, the secondary money market is delineated by the participating institutions. A key function of money markets within a national economy is to provide a means for transferring surplus household funds to deficit borrowers via the intermediation of banks. In Japan, a cartel of six short-term money dealers and brokers (the **Tanshi**), by effectively managing many of the short-term markets, acts as the vital link between the cash surplus produced by rural agriculture and small businesses on the one hand and the urban deficits of financial institutions on the other.

Although a money market is a securities market, it has several features that distinguish it from capital markets:

1. It is short term—one year or less.
2. It possesses a high degree of liquidity (money market instruments can be sold on demand) which resembles money.
3. The market makers are generally confined to financial institutions (such as banks, securities companies, and insurance companies) and the money market only exists because of their involvement.

By consensus, repurchase agreements (termed **gensaki** in Japan), which are *not* securities, are classified as money market instruments.

In Japan, during the quarter century following the war (1945–1970), the money market lacked the diversity of instruments available in the United States and Western Europe. Throughout this period, the short-term market consisted of three simple types of money market transactions: overnight borrowing, unconditional borrowing, and over-month-end funds. Interest rates, set by the Tanshi companies in consultation with the **Sanmeikai** (a special committee) and approved by the Bank of Japan ("the final arbiter of market funds"),[1] were kept low and were not permitted to fluctuate. The gensaki (repurchase agreement) market was created in 1949 but did not reach significant proportions until the early 1970s.

In 1971, the call market was divided into two distinct parts. The segment of the market with short-term maturities became the contemporary call-money market while the portion of the market with long maturities (two to four months) became the bill-discount market. One year later, in 1972, the Tokyo dollar call market was created and the Bank of Japan initiated open market operations in the bill discount market. Not until 1979 was a market in negotiable certificates of deposit established.

The May 1984 Joint Japan-U.S. Ad Hoc Group on Yen/Dollar Exchange Rate and Capital Market Issues resulted in the rapid liberalization of Japan's money market structure. In March 1985, money market certificates (MMCs) were introduced, followed by yen-denominated banker's acceptances (BAs) in June of that year, and short-term government bonds in February 1986. In 1985–86, interest rates on large denomination time deposits were deregulated, creating competition among banks for sums of ¥100,000 and larger.

In the United States, Treasury bills (TBs), commercial paper (CP), and a range of other short-term instruments constitute a market that represented roughly 40 percent of GNP in 1985. In Japan, by contrast, the aggregate value of the money market in

---

[1] The Bank of Japan, Economic Research Department, *The Japanese Financial System*, p. 48.

1985 was less than 8 percent of GNP. Because the interest rates on most deposits (see Appendix I) are set by the central bank and not by market forces, Japan's money markets lack the flexibility of their U.S. counterparts.

In 1986, gensaki, negotiable certificates of deposit (NCDs), large denomination deposits, money market certificates (MMCs), banker's acceptances (BAs), and Treasury bills had interest rates permitted to fluctuate in accordance with supply and demand. The Treasury bill market, because of the infrequency of short-term government debt, was of negligible proportions. In fiscal year 1986, an estimated 60 percent of the funds raised by city banks were derived from these floating rate money market instruments.

Interest rates in the interbank market, consisting exclusively of the bill-discount and call-money markets, are set through unofficial communication between the central bank and the short-term money brokers (Tanshi). Although a domestic commercial paper market has not yet been established (see below), the creation of a Euroyen commercial paper market is a harbinger of things to come.

Japan's short-term money markets can be divided into 11 distinctive sectors: call-money, bill-discounts, dollar call-money, gensaki, negotiable certificates of deposit, large denomination time deposits, money market certificates, yen-denominated banker's acceptances, nonresidents' yen deposits, foreign currency deposits, and Treasury bills.[2]

Since 1984, most of Japan's money markets have been expanding rapidly as a consequence of massive inflows of government and private sector capital. The call market, particularly, has been the recipient of institutional funds, with average daily transactions exceeding ¥10 trillion at the end of September 1986. At the end of fiscal year 1986, the outstanding balance of short-term money markets reached ¥130 trillion ($812 billion), an increase of ¥50 trillion over the level of the preceding year.

---

[2]At the time of writing, the Treasury bill *market* is a market in name only and therefore is not discussed in this chapter. However, the potential of a market in short-term bills (with no withholding tax) is enormous and an active Treasury bill market will almost certainly develop in Japan during the next several years.

The money markets are likely to experience continued growth in the late 1980s as the result of developments in the offshore banking market and the gradual expansion of the short-term government bond market. In addition, the progressive liberalization of domestic interest rates should eventually lead to increased opportunities for interest rate arbitrage transactions.

The following sections offer brief discussions of Japan's money market instruments. The reader desiring additional detail should consult two comprehensive English language studies listed in the Bibliography: Robert F. Emery's *The Japanese Money Market,* and Eisuke Sakakibara and Akira Kondoh's *Study on the Tokyo Capital Markets.*

TANSHI (SHORT–TERM BROKERS AND DEALERS)

The Tanshi are unique to Japan. In operation since the creation of the modern Japanese money market in 1902, the six Tanshi companies are licensed in perpetuity by the Ministry of Finance.[3] Although supervised by the Ministry's Banking Bureau, the Tanshi's banking records are audited by the Bank of Japan. The Tanshi function as intermediaries between lenders and borrowers in the money markets (excluding gensaki). Although private nonbanking organizations, the companies have borrowing privileges at the Bank of Japan and employ retired executives from the central bank. These former senior employees of the bank consult on a regular basis with bank officials regarding money market interest rates. In this way, the Tanshi companies assure that the government will have complete information and, ultimately, control of the markets in short-term funds.

Following the reestablishment of a foreign exchange market in Japan in 1952, the Tanshi became foreign exchange brokers. The largest of the firms, Tokyo Tanshi, established a foreign exchange subsidiary (Tokyo Forex) in 1978. Although they have both broking and dealing capabilities, the Tanshi operate pri-

---

[3]The six Tanshi companies are: Tokyo Tanshi, Ueda Tanshi, Yamane Tanshi, Nippon Discount and Call Money, Yagi Tanshi, Nagoya Tanshi.

marily as brokers and derive most of their income from their commission fees.

Together, the Tanshi constitute the **Tanshi Kyokai,** the Association of Call Loan and Discount Companies, created in 1962. The Association represents the solidarity of interests of the Tanshi in dealings with financial institutions, particularly the Bank of Japan and the Ministry of Finance. In addition, it establishes and standardizes the procedures as well as the dealing practices deployed by the Tanshi companies.

The four largest Tanshi are centered in Tokyo, Yagi Tanshi is located in Osaka, while the smallest Tanshi, Nagoya Tanshi, is Nagoya-based and only handles business in Nagoya. The Tanshi virtually supervise the bill-discount market, the call-money market, and the dollar call market.[4] Their offices provide a crucial marketplace for money market transactions and are indispensable to the flow of funds.

The Tanshi are the primary lenders of overnight funds to the city banks and are a major source of funds for the securities finance companies. Thus, the six companies together are a key part of Japan's interbank market. In addition, the Tanshi are used by the Bank of Japan as an agent for open market operations. As a result, the Tanshi can be viewed as an arm of the central bank and a witting implementor of monetary policy.

THE INTERBANK MARKETS

Structure

The interbank markets in Japan, unlike those of the United States and the United Kingdom, are not highly competitive open markets devoid of limitations regarding purchasers and sellers. In Japan, corporations as well as individuals are banned from call and bill transactions in the money markets. Interest rates, although subject to market forces, are artfully controlled by the Bank of Japan. The yen call-money market, long the only money market in Japan, is 70 years older than the bill-discount market.

---

[4]Excluding Tokyo Tanshi.

Call rates and bill-discount rates are prohibited by the central bank from falling below the official discount rate. The differential between the interbank money market rates and the discount rate fluctuates in accordance with Bank of Japan monetary policy: When monetary policy is loose, the differential contracts and the converse obtains when policy is tight. Ideally, the call and bill-discount rates are a mirror of the supply and demand conditions within the money market as a whole. The money market, in turn, is a sensitive indicator of fluctuations in private sector money supply.

The Bank of Japan succinctly summarizes the uniquely Japanese variations in the tightening and relaxation of the money market:

> Demand for bank notes expands: (1) in March to April when the farming season begins, when schools open, and when the recreation season commmences; (2) in June, when mid-year bonuses are paid; and (3) at the end of the year, when businesses settle accounts and pay year-end bonuses. Then, at the beginning of the new year, bank notes which were issued at the preceding year-end flow back. Also, receipts and payments in the Treasury accounts are influenced by seasonal variations in business activity and the following institutional factors: (1) Slight net payment in April–June in general; (2) slight net receipt in July–September; (3) large net payment in October–December; and (4) large net receipt in January–March. The increase in demand for bank notes and treasury net receipts cause the money market to tighten, and conversely, return-flows of bank notes and treasury net payments are factors which cause the money market to relax.[5]

During the past 15 years, an approximately inverse relationship has obtained between the yen call-money market and the bill-discount market on the one hand, and the city banks and nonbanking financial institutions on the other. Thus city banks have been the traditional borrowers in the call-money market and the customary lenders in the bill-discount market.

The outstanding balance of call-money and bill-discount interbank transactions was ¥24 billion at the end of 1986, an increase of ¥5 billion over 1985. It is likely that expansion of the offshore banking market as well as deregulation of interest

---

[5]The Bank of Japan. *The Japanese Financial System*, pp. 124–25.

rates in the late 1980s will result in a continuing rapid rate of growth in the use of the interbank markets.

Yen Call-Money Market

The call-money market in Japan is an interbank money market in which banks officially finance their *short-term* cash positions through the Tanshi companies. The market also enables banks to finance long-term liquidity shortages by means of perennial borrowing. Although they occasionally take positions, the Tanshi function primarily as brokers, deriving their profit from the spread (12.5 basis points) between the bid and offered interest rates. The Tanshi are sometimes bypassed by the city banks which may transact bank-to-bank fund transfers.

A call-money transaction in Japan—termed a *call-loan* transaction by the lender and *call-money* by the borrower—can be viewed as a simple exchange of promissory notes. Prior to the end of July 1985, the Bank of Japan required that these promissory notes be secured (with the exception of half-day transactions for which collateral would have been superfluous). The collateral regulation was abolished because the branches of foreign banks in Tokyo, which have far less collateral available than domestic institutions, encountered severe difficulties raising short-term funds in the local market during the 1980s. The central bank accommodation of this foreign problem was one facet of the deregulatory measures instituted during the period 1984–86.

City banks were the traditional borrowers in the call-money market until regional banks and securities companies joined them in the late 1970s.[6] The biggest lenders in the market have been trust banks, the Zenshinren Bank, financial institutions for agriculture and forestry, insurance companies, long-term credit banks, and regional banks.

In the typical call-money transaction, a lender transfers funds to a Tanshi company (a check drawn on its account at the Bank of Japan) and receives the Tanshi's promissory note, a negotiable instrument (formerly secured with legally acceptable

---

[6]Between 1965 (after the securities market crisis) and 1978, securities companies were prohibited from borrowing in the call-money market.

collateral). At the same time, the borrower delivers a promissory note to the Tanshi, receiving the lender's funds in exchange. The actual exchange of funds occurs at the Bank of Japan so that the borrowed funds are transferred from the Tanshi's account at the central bank to the borrower's account. In this way, for example, a city bank can telephone a Tanshi to request funds. The necessary promissory note can be delivered to the Tanshi office by a courier and the funds subsequently transferred to the bank's account by means of a telephone call placed by the Tanshi to the Bank of Japan. The unit of transaction in the call-money market is ¥100 million or more. There is no withholding tax.

Given its simple elegance, it is not surprising that the yen call-money market is the oldest money market in Japan. Created in 1902 after a U.S. and British model,[7] it gradually grew into a significant source of funds for the banking industry, representing 6 percent of the source of funds for the city banks. At the end of March 1986, the volume of the call-money market exceeded ¥4.5 trillion. In addition, the unsecured call-money market, fed by the participation of foreign banks in Japan, grew to ¥1.4 trillion.

Originally, the call-money market offered four types of maturities: overnight, unconditional, fixed maturity dates, and over-month-end. The latter two were abolished in 1972, although fixed maturity dates were reinstituted in 1978. Currently, overnight, seven-day unsecured, and three- to six-day maturities are commonly used.

Bill-Discount Market

Established in May 1971, the Japanese bill-discount market is an interbank market in bills of exchange. The market resembles the U.S. Federal Funds market. A discounted bill is literally a bill (or promissory note) of exchange from which a bank deducts in advance its interest for lending and its fees. Like the call-money market, the bill-discount market functions as a pipeline transferring liquidity between financial institutions with the Tanshi companies acting as brokers. Unlike call-money, bill-

---

[7] Particularly the London bill-discount market.

discounts have relatively long maturities (one to four months). Interbank transfers without the mediation of the Tanshi are ordinarily proscribed.

The bills traded in the bill-discount market are generally classified as belonging to one of two categories: *original bills* and *accommodation bills*. The bills of exchange (promissory notes) banks receive from blue chip borrowers are termed original bills. Accommodation bills are drafts drawn by financial institutions and made payable to a Tanshi. The accommodation bills are created in order to consolidate the variety of small denomination original bills which banks receive from their corporate clients. The face amount of an accommodation bill must be equal to a collection of original bills. If this were not the case, a bank would be producing its own domestic commercial paper which is currently prohibited.

Bill-discount transaction terms are usually one-month, two-months, three-months and four-months with secondary trading permitted after a 30-day holding period. Interest rates are based on the maturity of the bills and fluctuate in increments of 6.25 basis points. Ordinarily, the rate in the bill-discount market is between 25 and 125 basis points above the call-money rate. Rates for over-year-end bills (i.e. bills with maturities that occur the following year) are incrementally (perhaps 25 basis points) higher than bills that mature during the year.

The Bank of Japan uses the purchasing and sale of bills as a technique of intervention in order to adjust money market fluctuations. At times the central bank accounts for half of all transactions in the market. By limiting its purchases of bills, the bank tightens money supply and by increasing the volume of its purchases it eases credit conditions. Concurrently, the bank limits the transactions of the city banks in the gensaki market (see below) in order to maximize market control. In addition, the bank sometimes issues its own bills to absorb excess liquidity in the market.

The minimum market unit is ¥100 million and there is no withholding tax (although a small stamp duty may apply). The market operates in Osaka and Nagoya as well as Tokyo, but more than 90 percent of outstanding bills are in Tokyo.

Prior to 1985, financial institutions were prohibited from simultaneously issuing and procuring funds in the bill-discount market. In accordance with this system, the cash rich institutions (such as the Norinchukin bank and the Association of National Credit Banks) were suppliers of funds while the traditionally cash deficient city banks issued bills. This regulation was based on the assumption that simultaneous transactions for investment and procurement could destabilize the market. It also assumed that city banks were destined to have perpetual liquidity shortages. During the 1980s, however, many city banks had short-term liquidity surpluses. In March 1985, the Bank of Japan deregulated the market, authorizing banks to procure from and invest in the market at the same time.

Tokyo Dollar Call Market

Established in 1972 and limited to domestic banking institutions, the Tokyo dollar call market is an interbank market in short-term unsecured foreign currency loans. Despite the market's name, lending is not officially confined to dollar transactions. Nearly all transactions, however, are denominated in U.S. dollars with occasional recourse to other major currencies. The market was created in order to give regional banks without access to the Euromarkets (i.e., no overseas subsidiaries) opportunities to clear short-term foreign exchange positions when closing their books at the end of each business day. Thus, the Tokyo dollar call market can be viewed as a protected Eurocurrency enclave closed to nonresidents and to nonfinancial institutions.

The market has enabled regional banks, sogo banks, credit unions, and other smaller financial institutions to lend or borrow very short-term money (two to seven days) at freely moving interest rates. Long-term borrowing (one to five years) in the foreign currency market also exists (see Chapter 7). The bulk of the loans are U.S. dollar-denominated, although loans in other major currencies are also transacted. During fiscal 1984, market turnover reached $970 billion, a 34 percent increase from the preceding year.

During 1984–85, the monthly trading volume in the market averaged $80 to $90 billion. However, beginning in December 1985 and continuing throughout 1986, trading volume increased by roughly 50 percent. Small regional banks, with little foreign exchange experience, began to use the Tokyo dollar call market for practicing transactions in anticipation of the opening of the Japan offshore banking market.

The Tanshi companies function as brokers for the lending and borrowing of foreign currency deposits by the banking institutions authorized to participate in the Tokyo dollar call market. They charge a fixed commission of two basis points from both the borrower and the lender. Like the other interbank markets, transactions in the Tokyo dollar market are arranged by telephone. Most loan maturities (more than 90 percent) range from overnight to seven days, with roughly half on an overnight basis. In addition, there are term loans which extend from one month to any number of years. Although the minimum loan is $100,000, most loans are usually for $1 million or more.

Interest rates in the Tokyo dollar call market are usually incrementally higher than in the London Eurodollar market (usually 6.25 to 12.5 basis points). The central bank does not oversee interest rates in the Tokyo dollar call market as it does in the call-money and bill-discount markets. Nonetheless, the Bank *does regulate* the foreign exchange positions of the authorized foreign exchange banks and imposes swap quotas. Consequently, although interest rates are technically not controlled, the market itself has been tightly restricted.

The establishment of an offshore banking facility in Tokyo in 1986 created new opportunities for hedging. Authorized foreign exchange banks are now able to cover their positions on the Tokyo dollar call market through fund raising on the offshore market. Such relationships have wide ramifications. For example, a rise in dollar interest rates on the Tokyo dollar call market can cause a rise in dollar rates on the Asia dollar market through the Tokyo offshore market. The parallel existence of the Tokyo dollar call market, the Eurocurrency market, the Asia currency market, and the Tokyo offshore banking market— with their different time zones—provides domestic banking institutions with a choice of exchange rates and borrowing costs as well as arbitrage possibilities.

THE MAJOR "OPEN" MARKETS

Structure

The *gensaki* market, *large denomination time deposits,* and *negotiable certificates of deposit (NCDs)* tower above the other short-term instruments in the open market. At the end of fiscal year 1985, the outstanding balance of NCDs, at ¥9.8 trillion, was more than double the comparable figure for gensaki (¥4.34 trillion). NCDs have been preferred to gensaki because they do not involve a securities transaction tax and they are far easier to arrange. Together, the two types of transaction represented roughly 70 percent of the total outstanding balance of open market short-term vehicles in 1985. Their disproportionate size is partially a result of history. For decades, the gensaki was the only short-term instrument in the open market. NCDs, introduced eight years ago, provided institutions with a much needed alternative to the repurchase agreement.

In 1986, following successive cuts in the discount rate, corporations and government bodies seeking high yielding investments moved substantial funds to large-lot time deposits (deregulated in October 1985), making this instrument the single biggest short-term money market. Because large denomination time deposits offer interest rates from 10 to 30 basis points higher than NCDs, all types of entities switched funds to the deposits.

Enormous pools of funds held by investment trusts, pension funds, and tokkin are often parked in large denomination time deposits and NCDs. The enormous growth in the usage of large-lot time deposits, NCDs, and gensaki has been partly the result of domestic financial arbitrage operations (zaitek) by banks and nonfinancial institutions.

Gensaki Market

The gensaki market is a short-term money market for the conditional trading of bonds. The bonds traded are long-term but have attached agreements stating that the sellers will repurchase the securities at an indicated future date. In this way, a long-term security is converted into a short-term instrument. Thus, a gensaki is simply a short-term agreement between a buyer (lender) and a seller (borrower) to reverse a bond trade at a specified time at a specified price. Because the gensaki agreement involves a present transaction and a future transaction, the term, *gensaki,* is composed of two Chinese characters, *gen* ("present" or "spot") and *saki* ("future"). Gensaki is the least controlled of the money markets and functions independently of central bank intervention. It is currently the only money market in which nonfinancial institutions can borrow short-term funds.

The gensaki market was established in 1949 as a means of dealing with large inventories of unsold new debt issues. The repurchase agreement provided a technique for raising funds for new issues while older issues remained unsold. For decades, the Ministry of Finance classified gensaki transactions as collateralized loans. The increasing size and importance of the market during the early 1970s, however, motivated regulatory officials to reclassify gensaki as bond transactions in 1976.

Gensaki transactions occur on a 24-hour over-the-counter market and, unlike the interbank money markets, they are open to all institutions (individual transactions are banned, however).[8] All gensaki have maturities of less than one year and the majority mature in three months. Maturities of several days to one month are not uncommon.

The gensaki resembles, but is not based on, the U.S. bond repurchase agreement. It is noteworthy that the Tanshi companies do not participate in the gensaki market which was developed by, and is traditionally dominated by, the securities companies. Because the transactions have no upper limit (the minimum face value of a transaction is usually ¥100 million), the securities companies use gensaki as a convenient mode for raising short-term capital.

The Bank of Japan has traditionally underwritten virtually all short-term government securities and as a result a secondary market in Treasury bills never developed in Japan (such a market, however, will develop soon). Consequently, securities companies sought short-term financing from the securities finance companies (see Chapter 2) *and* through the trading of repurchase agreements attached to medium- and long-term government as well as corporate bonds. In this way, the gensaki market satisfied demands which would otherwise have been fulfilled by means of a short-term money market in Treasury bills (or commercial paper).

---

[8] Only corporations listed (or qualified to list) on the first section of the Tokyo Stock Exchange have traditionally been considered acceptable participants by the Ministry of Finance.

The gensaki market, by enabling institutions to borrow cash on a short-term basis, provides a means to compensate for short-term liquidity deficiencies. A byproduct of the borrowing, of course, is the opportunity for arbitrage in the money markets. Rarely, the gensaki market is used as a means for postponing the final sale of bonds in the hope that the bonds will be sold at a later date at a superior price. Although the gensaki market has also been used by domestic fund managers for hedging their fixed income portfolios, this function has been replaced by the bond futures market (see Chapter 5). Since October 1975, forward bond trading (**chakuchi**) in the gensaki market has been permitted.

The differential between a gensaki's sale price and its repurchase price governs the instrument's yield. Because a gensaki is both a security and a money market instrument, yields are influenced by bond market situations and money market rates.[9] Ordinarily, gensaki rates approximate the rates prevalent in the bill-discount market, although substantial differentials can occur because the rates in the bill-discount market are the product of central bank decision. As a direct result, gensaki sometimes offer one of the highest yields available for short-term funds in Japan. Yields move in increments of five basis points.

Excluded from the interbank market, corporations have utilized the gensaki market as a repository for short-term funds. As a result, the gensaki market became one of many symbiotic relationships cultivated between securities companies and their corporate clients. Thus securities firms, seeking to finance their long-term bond inventories, have accounted for more than 60 percent of all borrowing while nonfinancial corporations (followed by trust banks) have constituted the majority of lenders. The city banks, which prior to 1981 were allowed only negligible market lending participation, currently account for more than 10 percent of the lenders. In order to protect the integrity of Arti-

---

[9]The prices for bonds with repurchase agreements attached have historically not been precisely related to short-term interest rates, although they should have been. Instead, as a consequence of market activity in long-term bonds, the "time pattern of the market yield curve was distorted," impeding the development of the medium- and long-term bond markets. See Yoshio Suzuki, *Money and Banking in Contemporary Japan,* p. 55.

cle 65, the city banks have been required to arrange the gensaki transactions through a securities company.

There are two fundamental types of gensaki transaction:

1. In **dealing gensaki** or "one sided" gensaki (**jiko gensaki**) the securities company is one of the partners in the trade and utilizes bonds from its vaults. This type of transaction usually has a maturity of less than one month.
2. In **matched gensaki** (**itaku gensaki**) the securities company either
   1. Acts simultaneously as both the buyer and the seller of the securities, or
   2. Acts purely as an intermediary in the securities transaction.

   These transactions usually have two- to three-month maturities.

A gensaki variation emerged in the financial markets in 1985 which was designed to circumvent the interest or dividend withholding tax associated with the instrument. In this new, nameless market, a company lends bonds to another company for a specified holding period. The borrower pays a fee for the loan which, overall, is less than the cost of a bank loan. In this way, the recipient of the fee bypasses the 20 percent withholding tax which is levied on the interest and dividend income yielded by all securities. The borrower of the securities, in turn, sells the securities to a domestic tax-exempt institution (e.g. a temple or a school). At the end of the lending period, the borrower, instead of returning the borrowed bonds, gives the lender the cash equivalent of the bonds.

Negotiable Certificates of Deposit (NCDs)

During the 1970s, certificates of deposit became a vital part of the U.S. and U.K. money markets. Yen NCDs were not introduced in Japan until May 1979, following years of deliberation by the regulatory authorities. Although based on the American instrument, Japanese NCDs are issued in registered rather than bearer form (much to the chagrin of foreign bankers).

Because a market in NCDs was perceived as a potential threat to the gensaki market, the minimum denomination for the instrument was initially set at ¥500 million and maturities were set at three to six months in order to reduce the opportunities for direct competition. The minimum unit per certificate was reduced to ¥300 million in January 1984.

Like the gensaki market, interest rates in the NCD market are determined through market forces rather than government dicta. Thus, although the instrument is a form of bank deposit, it is not subject to Japan's Temporary Interest Rate Control Law and banks are free to determine their own rates. Because rates are not standardized, investors must negotiate the interest rate with the issuing institution. The bill-discount rate and the gensaki rate are used as guidelines in the bidding for NCD rates.

Issuance of NCDs is limited to the range of banking institutions, with the city banks by far the largest issuers. Private corporations are the major buyers of the instrument. Participation in the NCD secondary market is confined to financial institutions and the Tanshi companies. NCD gensaki agreements are the most common secondary market transaction. The NCD secondary market is not subject to transaction taxes and this factor enabled it to experience rapid growth, reaching ¥2.67 trillion at the end of 1981 and ¥9.8 trillion by the end of 1985.

NCD maturities range from three to six months with the majority less than 120 days. Initially, strict ceilings were imposed on issuing institutions, limiting the percent of net capital to 10 percent. During the course of deregulation, the ceiling was raised in successive increments, reaching 75 percent in 1984. Secondary trading in NCDs began in Arpil 1980. The Tanshi companies are major participants in this market, followed by the city banks (prohibited from trading in their own issues).

Large-Denomination Time Deposits

Interest rates on large-denomination time deposits were deregulated on October 1, 1985. On that day, alone, the city banks received 458 deposits, exceeding ¥955 billion. Initially, the large-lot deposits offered interest rates 10 basis points higher than NCD rates. The higher rate was provided because the vehicle is less liquid than NCDs and requires a larger minimum denomination.

The minimum deposit has been successively reduced from ¥1 billion to ¥500 million to ¥300 million and will be reduced to ¥100 million in 1987. Maturities range from three months to two years. Interest rate levels for the instrument are determined by the banks. In 1985–86, the city banks applied NCD rates plus 10 to 30 basis points to three-month and six-month time deposits and Euroyen rates to one-year time deposits. Two-year instruments bore interest rates tied to government bond yields.

At the end of June 1986, the outstanding balance of large denomination time deposits with freely moving interest rates exceeded ¥10 trillion, surpassing NCDs for the first time. By the end of December 1986, the market for the instrument was almost double that for NCDs, having reached ¥17.830 trillion— triple the level at the end of 1985. The increase can be ascribed to the growth in deposits made by corporations and government entities seeking the highest yielding deposit instruments. As a result of expanded use of large-denomination time deposits, the vehicle has become *the* central component of the short-term money markets.

The rapid development of two major open markets—large-denomination time deposits and NCDs—forced the Bank of Japan to consider altering its methods of monetary adjustment. Traditionally, the central bank used only the interbank markets for its open-market monetary adjustment operations. However, growing spreads between interbank and open market rates pressured the bank to consider a subtle alteration in monetary policy. By undertaking buying and selling operations in the open market, the Bank of Japan can cause interest rate arbitrage to occur more smoothly between the regulated interbank and the nonregulated open market.

In April 1986 (at the beginning of the new fiscal year), for the first time in 14 years, the Bank of Japan instituted a new method of monetary adjustment which involved the purchase and sale of NCDs through the Tanshi companies. Thus, the bank began to exert stronger influence on the open markets. In this way, monetary policy could stress adjustment in the nonregulated money markets in a manner resembling the approach of the Fed.

THE MINOR "OPEN" MARKETS

Money Market Certificates (MMCs)

Introduced in March 1985, money market certificates (MMCs) are large-denomination deposit instruments which currently have a minimum denomination of ¥30 million. Together with NCDs and large-denomination time deposits, MMCs provide the only means available to banks to compete for funds by offering competitive interest rates (see Appendix I).

MMCs, unlike NCDs, are nonnegotiable instruments and cannot be cancelled. When cancellations prior to maturity occur, the applied interest rate is reduced to the rate applicable to ordinary deposits. MMCs bear interest rates regulated by the Ministry of Finance and set at 0.75 percent below the average interest rate on NCDs. The maturities mirror the requirements for NCDs and have a minimum maturity of one month and a maximum of one year. While the market in MMCs is open to all financial institutions, only banks and Tanshi companies can sell the instruments.

It is probable that the ongoing relaxation of interest rate controls will result in successive extensions of the MMC maturity ceiling and reductions in the minimum deposit required. The ceiling has already been extended from six months to one year while the minimum deposit has been reduced from ¥50 million to ¥30 million. The maturity ceiling is likely to be raised to two years in 1987 and to three years by late 1988; similarly, the minimum deposit may be reduced to ¥20 million in late 1987 and to ¥10 million in 1988.

In order to compete with the MMCs, the securities companies began selling Money Market Funds (MMFs) that mimic the MMC. The funds are short-term bond investment trusts, with minimum denominations of ¥30 million and a rate of interest set to float with the MMC. Maturities for the MMF are also set to mirror the MMC. In this way, securities companies are able to offer a short-term instrument with market-determined interest rates which, technically, is not a money market vehicle and falls outside the purview of banks. One more blow for Article 65.

The Yen Banker's Acceptance (BA) Market

A yen banker's acceptance market was established in Japan on June 1, 1985. A direct result of U.S. pressure, the market was introduced in order to promote the "internationalization" of the yen and to expand the opportunities for short-term borrowing.

A banker's acceptance (BA) is a postdated instrument (a time draft) which transfers money from a buyer to a seller. The postdate deprives the seller of use of the money prior to the specified date. The instrument is converted into a money market vehicle by an attached payment guarantee provided by a bank. BAs are a convenient tool for trade financing. Manufacturers accept a discounted payment from a bank for goods yet to be delivered in exchange for a guaranteed time draft. Because the bank that buys the time draft will receive the face amount of the instrument at maturity, the discount is the effective interest rate.

The yen BA market is an open money market in which banks can purchase yen bills of exchange from importers and exporters and subsequently sell the bills to investors through the Tanshi. Yen-denominated BAs have maturities of six months or less.

Only a relatively small percentage of Japanese imports (3 percent) and exports (60 percent) have been denominated in yen. A purpose motivating the government to establish a yen-based BA market was to induce an expansion of the use of the yen in international trade and to facilitate the ability of domestic banks to raise funds for trade financing. The new market also promised to provide an additional tool for fund managers.

In 1984–85, the Ministry of Trade and Industry (MITI) publicly supported the establishment of a yen BA market which it described as a tool to increase imports and thus reduce trade friction with the United States and the EEC. Because a BA market could potentially increase the demand for yen funds in trade financing, it was believed that it would ultimately reduce the cost of imports. Later, the strong appreciation of the yen against the dollar reduced the need for MITI to promote imports so actively.

In 1985 when the banker's acceptance market was established, five types of bills were included within the BA category: banker's acceptance bills, accommodation bills, book bills (which combine accommodation bills issued by banks), the refinancing bills of foreign banks, and **jikihane** bills. Jikihane are bills used by Japanese corporations to procure yen funds in payment for their imports denominated in foreign currencies. Banks strongly opposed the inclusion of jikihane bills within the purview of the new market. Broad-based usage of jikihane bills in the BA market has the potential to undermine the banks' profitable foreign currency loan business.

In Japan, unlike the United States, the initial issuance of bills to the secondary market must go through banks. It is believed that if, as in the United States, bills were returned directly to the issuer, then they would virtually become a form of commercial paper. This would be the case because the issuers would procure funds in the BA market with their own returned bills. However, domestic commercial paper is prohibited in Japan, thus necessitating the intermediation of banks.

The Bank of Japan had its own vested interests in the development of the BA market. While the existence of a yen BA market complicated the central bank's task of monetary control, it also offered a challenging advantage. By conducting open market operations in the BA market (just as it does in the bill-discount market and the NCD market), the Bank can widen the breadth of its intervention. For example, in an open market purchase of bills the bank can distribute its buying between the interbank bill-discount market and the BA market.

Currently, the central bank buys and sells "eligible" BAs (those that meet the Bank's stringent criteria) through the Tanshi companies. This kind of market operation enables the Bank of Japan to use the open market (in which nonbanking corporations are allowed to participate) as a tool for the implementation of monetary policy. Because the interest rate for banker's acceptances offered by banks involves a spread with the interbank rates, any change in the market rate announced by the central bank is immediately manifested in the banker's acceptance lending rates. This rapid market penetrability of monetary policy provided the Bank of Japan with improved latitude for monetary adjustment.

Once established, however, the BA market proved to be a disappointment. Although the Ministry of Finance predicted it would reach a size of ¥100 billion within a month of opening and exceed ¥1 trillion within six months, the market barely reached ¥70 billion during its first month of operation and then fell to ¥30 billion, where it remained throughout 1985. The market's stunted development has been attributed to its lack of appeal to oil companies and steel producers which were able to raise short-term funds more cheaply with other instruments. Burdensome stamp duties, by adding to total borrowing costs, rendered the market noncompetitive. At the end of 1986 the market remained dormant.

Nonresidents' Yen Deposits

Placed with domestic authorized foreign exchange banks, non-resident deposits are made by sovereign bodies, central banks, and supranational institutions, with small numbers of foreign private financial institutions and corporations also participating. All foreign depositors, excluding sovereign entities, are subject to withholding tax on interest revenue.

Most nonresident deposits will eventually be siphoned into the offshore banking market established in Tokyo in late 1986. At the time of writing, however, the regulatory and tax structure of the offshore banking market (see Chapter 7) favor maintaining the status quo. Nonetheless, deregulation will eventually result in a vast expansion of the nonresident yen deposit base.

Residents' Foreign Currency Deposits

A foreign currency related short-term money market developed following the foreign exchange law of 1980. The deregulation of foreign currency deposits by residents of Japan provided institutions with a vehicle for the investment of short-term liquidity surpluses. It also offered opportunities for interest rate arbitrage. Because the Interest Rate Control Law does not apply, banks are free to use such rates as the London Eurodollar market rate. The opening of an offshore banking facility will eventually render this market superfluous.

THE YEN SWAP MARKET

A swap transaction involves the simultaneous sale and purchase of a currency with different purchase and sale dates. For example, a purchase of yen against U.S. dollars in the forward market (three-month delivery) is made while at the same time a sale of yen against U.S. dollars in the spot market (one-day delivery) is also made. In any swap position, the total volume of buy orders in a currency is always equal to the volume of sell orders in that currency. In this way, a swap transaction does not alter the net exchange position and its net effect is equivalent to two money market transactions. Yen swaps are a type of arbitrage transaction in which the real yen yield is equivalent to the dollar interest rate plus or minus the swap costs. Funding costs are roughly equivalent to the appropriate Euroyen interest rate. If a change occurs in a currency's spot rate, a foreign exchange gain or loss is not incurred. Thus, the swap enables institutions to convert yen into dollars (or vice versa) temporarily without establishing a net exchange position.

In Japan, swap funding transactions provide a vital short-term funding medium for foreign as well as domestic banking institutions. Prior to June 1984, ceiling restrictions inhibited the development of the yen swap market. The removal of these restrictions resulted in the rapid growth in the volume of swapping into yen of foreign currencies raised abroad by Japanese city banks or, alternatively, brought into Japan by the branches of foreign banks.

The outstanding balance of yen swapping (interest and currency transactions) grew from ¥250 billion at the end of May 1984 (before the deregulation) to more than ¥1 trillion two months later, at the end of July 1984. By the end of fiscal year 1985, the outstanding balance of the market exceeded ¥2.5 trillion and reached ¥4.9 trillion for the half year ending June 1986. Thus, in 1986, the Tokyo market was roughly the same size as the New York and London markets and represented about 25 percent of global interest rate swap transactions. As a result of this rapid expansion of the swap market, the structure of the short-term money markets are being weaned from their virtually total dependence on call-money, bill-discounts, NCDs and gensaki transactions.

THE COMMERCIAL PAPER MARKET

There is no domestic commercial paper market in Japan. Japanese companies have been issuing foreign-currency-denominated commercial paper in the United States and in the Euromarket for years and believe that overall funding costs would be lower in a domestic market in negotiable securities. In 1987, foreign corporations will be authorized to issue Euroyen commercial paper for exclusive sale in the Euromarkets and domestic companies are expected to join the market in 1988 (see Chapter 6). Since 1984, Japanese banks have been allowed to deal domestically in commercial paper issued by nonresident companies in foreign markets. For several years, the banks have been lobbying with the Ministry of Finance for authorization to sell in Japan the commercial paper issued overseas by Japanese companies. Permission is still pending.

When, in 1985, the design of the new banker's acceptance market was under consideration, the city banks objected that the proposed inclusion of jikihane bills (see above) in a yen-denominated banker's acceptance market would be a first step in the establishment of a domestic commercial paper market. From the banking perspective, the creation of a purely domestic commercial paper market would enable the securities companies to infringe on banking business. Thus, an indigenous commercial paper market would enable the Big Four to participate in a short-term money market other than the gensaki.

Current money market regulations prohibit nonfinancial institutions from *borrowing* short-term funds in all of the markets with the exception of gensaki. This prohibition was designed to assure that corporations would maintain their traditional dependence on banks for their short-term cash. The strong reluctance of regulatory authorities to introduce a domestic commercial paper market can be understood within this context. Indeed, in July 1986, the Commercial Banks Association issued an opinion that "it is too early to introduce commercial paper in the domestic market, since it is feared that this will upset Japan's financial order."[10] Japanese banks are persuaded that a market

---

[10] Quoted by Yoko Shibata, "Japan's banks fight domestic paper market," *Financial Times,* July 21, 1986.

in commercial paper possesses the potential to weaken relationships with their fellow keiretsu corporations. The banks also have voiced opposition to the development of a market in unsecured debt.

In 1982, new banking laws formally permitted the establishment of a domestic commercial paper market. The Ministry of Finance, however, postponed issuing regulations that would permit forming such a market. Nonetheless, the introduction of innovations such as the banker's acceptance market in 1985 and offshore banking in 1986 suggest that new money market instruments will be made available during the course of the late 1980s.

In May 1986, the Big Four attempted to prompt the Ministry of Finance to move on the commercial paper issue by creating a proposed body of draft rules for the market. The leading securities companies recommended the creation of a domestic commercial paper market which would *exclude* the participation of banks. The tentative rules outlined a new market in negotiable securities with denominations of ¥10 million, maturities of less than one year, and interest payments on a discount formula in order to circumvent the withholding tax. By suggesting that banks be excluded from the proposed market, the securities companies created a point of dispute which could only be resolved by means of direct government action. The ploy will probably prove successful.

In January 1987, the Bank of Japan released tentative regulations for a domestic commercial paper market. Classifying commercial paper in the same category as commercial bills, the central bank assured that banks and Tanshi companies as well as securities firms would be qualified participants. It is likely that a commercial paper market will be firmly established in Japan by 1988. Thus, one more instrument will be added to Japan's financial orchestra.

PART THREE

Fund Management

CHAPTER NINE

The Fund Management Industry in Japan[1]

OVERVIEW

Money is a big product in Japan. In 1986 corporate surplus funds exceeded $1.5 trillion while investment trusts totalled $188 billion, triple the spring 1983 level. Surplus corporate funds are managed by trust banks, life insurance companies, and via investment trusts (see Chapter 2). The nine foreign banks recently granted licenses to conduct trust business in Japan have not yet become an integral part of the fund management industry. Nonetheless, Japan Bankers Trust Company has already seized a portion of pension fund assets.

Life insurance companies are Japan's largest institutional investors. Although the 21 domestic companies invest only 14.7 percent (see Table 9–1) of their assets in equities, they own roughly 32 percent of the outstanding stock held by all Japanese financial institutions. This is about 10 percent of market capitalization. In addition, the life insurance companies hold about one-third of all the real estate controlled by financial institutions and account for one-third of all foreign institutional investment.

A handful of Japanese investment advisory firms provide indirect management services but they have been prohibited by

---

[1]Portions of this chapter previously appeared in an article by the author in *Euromoney Global Investor* 1 (April 1987).

TABLE 9–1   Investment Allocations of Life Insurance Industry Assets

Type of Investment	Percent
Domestic loans	39.5
Overseas loans	3.8
Domestic bonds	11.0
Foreign bonds	8.4
Domestic stocks	14.7
Foreign stocks	0.9
Domestic real estate	6.0

SOURCE: Yamaichi Research Institute

law from making discretionary decisions. Performance results are seldom announced and are known to be far below the indexes and often below the discount rate.

On November 25, 1986, all of this began to change irrevocably: A revolutionary investment advisory act became law. The Investment Advisory Act of 1986 allows any *licensed* entity to manage money (*excluding domestic pension funds*) on a discretionary basis. Thus, the Act gave birth to what will soon be a new investment management industry in Japan. More than 150 of the more than 400 domestic investment management firms applied for licenses to hang their shingles as discretionary managers in Tokyo's financial districts.

Simultaneously, for the first time in history, foreign management firms were legally permitted to have full discretionary management of Japanese institutional funds. At the time of writing, few Japanese institutions have the skills and experience to manage global stock and bond portfolios. Yet, Japanese recognition of the importance of international investments is growing. Japanese investors bought $100.1 billion of foreign securities in 1986, accounting for most of Japan's net long-term capital outflow (of these securities, 93 percent were bonds and 7 percent were equities).

North American and European capital management firms have been rushing to set up offices in Tokyo. Tie-ups between foreign and Japanese management companies have also been arranged and others are being negotiated. Thus, for example, in

1985 Okasan Securities Company and London-based Britannia Asset Management created an investment advisory company in London owned equally by the two firms. In 1986 Murray Johnstone, a Scots Investment Management Company, created a subsidiary in conjunction with Yamaichi International Capital Management Company. Yamaichi-Murray Johnstone Ltd., incorporated in the United Kingdom, is a 50/50 joint venture designed to invest Japanese domestic funds (provided primarily by insurance companies, regional banks, and sogo banks) in global securities portfolios.

Not only the Big Four have been involved in investment management tie-ups. Bank-affiliated third-tier securities firms have established linkages with foreign companies. For instance, Sumitomo Bank created Sumigin Bankers Investment Management Company in a joint venture with Bankers Trust Co. Similarly, Diamond Asset Management Company, an affiliate of the Mitsubishi Bank, tied up with the Boston-based Fidelity Group. Dai-ichi Securities, an affiliate of the Long-Term Credit Bank of Japan, established a relationship with Baring Brothers (the British merchant bank), designed to promote investment advisory activities aimed at Japanese institutional investors.

It is noteworthy that the first tie-up linking a Japanese investment adviser and a foreign firm was in 1984, between Nikko International Capital Management Company and Charterhouse J. Rothschild, a British investment bank. Aimed at the ultra-competitive American pension fund market, the alliance was designed to create a synergy between British management capability and Japanese marketing ability. The result of the marriage was divorce after a year. The reason: irreconcilable differences in management and style.

In late 1986, the Ministry of Finance indicated that it would demand that the parent companies of investment management subsidiaries register for licenses in applications separate from their Tokyo branches. This requirement was intended to strictly limit the number of foreign investment advisory firms able to procure licenses. However, outside pressure (particularly from the British government) to allow foreign financial institutions equal market access resulted in a softening of registration requirements. As a result, the parent companies (or affiliates) of foreign investment advisory companies will not be required to register under Japanese law. Thus, parent companies will be permitted to provide advisory services to subsidiaries while the subsidiaries will be authorized to subcontract advisory business to their parent firms. Not only will this allow portfolios of foreign currency–denominated securities to be managed abroad, but it will also effectively permit a large number of foreign investment advisers to market services through their Tokyo offices. (As this book goes to press, 135 investment advisory companies received approval of their registration applications. Sixteen of these were foreign companies.)

Soon the entire character of Japan's active institutional investing will be changed and new players will participate in the transformation. Meanwhile, although the stakes are considerable, the rules of the game are hazy and the impact of the Investment Advisory Act of 1986 remains to be seen.

What is the new Act? What are the rules of the investment management game and how will they change? Can foreigners win a portion of management commissions from those who have long considered noncompetition as certain and as institutionalized as the rule of law?

THE INVESTMENT ADVISORY ACT OF 1986

At the end of September 1986 there were more than 80 Japanese investment advisory companies which were the affiliates of domestic financial institutions (securities firms, banks, life and nonlife insurance companies) offering their services to Japanese investors (see Table 9–2). An additional dozen foreign investment advisory firms maintained representative offices in Tokyo. An estimated 400 investment advisory firms, many of them tiny companies publishing stock information newsletters, also plied their trade. By comparison, in the United States there are currently more than 11,000 firms registered as investment advisers.

As of March 30, 1986, the top 12 Japanese securities firms maintained capital management subsidiaries that managed a total of ¥5.7 trillion (roughly $38 billion). More than 40 percent of this amount was managed by subsidiaries of the Big Four securities firms.

Prior to the enactment of the Investment Advisory Act, there

TABLE 9–2	Numbers* and Type of Affiliation of Investment Advisory Firms

Type of Affiliation	Number
Securities company	19
Bank	25
Trust bank	4
Life insurance company	12
Nonlife insurance company	6
Foreign advisory firm	13
Others	2

*At the end of September 1986.
SOURCE: *Nihon Keizai Shimbun*

were no regulations in Japan regarding investment advisory companies. Although investment advisory firms were prohibited from managing funds on a *discretionary* basis, any entity could establish an *advisory* firm by complying with commercial law.

In 1984, the bankruptcy of the Toshi Journal (see Chapter 3) as well as several other well-publicized collapses of advisory firms, led the Ministry of Finance to consider establishing unequivocal investment advisory guidelines. In the late spring of 1985, a bill was introduced to the Diet and, after a year of deliberation, was approved on May 27, 1986, to become effective within six months.

The goal of the Investment Advisory Act is the establishment of a sound investment advisory industry. To this end, the Act includes a registration system and a licensing system. Companies that are mainly involved in the business of counseling by providing information on stocks and bonds need only to be registered. On the other hand, companies operating discretionary management accounts must obtain a license from the Ministry of Finance.

In order to obtain a license, an adviser must be an established corporation *including* corporations "based on foreign laws." A foreign corporation, however, is expected to maintain an office in Japan and satisfy the same requirements incumbent on domestic corporations. Although the general criteria to be fulfilled in order to obtain a license are detailed in the provisions of the Act, it is not yet known how the Ministry of Finance will exercise its considerable discretion. The Act itself does not specify minimum numbers of personnel and clients or levels of capitalization or years of experience. It is tacitly acknowledged that all qualified firms will not receive licenses and most small foreign firms will be excluded.[2]

Although the Investment Advisory Act will enable foreign management firms to participate in the Japanese market, foreigners will continue to find the bulk of Japanese corporate funds inaccessible. This is due to the special relationships among industrial and financial corporations (see Rule #1, below). As a result, it will be difficult for a corporation to change a manager, although new funds *will* be assignable to qualified foreign financial institutions. Indeed, several foreign investment management firms already "manage" (see Rule #6, below) billions of yen of "specified money trusts" or tokkin (*tokutei kinsen shintaku*), and foreign trust banks are managing some "fund trusts" (kingaishin funds) that closely resemble the tokkin accounts.

Since 1896, various investment advisory associations have been maintained in order to arbitrate disputes within the investment advisory industry. The Investment Advisory Act of 1986, in order to "insure investor protection and the sound development of the industry," provides for the creation of a National Federation of Investment Advisory Associations. Although its charter is vague, the new Federation will function as a liaison between licensed and registered investment advisors on the one hand and the Ministry of Finance on the other. The Investment Advisory Act does not preclude foreign membership in this Federation; however, it remains to be seen whether foreign investment management firms will be allowed to participate.

---

[2]At the time of writing (late 1986), the full guidelines of the Investment Advisory Act had not yet been determined by the Ministry of Finance. The Act itself, consisting of 61 articles described in a total of more than 10,000 words, is vague regarding the particulars of formal licensing requirements. It is expected, however, that minimum asset requirements will be set relatively low (in the ¥100–200 million range), while entrusted assets will also be quite low (¥20–30 billion). Similarly, personnel requirements for the Tokyo branches of foreign investment advisory firms are expected to be minimal.

BIG FUNDS ARE BIG BUSINESS IN JAPAN

Tokkin Funds

Specified money trusts or **tokkin** are funds handled by investment management firms and redeemable in cash. **Fund trusts** or **kingaishin** are managed by trust banks and redeemable in cash or assets. In the financial literature both types of funds are lumped together under the single rubric, tokkin. The tokkin are special transitory trust funds created by domestic industrial and financial corporations in order to provide a means through which capital gains achieved by the fund can be converted to dividends (thus transforming unrealized capital performance into income). In this way, tokkin provide significant tax advantages and add flexibility to accounting procedures.

Any institutional investor can create a tokkin by simply depositing a reserve with a trust bank and subsequently signing a specified money trust (tokkin) agreement. The agreement, which is standardized, states the type of portfolio management and reporting procedures intended, as well as the date and method of contract termination. The minimum life of a contract is one year. The investor can either appoint the trust bank to manage the newly created tokkin or select an investment advisory company to provide investment "advice."

Although tokkin, as a medium for investment, have been available for more than half a century, they have only recently become significant vehicles in Japan's investment management business. An amendment to corporate tax laws in late 1980 allowed the book value of securities within a tokkin to be assessed separately from identical securities taking the form of cross-shareholdings (which are ordinarily never liquidated— see Chapter 3 or Glossary). Furthermore, because the securities are held in the name of a trust bank, the identity of investors is fully concealed. This anonymity facilitates the secret trading and manipulation of the shares in affiliated companies.

In October 1984, insurance companies were authorized by the Ministry of Finance to invest up to 3 percent of their total assets in the domestic stock market through tokkin funds. It is likely that in 1987 this amount will be raised to 5 percent. The proviso that capital gains can be paid to policy holders in the form of dividends proved to be a boon to the insurance companies' fiscal management. Because the goal of tokkin investment is short-term capital appreciation, tokkin cash tends to be invested in speculative and volatile issues. In this way, the tokkin assets have contributed to stock market growth and market uncertainty. The total value of tokkin funds (including fund trusts) reached ¥17.3 trillion ($106 billion) at the end of October 1986, representing a significant and growing portion of the funds available for discretionary management under the new Investment Advisory Act.

More than half of the money directed into tokkin is derived from corporate surplus funds. Because of the outstanding bull stock market in 1986, it was rumored that many corporations gained more post-tax income from investments than from sales. As a result, some of the money raised in the Euromarket found its way into the Tokyo stock market via the anonymity of tokkin investments. It is likely, therefore, that a major decline in the stock market will result in some corporate disenchantment with the tokkin as a source of income. The short-term character of tokkin structure means that a change in climate could cause the oasis to disappear.

Meanwhile, the Ministry of Finance has given life insurance companies "administrative guidance" regarding the accounting method to be used in reporting tokkin investment valuation profits or losses. Beginning in fiscal 1987, life insurance companies will be expected to use the cost or market basis (whichever is lower) on their balance sheets. As a result, the insurance companies will be unable to conceal losses by listing the cost of shares purchased with tokkin funds rather than their market valuation.

In addition to the deepening reservoir of tokkin are **eigyo tokkin** funds. Eigyo tokkin are elusive blocks of money, of unknown but significant magnitude, given clandestinely by Japanese corporations (particularly life insurance companies) to the institutional sales departments of securities firms (which provide brokerage and underwriting services to the companies). The institutional sales departments provide a guaranteed rate of return (usually 7 to 8 percent) which is superior to that available from domestic fixed income securities.[3] All parties concerned deny the existence of the eigyo tokkin for three important reasons:

1. The institutional sales departments of securities companies are not authorized to act as investment advisors and therefore cannot legally invest funds on behalf of corporate clients.
2. On their books, corporations list their eigyo tokkin investments as deposits or bonds given to the securities companies and not as investments.
3. Thus, neither the securities companies nor the corporations inform the Ministry of Finance of the existence of the eigyo tokkin.

As the result of 1, 2, and 3, income derived from eigyo tokkin is concealed by all participants. The life insurance companies, for example, stockpile their profits in the form of hidden reserves. These reserves were used in 1986 to counterbalance severe foreign exchange losses incurred through the purchase of U.S. Treasury issues. Because the eigyo tokkin money does not officially exist, the institutional sales departments of securities companies are able to freely utilize it in a variety of creative and marginal "investment" activities such as ramping (see Chapter 3).

Pension Funds

In the Japan of 20 years ago, only 6.6 percent of the total population was aged 65 or older. In 1986, the ratio of the size of the cohort aged 65 or more to the total Japanese population was roughly 10.3 percent (lower than most industrialized nations). Demographers predict that this percentage will rise to 16 percent by the year 2000 (higher than the majority of industrial nations), reaching 22 percent by 2020. Perhaps it is thus appropriate that one of the most rapidly greying societies in history should own the fastest growing pension fund in the world.

---

[3] Such guarantees, which effectively transform a portfolio into a deposit instrument, are strictly illegal in Japan.

Nonetheless, the pension fund is not growing fast enough. In 1986, there were roughly seven contributors for each annuitant; by the year 2020 this figure will drop to about 2.7. Indeed, at their present rate of growth, Japan's pension fund reserves are likely to be exhausted in about 20 years.[4] So serious is this problem that in 1986 MITI (the Ministry for International Trade and Industry) proposed the creation of special new towns overseas for the elderly. The establishment of "Silver Columbia New Towns" is based upon the assumption that pension funds will soon be insufficient to support the aged (payment provisions have long been inadequate) and that the strong yen can go a long way in countries such as Spain, Portugal, and Mexico. That the suggested exportation of the elderly has been taken seriously by many in Japan is a powerful indicator of the gravity of the pension fund problem.

Pension fund assets in Japan, valued at approximately ¥24 trillion ($150 billion) at the end of September 1986, are currently increasing at the rate of 22 percent per year (and are expected to at least quadruple by the turn of the century). Much of the growth in private pension funds is the result of corporate contributions and *not* investment performance. In addition to the private pensions are public pension funds worth more than ¥70 trillion ($460 billion). Funded by employers and deductions from employees' salaries, the public pensions are handled by the government's Trust Fund Bureau and are used to subsidize the government's fiscal investment and loan program. Eventually, however, these funds will become available to banks and investment advisory companies.

Private pension funds are the exclusive preserve of the 16 trust banks, 1 city bank (Daiwa), and 21 domestic life insurance companies. At the end of 1985, the trust banks managed 63.6 percent of private pension fund assets with the balance handled by insurance companies. By 1988 or 1989, city banks will probably be allowed to manage private pension funds. A year or two after that, investment advisory companies, including foreign firms, will also be permitted to do so.

---

[4]See Mitsuhiro Fukao and Masatoshi Inouchi, "Public Pensions and the Saving Rate," *Economic Eye*, June 1985, pp. 236–43.

THE FUND MANAGEMENT GAME IN JAPAN

The Old Rules of the Game

RULE #1: *The management of money shadows the management of relationships.*

In Japan, relationships among corporate entities serve to delineate the entities themselves. This is particularly the case among the components of the keiretsu (the postwar groupings which replaced the pre-War zaibatsu—see Chapter 1). Each keiretsu consists of a diversified constellation of companies clustered around a bank. Thus, for example, the Fuyo Group, with Fuji Bank at its center, is made up of a financial tentacle (including Yasuda Trust & Banking Corporation and Yasuda Mutual Life Insurance) as well as a trading tentacle (Marubeni Corp.), and a dozen other tentacles ranging from construction to food. Each keiretsu member maintains its relationships with its fellows through interlocked cross-shareholding. The keiretsu bank provides loans to its members in a financial system that has long relied on indirect financing as the primary means of raising capital. Thus, the keiretsu bank is both a major shareholder and a major creditor of its member corporations.

In addition to the keiretsu, which include hundreds of the biggest companies listed on the first section of the Tokyo Stock Exchange, there are also smaller corporate groupings which mimic the keiretsu constellations. Each company within the group ideally attempts to rely as much as possible on group services. A company within the Fuyo group, for example, will usually borrow money from Fuji Bank and give its pension funds to Yasuda Trust & Banking Corporation. In this way, capital and goods flow like a current of electricity among the keiretsu members.

It is this flow pattern which has traditionally identified the group and determined where group members will seek financial services. Therefore, when fund management is necessary, the appropriate group member is sought. Concepts such as *investment philosophy* or *performance history* are irrelevant to the allocation of funds for management. Decisions regarding the selection of a fund manager are based upon the prior existence of relationships within a greater structure.

The group relationships are not perceived in terms of what they can accomplish for a particular member in a given situation. *Instead, relationships exist so they can be maintained.* Corporate relationships are not evaluated in terms of what they do but rather in terms of what they are. Although not articulated in Japan, this concept underlies much of the decision making that traditionally determined the flow of funds among industrial and financial institutions. Just as these relationships are not perceived in terms of *performance*, decisions regarding the allocation of funds for management are not made on the basis of anticipated performance results. *Fund managers are not selected:* the choice has already been made by virtue of the enduring relationship between the "client" and the manager.

RULE #2: *At trust banks and insurance companies: Portfolio performance = Gross yield.*

The clients of U.S. and European capital management firms focus their attention on the total return of a portfolio, which is simply the sum of capital appreciation and dividend (or interest) income. Although total return, by itself, can sometimes be a deceptive indicator of portfolio performance, it is generally considered to be the most meaningful and reasonable mode of appraising the results of management. Japanese trust banks and life insurance companies, however, have traditionally relied on a different yard stick for measuring portfolio growth: gross yield.

The yield (the total dividends or interest yielded annually and expressed as a percentage of the total portfolio) for each of the trust banks and insurance companies falls within the same narrow range of roughly 8 to 9 percent. Eight percent is the growth rate believed necessary to keep pace with the increasing pension demands of Japan's rapidly greying society. Is it suspicious that all the trust banks and insurance companies announce roughly identical annual portfolio performance results? Yes.

RULE #3: *Low return and low risk.*

The goal of fund managers and the institutions that employ them is not to achieve the highest return prudently possible. For decades, **administrative guidance** (see Glossary) from the Ministry of Finance, for example, directed trust banks and life insurance companies to curtail investments in equities (limited to a maximum of 30 percent), in real estate (limited to 20 percent) as well as in all nondomestic instruments (limited to 10 percent but raised to 25 percent in 1986). Indeed, the limitation on foreign securities exposure is partially responsible for the invention of sushi bonds (classified by the Ministry of Finance as Japanese, these foreign-currency-denominated bonds are sold in the Eurobond market by Japanese corporations and have higher interest rates than Japanese securities and lower rates than U.S. securities—see Chapter 6). However, the most conservative investment possible, long-term Japanese government debt, is necessarily the preferred investment vehicle for the pension funds of Japan's retired work force.

Traditionally, the quest for capital gain in the domestic equity market has been the special crusade of individual investors (who currently hold about 25.4 percent of outstanding shares and who accounted for roughly 40 percent of sales volume on the Tokyo Stock Exchange in 1986) and not of trust banks and life insurance companies. In 1985, most pension funds had only 7 to 10 percent of total assets invested in domestic equities with life insurance companies holding roughly double this percentage. Investment in high yielding U.S. and European equities is limited in accordance with the low risk philosophy and regulatory directives. In 1985, for example, 7 percent of the total net value of trust fund assets was invested in foreign stocks. Although the purchase of relatively high yielding foreign bonds has also not been altogether eschewed, the concept of tying domestic pension funds and corporate surplus funds with foreign instruments (dependent upon foreign economic and political forces) has long been viewed as distasteful by Japan's financial establishment. Indeed, a further appreciation of the yen against the dollar and other currencies is likely to result in a move away from foreign debt toward real estate and equity (see Chapter 2, note 1).

RULE #4: *Just as performance is not the goal of management institutions in Japan, it is also not the goal of individual fund managers.*

Portfolio managers in Japan are seldom evaluated by their employers in terms of performance. Managers are not rewarded for good performance results and are never fired for consistently poor results. Securities selection is conducted by committees with individual managers choosing particular issues from "buy lists." Fund managers are not encouraged to conduct securities research. After all, the buy lists are usually determined by executives who outrank the managers. A fund manager (or his assistant) investigating particular equities on the buy list could be perceived as challenging the wisdom of his superiors. Thus, the judicious fund manager avoids making unusual decisions and seeks, above all, to cultivate the appearance of stability and normality in his management behavior.

RULE #5: *At investment trusts: Portfolio performance = Brokerage commissions*

In 1985, there were 92 domestic open-ended investment trusts managed by 11 investment trust companies, each affiliated with one of the major securities firms. The average rate of return of the 92 funds at the end of fiscal 1985 was roughly 2.5 percent, significantly below the discount rate. Just six of the funds beat the Nikkei Stock Index Averages.

There are a number of reasons why Japanese investment trusts have performed so badly:

1. Churning. Because each of the investment trust companies is controlled by a securities firm whose primary source of revenue is brokerage commissions, fund managers at the investment trusts are encouraged to maximize portfolio turnover. Virtually all securities transactions are exercised by company traders. Many securities firms regularly have a special brokerage commission day in which fund managers within the group are encouraged to turn over their holdings. An annual portfolio turnover of 250 percent is not uncommon.

2. The parent securities firm (which also manages funds) routinely dumps poorly performing stocks on the subsidiary funds which are handled by the investment trust arm.

3. An insufficiency of experienced fund managers and the absence of training programs for managers contributes to poor management decisions which result in poor performance.

TABLE 9–3 Japanese Investment Management Companies

Name	Established
Pure investment advisory firms:	
Yamaichi International Capital Management	November 1971
Daiwa Capital Management	June 1973
Shin-Nihon Capital Management	September 1976
Nomura Capital Management	January 1981
Nikko International Capital Management	September 1981
Sanyo Investment Management	November 1983
Wako Capital Management	January 1984
Okasan Capital Management	September 1984
Kokusai Investment Management	December 1984
Cosmo Investment Management	August 1985
Kangyo Kakumaru Investment Management	October 1985
Yamatane Investment Management	December 1985
Kosei Investment Management	January 1986
Maruman Investment Management	July 1986
Research institutes also engaged as investment advisers:	
Dai-Ichi Investment Research Center	March 1971
Osakaya Research Center	October 1983
Tokyo Securities Research Institute	April 1985
Taiheiyo Research Institute	December 1985

RULE #6: *Japanese capital management firms, like the investment trusts, provide the parent securities company with a vital source of brokerage commissions.*

This is a corollary of Rule #5. Fourteen Japanese securities firms currently operate investment management subsidiaries (see Table 9–3). These subsidiaries, although theoretically prohibited from exercising discretionary management decisions, empirically do manage several different types of discretionary accounts. Non-Japanese institutions (including foreign governments) are permitted to give funds to the firms for discretionary management. In addition, Japanese institutional funds are managed by the firms on a de facto discretionary basis which is de jure advisory. This means that the investment management firms inform their Japanese clients of their buy and sell decisions and subsequently obtain a written "request" from the client specifying that the given order be implemented. These accounts, which represent billions of dollars, have annual portfolio turnovers in the 200 percent range. Transactions are ordinarily conducted through the parent securities firm, resulting in brokerage commissions which far exceed management fees.

With the exception of sample funds (belonging to non-Japanese institutions), which are routinely tracked by U.S. consultants (such as Frank Russell International or InterSec Research Corporation), the performances of the portfolios are unannounced. Thus, the performance history of the management firms is virtually unknown. However, the performances of the majority of nondomestic portfolios, which *have* been monitored by consultants during the past three years, have been relatively poor, often falling within the third or fourth quartiles. The performances of domestic portfolios (consisting largely of the tokkin funds) are rumored to be no better than the achievements of the trust banks and life insurance companies.

The Old Rules Must Make Way for the New

RULE #1A: *A new pragmatism will shift corporate vision to promises of improved portfolio performance, causing some old relationships to fall into desuetude.*

The trust banks and life insurance companies continue to enjoy the exclusive right to manage pension funds. However, because the Japanese population is aging faster than similar cohorts in other industrialized nations, obligations to provide for an expanding retired work force will be a big drain on pension fund growth. For this reason, there is a new anxiety that unless Japan's private pension funds are managed with the expectation of growth through performance, the day may soon come when Japan's retired workers will face penury in their retirement years.

In June 1985, the Finance Ministry authorized four city banks (Fuji, Sanwa, Mitsui, and the Bank of Tokyo) to create investment advisory companies. This move was interpreted as a signal by the government that banks will eventually be allowed access to pension fund management. Thus, it is virtually certain that within three to five years, pension funds, like corporate surplus funds, will become accessible to investment management firms, including foreign institutions. This will result in a search for management performance which will supersede the allocation of pension funds on the basis of relationships alone.

As decisions about the choice of fund manager become increasingly sophisticated, growing attention also will be given to fee scales. Trust banks, for example, currently charge a 1 percent management fee per annum and a 0.3 percent custodian fee for fund trusts. The management fees for pension funds are sometimes as high as 1.8 percent per year. Competition from life insurance companies (which charge up to 60 basis points less) and foreign trust banks will inevitably lead to reductions in management and custodial fees.

As with pension funds so with tokkin funds, investment trusts, and even individual accounts. The choice of manager, like the choice of vehicle, will be determined by performance history. Furthermore, Japanese professionals and individual investors will evaluate performance criteria with increasing discernment and will demand standardized methods of reporting and evaluation. Increased competition may also lead to discounted management and custodial fees.

Because many large corporations maintain overseas offices, they are sometimes more receptive to foreign approaches to investment management than Japanese institutions with relatively little international exposure. Although very few have done so, multinational Japanese corporations have the most latitude for selecting foreign managers when investing their corporate cash reserves. It is likely that giant multinationals will be among the first to regularly hire foreign managers.

Meanwhile, foreign investment management firms that set up offices in Tokyo will need local staff who are not only intimately familiar with the Japanese financial environment but also have developed relationships with top corporate executives. Qualified Japanese professionals are not easily poached by foreign institutions. Nonetheless, financial deregulation has given the Tokyo offices of executive search firms a booming business. At the same time, foreign capital management companies will utilize their own incentives to lure outstanding Japanese professionals to their camps. In September 1986, for example, ABD International (a subsidiary of Dresdner Bank) hired Masanori Yoshida as the managing director of its recently opened Tokyo office. Yoshida, who had been the president of Daiwa International Capital Management Company, resigned from Daiwa after more than 30 years of employment within the Daiwa group. Through this and similar moves in the future, foreign investment management companies will go native, buying and exploiting the inside knowledge and relationships that are indispensable to the effective marketing of management services in Japan.

RULE #2A: *Portfolio performance = Yield . . . but not forever.*

In May 1983, the Federation of Employee Pension Funds presented a formal complaint list to the Ministry of Health and Welfare (which oversees pension funds). The Federation objected to the near absence of disclosure and performance measurement as well as to high management fees (from 0.55 percent to 1.8 percent of assets under management). Federation representatives urged the Ministry to seek avenues to increase competition among managers. These objections were perhaps partly responsible for the decision to permit nine foreign banks to enter the pension fund management market through trust banking.

In 1986, the Foundation of Welfare Pension Funds, Japan's biggest administrator of pension funds, announced that it was instituting new management guidelines that placed particular stress on high returns. Under the guidelines, which will be used by all managers of pension funds in 1987, the portfolio performance of trust banks and insurance companies will be evaluated quarterly against a variety of standard equity and bond indexes. In addition, profit produced from growth in the book values of stocks will be taken into account. Recognition that income yield as a measure of portfolio performance is not only inadequate but also is easily susceptible to manipulation has become widespread among Japanese pension fund sponsors. It is likely that within a few years, mounting pressure from the Ministry of Health and Welfare conjoined with demands from the Foundation of Welfare Pension Funds will result in actions leading directly to the establishment of new measures of portfolio performance, including, perhaps, attention to total return. This in turn will result in the allocation of pension funds to investment institutions on the basis of a manager's performance history, leading to modifications of Rules #3 and #4.

RULE #3A: *Higher return and higher risk.*

means

RULE #4A: *New performance: the be-all and the end-all of the investment management business.*

Trust banks and insurance companies gradually will be forced to compete for funds to manage. Such competition will render inadequate the 8 to 9 percent return which for years has been the standard of performance expectations. In April 1985, in anticipation of the advent of foreign trust banks, Japan's trust banks cut by 10 percent the rates of commissions and processing fees charged for the management of pension funds. Although the move did not significantly lower the profit margins of the trust banks' pension fund management departments, it was an indication of internal concerns regarding foreign competition.

Meanwhile, the nine foreign trust banks will utilize the full magnitude of their management experience in order to outperform their Japanese colleagues. Simultaneously, each of the foreign trust banks will provide investment management training to the domestic trust bank with which it has established an affiliation.

It is a truism that higher return necessitates higher risk and, inevitably, the credo of Japan's pension fund management establishment will develop a rather different flavor from "low return and low risk." Although the allocation of funds will not change overnight, there will be a growing interest in higher yielding instruments, including nondomestic securities. In the spring of 1986, the Ministry of Finance substantially raised the ceiling restrictions on the proportion of international investments permissible for all domestic funds from 10 percent to 25 percent. As a result, fund managers, faced with new competition from foreign institutions, rushed to expand their exposure to higher yielding foreign securities, including equities.

Also in 1986, 16 Japanese life insurance companies as well as several foreign firms (Equitable Life Assurance and Sony-Prudential Life Insurance), introduced variable life insurance in Japan.[5] Variable life insurance policies are investment con-

---

[5] Equitable Seimei Hoken K.K. is the wholly owned Japanese subsidiary of Equitable Life Assurance Society of the United States.

tracts that provide investment in an underlying securities portfolio. The variable insurance premiums are exempted from most restrictions that encumber other types of insurance company investments. It is expected that the insurance companies will actively compete against each other for maximum portfolio performance which would result in optimal average yields on the policies sold to consumers.

RULE #5A: *At investment trusts, portfolio performance will rise while brokerage commissions decline.*

At the end of November 1986, total investment trust net assets stood at triple the March 1983 level. The catalyst for the enormous expansion was a growing investor preference for the promise of relatively high yields from the investment trusts. During the period ending June 30, 1986, interest rates for time deposits and postal savings plummeted to the lowest level since World War II (this followed three consecutive reductions of the official discount rate in January, March, and April). At the same time, new controls were added to tax exempt postal savings in an attempt to prevent those in the highest income brackets from evading taxes on savings.

Subsequently, another cut in the discount rate, bringing it to 3 percent in November 1986, further stimulated investor interest in the trusts. It is likely that additional discount rate cuts in 1987, followed by the abolishment of the tax exempt maruyu savings accounts (see Chapter 7 or Glossary), will result in massive disintermediation of funds from banks to securities investments.

Within the context of low bank deposit rates and a bull stock market, investors in 1985 and 1986 selected equity investment trusts as the ideal compromise between the security and low yield of bank deposits on the one hand and the risk and high yield of the equity market on the other. Investor demand for a return comparable to stock market performance has pressured the all-equity investment trusts to seek improved returns.

In the fall of 1985, the number of foreign equity markets sanctioned as investment territory by the Ministry of Finance was increased from 11 markets in 9 countries to 30 markets in 22 countries (including the roller coaster markets of Hong Kong and Italy). This was accompanied by a relaxation of a number of "self-imposed" guidelines for fund managers.

This liberalization of the number of foreign markets considered prudent hunting territory was the direct result of the exceptional relative performance of the four dozen foreign investment trusts being sold in Japan by the Big Four securities firms. Most of the foreign investment trusts sold to Japanese investors performed from 10 to 15 times better than the domestic investment trusts.

The superior performance of the foreign funds and growing consumer demand for them is forcing individual fund managers to seek improved returns on their investments. The managers, pressured by their employers to produce a domestic product competitive with foreign investment vehicles, are obliged to rationalize their portfolio management. Such rationalization necessarily involves a reduction in turnover which leads, of course, to a reduction in the brokerage commissions reaped by the parent firm.

RULE #6A: *Japanese capital management firms, gradually forced to compete with foreign managers in the domestic market, will be obliged to improve portfolio performance at the expense of brokerage commissions for their parents.*

Of the 12 biggest securities companies in Japan, only the Big Four maintain investment management subsidiaries with significant nondomestic client accounts. However, even these firms have encountered little success in marketing their management services to U.S. corporate pension funds. The greatest obstacle to the success of these management companies is not only the middling to poor performance of the portfolios they have managed but also the absence of coherent and consistent management styles and investment philosophies.

It will be many years before most fund managers employed by Japanese institutions will be able to produce a portfolio performance (even in portfolios consisting wholly of Japanese equities) competitive with the results of the leading U.S. and European capital managers. However, the inexorable pressure to compete in deregulated financial markets is already beginning to inspire the development of new investment approaches in Japan.

Japanese investment advisory firms are now becoming aware that fund management is a specialized activity requiring specialized training. As a result of this realization, Japanese investment management companies are exploiting their tie-ups with foreign capital management firms. The foreign firms are perceived as schools for young trainees. Thus, for example, after creating a joint venture subsidiary with Glasgow-based Murray Johnstone, Yamaichi International Capital Management Company immediately sent a trainee to Scotland. It is expected that, after three or four years, the trainee, having become experienced in foreign management methods, will return to Japan to manage international funds.

Only through prudent long-term investment guidelines which wholly disregard the production of brokerage commissions will Japanese investment management firms succeed in producing a world class product. The international capital management arm of at least one Japanese securities company has already begun to make this move and it is likely that other firms will follow.

MANAGING MONEY IN JAPAN

Today, vast pools of corporate surplus funds, tokkin funds, and pension funds are being managed by domestic institutions (and a few foreign firms) in Japan. The performance results have generally been poor. Simultaneously, there is a growing realization that international investments provide outstanding returns. The burgeoning market in foreign trusts is evidence of this new consciousness.

Japanese administrators and decision makers are bound by long-term keiretsu relationships that link companies in special groups. These relationships cannot be discarded easily, but they will be slowly vitiated by the recent arrival of foreign financial institutions. The importance of personal relationships in Japanese business (and Japanese culture generally), the critical value of existing corporate ties, and the long time period required to cultivate new relationships, render the marketing of foreign fund management services delicate and difficult. The Investment Advisory Act of 1986 will permit the licensing of many domestic and some foreign investment management firms in Japan. Competition for accounts will be keen.

Nonetheless, a strong and receptive client base exists in Japan. It represents a universe of potential business which has never before been available to investment advisory firms (domestic or foreign). U.S. and European firms that enter the market early and establish strong institutional relationships will gain an enduring access to corporate surplus funds. Given the expansion of Japan's international investments and the growth of Japan's institutional funds, a market of great promise and exceptional depth awaits the hungry foreign firms now applying to the Ministry of Finance for licenses.

Of course, the Japanese cultural features that led to the creation and continuance of the old system will not disappear. The importance of relationships within the keiretsu will not diminish. The embedded reluctance to give foreigners the power to make decisions about Japanese funds will not evaporate in the near future. Nonetheless, the cumulative effects of deregulation and the liberalization of Japan's financial institutions will overwhelm all obstacles. Tokyo will gradually join London and New York as a global financial marketplace. In the face of this ineluctable destiny, the Japanese investment management business will adjust and will someday come to resemble its U.S. and European counterparts.

ZAITEK

In the spring of 1984, the Ministry of Finance removed restrictions prohibiting nonfinancial institutions from participating in a range of financial activities in overseas markets.[6] As a result, major trading companies (**sogo shosha**) such as Mitsubishi, Sumitomo, Marubeni, and others set up finance corporations overseas, particularly in London. These were soon followed by finance corporations set up by other industries, such as Nippon Steel. By the end of 1986, more than 50 of these London-based finance companies had become participants in capital market activities.

---

[6]The proscription on domestic financial activities remained unchanged.

Zaitek (or zaitekku—see Glossary) is a hybrid term referring to the process of deriving money from relatively sophisticated techniques of financial management. In its current usage, the term refers almost exclusively to financial market arbitrage. The word connotes a new-age "technological" approach to cash management intended to improve corporate income and liquidity by means of investment rather than through production and marketing.

The cash balances of many Japanese corporations have reached record levels, despite losses resulting from the revaluation of the yen against the dollar. By investing a portion of cash balances in portfolios of money market instruments and long-term securities, Japanese corporations have often been able to reap handsome profits. This type of "financial engineering" is a novel concept in Japan and, not surprisingly, encountered some initial opposition from conservative factions within industrial circles.

Some traditionalists in the Japanese corporate community have stated that profit should be derived from the production of goods and not from financial arbitrage. They insist that finance departments should manage and not produce the company profits. According to this perspective, companies that devote their resources to trading financial instruments are analogous to rice farmers planting coffee trees in their rice fields when coffee prices are high. When the price of coffee declines, the share of the rice market is lost while the farmer is left with unneeded coffee trees. Thus, available funds are best invested in plant and equipment or R&D. Such cash-rich corporations as Toyota (long known as the "Toyota Bank" because of its approximately $12 billion cash surplus), Sony, and Matsushita have voiced distaste for investments in high yielding Euromarket instruments. Akio Morita, chairman and co-founder of Sony, observed in 1985 that "it is an unhealthy notion that money management is more profitable than investments in real goods."[7] In May 1985, Yoshihiro Inayama, chairman of Keidanren (the Federation of Economic Organizations) stated in a speech that

---

[7] Quoted by the *Japan Economic Journal*, July 16, 1985, p. 4.

a number of Japanese firms are floating convertible bonds in Switzerland where interest rates are low, and then they place the funds thus raised in the U.S. where interest rates are high. This is a pure money game of rolling over debts and these companies should be ashamed of themselves for making profits out of such a money game.[8]

The leaders in the art of zaitek, however, use surplus funds (or borrow funds domestically from their keiretsu bank) and subsequently reinvest these funds in a broad range of financial instruments.[9] In this way, the Euromarket is becoming the playground of Japanese corporate finance. The outstanding successes of dabblers in the arts of zaitek have begun to demonstrate to even the most obstinate that financial markets *can* be exceptional sources of revenue.

Indeed, in 1985 and 1986, despite loud claims to the contrary, Toyota and Matsushita Electric, as well as Sony, derived substantial pretax profits from zaitek operations (see Table 9–4). These corporations, however, deny that they are using money in order to conduct financial arbitrage. Instead, they insist that their cash management procedures simply involve conservative investments in such domestic money market vehicles as NCDs and foreign currency deposits. Nonetheless, their overseas subsidiaries (e.g. Sony Overseas SA in Switzerland) are actively engaged in foreign currency swaps and other types of arbitrage operations.

Among the trading companies, London-based Mitsubishi Finance Corporation has a $1 billion investment portfolio which in 1985 yielded more than $20 million in pretax profits. Portfolio investments have been funded by means of bonds floated in the Euromarket and swapped into floating rate notes. The finance houses created in London and New York by trading companies, as well as other Japanese industries, are growing rapidly. Eventually, such firms as Mitsubishi Finance International, C. Itoh

---

[8]*Ibid.*

[9]The domestic stock market contributed significantly to zaitek profits in 1986. Many corporations that raised funds through Euromarket debt issues subsequently invested the money, via tokkin funds, in the Tokyo stock market.

TABLE 9–4 Top 20 Zaitek Corporate Pretax Profits*

Company	Profits† 1986	Profits† 1985	Zaitek as a Percentage of Pretax Profit in 1986
Toyota	99,031	77,064	45.5
Matsushita Elec.	58,107	49,580	55.7
Nissan	53,355	35,700	151.1
Sharp	18,164	16,704	75.6
Sony	17,236	15,064	56.9
Toa Nenryo	16,914	−1,941	34.4
Hitachi Zosen	14,010	−3,255	n/a
Mitsubishi Shoji	10,567	5,522	46.5
Sanyo	10,058	17,175	85.9
Hitachi	9,580	16,428	21.0
Hanwa	9,366	1,076	75.9
Toshiba	8,698	−1,268	70.1
JVC	8,569	8,503	213.6
Canon	7,719	−4,160	55.4
Honda	6,785	2,690	16.3
Matsushita Trad.	6,757	6,593	40.0
Fuji Photo Film	6,581	3,548	11.4
Fujisawa	6,578	4,936	55.9

---

*Six months to September 30, 1986.
†¥ millions.
SOURCE: Wako Economic Research Institute.

Finance Europe, or Sumitomo Finance International may rival the overseas operations of the city banks.

Because the trading companies have a long history of international dealing, they possess far more expertise in the field of credit risk analysis than Japanese financial institutions. The more than 200 Japanese corporations that have participated in some form of zaitek have little experience in risk management. Unlike the trading companies and the banks, some corporations are rumored to have sustained major losses in their zaitek enterprises.

In 1986, a wide range of Japanese corporate and financial institutions used zaitek as a method for compensating for sharply declining revenues resulting from the revaluation of the yen against the dollar. As a consequence, the income for many Japanese corporations during fiscal year 1986 (ending March 31, 1987) will be deceptively high.

The financial markets were not the only frontier exploited by Japanese corporations in their search for nontraditional sources of profit. In 1985, for example, Mitsubishi Trust & Banking and the Mitsubishi Corporation, together with a group of U.S. individual investors, created a joint finance firm in New York. Named Spectrum Capital Ltd., the firm specializes in the leasing of aircraft as well as equipment for steel and petroleum plants. This undertaking represented the first joint venture between a Japanese trust bank or a Japanese trading house with U.S. interests. The first president of Spectrum Capital was an American, formerly employed by the leasing subsidiary of Chemical Bank.

Life insurance companies have also jumped on the bankwagon and are creating their own overseas investment companies registered in Luxembourg. For example, in April 1985, Kyoei Life Insurance Company created an investment firm intended to buy Eurodollar bonds to be managed by Daiwa International Capital Management Company. The foreign-based investment subsidiaries created by the life insurance companies are designed to provide an initial toehold in the Euromarkets with the expectation that future deregulation will render them vital to home operations.

Zaitek is the most obvious symptom of a profound problem haunting the banks. Japanese corporations no longer depend on the indirect financing provided by their traditional banking partners. The confluence of two factors has directed corporate activity away from borrowing and toward investment banking:

1. The level of the exportation of manufactured products has peaked. This has been caused by the strong yen as well as by market saturation.
2. Domestic demand has been weak for years and shows little indication of a dramatic turnaround.

Consequently, production capacity is static and the demand for investment in plant and equipment is therefore modest. As a result, major corporations no longer require significant funding from banks. Instead, they are in a position to utilize profits and depreciation to neutralize their bank debts. Thus, major blue chip manufacturing companies and trading companies (which have never had to worry about plant and equipment) can play the investment game. It is partly for this reason that banks, fearful that they will be left out in the cold, have been scurrying about the global financial sector, attempting to burrow into every nook and cranny of the investment banking world.

It is seldom possible to discuss the subject of Japanese financial markets with Japan's regulators or brokers or bankers without hearing three words spoken repeatedly in varying sequences. Like an incantation, these words quickly become so familiar that their meaning has been made subservient to the mode of usage and context: **INTERNATIONALIZATION, DEREGULATION, SECURITIZATION.** This trio of nouns is writ large upon the entire Japanese financial world.

Recently, a fourth term, **INNOVATION,** has been tentatively tossed around. The introduction of a yen-denominated banker's acceptance market, a bond futures market, an offshore banking market, a 24-hour foreign exchange market, and a stock average futures market[1] are the harbingers of greater innovations to come. Japan's investment community now stands poised, waiting for the chance to ride new vehicles to the promised land of greater financial opportunities.

The term internationalization has been popular in Tokyo since the late 1960s when Japan's current account surpluses triggered the first in an ongoing series of "trade frictions." As a result, the Ministry of Finance announced the new "internationalization of the yen," and promised an eventual relaxation of

---

[1]Scheduled to begin on the Osaka Stock Exchange in the spring of 1987 but not in existence as this book goes to press.

those regulations that excluded foreign financial institutions from participating on an equal basis with domestic institutions.

In 1968, for example, qualified North American and European banks were permitted to establish branches in Tokyo (see Chapter 7). A few restrictions were placed on these foreign banks:

1. They could not advertise.
2. They could not operate as savings banks (or trust banks).
3. Foreign currency loans could not be issued for less than one year.
4. The conversion of foreign currency to yen as well as the acceptance of yen deposits were determined by severe restrictions set by the Ministry of Finance.
5. Although not officially limited, the number of branches foreign banks could open in Japan was subject to approval by the Bank of Japan. (Ordinarily, the central bank only approved one or two branches for each bank. This compares with an average of more than 200 branches for each of the city banks.)

As a consequence of restrictions, foreign banks were rendered a segment apart from the indigenous banking system. A decade later, the more than 50 foreign banks in Japan together controlled roughly 2 percent of total domestic loan volume.[2] Deregulation was underway.

The first oil crisis of 1973–74 ploughed deregulatory intentions deep into the financial soil. Meanwhile, the government bonds that had been issued in modest volumes since 1965 were made into a major vehicle of deficit financing in 1975. Today, bureaucrats at Japan's Ministry of Finance are quick to point out that although foreign pressure provided an impetus for current deregulatory trends, the ultimate power behind market liberalization was the government's debt (see Chapter 5).

Nonetheless, the "Report by the Working Group of the Joint Japan–U.S. Ad Hoc Group on the Yen/Dollar Exchange Rate, Financial and Capital Market Issues" provided the canon for the plethora of deregulatory measures instituted during the period

---

[2]Today, this paltry figure has risen to 3 percent for the 79 foreign banks with full-service branches in Japan (see Chapter 7).

1984–87. This document promised to "liberalize Japan's capital markets, internationalize the yen, and allow the yen to more fully reflect its underlying strength."[3] Since the report was released in May 1984, the financial markets have begun to open to foreign participation and the yen has appreciated against the dollar by roughly 45 percent.

In a 1984 meeting, which preceded the report, U.S. undersecretary of state for monetary affairs Beryl Sprinkel said to deputy director general of the Banking Bureau of the Ministry of Finance Toyoo Gyohten, that the only way to cut the tail off a dog is with a single chop. This perspicacious observation led the Japanese negotiator to reply that when making a wheel, it is necessary to gently bend the wood into shape. Three years later, the American demands for instant structural change and Japanese insistence on gradual systemic adjustment have resulted in either sluggish change or exceptionally swift accommodation. American and Japanese perspectives have neither become more compatible nor more mutually intelligible.

Nonetheless, the flow of funds, unlike the flow of words, permits little ambiguity. That there has been a major change in the regulatory structure of Japan's capital markets and money markets is beyond question. During the past several years, the guidelines regulating the issuance of unsecured bonds were relaxed, and dozens of foreign securities companies have opened branches in Tokyo with six now members of the Tokyo Stock Exchange.

Meanwhile, some interest rates, money market instruments, and financial transactions have been deregulated. Thus, interest rate ceilings on large deposits have been removed while, simultaneously, money market certificates and negotiable certificates of deposit can be freely issued by banks. As a result, the range of money market instruments has broadened and now includes banker's acceptances. A domestic commercial paper market may soon be permitted while there is hope that interest rates on small deposits will someday be free.

---

[3]*Report by the Working Group of Joint Japan–U.S. Ad Hoc Group on Yen/Dollar Exchange Rate, Financial and Capital Market Issues to Japanese Minister of Finance Noboru Takeshita and United States Secretary of the Treasury Donald T. Regan*, Tokyo, 1984, p. 1.

At the same time, while deregulation has been dawdling or racing along, external transactions have been internationalized. Restrictions on forward exchange transactions were relaxed and limitations on swaps into yen were removed. Yen-denominated loans to foreign institutions (Samurai loans) became the province of the banks that provided them rather than the domain of the bureaucrats who regulated them. Faced with a moribund market in Samurai and Shogun bonds, the Ministry of Finance eased some of the restrictions impeding the market.

Concurrent with these changes, a shift away from indirect financing to direct tapping of the capital markets became increasingly pronounced. The disintermediation of funds from the banks and the intermediation of funds into the instruments sold by securities companies has resulted in the first signs of a significant future securitization in Japan. Beginning in the 1970s and gaining momentum in the 1980s, this change in financing has been forcing banks to choose a new destiny.

The giant city banks, determined to trample Article 65 into the dust of history, are using their financial and political power to become all-service financial institutions. They are planning for a future where no regulations will inhibit their deployment of domestic and international resources into the full spectrum of financial activity. The small commercial banks are reaching toward international business, including foreign exchange trading, as their only salvation. The joint evil of disintermediation and securitization is a Janus-faced monster promising to consume every regional bank anchored in nonurban domestic deposits and lending. Even the most optimistic of Japan's bankers and regulators expect some regional or sogo bank insolvencies during the course of the next decade.

Although the Bank of Japan will not admit it, during the remaining years of this century, the central bank's iron grasp of the money supply will be weakened. The emergence of a fully mature Euroyen market, an offshore banking center which will gradually come to resemble the U.S. IBF in *all* respects, and "open" money markets dwarfing the interbank market will together contribute to the transformation of the yen. Foreign trade will increasingly be billed in yen. Simultaneously, the yen will grow as a reserve currency and eventually will become fully internationalized.

As a result of these developments, the Bank of Japan's relationship with the yen will be changed. Instead of directing the money supply with a whip, the central bank will be obliged to coax and cajole it by a variety of means. Indeed, this has already begun to happen. The Bank of Japan is slowly coming to resemble its American counterpart, the Fed. Japan's monetary policy will continue to be implemented through interest rates and market operations, but the central bank's power over the money supply will be diluted.

This is just one instance of the current trend in which Japanese regulators are losing their accustomed control of Japan's financial markets and market instruments. Like a domineering and possessive parent responding to the behavior of an independent and occasionally unruly offspring, Japanese government entities are loath to allow their "guidance" of the markets to dwindle. However, financial markets, like wayward children, go where they must—and, if they are healthy, will outlive their parents.

A Note Regarding Japanese Interest Rates

Japanese interest rates were strictly regulated during the post-war period. The May 1984 agreement between the Ministry of Finance and the U.S. Treasury Department (the "Yen-Dollar Accord") resulted in the announcement of deregulatory measures leading to the introduction of market rates for large denomination deposits. Regulations applying to NCD interest rates have been a first step in a gradual process of what may eventually be total interest rate deregulation.

Money market certificates (MMCs) were introduced in March 1985. Interest rates on large denomination time deposits of ¥1 billion or more were deregulated in October 1985. This was followed by the reduction of the minimum deposit to ¥500 million in April 1986, to ¥300 million in September 1986, and a planned reduction to ¥100 million in 1987. The deregulation of small denomination deposits is currently under consideration.

The long-term prime rate has been used as a standard for Japan's long-term interest rate system. As financial deregulation proceeds, long-term interest rates on corporate loans will be diversified. Both short- and long-term interest rates have become instruments for the Ministry of Finance to adjust the capital market structure in order to bring Japan's system closer to standards existing in the United States and key Western nations in accordance with the first G-5 summit.

Japan's official discount rate is set by the Policy Board of the Bank of Japan and applies to the discount rate on commercial

Japanese Interest Rates

Regulated Rates	*"Free" or Market Rates*
Long-term prime rate	Industrial bonds (12-year class AA, 11
Industrial bonds	years and four months remaining)
(12-year class AA)	Circulation yields
Postal savings fixed deposits	Interest bearing bank debentures
Time deposits below ¥300 million	(five-year with four years and 10
Standard interest rate	months remaining)
Short-term prime rate	Large denomination time deposits
Bank fixed deposits	Certificates of Deposit
Official bank rate	Money Market Certificates
Postal deposits (ordinary)	Gensaki
General deposits	Banker's acceptances
	Bill-discount
	Call-money

bills and the interest rate on loans secured by government bonds. Changes in the discount rate directly affect bank rates. The city banks customarily set their prime rate at 0.25 percent above the discount rate. Call-money and bill-discount rates are set by the Tanshi companies in consultation with the Bank of Japan "the final arbiter of market funds" (see Chapter 8).

The interest rates offered by private financial institutions (for deposits and loans) fall under the control of the Temporary Interest Rate Adjustment Law. Promulgated 40 years ago, in 1947, the term "temporary" is a misnomer. The Ministry of Finance and the Bank of Japan have roles to play in the determination of these rates. The Bank of Japan strongly supports interest rate deregulation, which it perceives as a vital instrument for the production of increased liquidity in the money markets. Such liquidity would enable it to strengthen its control of the interest rate structure.

At the end of 1986, roughly 80 percent of deposits in Japanese banking institutions fell under fixed interest rate regulations. Although the eventual deregulation of small deposit interest rates is anticipated, such a move will undermine the primary funding of regional, sogo, and cooperative institutions. This will result in an epidemic of bank insolvencies, restructurings, and mergers.

The Bank of Japan identifies two types of interest rates: regulated and market. These two categories are perceived as leading parallel and mutually variable existences. Together the interest rates can be grouped according to the simple classification summarized in the table on page 307.

These parallel interest rate systems manifest considerable disparities. For example, at the end of 1986, demand deposits paid 0.26 percent interest (before withholding tax) while three-month small time deposits (less than ¥300 million) yielded 1.76 percent, nearly seven times more. Meanwhile, three-month NCDs yielded 4.59 percent—nearly 2.5 times more than *equivalent* small time deposits and about 17.5 times more than demand deposits.

Japanese ADRs[1]

Company Name	Market	ADR Ratio	Bank
Aida Eng., Ltd.	OTC	10 to 1	Morgan Guaranty
Ajinomoto Co.	OTC	10 to 1	Morgan Guaranty
Akai Elec. Co.	OTC	10 to 1	Morgan Guaranty
Alps Elec Co.	OTC	2 to 1	Morgan Guaranty
Amada Co.	OTC	4 to 1	Morgan Guaranty
Asahi Chem. Ind. Co.	OTC	10 to 1	Citibank
Asahi Glass Co.	Pk Sheet	10 to 1	Morgan Guaranty
Ashikaga Bank	OTC	2 to 1	Morgan Guaranty
Bank of Fukuoka	OTC	10 to 1	Citibank
Bank of Tokyo	Pk Sheet	10 to 1	Morgan Guaranty
Bank of Yokohama	OTC	10 to 1	Morgan Guaranty
Banyu Pharm. Co.	OTC	20 to 1	Chemical Bank
Bridgestone Corp.	Pk Sheet	10 to 1	Irving Trust
Brother Ind., Ltd.	OTC	10 to 1	Morgan Guaranty
Calpis Food Ind. Co.	Pk Sheet	10 to 1	Morgan Guaranty
Canon Inc.	NASDAQ	5 to 1	Morgan Guaranty
Casio Computer Co.	Pk Sheet	10 to 1	Citibank
Computer Services	NASDAQ	1 to 1	Citibank
C. Itoh & Co.	OTC	10 to 1	Citibank
Dai Nippon Printing	Pk Sheet	10 to 1	Citibank
Daiwa House Ind.	OTC	10 to 1	Morgan Guaranty
Daiwa Securities Co.	OTC	10 to 1	Morgan Guaranty
Daiwa Seiko Inc.	Pk Sheet	10 to 1	Morgan Guaranty
Dai'ei, Inc.	NASDAQ	2 to 1	Citibank
Dai-Ichi Kangyo Bank	OTC	10 to 1	Morgan Guaranty
Ebara Corp.	OTC	10 to 1	Morgan Guaranty
Eisai Co.	OTC	10 to 1	Chemical Bank
Fuji Bank	OTC	10 to 1	Morgan Guaranty
Fuji Heavy Ind.	Pk Sheet	10 to 1	Morgan Guaranty

[1]As of March 1986. Listed in alphabetical order by company.

Company Name	Market	ADR Ratio	Bank
Fuji Photo Film	NASDAQ	2 to 1	Morgan Guaranty
Fujita Corp.	OTC	10 to 1	Citibank
Fujitsu Ltd.	Pk Sheet	5 to 1	Morgan Guaranty
Furukawa Elec. Co.	OTC	10 to 1	Morgan Guaranty
Hachijuni Bank	OTC	10 to 1	Citibank
Hitachi Cable Ltd.	OTC	10 to 1	Morgan Guaranty
Hitachi Koki Co.	OTC	10 to 1	Morgan Guaranty
Hitachi Metals Ltd.	OTC	10 to 1	Morgan Guaranty
Hitachi Ltd.	NYSE	10 to 1	Citibank
Hochiki Corp.	OTC	10 to 1	Morgan Guaranty
Hokuriku Bank	OTC	10 to 1	Morgan Guaranty
Honda Motor	NYSE	10 to 1	Morgan Guaranty
Isuzu Motors	Pk Sheet	10 to 1	Bank of New York
Ito Yokado Co.	NASDAQ	4 to 1	Morgan Guaranty
Japan Air Lines	NASDAQ	2 to 1	Morgan Guaranty
Japan Steel Works	OTC	10 to 1	Morgan Guaranty
Jusco Co.	OTC	10 to 1	Morgan Guaranty
Kajima Corp.	OTC	10 to 1	Morgan Guaranty
Kanebo Ltd.	OTC	10 to 1	Morgan Guaranty
Kao Soap Corp.	OTC	10 to 1	Morgan Guaranty
Kashiyama & Co.	OTC	5 to 1	Morgan Guaranty
Kawasaki Steel Corp.	Pk Sheet	10 to 1	Morgan Guaranty
Kirin Brewery Co.	NYSE	10 to 1	Morgan Guaranty
Komatsu Ltd.	Pk Sheet	20 to 1	Citibank
Konishiroku Photo Ind.	OTC	10 to 1	Chemical Bank
Korakuen Stadium Co.	OTC	10 to 1	Morgan Guaranty
Kubota, Ltd.	NYSE	20 to 1	Morgan Guaranty
Kumagai Gumi Co.	OTC	10 to 1	Chemical Bank
Kyocera Corp.	NYSE	2 to 1	Citibank
Kyowa Bank	OTC	10 to 1	Morgan Guaranty
Makita Electric Wks	NASDAQ	5 to 1	Chemical Bank
Marubeni Corp.	Pk Sheet	10 to 1	Citibank
Marui Co.	Pk Sheet	2 to 1	Morgan Guaranty
Matsushita Elec. Ind.	NYSE	10 to 1	Morgan Guaranty
Matsushita Elec. Wks.	Pk Sheet	10 to 1	Morgan Guaranty
Meiji Seika Kaisha	OTC	10 to 1	Citibank
Minebea Co.	OTC	5 to 1	Morgan Guaranty
Mitsubishi Bank	OTC	10 to 1	Morgan Guaranty
Mitsubishi Chem. Mfg.	OTC	10 to 1	Morgan Guaranty
Mitsubishi Corp.	Pk Sheet	10 to 1	Morgan Guaranty
Mitsubishi Elec. Corp.	Pk Sheet	10 to 1	Morgan Guaranty
Mitsubishi Estate Co.	OTC	10 to 1	Morgan Guaranty
Mitsubishi Trust	OTC	10 to 1	Morgan Guaranty
Mitsui Bank	OTC	10 to 1	Morgan Guaranty
Mitsui & Co., Ltd.	NASDAQ	20 to 1	Citibank
Mitsukoshi	Pk Sheet	10 to 1	Morgan Guaranty
Nagoya R. R.	Pk Sheet	10 to 1	Citibank
NEC Corporation	NASDAQ	5 to 1	Irving Trust
Nifco Inc.	Pk Sheet	1 to 1	Morgan Guaranty
Nikko Securities Co.	OTC	10 to 1	Morgan Guaranty
Nippon Kokan K. K.	OTC	10 to 1	Morgan Guaranty

Company Name	Market	ADR Ratio	Bank
Nippon Optical Co.	Pk Sheet	10 to 1	Morgan Guaranty
Nippon Seiko K. K.	OTC	10 to 1	Citibank
Nippon Shinpan Co.	OTC	10 to 1	Citibank
Nippon Suisan Kaisha	OTC	10 to 1	Morgan Guaranty
Nippon Yusen Kab. Kaisha	OTC	10 to 1	Morgan Guaranty
Nippondenso Co.	OTC	4 to 1	Citibank
Nissan Motors Co.	NASDAQ	2 to 1	Morgan Guaranty
Nisshin Steel Ltd.	OTC	20 to 1	Bank of N.Y.
Nitto Elec. Ind.	OTC	10 to 1	Morgan Guaranty
Nomura Securities	OTC	10 to 1	Chemical Bank
Oji Paper Co.	OTC	10 to 1	Citibank
Omron Tateishi Elec.	OTC	10 to 1	Morgan Guaranty
Pioneer Electronic	NYSE	2 to 1	Chemical Bank
Ricoh Co.	OTC	10 to 1	Chemical Bank
Saitama Bank	OTC	10 to 1	Morgan Guaranty
Sanwa Bank	Pk Sheet	10 to 1	Morgan Guaranty
Sanyo Electric Co.	NASDAQ	5 to 1	Morgan Guaranty
Secom Co.	OTC	2 to 1	Morgan Guaranty
Sekisui House Ltd.	Pk Sheet	10 to 1	Morgan Guaranty
Seven Eleven Japan	OTC	1 to 1	Morgan Guaranty
Sharp Corp.	Pk Sheet	10 to 1	Citibank
Shiseido Co.	OTC	5 to 1	Morgan Guaranty
Shizuoka Bank	OTC	10 to 1	Morgan Guaranty
Showa Sangyo Co.	OTC	20 to 1	Morgan Guaranty
Sony	NYSE	1 to 1	Morgan Guaranty
Sugiura Bank	OTC	10 to 1	Citibank
Sumitomo Bank	OTC	10 to 1	Morgan Guaranty
Sumitomo Elec. Ind.	OTC	10 to 1	Morgan Guaranty
Sumitomo Metal Ind.	OTC	20 to 1	Citibank
Taisei Corp.	OTC	10 to 1	Citibank
Taisho M/F Ins.	OTC	10 to 1	Morgan Guaranty
Taiyo Yuden Co.	OTC	4 to 1	Morgan Guaranty
TDK	NYSE	2 to 1	Morgan Guaranty
Teijin Ltd.	OTC	10 to 1	Morgan Guaranty
Toa Harbor Works	OTC	10 to 1	Citibank
Tokai Bank	OTC	20 to 1	Chemical Bank
Tokyo M/F Ins. Co.	NASDAQ	50 to 1	Citibank
Tokyo Sanyo Elec.	OTC	5 to 1	Morgan Guaranty
Tokyu Land Corp.	OTC	10 to 1	Morgan Guaranty
Toppan Printing Co.	OTC	5 to 1	Citibank
Toray Ind.	OTC	10 to 1	Morgan Guaranty
Toto Ltd.	OTC	10 to 1	Morgan Guaranty
Toyo Suisan Kaisha	OTC	10 to 1	Morgan Guaranty
Toyota Motor Corp.	NASDAQ	2 to 1	Morgan Guaranty
Tsubakimoto Prec.	OTC	4 to 1	Morgan Guaranty
Tsugami Corp.	OTC	10 to 1	Morgan Guaranty
Victor Co. of Japan	OTC	2 to 1	Morgan Guaranty
Wacoal Corp.	NASDAQ	1 to 1	Chase Manhattan
Yamaichi Securities	OTC	10 to 1	Chemical Bank
Yamazaki Baking	OTC	10 to 1	Citibank
Yasuda Trust	OTC	10 to 1	Citibank

Foreign Corporations Listed on the Tokyo Stock Exchange at the End of 1986

At the end of 1986 there were 52 foreign companies listed on the First Section of the Tokyo Stock Exchange (TSE). More than 60 percent (32) of these listings were U.S. corporations. More than one-third (19) were banks or financial service institutions. About two dozen foreign corporations are expected to list their shares on the Tokyo Stock Exchange in 1987, while at least 80 more have applications pending. To date, all listed foreign firms have been sponsored by one of the Big Four. See Chapter 3 for a detailed discussion of foreign listings on the TSE.

Company	Listed	Nationality	Classification
AGA	1986	Sweden	Chemical
American Express	1985	U.S.A.	Financial Service
Ameritech	1986	U.S.A.	Telecommunication
BankAmerica	1975	U.S.A.	Bank
Barclays Bank	1986	U.K.	Bank
Bell Atlantic	1986	U.S.A.	Telecommunication
Bell Canada Enterp.	1985	Canada	Communication
British Telecom	1986	U.K.	Telecommunication
British Tire & Rubber	1986	U.K.	[Conglomerate]
Cable & Wireless	1986	U.K.	Telecommunication
Canadian Imperial Bank of Commerce	1986	Canada	Bank
Chase Manhattan	1973	U.S.A.	Bank
Chrysler	1986	U.S.A.	Automobiles
Citicorp	1973	U.S.A.	Bank
Commerz Bank	1986	Germany	Bank

Company	Listed	Nationality	Classification
Disney	1985	U.S.A.	Entertainment
Dow Chemical	1973	U.S.A.	Chemicals
Dresdner Bank	1985	Germany	Bank
Eastman Kodak	1986	U.S.A.	Photo Products
E. I. Dupont	1986	U.S.A.	Chemicals
Eli Lilly	1986	U.S.A.	Pharmaceutical
Exxon	1986	U.S.A.	Oil
First Chicago	1973	U.S.A.	Bank
F. P. L. Group	1986	U.S.A.	Utility
General Motors	1974	U.S.A.	Automobiles
IBM	1974	U.S.A.	Elec. Equipment
ITT	1974	U.S.A.	[Conglomerate]
IU International	1986	U.S.A.	[Conglomerate]
McDonald's	1986	U.S.A.	Service
Merrill Lynch	1986	U.S.A.	Financial Service
Minnesota Mining & Manufacturing	1985	U.S.A.	Chemicals
National Australia Bank	1985	Australia	Bank
Northern Telecom	1986	Canada	Bank
Pepsico	1986	U.S.A.	Consumer Products
Philip Morris	1985	U.S.A.	Consumer Products
Procter & Gamble	1986	U.S.A.	Consumer Products
R. J. Reynolds-Nabisco	1986	U.S.A.	Consumer Products
Robeco	1976	Netherlands	Financial Service
Royal Bank of Canada	1986	Canada	Bank
Royal Trust	1986	Canada	Bank
Sears Roebuck	1984	U.S.A.	Retail Sales
Security Pacific	1986	U.S.A.	Bank
Smithkline Beckman	1986	U.S.A.	Pharmaceutical
Standard Chartered Bank	1986	U.K.	Bank
Telephonica	1985	Spain	Telecommunication
Toronto Dominion Bank	1986	Canada	Bank
Union Bank of Switzerland	1985	Switzerland	Bank
U.S. West	1986	U.S.A.	Telecommunication
Volvo	1986	Sweden	Automobiles
Waste Management	1986	U.S.A.	Service
Westpac Banking	1986	Australia	Bank
Weyerhaeuser	1986	U.S.A.	Pulp

SOURCE: Tokyo Stock Exchange

Samurai and Shibosai Bond Issues in 1986

Samurai Bonds (domestic yen bonds floated by foreign entities in 1986)

Date Signed	Name of Entity	Amount ¥ bil.	Life Years	Lead Manager
1-17-86	E.I.B.	30	12	Daiwa
1-22-86	Korea Exchange Bank	30	10	Daiwa
1-27-86	Shanghai ITIC	25	10	Nomura
1-28-86	Ireland	20	10	Daiwa
1-30-86	OKB	30	12	Nomura
2-06-86	Sweden	50	10	Nomura
2-16-86	I.A.D.B.	30	12	Nomura
2-18-86	CITIC (China)	40	10	Daiwa
3-06-86	EDF (France)	30	10	Nikko
3-12-86	Export Development Corporation (Canada)	20	10	Daiwa
4-09-86	Bank of China	50	12	Nomura
5-09-86	Korea Power Electric	20	10	Nikko
5-12-86	Africa Development Bank	15	10	Nomura
6-12-86	World Bank	30	15	Nikko
7-09-86	Portugal	20	10	Daiwa
9-09-86	Guangdong Int'l Trust Inv. Corp.	20	10	Nomura
9-12-86	I.A.D.B.	30	15	Daiwa
10-30-86	E.I.B.	40	10	Nomura
11-06-86	Ireland	20	12	Daiwa
12-11-86	Tianjin Int'l Trust	10	10	Nikko
12-12-86	A.D.B.	30	15	Daiwa

Shibosai Bonds (domestic yen bonds issued by foreign entities and privately placed in Japan in 1986)

Date Signed	Name of Entity	Amount ¥ bil	Life Years	Lead Arranger
1-23-86	Gabiente de Area de Sines	5	10	LTCB
1-30-86	Nauru Finance Corp.	4	7	Daiwa
2-26-86	World Bank	30	20	Daiwa
3-07-86	A.D.B.	20	20	IBJ
4-15-86	National Bank of Hungary	10	10	IBJ
4-28-86	Greek Industrial Development	5	10	DKB
5-30-86	Hong Kong Subway	10	7	Sanwa
6-09-86	Empresa Nacional du Autopistas	7.5	10	NCB
6-19-86	State Investment Bank of Turkey	10	7	Nomura
6-19-86	Industrial Finance Corporation of India	5	10	Mitsui
6-27-86	Forsmarks Kraftgroupp	4	5	Yamaichi
7-29-86	Columbia	6	8	IBJ
9-24-86	Barbados Central Bank	4.3	5	Nikko
11-21-86	DSL Bank	3.2	5	M-H*
12-10-86	Siderurgia	5	10	Daiwa
12-15-86	World Bank	20	20	IBJ

*Manufacturers-Hanover

Nikkei Stock Average

A. 225 STOCKS*

Code	Name	Expected Return	Beta Value	Code	Name	Expected Return	Beta Value
1301	KYOKUYO	2.07	0.118	3111	OMIKENSHI	1.10	0.374
1331	NICHIRO GYOGYO	2.12	0.716	3201	JAPAN WOOL TEXTILE	1.98	0.344
1332	NIPPON SUISAN	1.52	0.263	3202	DAITO WOOL SPINNING	2.04	0.075
1501	MITSUI MINING	0.55	0.019	3302	TEIKOKU SEN-I	1.82	0.631
1503	SUMITOMO COAL MINING	1.26	0.696	3401	TEIJIN	2.43	1.224
1601	TEIKOKU OIL	0.24	0.013	3402	TORAY INDUSTRIES	1.68	1.106
1801	TAISEI	1.97	0.407	3403	TOHO RAYON	1.27	0.423
1802	OHBAYASHI-GUMI	2.75	0.880	3404	MITSUBISHI RAYON	1.65	1.208
1803	SHIMIZU CONSTRUCTION	2.12	0.581	3405	KURARAY	5.02	1.220
1804	SATO KOGYO	2.20	0.461	3407	ASAHI CHEMICAL IND.	2.77	0.671
1805	TOBISHIMA	1.85	0.076	3702	SANYO-KOKUSAKU PULP	1.91	0.472
1806	FUJITA	2.93	0.643	3861	OJI PAPER	2.03	1.066
1812	KAJIMA	2.29	0.632	3862	HONSHU PAPER	1.90	0.704
1815	TEKKEN CONSTRUCTION	2.37	0.205	3863	JUJO PAPER	1.81	0.913
1885	TOA HARBOR WORKS	2.24	0.110	3864	MITSUBISHI PAPER	2.03	0.648
1925	DAIWA HOUSE INDUSTRY	3.08	0.415	3865	HOKUETSU PAPER MILLS	1.64	0.107
2001	NIPPON FLOUR MILLS	1.43	0.477	4001	MITSUI TOATSU CHEMIC	1.59	0.626
2002	NISSHIN FLOUR MILL.	1.32	0.396	4004	SHOWA DENKO	1.50	0.926
2102	TAITO	1.32	0.304	4005	SUMITOMO CHEMICAL	1.67	1.132
2108	NIPPON BEET SUGAR	1.04	0.156	4010	MITSUBISHI CHEMICAL	1.85	0.985
2201	MORINAGA	2.01	0.305	4021	NISSAN CHEMICAL IND.	2.66	0.344
2202	MEIJI SEIKA	0.93	0.219	4022	RASA INDUSTRIES	1.43	0.520
2261	MEIJI MILK PRODUCTS	1.75	0.345	4041	NIPPON SODA	1.19	0.355
2501	SAPPORO BREWERIES	2.65	0.928	4042	TOYO SODA MFG.	1.92	0.613
2502	ASAHI BREWERIES	1.87	0.826	4045	TOA GOSEI CHEMICAL	2.30	1.132
2503	KIRIN BREWERY	2.22	1.050	4061	DENKI KAGAKU KOGYO	1.52	0.936
2531	TAKARA SHUZO	2.00	0.266	4063	SHIN-ETSU CHEMICAL	2.91	1.303
2533	GODO SHUSEI	2.21	0.031	4064	NIPPON CARBIDE IND.	1.87	0.180
2536	SANRAKU	1.74	0.020	4092	NIPPON CHEMICAL IND.	2.01	0.486
2601	HOHNEN OIL	1.96	0.440	4151	KYOWA HAKKO KOGYO	3.02	1.493
2602	NISSHIN OIL MILLS	1.67	0.257	4201	NIPPON SYNTHETIC	3.28	0.285
2801	KIKKOMAN	1.71	0.297	4208	UBE INDUSTRIES	0.68	0.887
2802	AJINOMOTO	1.78	0.852	4272	NIPPON KAYAKU	1.47	0.521
2871	NICHIREI	2.49	0.363	4401	ASAHI DENKA KOGYO	2.74	0.208
3001	KATAKURA INDUSTRIES	1.98	0.263	4403	NIPPON OIL AND FATS	2.42	0.242
3101	TOYOBO	2.41	1.060	4501	SANKYO	2.04	1.109
3102	KANEBO	2.66	0.224	4502	TAKEDA CHEMICAL IND.	1.50	1.075
3103	UNITIKA	1.96	0.611	4503	YAMANOUCHI PHARMACEUTICAL	3.45	0.696
3104	FUJI SPINNING	2.16	0.322				
3105	NISSHINBO INDUSTRIES	1.98	1.204	4506	DAINIPPON PHARMACEUTICAL	5.99	0.208
3110	NITTO BOSEKI	1.02	0.664				

*April 1986.

Code	Name	Expected Return	Beta Value	Code	Name	Expected Return	Beta Value
4901	FUJI PHOTO FILM	1.54	1.300	6504	FUJI ELECTRIC	1.10	1.042
4902	KONISHIROKU PHOTO	0.78	0.665	6508	MEIDENSHA ELECTRIC	2.60	0.585
5001	NIPPON OIL	0.52	0.376	6701	NEC	2.03	1.191
5002	SHOWA SHELL SEKIYU	1.97	0.776	6702	FUJITSU	2.08	1.105
5004	MITSUBISHI OIL	1.04	0.527	6703	OKI ELECTRIC IND.	1.72	0.843
5005	TOA NENRYO KOGYO	1.51	0.522	6752	MATSUSHITA ELECTRIC	1.36	1.359
5101	THE YOKOHAMA RUBBER	1.12	0.567	6753	SHARP	0.59	0.736
5108	BRIDGESTONE	1.13	0.918	6758	SONY	0.58	1.019
5201	ASAHI GLASS	1.68	1.162	6764	SANYO ELECTRIC	0.05	0.911
5202	NIPPON SHEET GLASS	1.64	0.784	6841	YOKOGAWA HOKUSHIN	2.14	1.253
5231	NIHON CEMENT	1.54	0.399	6902	NIPPONDENSO	2.07	1.133
5232	SUMITOMO CEMENT	1.57	0.554	6933	YUASA BATTERY	1.11	0.537
5233	ONODA CEMENT	2.54	1.257	7003	MITSUI ENGINEERING	0.12	0.694
5238	MITSUBISHI MINING	1.08	0.634	7004	HITACHI ZOSEN	0.48	0.479
5301	TOKAI CARBON	2.12	0.417	7011	MITSUBISHI HEAVY IND.	1.80	1.339
5302	NIPPON CARBON	0.51	0.814	7013	IHI	0.88	1.175
5331	NORITAKE	1.38	0.526	7102	NIPPON SHARYO SEIZO	1.01	0.130
5332	TOTO	2.03	0.877	7201	NISSAN MOTOR	0.32	0.939
5333	NGK INSULATORS	1.97	0.822	7202	ISUZU MOTORS	1.47	0.991
5351	SHINAGAWA REFRACTORY	0.88	0.299	7203	TOYOTA MOTOR	1.80	1.137
5401	NIPPON STEEL	0.69	1.014	7205	HINO MOTORS	0.63	0.292
5403	KAWASAKI STEEL	0.37	1.181	7261	MAZDA MOTOR	0.86	0.694
5404	NIPPON KOKAN	0.28	0.886	7267	HONDA MOTOR	1.71	1.068
5405	SUMITOMO METAL IND.	0.06	0.920	7269	SUZUKI MOTOR	0.87	0.508
5406	KOBE STEEL	0.68	0.734	7731	NIPPON KOGAKU	2.62	1.129
5478	NIPPON STAINLESS	0.76	0.423	7751	CANON	1.37	1.206
5479	NIPPON METAL IND.	0.52	0.219	7752	RICOH	1.42	1.083
5480	NIPPON YAKIN KOGYO	0.82	0.104	7762	CITIZEN WATCH	1.05	0.787
5563	NIPPON DENKO	3.16	0.186	7911	TOPPAN PRINTING	2.30	1.091
5631	THE JAPAN STEEL WORK	0.86	0.822	7912	DAI NIPPON PRINTING	2.42	1.261
5632	MITSUBISHI STEEL MFG.	1.86	0.520	7951	NIPPON GAKKI	1.72	0.471
5701	NIPPON LIGHT METAL	1.34	0.413	8001	C. ITOH	1.01	0.883
5706	MITSUI MINING & SMELT	2.96	0.225	8002	MARUBENI	0.47	0.506
5707	TOHO ZINC	1.39	0.516	8031	MITSUI	1.07	0.575
5711	MITSUBISHI METAL	2.89	0.964	8053	SUMITOMO	1.91	1.043
5712	NIPPON MINING	2.09	1.360	8058	MITSUBISHI	0.74	0.806
5713	SUMITOMO METAL MINING	5.20	0.313	8088	IWATANI	0.76	0.187
5714	DOWA MINING	1.18	0.427	8231	MITSUKOSHI	1.72	0.803
5715	FURUKAWA	1.90	0.683	8232	TOKYU DEPARTMENT	1.86	0.541
5721	SHIMURA KAKO	1.56	0.097	8233	TAKASHIMAYA	1.37	0.188
5801	FURUKAWA ELECTRIC	1.31	1.067	8235	MATSUZAKAYA	1.88	0.113
5802	SUMITOMO ELECTRIC	2.27	1.147	8236	MARUZEN	2.13	0.399
5803	FUJIKURA	2.08	0.783	8311	DAI-ICHI KANGYO BANK	2.94	1.202
5805	SHOWA ELECTRIC WIRE	1.28	0.603	8313	THE BANK OF TOKYO	2.82	0.709
5901	TOYO SEIKAN	3.11	1.088	8314	THE MITSUI BANK	2.73	0.946
5981	TOKYO ROPE MFG.	1.05	0.058	8315	THE MITSUBISHI BANK	2.86	1.298
6011	NIIGATA ENGINEERING	0.04	0.064	8317	THE FUJI BANK	2.95	1.430
6103	OKUMA MACHINERY WORK	0.60	0.709	8318	THE SUMITOMO BANK	3.50	1.648
6301	KOMATSU	0.94	0.743	8401	MISUI TRUST & BANK	4.07	1.841
6326	KUBOTA	0.36	0.409	8402	MITSUBISHI TRUST	4.44	1.840
6361	EBARA	1.23	0.696	8511	JAPAN SECUR. FINANCE	2.56	1.485
6366	CHIYODA CHEMICAL	1.00	0.565	8583	NIPPON SHINPAN	1.61	1.087
6461	NIPPON PISTON RING	1.20	0.537	8603	THE NIKKO SECURITIES	2.65	1.631
6471	NIPPON SEIKO	0.94	1.163	8604	NOMURA SECURITIES	3.70	2.551
6472	NTN TOYO BEARING	0.72	0.823	8751	TOKYO MARINE & FIRE	2.51	1.903
6473	KOYO SEIKO	0.27	0.488	8752	TAISHO MARINE & FIRE	2.88	1.885
6474	NACHI-FUJIKOSHI	1.06	0.885	8755	YASUDA FIRE & MARINE	2.63	1.763
6501	HITACHI	1.63	1.224	8801	MITSUI REAL ESTATE	3.05	1.665
6502	TOSHIBA	1.06	1.245	8802	MITSUBISHI ESTATE	3.59	1.791
6503	MITSUBISHI ELECTRIC	1.05	1.311	8803	HEIWA REAL ESTATE	1.42	0.746

Code	Name	Expected Return	Beta Value	Code	Name	Expected Return	Beta Value
9001	TOBU RAILWAY	2.95	0.778	9202	ALL NIPPON AIRWAYS	2.06	0.394
9005	TOKYU	3.18	0.878	9301	MITSUBISHI WAREHOUSE	3.61	0.887
9006	KEIHIN ELECTRIC RAIL	2.78	0.691	9302	THE MITSUI WAREHOUSE	2.79	0.672
9007	ODAKYU ELECTRIC RAIL	2.72	0.497	9501	TOKYO ELECTRIC POWER	3.37	1.129
9008	KEIO TEITO RAILWAY	2.42	0.455	9503	KANSAI ELECTRIC POWER	2.63	0.951
9009	KEISEI ELECTRIC RAIL	3.47	0.590	9531	TOKYO GAS	3.15	0.956
9062	NIPPON EXPRESS	3.93	1.341	9532	OSAKA GAS	2.48	0.828
9101	NIPPON YUSEN	1.61	1.242	9601	SHOCHIKU	2.49	0.355
9103	JAPAN LINE	0.40	0.223	9602	TOHO	3.13	0.634
9104	MITSUI O.S.K. LINES	0.93	0.707	9605	TOEI	2.64	0.585
9105	YAMASHITA-SHINNIHON	0.22	0.066	9606	NIKKATSU	0.54	0.140
9107	KAWASAKI KISEN	0.32	0.030	9681	KORAKUEN	1.97	0.374
9126	SHOWA LINE	0.13	0.073				

B. THE PROCEDURE FOR CALCULATING THE NIKKEI STOCK AVERAGE

$$\text{Nikkei stock average} = \frac{\text{Aggregate of the 225 stock prices}}{\text{Divisor}}$$

The divisor was originally 225 but has been adjusted downward. When aggregating stock prices, prices of ¥500 par value stocks are adjusted downward as if they are ¥50 par value issues. The divisor is adjusted when any of the stocks is replaced or has exercised its rights for stock splits or gratis issues.

When a right is exercised:

$$D = d \times \frac{A - W}{A}$$

$$= A - \text{Aggregate of theoretical stock prices ex-rights}$$

Such that: D is the new divisor,
d is the divisor before adjustment
A is the aggregate of stock prices with rights
W is the value of the rights

The stock price ex-rights is determined as follows:

Theoretical stock price ex-rights $= T$
Capital contribution $= C$
Ratio of capital contribution to par value $= R$
Right for subscription per share $= S$

$$T = \frac{A + C \times R}{1 + S} \text{ (Both subscription and free distribution)}$$

In cases of deletion and addition of companies:

Rights price $=$ Stock prices of deleted companies $-$ Stock prices of added companies

C. PERFORMANCE RECORD FOR THE NIKKEI STOCK AVERAGE (225 STOCKS)

TABLE A–1 Comparison of Peak Stock Price Levels

Date	Nikkei Average	Arithmetic Average	Yield (percent)	PER	PBR
5-04-57	595.46	128.41	5.06	8.77	0.90
7-18-61	1,829.74	219.19	2.92	20.06	2.23
4-05-63	1,634.37	146.69	3.50	19.54	1.73
4-01-66	1,588.73	129.65	3.68	16.37	1.62
4-06-70	2,534.45	179.11	3.17	12.76	1.98
1-24-73	5,359.74	324.73	1.57	25.10	3.07
8-17-81	8,019.14	419.92	1.35	24.18	2.38
5-04-84	11,190.17	624.57	1.06	28.77	2.80
8-20-86	18,936.24	962.98	0.64	59.55	4.31

TABLE A–2   Growth in Yen and Dollar Terms

End of Period	Nikkei Average	Growth	Exchange Rate (U.S.$)	Growth in U.S.$
1974	3,817.22		300.95	
1975	4,358.60	14.2	305.15	12.6
1976	4,990.85	14.5	292.80	19.3
1977	4,865.60	-2.5	240.00	18.9
1978	6,001.85	23.4	194.60	52.1
1979	6,569.47	9.5	239.70	-11.2
1980	7,116.38	8.3	203.00	27.9
1981	7,681.84	7.9	219.90	-0.4
1982	8,016.67	4.4	235.00	-2.5
1983	9,893.32	23.4	232.20	24.9
1984	11,542.60	16.7	251.10	7.9
1985	13,113.32	13.6	200.60	42.2
1986	18,701.30	42.6	159.50	

FIGURE A–1   Nikkei (225) Stock Average

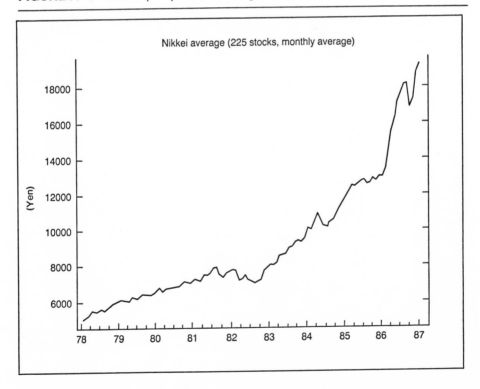

Nikkei average (225 stocks, monthly average)

FIGURE A–2   Comparison of Nikkei (225) Stock Average and the S&P 500

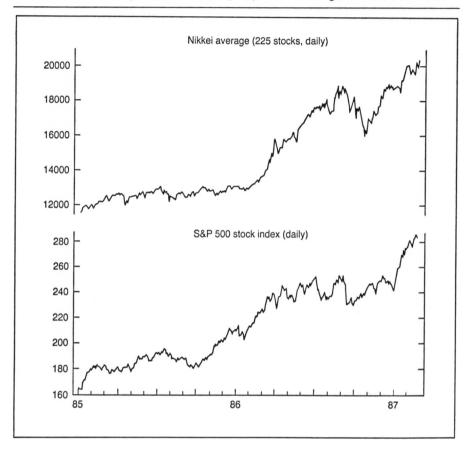

FIGURE A–3 Comparison of Nikkei (225) Stock Average and the S&P 500 in Dollar Terms

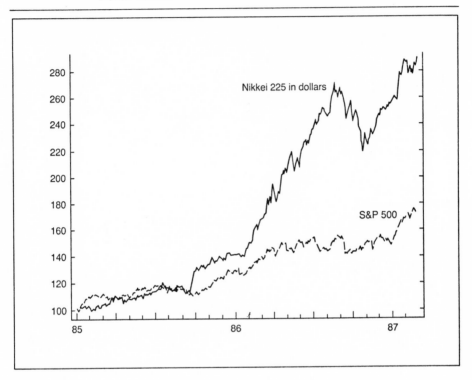

FIGURE A–4 Comparison of the Nikkei (225) Stock Average and Volume Traded on the Tokyo Stock Exchange First Section

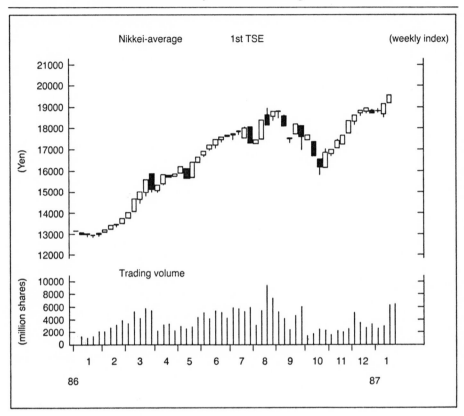

Accommodation Bills. A component of the yen-denominated banker's acceptance market, these issues combine small amount bills issued by corporations.

Administrative Guidance (Gyosei Shido). The tacit authority of the Ministry of Finance and other ministries to establish and "enforce" (with indirect and delayed negative sanctions) unwritten regulations. The Bank of Japan does not have this authority.

Agriculture and Forestry Debenture. Issued exclusively by the Norinchukin Bank and the Shoko Chukin Bank. See also **Bank Debenture** and **Debenture.**

Amakudari. The term (literally, "descent from heaven") refers to the acceptance of private sector positions by bureaucrats retiring from the ministries. The majority of companies providing the jobs have been regulated by the officials during their government service.

Anti-Monopoly Act. Revised in 1977, the Act prohibits banks from holding more than 5 percent of any company's equity. Banks were given until December 1987 to divest excess holdings. In the event, many banking institutions are expected to swap shares with affiliates.

Article 65 (of the Securities and Exchange Act of 1948). Prohibits banks from participating in the domestic securities industry and bans securities companies from domestic banking activities. Banks are not permitted to own more than 5 percent of a Japanese securities company and they are banned from selling equity or underwriting primary securities issues in Japan. At the same time, securities companies are not allowed to take deposits or give loans in the home market. The Act also required the registration of securities and the registration of broker-dealers. In addition, the Act separates the insurance industry from the securities industry.

Asia Dollar Bond. An Asia dollar market developed in Singapore in 1968. In 1971 the first Asia dollar bond was issued by the Development Bank of Singapore. Although still a minor market, there is a promise of growth (see Chapter 6).

Asia Yen Bonds. Yen-denominated bonds sold in the Singapore and Hong Kong markets. A market in these instruments developed concurrently with the market in Euroyen bonds. Bonds denominated in Asia yen have competed on a small scale with the Samurai and Euroyen bond markets for Japanese institutional investor business. See also **Asia Dollar Bonds.**

Authorized Foreign Exchange Bank. A bank that holds a license from the Ministry of Finance allowing it to engage in the lending and borrowing of short-term foreign currency funds in Japan. Although this was not always the case, today virtually all commercial banks in Japan are authorized foreign exchange banks. In addition, the long-term credit banks, trust banks, and sogo banks also fall within this category.

Bank Debenture. Issuance is confined to six banks: the three long-term credit banks, the Norinchukin Bank, the Shoko Chukin Bank, and the Bank of Tokyo. The three long-term credit banks account for nearly three-fourths of all issues. Types include three- and five-year interest bearing, discount (one year), and, less common, interest-bearing securities with lump sum interest payments. Interest-bearing obligations account for one-third of the issue amount and two-thirds of all outstanding issues. See also **Agriculture and Forestry Debenture,** and **Debenture.**

Bank of Japan. Japan's central bank. The sole issuer of currency and the lender of last resort, the bank determines and implements monetary policy and is the defender of the yen. Sometimes abbreviated as BoJ.

Bank of Tokyo. Classified as a city bank, it is a specialized foreign exchange bank. In the postwar financial system, it dominated international banking activities as well as domestic foreign exchange transactions. Sometimes abbreviated as BoT.

Big Four. The four largest securities companies in Japan: Nomura, Nikko, Daiwa, and Yamaichi. (Discussed in Chapter 2 in some detail.)

Book Bills. A component of the yen-denominated banker's acceptance market, these issues combine accommodation bills issued by banks. See also **Accommodation Bills.**

BoJ. See **Bank of Japan.**

BoT. See **Bank of Tokyo.**

Capital Gains on Equity Tax. Capital gains procured by domestic institutional investors are taxed as a component of corporate taxes. For all good purposes, there is no capital gains tax for individuals. Individual investors *are* taxed on capital gains only if transactions with one broker exceed 50 per year or the individual buys (or sells) a minimum of 200,000 shares in a single company in a single transaction. Although it is likely that a capital gains tax will be introduced in Japan in the near future, it will be difficult to enforce. Nonetheless, market impact could be considerable.

Central Government Bond. Securities issued by the Japanese government consist of two basic types: deficit financing bonds and construction bonds. Deficit financing bonds, which must be redeemed in cash at maturity, are expected to be discontinued in 1991. See also **Construction Bond, Deficit Financing Bond, Municipal Bond, Public Bond,** and **Public Corporation Bond.**

Central Stock Exchanges. This term refers to the Tokyo, Osaka, and Nagoya stock exchanges, which together account for 99 percent of the trading in Japan's listed stocks. Of the eight stock exchanges in Japan, only these three have second sections (established in 1961). See also **Regional Stock Exchanges** and **Stock Exchanges.**

Chakuchi. Forward bond trading in the gensaki market. See also **Gensaki.**

Churning. The term maintains the same meaning in Japan as in the West. Excessive trading in an account by brokers for the purpose of generating commissions, although technically actionable by Japanese law, is far more frequent in the Japanese brokerage industry than in the United States or United Kingdom. However, in only one known instance has a Japanese court decided for the plaintiff in litigation by an offended party against a Japanese securities company (see Chapter 2).

Chusho Shoken. Referring to second- and third-tier securities companies, the term, in effect, designates any domestic securities company other than the Big Four. See also **Big Four, Second-Tier Securities Company,** and **Third-Tier Securities Company.**

City Bank. A classificatory term for the 13 largest domestic commercial banks (see Table 7–1). So called because they are based in cities, the term includes the Bank of Tokyo which is also classified as a foreign exchange bank. See also **Bank of Tokyo, Commercial Bank,** and **Regional Bank.**

Commercial Bank. This is a legal term that refers to the 13 city banks, the 64 regional banks, and the 79 full-service foreign banks in Japan. See also **Bank of Tokyo, City Bank,** and **Regional Bank.**

Commercial Banks Association. A lobbying body with membership consisting of the city banks. See also **City Bank.**

Commissioned Company. A bank entrusted with handling issuance and subscription of a corporate bond issue. Acting as trustee, the commissioned company undertakes at the time of issue all paperwork as well as other matters pertaining to the repayment of bond holders. Only commercial banks, long-term credit banks, and trust banks can act as commissioned companies (securities companies are specifically excluded). The commissioned company holds the liens on all property used as collateral for secured bonds. See also **Trustee.**

Construction Bond. One of two types of government bonds issued by the Ministry of Finance. These bonds do not require consideration by the Diet. See also **Deficit Financing Bond.**

CORES. Computer Assisted Order Routing and Execution System. An automated system for trading equities on the Tokyo Stock Exchange which replaced floor trading on the second section in 1974 and on the first section in 1985 (excluding 250 of the most actively traded issues).

Corporate Debenture. Currently, about 70 Japanese blue chip corporations are allowed to issue unsecured debentures and roughly 180 can issue unsecured convertible debentures. In order to revivify the domestic bond market, in January 1987 the Ministry of Finance announced a relaxation in issuing requirements and an increase in the number of companies permitted to issue domestic unsecured debt. In April 1987, the number of companies allowed to issue straight unsecured bonds will more than double to 170.

Credit Association. See **Shinyo Kinko.**

Credit Cooperative. See **Shinyo Kumiai.**

Cross-Shareholding. A continuation of the zaibatsu heritage, Japanese corporations own shares in all of the companies within their groups (as well as other firms). The percentage of share ownership in individual corporations is limited for banks and securities companies by antitrust regulations. Nonetheless, in Japan, corporations and financial institutions together currently hold about 65 percent of all stock listed on all stock exchanges. Often the majority of shares in a corporation are collectively owned by members of the same keiretsu. This is **Interlocked Cross-Shareholding.** As a result of institutional share ownership, only an average 30 percent of the total float of shares in listed companies is traded. See also **Keiretsu** and **Zaibatsu.**

Daimyo Bond. Introduced by the World Bank in 1987, the instrument was designed as a response to illiquidity in the Samurai bond market. Issued as a bearer instrument and listed on the Luxembourg

Stock Exchange, the bond may be sold in Japan *and* in the Euromarket. Market makers are authorized to take short positions (short positions are prohibited in the **Samurai Bond** market).

Debenture. There are two types: (1) **Financial Debentures** (**Bank Debentures** issued by the long-term credit banks and **Agriculture and Forestry Debentures** issued by the Norinchukin Bank and the Shoko Chukin Bank), and (2) **Corporate Debentures.**

Deficit Financing Bond. Also known as revenue bonds. One of two types of central government bonds issued by the Ministry of Finance. The government expects to discontinue the use of these bonds by fiscal 1991 and will reduce its dependence on them during the next several years. See also **Central Government Bond, Construction Bond, Municipal Bond, Public Bond,** and **Public Corporation Bond.**

Deposit Insurance Corporation (DIC). Controlled by the Ministry of Finance, the corporation has never rescued a bank and employs fewer than 20 staff members (compared with 5,000 employed by the U.S. FDIC). Strengthened by the Ministry of Finance in 1986, it insures deposits for up to ¥10 million.

Diet. The Japanese parliament consisting of 511 seats of which more than 50 percent are controlled by the Liberal Democratic Party (LDP) which has governed Japan for more than 30 years. Together with the House of Councillors (252 seats and also dominated by the LDP), it constitutes the Japanese legislature.

Discount Bond. A government or a corporate issue of less than five-year maturity issued at a discount. Taxed at issue so that there are no taxes on the secondary market.

Discount Broker. Provides execution-only services for clients and therefore charges discounted commissions. Currently only trust banks and foreign banks are authorized by the stock exchanges to receive 20 percent of the commission clients pay to securities companies. In 1986, the city banks undertook efforts to persuade the Ministry of Finance to permit them to become discount brokers.

Dead Cross. A technical term used by chartists. Two moving averages (e.g. the 21- and 90-day moving averages) cross in decline, thus indicating a depreciating trend. See also **Golden Cross** and **Keisen Bunseki.**

DKB. Abbreviation for Dai-Ichi Kangyo Bank, one of the 13 city banks and the largest commercial bank in the world in terms of assets.

Dual Currency Bonds. A further liberalization of the issuing regulations for Euroyen bonds in April 1985 made these issues possible. They usually carry a yen coupon roughly 150 to 200 basis points higher than straight yen bonds and are redeemable in dollars. They are ordinarily swapped into fixed-rate dollar obligations at the spot rate. In such issues, the borrower swaps the yen interest while the principal is paid in dollars. Theoretically, the dual currency issues can be viewed as dollar obligations by borrowers and as yen securities by investors.

Doyukai. The Japan Committee for Economic Development. A group of selected individual representatives of major industrial and financial corporations in Japan.

Eigyo Tokkin. Funds of unknown but significant magnitude, given by Japanese corporations to the institutional sales departments of securities firms (which ordinarily provide underwriting services to the companies). The institutional sales departments provide a guaranteed rate of return superior to that available from domestic fixed income securities. All parties concerned deny the existence of these funds (discussed in Chapter 9). Enforcement of the provisions of the new **Investment Advisory Act** should render these funds defunct. See also **Tokkin Fund** and **Kingaishin Fund.**

Eligible Bills. These are yen-denominated banker's acceptances that satisfy the Bank of Japan's eligibility requirements. The central bank buys and sells these bills in the open market through **Tanshi** companies.

Endaka. Literally, the "high yen," the term refers to the substantial appreciation of the yen, against the dollar and other currencies, which occurred after the September 1985 meeting of the Group of Five at the Plaza Hotel in New York.

Euroyen. Yen deposits and yen currency held outside Japan (currently equal to about 2.7 percent of international banking assets).

Euroyen Bond. The first Eurobond issue denominated in yen was not floated until 1977, more than a decade after the emergence of the Eurobond market. Domestic entities were prohibited from issuing Euroyen instruments and inhibiting regulations were not significantly altered until December 1984. Further relaxation of regulatory controls in 1985 caused the market to exceed the **Samurai Bond** market in volume and number of issues. In 1986 foreign banks in Tokyo were authorized to issue the securities.

Euroyen Loan. Yen-denominated loans issued in the Euromarket by resident and nonresident institutions. Scheduled to be fully deregulated in April 1987, these loans are viewed as a vital means for promoting the international use of the yen. Because city banks will be authorized to issue long-term yen-denominated loans in the Euromarket, the distinction between long-term credit banks and commercial banks will be further eroded.

Financial Debenture. Currently limited to **Bank Debentures** and **Agriculture and Forestry Debentures.**

Futures. In 1986, the only financial futures market in Japan was the bond futures market on which a single contract was traded. Stock average futures will be introduced on the Osaka Stock Exchange in 1987 (an average of 50 issues) and will be followed by index futures on the Tokyo Stock Exchange in 1988. There is also a possibility that commodity index futures will be introduced on the Tokyo Commodities Exchange (TCE) in 1988. See also **Osaka Stock Exchange, Tokyo Commodities Exchange**, and **Tokyo Stock Exchange.**

Gai Atsu. Foreign pressure. A term used to denote foreign political and economic demands for alterations in Japanese financial or trade activities.

Gaimuin. Full-commission stockbrokers from small securities firms.

Gensaki. The conditional purchase (or sale) of an authorized bond for a specified duration with the stipulation that the bond will be re-sold (or repurchased) at an agreed-upon price. The price differential establishes the gensaki yield on an annualized basis. Gensaki agreements cannot be offered publicly in the United States.

Golden Cross. A technical term used by chartists. Occurs when two moving averages (e.g. the rising 13-week moving average and the 26-week moving average) cross, thus indicating an increased probability of continued upward movement in stock or commodity price. See also **Dead Cross.**

Government Guaranteed Bond. Government guaranteed securities issued in the domestic market by special government-owned corporations. See also **Public Bond.**

Gratis Issue. An issue similar to a stock dividend but not taxable as income.

Harakiri. Harakiri (properly termed *seppuku* from the Chinese) is an obsolete method of Japanese ritual suicide formerly utilized as a method of execution. When used as a prefix in a financial term (see **Harakiri Swap**), it refers to losing terms provided by an issuer in order to procure market share. Synonymous with predatory pricing. See also **Kamikaze Pricing.**

Harakiri Swap. A swap transaction in which the Japanese bank or broker has no spread.

Housing Loan Public Corporation. Provides low-interest, long-term loans to individuals for the purpose of financing the purchase (or construction) of homes. Funds are supplied by the Trust Fund Bureau. See also **Trust Fund Bureau.**

IBJ. See **Industrial Bank of Japan.**

Ichibu. First section of the Tokyo, Osaka, or Nagoya stock exchanges.

Impact Loans. Controlled foreign currency loans to residents of Japan by authorized foreign exchange banks with no restrictions imposed on use of the funds. Prior to 1980, impact loans were the exclusive and profitable preserve of foreign banks in Japan. In 1986, the market was dominated by domestic banks. In 1984, many corporations and financial institutions in Japan began to borrow foreign currencies, particularly dollars, in large volume in order to invest in foreign bonds.

Incentive Issue. This is a vague term that denotes any stock liable to attract individual investor interest because of rumored or actual market trends or company specific developments.

Industrial Bank of Japan (Nippon Kogyo Ginko). The oldest and biggest of the three long-term credit banks. See also **Long-Term Credit Banks.**

Interbank Market. The short-term money markets consisting of call-money, bill-discount, and the Tokyo dollar call market.

Interlocked Cross-Shareholding. Mutual ownership of stock among members of the same keiretsu. Often the majority of a corporation's equity is held collectively by the keiretsu. See also **Cross-Shareholding** and **Keiretsu.**

Investment Advisory Act of 1986. The act provides for the registration and approval of investment advisers and is intended to protect investors from fraudulent management (see Chapter 9). Under the enforced provisions of the Act, all fund managers are required to hold a license issued by the Ministry of Finance. Previously, only trust banks and life insurance companies were permitted to manage funds for others. However, passage of the Act enables domestic and foreign investment advisory firms to obtain a license authorizing them to manage funds on a discretionary basis.

Investment Trust Company. Among the biggest institutional investors in Japan, all 11 companies are operated by the subsidiaries of securities companies. They function as a means of channeling private savings into the securities markets through pooled **Investment Trusts.** Buying and selling activity of the 11 companies has a major impact on the capital markets.

Investment Trusts (Toshi Shintaku). There are two types: unit type (**tanigata toshi shintaku**) and open type (**tsuikagata toshi shintaku**); a third form of investment trust, foreign mutual funds, has been growing rapidly.

Itaku Gensaki. A matched gensaki agreement between two customers. See also **Gensaki** and **Jiko Gensaki.**

Itayose Method. Used in the stock exchanges for the execution of opening trades. Orders reaching the floor before the market opens are regarded as simultaneous, permitting the matching of all buy and sell orders.

Japan Bond Trading Company. See **Nihon Sogo Shoken.**

Japan Committee for Economic Development. See **Doyukai.**

Japan Development Bank. A government financial institution intended to finance industrial development projects through the provision of long-term loans.

Japan Export-Import Bank. A government financial institution intended to finance Japan's exports, imports, and overseas investments. In addition to financing exports, the bank provides loans to foreign entities.

Japan Offshore Market. See **Tokyo Offshore Banking Market.**

Japan Securities Clearing Corporation. A wholly owned subsidiary of the Tokyo Stock Exchange which handles clearing procedures.

Japan Securities Dealers Association. An organization of securities companies intended to provide a self-regulatory mechanism within the securities industry.

Japan Securities Holding Association. Created in January 1965 by Japan's securities companies in order to buy stock market issues and prevent an impending market collapse. Dissolved in January 1969 (see Chapter 3).

JCB. The largest credit card company in Japan. JCB Company, Ltd., formerly the Japan Credit Bureau, is a franchise owned by Sanwa Bank. There are currently more than eight million JCB card holders.

Jikihane Bills. Bills drawn by Japanese companies to obtain yen funds in payment for their imports denominated in foreign currencies. These bills were made a part of the new banker's acceptance market in 1985.

Jiko Gensaki. A gensaki agreement between a securities company and an institution in which the broker is almost invariably borrowing short-term funds. See also **Gensaki** and **Itaku Gensaki.**

JOM. Abbreviation for **Japan Offshore Market**, the official name of the **Tokyo Offshore Banking Market.**

Kabushiki Hyoronka. Stock market journalists ("stock evaluators"), who write freelance articles for newspapers and sometimes appear on television.

Kabushiki Kaisha. A joint stock company.

Kaishime. "Corner groups." Groups of speculators, often operating under separate names, which systematically purchase on margin substantial blocks of shares in listed corporations. Subsequently, the speculator group resells the block of shares at a premium. In rare cases, corner groups will purchase most of the float of listed corporations.

Kamikaze Pricing. Slang for predatory pricing of securities by Japanese institutions in order to gain market share. See also **Harakiri.**

Keidanren. The Federation of Economic Organizations. Comprised of more than 700 major domestic corporations as well as about 30 foreign firms, this is the leading representative organization of private sector Japanese industry. The organization's chairman has often been referred to as the "Prime Minister of Japanese Industry."

Keiretsu. Groupings of companies. Some groupings were successors of the prewar zaibatsu while others developed during the postwar period. Usually bank centered and invariably using interlocked cross-shareholding, credit, management, and marketing as cohesive devices, the groups continue to exercise a decisive influence on Japanese financial markets.

Keisen Bunseki. An indigenous technique for charting and analyzing stock and commodity prices. See also **Rosokuashi.**

Kingaishin Fund. "Fund trusts" managed by trust banks and redeemable in cash or assets. Sometimes classified as a component of tokkin, a special trust fund created by domestic industrial and financial corporations in order to provide a means through which capital gains achieved by the fund can be converted to dividends. See also **Tokkin Fund.**

Kisaikai (Kisai Chosei Kyogikai). The Council for the Regulation of Bond Issues. Comprised of those bond-related institutions in banking (22 banks) and securities (7 major securities companies). As an institution it has existed since World War II, but its present form was the result of a 1968 restructuring. It operates under the aegis of the Ministry of Finance and the Bank of Japan. Performs quantitative adjustment of bond issues. Determines bond-issuing procedures and practices. Approves monthly designations.

K.K. Abbreviation for **Kabushiki Kaisha.**

Labor Credit Association. See **Rodo Kinko.**

Long-Term Credit Banks. The three long-term credit banks constitute Japan's long-term credit bank system, intended to supplement the function of commercial banks. The long-term credit banks are, theoretically, restricted to long-term instruments: loans and bonds on the asset side and debentures on the liability side. Only the government and borrowers are permitted to place deposits with the institutions.

LTCB. Long-Term Credit Bank of Japan (Nippon Choki Shinyo Ginko). One of the three long-term credit banks. See also **Long-Term Credit Banks.**

Maruyu. A national system for tax exemption for interest on small savers' deposits. Each individual is allowed a tax-free savings account to a maximum of ¥3 million. Additional tax-free savings allowances apply to government bond accounts (to a maximum of ¥3 million) and postal savings (also to a maximum of ¥3 million). An additional ¥5 million in contributions to employee savings plans also falls under the tax-free umbrella. Thus, each individual saver is allowed ¥14 million of tax-exempt savings. Because the Ministry of Posts and Telecommunications has not monitored depositors, multiple illicit accounts were established in the postal savings system. These deposits were crucial to the massive growth of the post office savings bank. The total system *will soon be abolished* under the new tax laws. See also **Postal Savings System.**

Meiji Restoration. A period in Japanese history that began in January 1868 following the surrender of power by the Tokugawa shogunate directly to Emperor Meiji and indirectly to the Imperial family. The period ended in 1912 with the death of Meiji and the beginning of the Taisho Era. This "restoration" of Imperial power lasted until 1945 when it was terminated by the Occupation and a "democratic" government was introduced.

Ministry of Finance. The Ministry of Finance regulates all financial institutions in Japan, including the budgets of all government ministries. It also establishes and administers the national tax structure. This comprehensive authority has made it the most powerful and prestigious arm of the Japanese government.

Ministry of Posts and Telecommunications. Among other functions, administers the postal savings system, the largest deposit-taking institution in the world. Abbreviated MPT.

MITI. Ministry for International Trade and Industry.

MoF. Ministry of Finance.

MMC. See **Money Market Certificate.**

MMF. See **Money Market Fund.**

Money Market Certificate (MMC). Large denomination deposit instrument which currently has a minimum denomination of ¥30 million and offers interest rates free from official controls. Minimum maturity is currently set at one month with a maturity ceiling of one year. It is expected that the Ministry of Finance will authorize the introduction of a small denomination MMC in 1988. See also **Money Market Fund.**

Money Market Fund. Short-term bond investment trusts sold by securities companies in order to compete with the money market certificates (MMCs) sold by domestic banks. The funds have minimum denominations of ¥30 million and interest rates set to float with domestic MMCs. Maturities are also set to mirror the MMC. See also **Money Market Certificates.**

MPT. Ministry of Posts and Telecommunications.

Municipal Bond. Securities issued by one of more than 3,000 prefectural and municipal entities in Japan. The vast majority of these issues are floated in order to raise funds for specified construction projects. See also **Public Bond.**

Nakadachi. Saitori on the Osaka Stock Exchange. See also **Saitori.**

Nakasone Bonds. Foreign currency-denominated Japanese government bonds. The Nakasone bond was first proposed by Prime Minister Nakasone in 1982. With the 1984 amendment of the law concerning the issuance of foreign currency denominated public bonds, the Japanese government can now issue such bonds overseas.

NCB. Abbreviation for Nippon Credit Bank (Nippon Saiken Shinyo Ginko). The smallest of the three long-term credit banks.

Negotiable Certificates of Deposit. Introduced in 1979 with a minimum denomination of ¥500 million, severe maturity limitations, and a ceiling of 100 percent of net worth on the amount any bank could issue. Subsequently, the minimum denomination was reduced to ¥100 million while the net worth requirement was relaxed to 250 percent (see Chapter 8). The interest is untaxed.

Negotiable Loan Trust Certificate (Kashitsuke Shintaku). The Loan Trust Law of 1952 authorized the trust banks to issue these instruments in order to raise long-term funds to help finance the postwar reconstruction. Usually issued in ¥10,000 denominations, the certificates have maturities of two to five years. Penalties apply to early withdrawals.

Nikkei Stock Average. The arithmetic mean of the stock prices of 225 representative issues multiplied by a constant which is regularly adjusted (see Appendix Five for formula). Previously named the Nikkei Dow Jones Average, it was established on May 16, 1949 with an opening average of 176.21.

Nikkei Stock Index Futures. Traded on the Singapore Monetary Exchange (SIMEX), the futures contract based on the Nikkei 225 may be traded on the Tokyo Stock Exchange in 1988.

Nihon Sogo Shoken. The Japan Bond Trading Company. Functions as a broker's broker for the Big Four securities companies.

Nibu. Second section of the Tokyo, Osaka, or Nagoya stock exchanges.

Nixon Shock. In August 1971, the U.S. government eliminated the gold standard. Immediately thereafter, Japan allowed the yen to float in the international foreign exchange market. The yen, which had been fixed at 360 to the U.S. dollar since the beginning of the Occupation, was revalued by 16.88 percent by the end of 1971.

Norinchukin Bank. The Central Cooperative Bank for Agriculture and Forestry. The sixth largest bank in Japan and the ninth largest in the world in terms of assets (at the end of September 1985), it is a specialized private financial institution (see Chapter 7).

Options. There are no options available in Japan. However, options trading on commodity contracts may be introduced as early as 1988. Once this precedent is set, options on securities are likely to be introduced.

Over-the-Counter Market. Registered stocks and stocks delisted from the exchanges are traded in this market (see Chapter 3). In 1976, the Japan Over-the-Counter Securities Company was created in order to promote trading. The primary function of the OTC market has been secondary trading in government bonds (see Chapter 5).

Par Value. Prior to October 1, 1982, the par values of *all* Japanese shares varied from ¥50 to ¥500, with some shares issued prior to 1952 having par values of ¥20. However, the par value of the shares of corporations created after October 1, 1982, are required to be a minimum of ¥50,000. Thus, for example, the recent NTT shares were issued at a par value of ¥50,000 and were sold in single share units (see Chapter 3).

Political Stock (Seiji Kabu). An issue traded on the stock exchanges rumored to be selected by politicians as an investment. In such cases, it is widely assumed that the stock in question will be ramped by securities firms or special interest groups. See also **Ramp**.

Postal Savings System. Although technically not a bank, in effect a national banking system administered by the Ministry of Posts and Telecommunications. Approximately 19,000 of Japan's 23,673 post offices provide banking services. The largest deposit-taking institution in the world, the system deposits its holdings with the Trust Fund Bureau of the Ministry of Finance. Higher than average interest rates conjoined with unmonitored tax-free savings accounts (limited to ¥3 million per depositor) have motivated individuals to illicitly open multiple accounts under false names. At the end of fiscal 1985, total deposits exceeded ¥104 trillion ($670 billion), representing 26 percent of Japan's national savings. See Chapter 7 for a discussion of ongoing changes. See also **Maruyu.**

Public Bond. A general term subsuming central government bonds, municipal bonds (which are issued by local public entities), and bonds issued by public agencies. See also **Deficit Financing Bond** and **Public Corporation Bond.**

Public Corporation Bond. Security issued by special institutions including public corporations and government corporations. The term subsumes government guaranteed public offers and nongovernment guaranteed private placements by public corporations. See also **Public Bond.**

Quick. Quotation Information Center K.K., wholly owned by the Nihon Keizai Shimbun Co., Inc.

Ramp. The term has the same meaning in Japan as in other equity markets: Stock price manipulation induced through a variety of means, resulting in dramatic increases in the share price of issues listed on the stock exchanges. Usually prices that have been inflated through this type of manipulation eventually return to prior price levels.

Regional Banks. Commercial banks (there were 64 at the end of 1986) scattered throughout Japan. Smaller than the 13 city banks, these institutions specialize in lending to small- and medium-size businesses (see Chapter 7).

Regional Stock Exchanges. The five smallest stock exchanges in Japan (Kyoto, Hiroshima, Fukuoka, Niigata, and Sapporo) in contrast to the three largest which are classified as **Central Stock Exchanges.** See also **Stock Exchanges.**

Regular Stock Exchange Member. Securities companies that have purchased membership on one of the eight stock exchanges in Japan. The Tokyo Stock Exchange, for example, currently has 93 members. Traders on the stock exchange floor representing the member firms wear blue jackets which distinguish them from the brown jackets of the saitori. See also **Saitori.**

Repotoya. Companies that publish one or several stock market reports on a weekly (or sometimes biweekly) basis. Varying in quality and accuracy, the reports frequently take the form of newsletters designed to inform subscribers about market rumors and suspected corporate developments.

Revenue Bond. See **Deficit Financing Bond.**

Rodo Kinko. Labor credit associations. A specialized form of banking institution for small businesses. There are 47 labor credit associations which belong to the National Federation of Labor Credit Associations.

Rosokuashi. Literally translated as "the trend of burning candles," a technique (developed in Japan) of charting stock or commodity prices. In accordance with this method, the charts employed use boxes to represent spans of time. White boxes indicate a closing price that is higher than an opening price while the converse is indicated by black boxes. The range between high and low prices is indicated by a thin, black vertical line.

Saitori. Securities firms operating in an intermediary capacity in securities trading for regular stock exchange members. Limited to 12 in Tokyo, 5 in Osaka, and 3 in Nagoya. This intermediary function is analogous to the activities of specialists on the New York Stock Exchange. Saitori are not permitted to compete with regular members for commission business by taking orders from ordinary investors. Unlike specialists on the New York Stock Exchange, they are proscribed from trading for their own accounts. Representatives of the saitori firms actively trading on the exchange floor wear brown jackets which distinguish them from the blue jackets of the regular members (and the black jackets of the exchange staff).

Samurai Bond. A yen-denominated foreign issued security floated in Japan.

Samurai Loan. Yen-denominated long-term loans issued to foreign borrowers. Pioneered by the Bank of Tokyo and refined by the long-term credit banks.

Samurai Private Placement. See **Shibosai Bond.**

Sanmeikai. A special committee (to which all city banks belong) that participates in determining short-term interest rates.

Sarakin. Consumer finance companies that lend funds to individuals at usurious rates. Many of the firms are known to use intimidation and strong-arm methods as collection tactics. The activities of these companies were curtailed by government regulations in 1985. These regulations reduced the maximum interest rate from 109.5 percent to the current 73 percent and set a limit of ¥500,000 (or 10 percent of annual salary) to the amount a customer can borrow. There are an estimated 40,000 of these companies registered in Japan.

Second-Tier Securities Company. One of a small number of domestic securities companies that are significantly smaller than the Big Four but larger and more profitable than the several hundred third-tier securities companies. See also **Big Four** and **Third-Tier Securities Company.**

Securities and Exchange Council. An advisory body to the Minister of Finance. (Responsibilities include recommending changes in the financial markets.)

Securities Holding Company Liquidation Commission. Created by the Occupation authorities, the committee was responsible for the mass release of stocks that accompanied the liquidation of the zaibatsu. See also **Zaibatsu.**

Securities Exchanges. See **Stock Exchanges.**

Shibosai Bond. A privately placed Samurai bond. Currently, limited to one-third the amount of public Samurai issues. See also **Samurai Bond.**

Shinkin Bank. See **Shinyo Kinko.**

Shinyo Kinko. Credit associations. A type of specialized banking institution for small businesses. There are 470 credit associations in Japan operating more than 5,000 branches. They all belong to the National Federation of Credit Associations. The credit associations are similar in structure and function to credit unions in the United States. See also **Shinyo Kumiai.**

Shinyo Kumiai. Credit cooperatives. Smaller than credit associations, they are a type of specialized banking institution for small businesses. There are 489 credit cooperatives in Japan, all belonging to the National Federation of Credit Cooperatives. See also **Shinyo Kinko.**

Shogun Bond. Foreign currency-denominated straight bond issued in Japan by a foreign entity. The current market in these issues began in 1985.

Shoko Chukin Bank. The Central Bank for Commercial and Industrial Cooperatives. The 20th largest bank in Japan and ranked 48th in the world in terms of assets (at the end of September 1985), it is a specialized private financial institution for small business (see Chapter 7).

Small Business. This term refers specifically to enterprises with capital of less than ¥50 million or employing fewer than 300 people. In the service industries, the criteria are lower and the term denotes businesses with capital of ¥10 million or less and employing 50 or fewer people.

Sobashi. An unaffiliated stock market expert (often with considerable cash backing for cornering operations).

Sogo. Mutual loan and savings bank.

Sogo Shosha. General trading companies (such as Mitsubishi Corporation, Mitsui & Co., and Marubeni Corporation).

Sokaiya. Directly translated as "shareholders' meeting men" or "specialists," the term refers to a type of financial racketeer specializing in attending *sokai*, shareholders' meetings.

Sprinkel Bond. U.S. government treasury bond issued for Japanese (and European) investors in the New York market.

Stable Stockholders (Antei Kabunushi). The corporate and financial holders of interlocked cross-shareholdings. The holdings are stable because they are seldom, if ever, traded.

Stock Exchanges. Technically referred to as "securities exchanges," Japan's eight stock exchanges are: Tokyo, Osaka, Nagoya, Kyoto, Hiroshima, Fukuoka, Niigata, and Sapporo. The Tokyo Stock Exchange represents 83 percent of all stock exchange business, followed by Osaka (13 percent) and Nagoya (3 percent). The stock exchanges are nonprofit, autonomous organizations regulated by the Securities and Exchange Law of Japan. Members must be securities companies. See also **Central Stock Exchanges.**

Sushi Bond. Straight bonds denominated in foreign currency (usually dollars), floated by Japanese institutions or corporations, and intended for the portfolios of Japanese trust banks and insurance companies. Japanese institutions are restricted in the amount of foreign bonds they can hold; however, foreign currency bonds issued by Japanese corporations are regarded as Japanese bonds and thus do not count against limits on holdings.

Tanshi Company. Short-term broker and dealer in the money markets and the foreign exchange market (see Chapter 8).

Tanshi Kyokai. The Association of Call Loan and Discount Companies. Comprised of the six Tanshi firms. Determines dealing practices and procedures.

TCE. See **Tokyo Commodities Exchange.**

Teigaku. A type of long-term (10-year maturity) deposit certificate issued by post offices throughout Japan. A highly liquid vehicle, these certificates can be cashed in without penalty after six months. After one year, the certificates yield a minimum annual interest rate of 4 percent and, after three years, the rate rises to a maximum of 5.75 percent.

Third-Tier Securities Company. All securities companies in Japan that are smaller than the handful of second-tier firms. See also **Big Four, Second-Tier Securities Firms**, and **Chusho Shoken.**

Three Bureaux Agreement. An accord reached by the Ministry of Finance's (1) banking, (2) securities, and (3) international finance bureaux in 1975 to ban the overseas branches of domestic banks from becoming lead managers in underwriting bonds issued overseas by Japanese corporations.

TIBOR. Tokyo Interbank Offered Rate.

Tokkin Fund (*Tokutei Kinsen Shintaku*). Special transitory trust fund created by domestic industrial and financial corporations in order to provide a means through which capital gains achieved by the fund can be converted to dividends. In this way, the trust fund provides significant tax advantages and adds flexibility to accounting procedures. The funds are handled by investment management firms and are redeemable in cash. See also **Kingaishin Fund.**

Tokyo Commodities Exchange. The exchange is sponsored by the Ministry for International Trade and Industry (MITI) because its origin is industrial rather than financial: the exchange was originally a market in rubber and textiles. Precious metals were not traded on the exchange until gold was introduced in 1982, followed by platinum and silver in 1984. Options on gold and platinum contracts are likely to be introduced in 1988.

Tokyo Dollar Bond Market. The name for the Tokyo market in over-the-counter U.S. dollar-denominated bonds. Many foreign securities firms in Japan have quoted the purchasing and selling prices of dollar bonds. The Big Four securities firms began to do the same in 1986. Commercial banks are currently prohibited from participation. Contracts and settlements are often conducted overseas in order to avoid taxes on securities trading. During fiscal year 1985, the trading volume of foreign bonds in the Tokyo market reached ¥55 trillion, triple the level achieved during the preceding year.

Tokyo Dollar Call Market. Established in 1972 and limited to domestic banking institutions, the Tokyo dollar call market is an interbank market in short-term unsecured foreign currency loans. Despite the market's name, lending is not officially confined to dollar transactions.

Tokyo Offshore Banking Market. Officially termed the Japan Offshore Market (JOM), Japan's first offshore banking facility was launched on December 1, 1986. The imposition of stamp duty as well as local taxes distinguish it from other offshore banking markets which are ordinarily free of tax encumbrances.

Tokyo Stock Exchange Yield Average. Determined by dividing the total dividends paid by all first-section and most second-section issues by the total market value of those issues.

Toshi Journal. A monthly publication designed to provide its readers with stock market tips, the journal also functioned as an investment advisor to its readers, inviting them to let it invest their money. When the publication went bankrupt in 1984, more than 10,000 individual Japanese investors lost a total of ¥350 billion (about $1.5 billion at 1984 exchange rates). The publication and the company that produced it became a symbol of the exploitation of naive individual investors by fraudulent investment advisors. The episode helped prompt the Ministry of Finance to introduce the **Investment Advisory Act** to the Diet.

Treasury Bills (TBs). Although a market in short-term government bonds was created in Japan in 1985, it represented only a marginal segment of the short-term money markets at the end of 1986. TBs in circulation at the end of December 1986 totalled an estimated $13.2 billion (¥2 trillion). By contrast, the comparable figure for the United States was $400 billion. Interest yields on the issues are subject to withholding tax for residents and nonresidents.

Trust Banks. Japan's seven domestic and nine foreign trust banks engage in both banking and trust business. Together with the 21 life insurance companies, they manage private pension funds.

Trust Fund Bureau (Shikin Unyobu). An arm of the Ministry of Finance organized in 1951, and largely funded through the assets of the Postal Savings System. Manages public pension funds and finances a broad range of government financial institutions.

Trustee. Japanese law does not clearly distinguish between the underwriter and the trustee. As a result, the **Commissioned Companies** fulfill most of the roles of both categories. If a bond issuing company fails, the commissioned bank is expected (although not legally enjoined to) protect the investor by purchasing outstanding bonds at par value.

TSE. See **Tokyo Stock Exchange.**

Tokyo Stock Exchange (TSE) Stock Price Index. The Tokyo Stock Exchange's stock price index is determined according to a total market price method which takes into account all issues listed on the exchange. January 4, 1968, was set as the base level with a value of 100 given to the total market value of all listed issues on the first section.

Underwriter. Corporate bonds can only be underwritten by securities companies possessing an underwriting license. Such companies must fulfill minimum capital requirements. Publicly offered corporate bonds are underwritten jointly by a securities company underwriting group made up of 10 to 20 companies. The Big Four account for roughly 75 percent of all underwriting.

Unit of Shares.   A round lot. The round lot can vary in size from one share (recently listed NTT) to 1,000 shares (see Chapter 3). The majority of round lots are 1,000 share units.

Window Guidance.   A method used by the Bank of Japan to direct the disposition of the funds held by the city banks. Through unofficial direction, which resembles the "administrative guidance" of the Ministry of Finance, the central bank "advises" commercial banks regarding lending policy. See also **Administrative Guidance, Bank of Japan,** and **City Bank.**

Yankee Yen Bond.   A yen-denominated bond sold in the United States market. The first such issue, for ¥25 billion, was floated by the Asian Development Bank in 1985.

Yen Bond.   Any yen-denominated security issued outside Japan. See also **Asia Yen Bond, Euroyen Bond**, and **Yankee Yen Bond.**

Yen-to-Yen Swap.   The procedure of exchanging yen long-term fixed interest liabilities for yen short-term floating interest liabilities.

Yondai Shoken.   The **Big Four** securities companies (Nomura, Nikko, Daiwa, and Yamaichi).

Yugen Kaisha.   Far smaller than a **Kabushiki Kaisha**, this is the form of business organization usually adopted by small businesses. Ownership certificates are issued in lieu of capital stock. Abbreviated Y.K.

Y.K.   See **Yugen Kaisha.**

Zaibatsu.   Literally, "financial cliques." Pre-1945 conglomerates clustered around a central bank or a trading company or both. Mitsui and Sumitomo, the two largest zaibatsu, developed from merchant families that had risen to prominence during the Tokugawa period. Other major zaibatsu, such as Mitsubishi, Yasuda, and Dai-Ichi, were created by entrepreneurs during the first 20 years of the Meiji Restoration. Dismantled but not destroyed by the Occupation. See also **Keiretsu** and **Securities Holding Company Liquidation Commission.**

Zairyo Kabu.   This is a gloss for "incentive issues," also known as "story stocks." See also **Incentive Issue.**

Zaitek (also Zaitech or Zaitekku).   A slang neologism coined from the root of the Japanese word for finance (*zaimu*) and the Greek prefix of the English word, technology. A vague term referring to domestic and international financial arbitrage conducted by treasurers of Japanese corporations.

Zaraba Method. The "auction method" of trading, which is the primary method of stock transaction on the Japanese stock exchanges. Transactions are consummated on the basis of price priority so that the sell order with the lowest price and the buy order with the highest price take precedence.

Zen Noh. The National Federation of Agricultural Cooperative Associations.

Zenshinren. The National Federation of Credit Associations. A private organization that functions as a central bank for the credit associations. Invests surplus funds and extends loans to members.

BIBLIOGRAPHY

Adams, T. F. M. and Iwao Hoshii. *A Financial History of the New Japan*. Tokyo: Kodansha, 1972.

Bank of Japan, Economic Research Department. *The Japanese Financial System*. Tokyo, 1978.

Bennett, John B. and Norman Doelling. *Investing in Japanese Securities*. Rutland, Vermont: Tuttle, 1972.

Emery, Robert F. *The Japanese Money Market*. Lexington, Mass.: Lexington Books, 1984.

Goldsmith, Raymond W. *The Financial Development of Japan, 1868–1977*. New Haven: Yale University Press, 1983.

Hadley, Eleanor M. *Antitrust in Japan*. Princeton: Princeton University Press, 1970.

Hofheinz, Roy, Jr. and Kent E. Calder. *The East Asia Edge*. New York: Basic Books, 1982.

Japan Securities Research Institute. *Securities Market in Japan*. Tokyo, 1985.

Japanese Ministry of Finance and the United States Department of the Treasury Working Group on Yen/Dollar Exchange Rate Issues. *Report by the Working Group on Yen/Dollar Exchange Rate, Financial and Capital Market Issues to Japanese Minister of Finance Noboru Takeshita [and] U.S. Secretary of the Treasury Donald T. Regan*. Tokyo, May 1984.

Kaplan, David E. and Alec Dubro. *Yakuza, the Explosive Account of Japan's Criminal Underworld*. Reading, Mass.: Addison-Wesley, 1986.

Prindl, Andreas R. *Japanese Finance, a Guide to Banking in Japan*. New York: John Wiley & Sons, 1981.

Sakakibara, Eisuke and Akira Kondoh. *Study on the Internationalization of Tokyo's Money Markets*. (JCIF Policy Study Series, No. 1) Tokyo: Japan Center for International Finance, June 1984.

Sakakibara, Eisuke and Yoriyuki Nagao, eds. *Study on the Tokyo Capital Markets.* (JCIF Policy Study Series, No. 2) Tokyo: Japan Center for International Finance, March 1985.

Shibata, Tokue, ed. *Public Finance in Japan.* Tokyo: University of Tokyo Press, 1986.

Suzuki, Yoshio. *Money and Banking in Contemporary Japan.* New Haven: Yale University Press, 1980.

Wallich, Henry C. and Mable I. Wallich. "Banking and Finance." In Patrick, Hugh and Henry Rosovsky, eds. *Asia's New Giant, How the Japanese Economy Works.* Washington, D.C.: The Brookings Institution, 1976, pp. 251–315.